THE REVOLUTION REMEMBERED

Clements Library Bicentennial Studies

This series is made possible by a grant from Lilly Endowment, Inc.

THE TOLL OF INDEPENDENCE
Engagements & Battle Casualties of the American Revolution
Howard H. Peckham, editor

THE SINEWS OF INDEPENDENCE
Monthly Strength Reports of the Continental Army
Charles H. Lesser, editor

FIGHTERS FOR INDEPENDENCE
A Guide to Sources of Biographical Information on Soldiers and Sailors of the American Revolution
J. Todd White and Charles H. Lesser, editors

THE REVOLUTION REMEMBERED
Eyewitness Accounts of the War for Independence
John C. Dann, editor

SOURCES OF AMERICAN INDEPENDENCE
Selected Manuscripts from the Collections of the William L. Clements Library
(In two volumes)
Howard H. Peckham, editor

THE REVOLUTION REMEMBERED

Eyewitness Accounts of the War for Independence

Edited by
JOHN C. DANN

THE UNIVERSITY OF CHICAGO PRESS
Chicago *London*

JOHN C. DANN has been director of the Clements Library at the University of Michigan since 1977. He is the author of numerous articles and book reviews on early American history.

THE UNIVERSITY OF CHICAGO PRESS, CHICAGO 60637
THE UNIVERSITY OF CHICAGO PRESS, LTD., LONDON

Printed in the United States of America
84 83 82 81 80   5 4 3 2 1

LIBRARY OF CONGRESS CATALOGING IN PUBLICATION DATA
Main entry under title:
The Revolution remembered.
(Clements Library Bicentennial studies)
Bibliography: p.
Includes indexes.
1. United States—History—Revolution, 1775–1783—Personal narratives. I. Dann, John C. II. Series.
E275.A2R48   973.3'8   79–19254
ISBN 0-226-13622-1

To James S. Schoff of New York,
friend, advisor, and
unselfish benefactor of the
William L. Clements Library,
who with characteristic vision
conceived this project

CONTENTS

ILLUSTRATION CREDITS

The illustrations in the text are reproduced, by permission, from the following sources:

Page 3 The New-York Historical Society. New York City
5 The Library of Congress, Washington, D.C.
7 J. Barber, *Incidents in American History,* 1854
11 The Massachusetts Historical Society, Boston
16 J. Barber, *Incidents in American History*
20 The Library of Congress
32 The Clements Library, University of Michigan, Ann Arbor
49 The Library of Congress
59 J. Barber, *Incidents in American History*
64 The Boston Public Library
66 D. Humphreys, *Life, Anecdotes and Heroic Exploits of Israel Putnam,* 1833
74 The Library of Congress
79 The Library of Congress
105 The Newberry Library, Chicago
106 D. Humphreys, *Life . . . of Israel Putnam*
107 The Library of Congress
115 J. Barber, *Incidents in American History*
138 The Library of Congress
140 J. Barber, *Incidents in American History*
148 The Clements Library
153 The Library of Congress
163 The Massachusetts Historical Society
173 The Library of Congress
176 The Library of Congress
180 The Library of Congress
188 The Clements Library
200 The Newberry Library
212 The Clements Library
223 The Clements Library
246 J. Barber, *Incidents in American History*
247 The Newberry Library

FOREWORD

The final volume in the Clements Library Bicentennial Studies taps the little known and less used collection of Revolutionary War pension applications held in the National Archives. Those records have mainly served genealogists; yet they contain fascinating details and personal views of the war itself by participants.

While most of the aged veterans were content to list the periods of their service, the units in which they were enrolled, and the names of their commanding officers, there were always some garrulous souls who wanted to describe the actions they were in, or other events, and to comment on certain commanders and buddies. The articulate always have more to say and usually say it better than the taciturn. They dictated, or wrote without revision, page after page of military experiences. We hear—indeed, we are privileged to overhear—what their children and grandchildren must have heard.

As Dann points out, this is oral history, perhaps the first of its kind gathered in our country and on an immense scale: there are some eighty thousand applications, short, medium, and long, dated in the nineteenth century. He has selected seventy-nine of the longer accounts, with consideration for geographical spread (and the limits of one volume), as examples of the most historically significant reminiscences. They are eyewitness narratives, of course, but are not contemporary with the events related. Yet by no means does that delay render them unreliable. They constitute source material, nevertheless, and supply the colorful impressions and indelible details that stuck in memory. Dann discusses the cautions that apply to evaluation of this type of source.

Diaries and memoirs of more than fifty veterans have been published since the Revolution, but they are preponderantly by officers; only nine or ten were written by privates. Thus the pension applications add to this store dozens more of personal accounts. This volume will take its place beside those earlier published sources. Readers will gain a sense of the Revolutionary War not available from textbooks. Not strategy or tactics, not campaigns are discussed here, but what it meant to be a soldier and see camp life and battles at close range.

Again the Clements Library readily acknowledges its debt to the Lilly Endowment for funding this volume, and indeed the whole series of Bicentennial Studies, now concluded.

Howard H. Peckham
Director Emeritus, Clements Library

ACKNOWLEDGMENTS

I am indebted to many people for making this volume possible: James S. Schoff and Howard H. Peckham for encouraging the project from its inception; Christine Vroom for masterly typing of a difficult text; John G. Gantt for aiding copying and providing a microfilm reader. J. Todd White shared his knowledge of federal records and searched at the National Archives for texts omitted from the films. Barbara Mitchell supplied editor's skills on numerous occasions, and Arlene Shy typed material and critically read the Introduction, improving it greatly. John Shy was frequently called on to deal with the most difficult historical problems, and he never failed to find answers. Orelia Dann provided encouragement for the book and cheerfully put up with many eighty-hour workweeks while the film was being read and the texts edited. The picture research for the illustrations in the text was done by Annette Fern. Galen Wilson assisted the author in preparing the index. Andy Wyeth provided enthusiastic support throughout the years this volume was in preparation.

The Lilly Endowment, through a grant for the Clements Library's Bicentennial publications, provided the funds necessary to bring the project to a successful conclusion.

INTRODUCTION

The military pension records, now kept at the National Archives, contain some of the most valuable, yet least explored, sources for studying the American Revolution. There are eighty thousand applications for pensions and bounty land on file, part of Record Group 15 of the Records of the Veterans Administration. They can be purchased on microfilm from the National Archives: Microfilm Publication M804, comprising 2,670 reels, contains the entire body of pension files; Microfilm Publication M805, 898 reels, contains the applications themselves, contemporary supporting data, and selected correspondence of later date. To complete this volume, I read through the entire 898-reel series. The records are listed by name and by the state for which the veteran served in the *Index of Revolutionary War Pension Applications in the National Archives* (Washington, D.C.: National Genealogical Society, 1976).

Congress enacted pension legislation in the early days of the war, providing half pay in 1776 for officers and servicemen disabled in United States service. In 1778 those officers agreeing to remain in service for the duration of the war and for seven years more were to receive half pay (changed in 1783 to five years' full pay), and in 1780 pensions were provided for widows and orphans of Continental army officers who had enlisted for the war and the seven additional years. This early legislation was largely designed to encourage enlistment, and it affected relatively few persons.

After its institution in 1789, the federal government gradually took over invalid pensions from the states. In 1818, attempting for the first time to reward veterans rather than entice men to enlist, Congress granted half pay to all Continental officers and enlisted men, to members of the United States naval service, and to marines, if they were now in need of financial assistance. A supplementary act of 1820 required that the applicant submit a certified schedule of personal property and of income.

With Lafayette's visit to the United States in the 1820s and a growing spirit of nationalism, the Revolution took on a romantic aspect in the minds of Americans who had not lived through the conflict. The youngest veterans were now in their sixties, grandfathers with stories to tell, and the country was wealthy and secure enough to show its gratitude. In 1832, Congress passed the first comprehensive pension act, providing a yearly grant to every man who had served for six months or more. To be eligible, a soldier no longer had to be disabled or poor, and service in any military organization was satisfactory, as long as this service could be proved beyond a reasonable doubt. An individual with two years of active duty was eligible for full pay during his lifetime, and a proportion of this was awarded for any service of more than six months. Widows married at the time of the war were also eligible. Provisions for wives were extended during the next forty-six years; widows who had married the veteran before 1795 in 1838; those married before 2 January 1800, in 1848; all wives, no matter when they had married, in 1855. In 1878 widows of Revolutionary soldiers who served in any single engagement or had fourteen days of service were declared eligible.

With only two exceptions, the narratives presented here were recorded in response to the act of 1832. The earlier pension legislation, which, except for the disabled and the poor, had applied only to Continental officers and soldiers, was based on service records readily available at the War Department. Applicants therefore did not usually need to prove their service, and their descriptions of wartime action are sketchy or nonexistent. Those responding to the 1818 act devoted most of their statements to proving financial need.

The 1832 act created a remarkable body of historical data, unique in its volume, on one of the most unusual armies ever to win a war. In a very real sense, the American force was a highly democratic conglomerate of many armies—voluntary corps at the beginning of the conflict, Continental units, state lines fighting with the main army, state militia units, usually organized on the county or town level, companies of Indian spies, and "coast guards" organized to meet particular crises. Sea defense was also diversified, with men serving in the United States navy, state navies, and on privateers.

To qualify for a pension under the 1832 act, a soldier had to indicate in his application the time and place of service, the names of units and officers, and engagements in which he had participated. The narrative was presented and sworn to in a court of law, and it had to be supported by the statements of two or more character witnesses, including a clergyman if possible. Unlike Continental and high-ranking officers, very few common soldiers had any proof of service other than their memories. Discharge papers were not systematically given out at the end of the war, and they were easily lost. Pay certificates were thrown away or sold to speculators who later used them to acquire bounty lands and money. The regulations governing applications under the 1832 act urged that veterans lacking strong documentary evidence or the testimony of contemporary witnesses submit "a very full account" of their service.

A relatively small percentage of the applicants wrote out narratives themselves. In many cases the soldier would go to the courthouse and tell his story to a clerk or a court reporter. Some of them seem to have presented their stories in open court, which must have been very entertaining to the courthouse crowd. Many others went to a lawyer, related their experiences, and attested to the narratives in court. The 1832 act also encouraged the multiplication of pension agents who sought out veterans, took down narratives, and filled out applications as a regular business. In reality, then, the pension application process was one of the largest oral history projects ever undertaken, with thousands of veterans being interviewed. The historical quality of the applications, therefore, depended upon the expertise and honesty of two persons: the veteran, who had to have a good memory and the ability to relate his recollections; and the transcriber, who had to get down not only the facts but the mood and the language of the old man he was listening to. Fortunately, the arts of shorthand and court reporting were fairly well advanced by the 1830s, and now and then a veteran produced a masterpiece of the sort contained in this volume. The seventy-nine narratives presented here were selected for their historical significance, literary value, and geographical balance. In general, those chosen were longer than average—ones in which the applicant tried not merely to document his service but to tell a story.

How significant are the pension records as historical sources? On the most basic level, they provide firsthand descriptions of important events and persons. Narratives included in this book tell, for the first time, how Col. William Ledyard was killed at Fort

Griswold, how the Boyd party was massacred in the course of the Sullivan expedition, and the truth behind the legendary ride of Gen. Israel Putnam down the stone steps at Greenwich, Connecticut. There is a wonderful account of the Sag Harbor raid by the man who seems to have conceived the plan, and there are eyewitness descriptions of Arnold's escape and André's execution. Dozens of soldiers quote Montgomery, Greene, Arnold, Putnam, and Washington, and they provide portraits of these men as the common soldier saw them. The book contains six confessions of spies, three Indian captivity narratives, two accounts by black veterans, and two autobiographical sketches by women involved in the war. One of these, by Sarah Osborn, is the first known account by a female who traveled with the army.

Beyond the description of events, the veterans' narratives provide us with a staggering quantity of factual information about battles, dates when forts were constructed and how long it took, the locations of headquarters, the food consumed, and weather conditions before engagements. The movements of companies are recorded, providing great potential for writing regimental histories. Crops made a strong impression on farmers away from home, and incidents are often dated "when the corn was in roasting ears" or "when the wheat was knee high." Hundreds of minor skirmishes are noted here, many undoubtedly unrecorded elsewhere.

Militia units were often assigned the duty of "putting down" Tories, and descriptions of these efforts provide a great deal of information about the loyalists themselves—not just the wealthier ones who escaped the country and made claims against the British government, but also those who succumbed to American pressure and switched sides.

Buried among the thousands of applications are unique descriptions of dishonorable behavior on not only the British but the American side—soldiers shooting at their own officers, torturing and killing prisoners, deserting, and scalping. Such activities were not widespread, but they are documented in few other bodies of source material. It helps put the Revolution in perspective with other American wars.

Away from the fields of battle, the narratives tell a great deal about the Revolutionary army and the soldiers that made it up. There are descriptions of uniforms and equipment and of all the everyday details of camp life—sore feet, lack of water, tricks played on officers, and the games and diversions the soldiers thought up to pass the time.

Wounds, diseases, injuries, and treatment are carefully described in almost every application and could provide important statistical data. Smallpox and inoculations are regularly mentioned. Substitution was widespread in the war, and the pension applications, containing both substitutes and those who paid them, are the best narrative source for this process. It is an excellent place to go for information on the disposal after the war of the pay certificates that became so important in Hamilton's financial plan some years later.

The complete pension files, one must remember, contain far more than just the narratives of military service, although little of that material is included in this volume. As the generations of genealogists who have used the records know, there is much information on the family: names of parents, wives, and children, and dates of birth and death. For the modern historian as well, there is a vast, untouched body of demographic source material that precedes the informative census of 1840 by more than half a century. There are detailed, concrete data on population mobility, occupational patterns, poverty, and health. In the process of proving pension eligibility, veterans and their widows trace their individual family histories over time and place as periodic censuses cannot do. Military service was restricted to males, but the pension applications and accompanying documents and letters tell much about marriage, childbearing, and widowhood. The vastness of the records created makes these files a source whose potential historical significance cannot be overemphasized.

Like any historical data, the pension records must be used cautiously. The percentage of Revolutionary America's population documented is, by modern sampling standards, remarkably large, but the group is not entirely representative. Civilians of the Revolutionary era, except for widows and orphans, were obviously not eligible. The war itself and the subsequent half-century had already weeded out the less healthy and the older soldiers. Most of the applicants of the 1830s were between sixty-five and eighty-five, younger than the average age of men who bore arms, though only slightly so. In terms of the quality of the narratives themselves, this youthfulness is a distinct advantage, because at the time of service the applicants were impressionable, enthusiastic for military life, and observant.

It is obvious that wealthier men did not generally apply for pensions, in spite of eligibility. Certain church denominations frowned upon accepting public funds, feeling that charity should be kept within the congregation, and the inability of many applicants to find clergymen as character references suggests that churchgoers were somewhat underrepresented. Yet, when all the qualifications are taken into account, it must still be accepted that the pension files as a whole present a fairly good composite of the average soldier in the Revolutionary War.

The pension narratives must also be weighed on the basis of credibility. They are reminiscences set down half a century after the events, not contemporary primary sources, and one must always keep this in mind when using them.

In the most obvious sense, they are latter-day factual records of occurrences that took place years before. Anyone who has listened to the stories of his grandparents is aware that such recollections are uneven—often weak for recent events but exceptionally detailed for selective incidents in the distant past, and this was equally true with the veterans. As any older person can document, memory for names and for time sequence is often the first to fail, and statements of this sort must be used with particular caution. Years are more quickly forgotten than months or seasons, pinned down by changes in nature. On the other hand, for many of the veterans the war was the great event of their lives. These were the times that raised these men above ordinary existence; these were the events most deeply imprinted on their minds.

The pension narratives must also be considered not simply as reminiscences, but as views of the war from the vantage point of the 1830s. These men could not discard fifty years of intervening personal experiences, and their memories could not help but be touched by the march of time. This subjective element has little effect on the recollection of factual details, but it does affect attitudes. In summary, the pension narratives must be used with the circumspection due any reminiscence of events in the distant past.

If one gets any dominant impression from reading all the pension narratives, it is that the militia deserves far more credit for winning the Revolutionary War than it has received. Collectively, the militia possessed ingenuity surpassing anything a regular, unified army could muster when fighting a war stretching over a continent. Its members may have served with only limited distinction as regular soldiers, but they performed remarkable service in holding territory and consolidating gains beyond the reach of the main armies.

Organized on the local level, town by town and county by county, militiamen knew their localities and their particular needs. In the coastal areas they stood sentry mile after mile to watch for enemy ships, privateers, and landing parties. On the frontier they garrisoned forts and conducted continual scouting expeditions, matching the Indians in stealth and viciousness. They knew the local population and were efficient in ridding the country of Tories.

Large numbers of men were in the field throughout the war, and a crisis could bring out many more on a moment's notice. The mere omnipresence of the draft solidified American political control in areas distant from the main armies by requiring male citizens to stand up and be counted. Practically no one could avoid being drafted, few could continually afford to pay substitutes, and as call after call for men was issued by each state and county, neutrality became impossible.

The tenacity of the men represented in this volume is striking. Many had been drafted a dozen times, and there is every reason to think they would have continued to serve as long as the conflict might last. It is hard to imagine that the British could ever have won the war.

Not the least of the soldiers' accomplishment was to document their experiences in great numbers in the pension files. The reader who has the patience to read the narratives presented here will come away with a new understanding of what Revolutionary service was like for the average man and an appreciation of what these men accomplished in gaining us our political independence.

The pension applications, although diverse in appearance, organization, and style, are typical early nineteenth century manuscripts. They contain archaic spelling and a minimum of punctuation and paragraphing.

A fairly standard editorial method has been employed to eliminate as many stylistic archaisms as possible without disturbing the original text. Punctuation, capitalization, abbreviation, paragraphing, and spelling have been regularized and corrected without comment. Names of persons and places have been corrected when identity was certain. Unreadable portions of the text and material inadvertently omitted by the author but needed to complete sentences have been reconstructed and placed in square brackets. Blanks left by the authors and illegible words are noted with "blank" or "illegible" in square brackets. Quotation marks have been added by the editor.

In six of the narratives included in this volume—those of Abel Potter, Joseph Wood, Michael Graham, Alpheus Parkhurst,

James Hawkins, and Jacob Zimmerman, an exceptional method has been employed to make the material readable. Most of the depositions begin with some phrase like "the applicant deposeth that" and then go into a regular narrative form. In these six instances, "the applicant deposeth" or some equivalent introduces the application, and "That" begins a majority of the sentences thereafter. Such "thats" have been omitted without mark. Those interested in purity of text should consult the original manuscript copies, easily obtainable on film from the National Archives.

In publishing the narrative portions of the applications, preceding and succeeding nondescriptive text has been omitted. Major deletions within texts and significant errors by authors are mentioned. To keep the texts as clean and straightforward as possible, this and other information normally relegated to footnotes is given in the brief introductions preceding the narratives. What footnotes there are are the authors', not the editor's.

CHRONOLOGY OF EVENTS

This brief chronology of events mentioned in the narratives will help the reader place particular incidents in the context of the war as a whole. Anyone desiring a more detailed list should consult the first volume in the Clements Library Bicentennial Studies series, Howard H. Peckham's *The Toll of Independence: Engagements & Battle Casualties of the American Revolution* (Chicago: University of Chicago Press, 1974).

1775

Apr. 19	Battles of Lexington and Concord
June 17	British seize Bunker Hill
July 3	Washington takes command of the army
Nov. 13	Montreal occupied by Montgomery
Dec. 9	Skirmish at Great Bridge, Virginia
Dec. 31	American attack on Quebec fails

1776

Mar. 17	Boston evacuated by British
June 21–28	Clinton-Parker siege of Charleston, South Carolina
July 4	Declaration of Independence
Aug. 27	British victory at Battle of Long Island
Sept. 16	Battle of Harlem Heights
Oct. 28	Battle of White Plains
Nov. 16	Fort Washington captured by British
Nov. 20	Fort Lee abandoned to British
Dec. 26	Washington's surprise of Trenton

1777

Jan. 3	Battle of Princeton

Apr. 11	Destruction of U.S.S. *Morris* off Lewes, Delaware
1777	
Apr. 25–27	Tryon's Danbury raid
May 23–24	Sag Harbor raid
July 5	Fort Ticonderoga evacuated
July 10	Barton's raid to capture General Prescott
Aug. 6	Battle of Oriskany
Aug. 16	Germans crushed at Battle of Bennington
Aug. 25	Howe's army lands at head of Elk River, Maryland
Sept. 11	Americans thrown back at Battle of Brandywine
Sept. 19	Burgoyne checked at Freeman's Farm
Sept. 21	Surprise attack on Americans at Paoli
Sept. 26	Howe occupies Philadelphia
Oct. 4	Battle of Germantown
Oct. 7	Burgoyne turned back at Bemis Heights, or second Battle of Freeman's Farm
Oct. 17	Burgoyne surrenders at Saratoga
Nov. 8	British evacuation of Ticonderoga
Nov. 15	Fort Mifflin captured by British
1777–78	
Dec. 19 to June 19	American encampment at Valley Forge
1778	
Feb. 6	Franco-American alliance signed in Paris
May 30	Engagement at Cobleskill
June 28	Battle of Monmouth
July 3	Wyoming Valley massacre
July 4	George Rogers Clark seizes Kaskaskia
Aug. 29	Battle of Rhode Island
Nov. 11	Cherry Valley massacre
Dec. 29	British occupy Savannah
1779	
Feb. 23–24	George Rogers Clark recaptures Vincennes
Mar. 3	Americans surprised at Briar Creek, Georgia
May 8	Spain enters the war
May–Nov.	Sullivan expedition against the Iroquois
July 11	Tryon's raid on Norwalk, Connecticut
July 15	Wayne takes Stony Point

July 26	Unsuccessful American offensive at Penobscot Bay, Maine
Aug. 14	Massachusetts expedition against Penobscot Bay fails
Oct. 9	Franco-American attack on Savannah repulsed

1780

May 12	Charleston falls to month-and-a-half siege
June 7	Battle of Connecticut Farms
June 20	Battle of Ramsour's Mill
July 11	Rochambeau's French troops arrive at Newport
Aug. 1	Skirmish at Rocky Mount, South Carolina
Aug. 6	American victory at Hanging Rock, South Carolina
Aug. 16	Gates defeated at Camden
Sept. 25	Arnold deserts American cause
Oct. 2	Execution of André
Oct. 7	British defeat at Kings Mountain
Oct. 15–19	Schoharie raids

1781

Jan. 1	Mutiny of the Pennsylvania line
Jan. 17	Morgan's victory at the Cowpens
Feb. 23	Battle of Haw River, North Carolina
Mar. 15	Battle of Guilford Courthouse
Apr. 25	Greene forced off Hobkirk's or Hobkick's Hill
May 22 to June 19	Unsuccessful siege of Ninety Six
July 29	Loyalist victory at Deep River, North Carolina
Sept. 5	French fleet drives British fleet away from Chesapeake Bay
Sept. 6	Arnold's raid on New London and Fort Griswold massacre
Sept. 8	Greene drives British from Eutaw Springs
Oct. 6–19	Siege of Yorktown
Oct. 19	Cornwallis surrenders at Yorktown
Oct. 25	Battle of Johnstown
Nov. 13	East Chester raid

1782

May 25 to June 14	Crawford expedition to Sandusky
June 4	Crawford defeated at Sandusky
July 11	Savannah evacuated by British

Aug. 19	Kentuckians overwhelmed at the Blue Licks
Nov. 30	Preliminary peace treaty signed in Paris
Dec. 14	British evacuate Charleston

1783

Apr. 3	Tories and militia fight at Clam Town (Tuckerton), New Jersey
Apr. 19	Congress proclaims cessation of hostilities
Sept. 3	Final peace treaty signed
Nov. 25	British evacuate New York City
Dec. 23	Washington retires from command

1
NEW ENGLAND IN ARMS

JONATHAN BRIGHAM *(b. 1754) was born and grew up in Marlborough, Massachusetts. He entered the local minute company in April 1774, served two terms of active service, and paid a substitute for another three-month period.*

New England, with its Puritan origins and articulate leadership, was quick to react to discriminatory British actions. By 1774 many citizens were ideologically prepared for war. It was the town minute companies like that formed in Marlborough in April, organized and dominated entirely by individuals hostile to the Crown, that paved the way for armed conflict on Lexington Green a year later.

Brigham's memory of the incident surrounding the removal of military stores from Cambridge is somewhat faulty. On 1 September 1774 a detachment sent out by General Gage seized gunpowder from Charlestown and two cannons from Cambridge. The populace reacted with predictable vigor. A group of three or four thousand did surround the house of the lieutenant-governor, Thomas Oliver (not Thomas), and force him to sign a paper resigning his seat as president of the council. The mob dispersed quietly.

Brigham remained in Marlborough until 1796, when he joined the Yankee exodus to New York. He lived at Madison until 1802, then at Augusta in Oneida County, and moved to Chautauqua in 1810. He submitted this deposition in 1832 and was granted a pension.

In the year 1774 he was residing in the town of Marlborough, Middlesex County, Massachusetts. The British troops were then in Boston and their fleet lying off and blockading the harbor. Excitement was high and the moment of actual hostilities constantly anticipated by the inhabitants. Under these circumstances, he, with others of his townsmen, voluntarily formed themselves into a military company, and in the month of April in that year chose the following company officers: Daniel Barns, captain, William Morse, 1st, and Paul Brigham, 2d lieutenants. The company attached itself to a regiment raised in like manner, of whom one Henshaw was chosen colonel, Jonathan Ward, lieutenant colonel, and Timothy Bigelow and Edward Barns, majors. That he and the company to which he belonged equipped themselves and met punctually through the year two days each week for the purpose of military exercise and improvement and, as a minuteman, continued to serve until his regular enlistment in the month of May, 1775, a period of about one year and about one month. Among his first companions in the service he recollects Benjamin Stevens, John Loren, Ephraim Barber, and Moses Roberts, who was afterwards killed at the Battle of White Plains.

While in the service as such minuteman, and in the early part of April 1775, word was brought to Col. Cyprian How of the militia that the colonial lieutenant governor, Thomas, had caused the Cambridge town house, in which the inhabitants had deposited a quantity of ammunition and military stores, to be broken open and the articles it contained removed in the night to Boston. He immediately requested those who were willing to volunteer and go with him to punish the aggressor and take measures to prevent the like occurrences in other towns. The declarant and others, to the number of about twenty-five, offered their services and went on horseback under the command of Colonel How to the lieutenant governor's residence, a distance of some twenty-five miles. On arriving there, a committee was appointed to wait upon the lieutenant governor and make known their business, who, in discharge of their duty, went to his front door and knocked for admittance. But the door was fastened and all silent in the house. They then went to the rear door and knocked, on which the lieutenant governor put out his head from a chamber window and demanded their business. They told him they did not come to do him any personal injury, but to obtain information and satisfaction in relation to the removal of the stores from Cambridge. He replied that they were removed by the express orders of Governor Gage, commander of the king's troops in Boston, that he was sorry that he had removed them, and would not remove any more, and consented to give a written pledge to that effect. That he then came out, marched with uncovered head through the company, and then signed the written pledge that he would not in

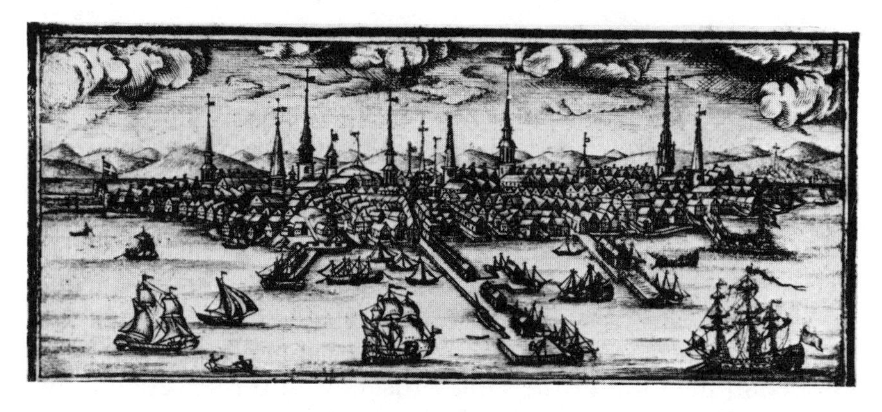

Boston Harbor under siege

future interfere or intermeddle with any of the town stores and would remain quietly and peaceably at home, and that he was sorry that he had had anything to do with the removal of the Cambridge stores. On this he was dismissed, and the company returned, not knowing but that they would be immediately arrested and transported beyond the seas for trial for so hazardous an action. At other times before the actual commencement of hostilities, declarant was engaged in other similar enterprises, and on one occasion dispersed a gang of the king's adherents who had collected to destroy the property, if not the person, of Colonel Bailey of Berlin, an ardent Whig who had become obnoxious to the enemies of liberty. And, as a minuteman, declarant was ever ready on all occasions to defend his country and her rights.

On the nineteenth of April, 1775, declarant, under the same officers as the preceding year, marched to Concord for the protection of the military stores on the first notice of the hostile approach of the British forces. Great efforts were made to keep secret the march and the objects of these troops, but the battle at Lexington roused the country. Declarant heard of the affair at Lexington about nine or ten o'clock in the forenoon and arrived at Concord, a distance of about sixteen miles, at about two or three o'clock in the afternoon. When declarant arrived, the British had effected their object and were retreating, when declarant and his company immediately pursued. They could hear, as they advanced, various accounts of the retreating foe. Sometimes they were told they were nearly upon them and would then march upon a run for some distance till other accounts would induce them to believe they could not be overtaken and would then resume their ordinary march. When in pursuit, they saw numbers of dead bodies, as the enemy's retreat was harassed by the yeomanry firing upon them from behind walls, hedges, and buildings. The British, reinforced at Lexington by Lord Percy, continued their retreat to Bunker's Hill and the next morning crossed to Boston. Declarant and company encamped overnight at a place called Menotomy, about four miles from Cambridge, and the next morning joined the American army at Cambridge. Declarant remained at Cambridge with the troops until sometime in May thereafter, when enlisting orders were published, and then declarant and his company enlisted for eight months and were continued under the same officers with this exception, that Artemas Ward was colonel of his regiment instead of Colonel Henshaw.

On the seventeenth June, 1775, declarant was engaged in the battle at Bunker's Hill. The firing on the part of the British commenced at an early hour in the morning from their ships and batteries. But the engagement did not become general until a little after noon, when their forces crossed Charles River and attempted to dislodge the Americans from the redoubt which they had erected the preceding night. The battle was severe and the British repulsed at every charge until, for want of ammunition, the Americans were compelled to retire. The awful solemnities of that day are still deeply impressed upon declarant's mind, and the scenes of carnage and death and the inconceivable grandeur of the immense volume of flames illuminating the battlefield from the burning of Charlestown appear as vivid as if the events of yesterday. He was acquainted with every captain in his regiment who was in the battle, viz., Captain McMillan of Hopkinton, Captain Fay of Southborough, Captain Barns of Marlborough (declarant's company), Captain Wood of Northborough, who was wounded in the shoulder, Captain Wheelock of Westborough, Captain Drury of Grafton, Captain Cushing of Shrewsbury, Captain Hubbard (who was afterwards killed at Quebec), Captain Kellogg of Hadley, and Captain Washburn of Leicester, who, then an aged man and being himself wounded in the shoulder, brought off from the field Sergeant Brown, who was wounded in the thigh.

When Col. Artemas Ward assumed the command-in-chief of the army, declarant's regiment continued under the command of Col. Jonathan Ward, no colonel being appointed in the place of Artemas. On the second day of July, 1775, General Washington arrived at Cambridge as commander-in-chief. The army was reorganized by him and declarant's regiment removed from Cambridge to Dorchester Neck, where declarant remained until sometime in February, 1776, thirty days after his period of enlistment had expired. The last thirty days' service was rendered at the express request of the commander-in-chief and with the assurance that it should in all respects be deemed the same as if the original term of enlistment had not till then expired. The company was called together at the expiration of the last thirty days and dismissed without any written discharges, having served nine months after his regular enlistment.

A Correct View of The Late Battle at Charlestown June 17th 1775.

In March or the forepart of April 1776, declarant enlisted, under a captain whose name he does not now recollect, as he was a stranger to him and as he did not serve personally under him, for a period of three months to guard the town of Boston, which had then been recently evacuated by the enemy. He hired Charles Hudson to serve this period for him, who was accepted as his substitute, answered, and did duty in his name. Declarant went to Boston during his service and understood and believes he served the said term of three months faithfully and was regularly discharged at the expiration thereof and was paid his wages by declarant in addition to his regular pay which he drew as such substitute in declarant's name.

In the beginning of October 1777, when General Burgoyne was advancing from the north and Sir Henry Clinton from the south, threatening a total dismemberment of the states, a call was made for volunteers from Marlborough, where declarant was still residing, to march against Burgoyne. Declarant volunteered in this service, and a company of his townsmen was organized under William Morse as captain, and Ephraim Barber and Obadiah Bass, lieutenants, and declarant marched with them through Springfield and Northampton, Massachusetts, Brattleborough and Bennington, Vermont, Hoosick and Cambridge to Saratoga, New York, where they arrived two or three days before the surrender of Burgoyne. Declarant's regiment was commanded by Colonel Reade on this occasion. After the surrender of Burgoyne, declarant and his regiment returned, having in their charge the Hessian prisoners in one party and the British prisoners in another, the regiment having divided and taken different routes for that purpose. At Charlestown in Massachusetts the regiment united, but the British prisoners not being willing to go on in company with the Hessians, that part of the regiment with which declarant was and who had the Hessians in charge remained there until the other party had first advanced, when they proceeded with their prisoners to Winter Hill, near Boston, and then returned to their homes. On this service, declarant was absent thirty days.

SYLVANUS WOOD *(d. 1840), a lifelong resident of Woburn, Massachusetts, was one of the minutemen who stood the British fire on Lexington Green the fateful morning of 19 April. In this narrative, and in a separate deposition taken three years earlier for publication in Ezra Ripley's* History of the Fight at Concord *(1827), he claims the distinction of taking the first prisoner of the war.*

Wood was a shoemaker by trade and served three tours in the Massachusetts state units of the Continental army, successively as sergeant, ensign, and lieutenant. He retired to make shoes for the army, later farmed, and successfully submitted this pension application in 1830.

Whoever these lines come before may depend upon facts that I, Sylvanus Wood, was born in Woburn, but in that part now called Burlington, Middlesex County, Massachusetts, twelve miles from

Boston, and there I learned to make boots and shoes. There I joined a minute company, disciplined with activity by a man who was in the fight on Abrahams Plains with the brave General Wolfe, and in fifteen months hostilities commenced. I was then established at my trade two miles east of Lexington meetinghouse, on west border of Woburn, and on the nineteenth morn of April, 1775, Robert Douglass and myself heard Lexington bell about one hour before day. We concluded that trouble was near.

BATTLE OF LEXINGTON

We waited for no man but hastened and joined Captain Parker's company at the breaking of the day. Douglass and myself stood together in the center of said company when the enemy first fired. The English soon were on their march for Concord. I helped carry six dead into the meetinghouse and then set out after the enemy and had not an armed man to go with me, but before I arrived at Concord I see one of the grenadiers standing sentinel. I cocked my piece and run up to him, seized his gun with my left hand. He surrendered his armor, one gun and bayonet, a large cutlash [cutlass] and brass fender, one box over the shoulder with twenty-two rounds, one box round the waist with eighteen rounds. This was the first prisoner that was known to be taken that day.

I followed the enemy to Concord and to Bunker Hill that day. Next morning I agreed to stay the first campaign and served as sergeant, and when my first term was expired Col. Loammi Baldwin of the same town of myself gave me an ensign's commission for 1776 and marched to New York, when General Sullivan [and] General Lord Stirling were made prisoners. I was in the reinforcement on Long Island when we evacuated the island. General McDougall commanded the flotilla when we left the island of New York. The baggage was carried to the North River, with an officer and ten privates to guard the chests, but a British ship came up the river and cut off ours, and all was lost. The next day we crossed the river and went over to Fort Lee. Soon after, we crossed back and landed above Kingsbridge. We marched on and came to a place called Frog's Point. There we had a small brush with the enemy. I received a ball through my left shoulder, Colonel Shepard through his double chin. Our wounds were dressed at Dr. Graham's, White Plains.

My wound soon got well, and at the end of 1776 campaign, Colonel Baldwin leaving the army, Colonel Wesson took the command, and he placed me as first lieutenant in Capt. John Wood's company during the war. I told the colonel I would stay with all my heart if I was not overpowered at home, and when four months was elapsed I saw my parents and offered them all I was worth if they would be willing I should stay in the army. But no offer whatever would answer. I then concluded to leave the army, but with great reluctance.

Colonel Wesson asked me what I was agoing to do. I told him I did not know what to set myself about, but, having a chance to make shoes for the army, I bought leather, hired journeymen, made shoes, and delivered them for the soldiers. And after some time was elapsed I took my money, and it would not purchase my stock, so I lost my time for 1777. After this, it came into my mind to purchase a small farm about forty acres, and my custom was to make a pair of plow-joggars in the forenoon and work on the farm in the afternoon, so that I got no time to go ahawking. And about thirty years ago, I becoming acquainted with the Honorable Abraham Bigelow Clarke of Middlesex County courts, he offered me a farm in the town of Woburn, 5,333 dollars purchase, about twenty-six years ago. I labored nights as well as days and have paid for the same.

It is true but my lifting logs of wood, barrels of cider, has caused a breach of body which all physicians on earth cannot make whole. This infirmity I have been troubled with about fifteen years, and now I am not able to do anything by reason of the breach. I am past seventy-six years of age.

I sent an application with my commission eight or nine years ago to Congress. I am worth nothing but what has been drawn from my fingers' ends. If I am favored ever with anything for service done in the army, I need it now as well as my fellow soldiers who have done no more than I have. I think I have been neglected. If I have said anything wrong, I will seal my lips and say no more, but I am willing to publish this to the United States.

SAMUEL LARRABEE *(b. 1753), a resident of North Yarmouth, Maine, who claims to have participated in the Boston Tea Party in 1773, joined a state militia company two months after Lexington and Concord. He served on a government vessel in Casco Bay and at Falmouth and enlisted, in February 1776, in a Massachusetts regiment with the Continental army.*

After a siege of about a year, Washington's troops occupied Dorchester Heights on the night of 4 March 1776. The British commander Howe had no choice but to evacuate Boston. This narrative conveys the excitement with which the Americans reoccupied the town. It was the first and one of the most brilliant American successes of the war.

Larrabee filed this account and received a pension in 1837.

In the month of June, 1775, at North Yarmouth, he enlisted in a company of the state militia commanded by Capt. Benjamin Parker and served in said company till the last of November or first of December following. The first part of the time he served on Chebeague Island in Casco Bay. Then, accompanied by Captain Parker, he went on board a government vessel commanded by Capt. John Wyman which was employed in cruising between Cape Elizabeth and Monhegan. On one of these cruises we fell in with General Arnold's transports on their way up the Kennebec, near Seguin Island. At the time Falmouth (now Portland) was burnt, in October 1775, a part of our company was there, and the rest followed immediately after. The last duty we did on that enlistment was to build a fort near the foot of King Street, a British armed vessel having made its appearance in the harbor. This fort was thrown up in one night by said Parker's company, assisted by soldiers from other companies which were stationed there. The British vessel, the next morning seeing our fort mounted with two long eighteen-pounders, immediately made sail without changing a shot. This was about the last of November or first of December, when our company were discharged, having served not less than five months.

The said Samuel Larrabee farther states that early in the month of February, 1776, at North Yarmouth, he again enlisted under John Webster, an orderly sergeant, and marched to Dorchester, near Boston, and there joined a company commanded by Captain Cranston in the regiment commanded by Colonel Whitcomb and served on Dorchester Heights, the road to which was across a low piece of land where we were exposed to the fire of Lord Howe's guns, to protect ourselves from which we placed bundles of hay. The last fortnight before Howe evacuated Boston, we kept up a smart cannonading every pleasant night from twelve o'clock till sunrise. The night before Howe left, we threw up a fortification on the point opposite South Boston. In this new fortification were myself and three hundred others who received a heavy fire as soon as we were discovered in the morning from guns placed on May's Wharf and those around it. About sunrise and on a day in the middle of March, the seventeenth I believe, Howe's fleet began to move. The drums beat to arms from Dorchester Heights all round to Cambridge, and we instantly left our fort and hastened to our regiment, which was barracked at Governor Hutchinson's house, where we found them parading. We immediately formed, took up our line of march and, a few rods from the trench on Roxbury Neck, were met by two men who had just thrown open the gates and let down the bridge to receive us into the town. At twelve o'clock we were in the State House at the head of King Street. At half past twelve all the English were embarked, and while the fleet were sailing out of the harbor I heard the explosion of Castle William and the lighthouse as they were blown up by the English.

Lord Howe left ten or twelve transports and other armed vessels to blockade the harbor. Ten or twelve days after this, Captain Mugford of Marblehead, a privateersman having just returned with a prize, a powder ship, went down in company with the schooner *Lady Washington,* another privateer, to Pudding Point Gut on his way out on another cruise. They were attacked by boats from the fleet, which were finally repulsed, though Captain Mugford lost his life in the engagement. On this our officers immediately sent down a number of boats and gondolas, on board of which they put two eighteen-pounders and a mortar with three hundred or four hundred men, among whom I was, to Castle William. From thence we proceeded to Long Island and there during the night threw up a breastwork on the head and planted our cannon on it, having first placed our mortar on the north side of the island. At daylight we opened a fire from our eighteens and tossed three or four dozen shells from our mortar. In a short time the blockaders cut their buoys, slipped their cables, and cleared.

The evacuation of Boston

In a day or two after, we returned to Boston, where our regiment, Colonel Glover's, and Colonel Phinney's were employed during the summer in repairing the Castle and building a fort and blockhouse on Governor's Island and a fort on Fort Hill. In July we were paraded on the east side of the State House and heard the Declaration of Independence read.

In August the smallpox prevailed, and the three regiments were inoculated, which took in every instance in our regiment except on myself. When the regiment had recovered, we were ordered to Ticonderoga and, before marching, were drawn up on the common to hear a sermon and prayers. This day I had the symptoms of smallpox, and the day the regiment marched I was broke out with it. Not having anyone to take care of me, there being no hospitals, I was ordered back to Widow Dimond's, with whom I was quartered when inoculated, who nursed me and got me well of the smallpox though I was long after very feeble and afflicted with boils. After recovering from smallpox, I sold my watch to pay the widow and returned my gun and equipments to the gunhouse where I drew them, not being fit for military duty, and returned to Falmouth (now Portland) by water, not being able to walk that distance.

I know not of any living witness to my last service above stated except my wife. It was in September that I returned my gun and equipments, making seven months from the time I enlisted in February and twelve months service in all on both enlistments. When he enlisted with John Webster, he received four or five dollars and has never received anything since for his services. He would also state that in December 1773 he went to Boston in a coaster with a load of wood and was there when the tea was destroyed, and that he assisted that night in throwing the tea overboard.

EPHRAIM CHASE *(b. 1744), son of a ship's captain, was born at Bristol, Massachusetts. He served an apprenticeship as a carpenter there and practiced his trade on Nantucket and at Machias, Maine.*

In towns removed from the center of conflict, it often took an incident such as the one here described with Ichabod Jones to confront the citizens with the issue of political loyalties. Dramatically and quickly, Machias was transformed from a village going about routine business into a loyal, active supporter of the American cause.

Chase was engaged in "coast guard" service throughout the war and was pensioned in 1834 at age eighty-nine.

I was born in Freetown, county of Bristol, province of Massachusetts, June 1st, A.D. 1744. At the age of seven years my father took me to sea as cabin boy, in which capacity I continued nine years. I was then apprenticed to a carpenter, with whom I served my time. At the age of twenty-one I married and removed to Nantucket, where I lived four years, working at my trade.

I then removed to Machias, where I arrived June 1st, 1769, and where I have resided till the present time. I labored at my trade six years, when the disturbance between England and America commenced. At that time one Ichabod Jones, who for several years had furnished the town with provision, being disaffected towards the American cause, applied to Admiral Graves, who had possession of Boston Harbor, for a tender to convoy him into our river.

The admiral granted him one, which accompanied him [to] White's Point, where he unloaded and stored his provisions. He then desired a town meeting. Being asked for what purpose, he replied, "I will inform you at the meeting." The town having met, he proposed our trading as usual and paying according to contract. A few only voted in favor of his proposal. And so he withheld his provisions from all excepting those few. These circumstances, in connection with the situation of Boston, provoked our jealousy and aroused us to assert and defend our rights. Mr. Benjamin Foster proposed taking Jones and his vessels by force of arms.

He collected twenty-five of the most resolute of the inhabitants on Sunday, intending to seize upon Jones and the captain of the tender, both in meeting. Having approached within a few rods of the meetinghouse, the captain espied us. He arose and exclaimed, "An army is approaching," upon [which] Jones, accompanied by a friend, fled into the wood. His captain made the best of his way to the shore. We pursued, but he escaped and got on board his vessel. He had four cannon, and we gave up the pursuit through fear of them. Jones's sloop lay about three miles below, loading with boards. We suspected the captain would endeavor to escape out of the river and take the sloop in company. We therefore repaired to her in order to prevent him.

He arrived according to our conjectures, and when within a short distance we caused him to sheer off by telling him a ledge lay in his way. Being unacquainted with the river, he ran aground, where he was obliged to lay till flood tide. This gave us an opportunity of adding twenty-five more men to our little company. Next morning, we manned the sloop we had then got into our power and another smaller one and pursued the enemy. We got pretty near before she began to float. We overtook her at the outer islands, where we attacked and captured her. A number were killed and wounded on both sides. The captain of the tender expired on the third day. We removed the guns and ammunition of the prize on board our sloop.

A few days after, a vessel which had been sent out from Halifax to survey the coast entered our river to inquire into the affair and espouse the cause of our enemies. As she lay at anchor in Bucks Harbor, we ran our sloop alongside and boarded her, meeting with no resistance whatever from her crew. We then carried her up the river, where we fitted her for our service. The Committee of Safety selected Benjamin Foster, George Stillman, Abiel

Sprague, Nathan Longfellow, myself, and three others whose names I have forgotten to carry our prisoners to Cambridge and deliver them to George Washington. Two small vessels were fitted for the purpose, when we set sail and reached Cambridge in safety. We left our prisoners with Washington and returned.

After the British evacuated Boston, March 1776, I commenced coasting from Machias to that place. In March 1777 or 1778 (I am not positive which), Col. John Allen, commander of the troops in Machias and superintendent of the Indians, presented me with a commission from Congress wherein I was authorized to take command of the *Salute,* mounting ten guns, and cruise in the states' service and capture the enemy. The *Salute* was taken from the English at Moose Isle and by Francis Joseph, governor of the Indians in Machias. He called his prize the *Neshquoit.*

Before I entered the cruising service, Congress countermanded my orders and stationed me at Machias to "defend the harbor and supply the troops and Indians with provisions and other necessaries." I engaged in the service and performed my duties to the extent of my abilities till 1782. Colonel Allen then received orders from the General Court at Cambridge to send the *Salute* or *Neshquoit* to them. As I was out of health at that time, the command devolved on Elijah Ayres, my first lieutenant.

My commission and journal were both unfortunately burnt about this time under the following circumstances. In my absence, the dry forest which surrounded my house having accidentally caught fire, my furniture was removed into the greenwood as a place of safety. But the wind blowing very hard, even the green trees were consumed, together with many of my effects, among which were my commission and journal.

The above narrative is the simple truth according to the best of my remembrance.

RICHARD VINING *(b. 1753) was born at East Windsor, Connecticut, and indentured at age nine in Enfield. He was residing at Loudon, Massachusetts, when the war broke out. He served for five months in a Massachusetts regiment with the Continental army besieging Boston. He volunteered in September 1775 for Arnold's daring expedition to Quebec.*

Although illness forced Vining to leave the army before the actual attack of 31 December, he describes some of the difficulties and privations that marked the remarkable trek through the wilderness. The previously known narratives of the expedition, which support the accuracy of Vining's de-

tails, were collected in Kenneth Roberts's March to Quebec *(1938) and were used as sources for his novel* Arundel *(1930).*

Vining served one more brief term of service, guarding the Hudson at the time of the abortive Vaughan expedition. He resided at Granby, Connecticut, Salisbury, Ohio, Granby again, and finally Boonville, Oneida County, New York. He submitted this narrative and was granted a pension in 1833.

That he entered the service of the United States under the following-named officers and served as herein stated. That Colonel Patterson commanded the regiment of volunteers in which this deponent enlisted after he arrived at Boston on or about the first of May in the year 1775. Does not recollect the lieutenant colonel's name nor that of the major's name belonging to said regiment. The captain's name was William Goodrich; lieutenant's name was David Picksley. Thinks the name of the ensign was William Picksley, is not certain. The first sergeant's name was Joshua Finch. The deponent continued in the service of the army in this regiment until the first of September or about that time as a private. They were stationed at Cambridge in Massachusetts. Says he lived in the town then called Loudon but now called Otis in the state of Massachusetts when he first went as volunteer to Cambridge into the service.

About the first of September (1775), General Arnold had orders to march to Quebec, when deponent volunteered his services into the same company under the same officers except the colonel, whose name he does not now recollect. After they had started, he got acquainted with Lieutenant Colonel Greene and Major Meigs: does not recollect their Christian names. The orders then came to [march to] Newburyport, which they did and lay some days in preparing sloops to carry the army across the Bay of Fundy into the mouth of Kennebec River. They next set sail and went up the Kennebec River as far as an Indian fort called Fort Western. They there landed and lay some days making preparations for marching through the woods. Then they took up the line of march up the river aforesaid until the stream got so small that trees reached across, so that they crossed and left the Kennebec and went through the woods to Chaudiere River, should think about fifteen miles from Kennebec.

Previous to this time, by undertaking to go round a creek which was not fordable (the company with me), I, having occasion to stop, was left by my company and got lost and was in the woods alone three days without a mouthful of provisions. In this time I did not travel much, as I thought I should not gain the river by traveling until the sun could be seen. It was then cloudy. When the sun shone again, I then struck for the river and came up with the rear company of the army, and there I got half allowance which was allotted to the army on account of the scarcity of provisions.

ARNOLD'S MARCH *through the* WILDERNESS

The day after I came up with the company aforesaid, I started at sunrise and overtook my own company. I continued on half rations for nine days when I come to Chaudiere River. Then we went down Chaudiere River until we came to a marsh which by a previous rain had been overflown. We waded the marsh some places to our middles and ice as thick as a window glass. After we had got across the marsh, we came onto a rise of ground, and a creek which we could not cross presented itself, and the company was ordered to fire three rounds as a signal of distress. Major Meigs procured from some Indians a bark canoe on hearing the firing and crossed a pond which lay upon the west side of us and took Captain Goodrich and went back to where the bateaux was which belonged to the army and carried our company across.

General Arnold took five or six men, pushed on to the French inhabitants as fast as possible to provide provisions for us. The general, on coming to the first inhabitants, procured a cow and sent back to relieve the army. Previous to this, our company was obliged to kill a dog and eat it for our breakfast, and in the course of that day I killed an owl, and two of my messmates and myself fared in the repast. However, we came up with the cow and cooked a portion of it and drinked the broth of the beef and owl cooked together, and the next day eat the meat. The second day after we got the beef, it rained heavily and turned to a snowstorm, and the snow fell needleg deep. The day following, we waded a river thirty rods wide. We came soon to a house where we drew a pound of beef and three potatoes each. I do not recollect the name of the man owning the house. Went from the house into the woods and found an Indian camp and lodged for the night. Next day started, and I was taken sick of a kind of camp distemper. Could not walk far in a day. Went on five miles and came to another house where we got one pound of beef, three potatoes, and a pint of oatmeal each. We then went on, when I became so feeble that myself and two more hired a Frenchman to carry us on at our own expense for thirteen miles. There we found common rations. We then went on, all very much enfeebled by reason of sickness and hardship, for four or five days until we reached Quebec.

At Quebec we lay on the opposite side of the river from the town about one week. General Arnold ordered all who were fit for duty to cross the river, who crossed and presented themselves in front of the fort when the British fired upon them. No injury done except that one man had a leg shot off by a cannonball. The general then ordered a retreat. We retreated up the river towards Montreal to a place called Point Trumbull, twenty-four miles from Quebec. We lay there about four weeks until General Montgomery had secured Montreal, when he came and joined us, and we returned to Quebec.

I was sick and left at Point Trumbull and left in a hospital at that place. Stayed at that place about two weeks. Then my physician told me that he would give me a recommend for a discharge, as did the other physicians when I got to Quebec. But I refused it, as I thought I might get better. I went to Quebec, and my captain went with me to the physician, who gave me a recommend for a discharge, which I presented to General Arnold, who told me I had not better take a discharge but had better take a furlough until I gained health and soundness, which furlough he gave me, which furlough is lost. The general gave me five dollars to bear my expenses. I bought a horse of my captain, for which I was to let him have ten dollars out of my wages. After I left, the captain was taken prisoner in an attempt to scale the walls of Quebec, as I understood. My lieutenant received the pay for the company to which I belonged and sent word to me that your money was ready. I went to Stockbridge in Massachusetts and received my pay. This was after the lieutenant had returned home. I then went and paid the ten dollars due my captain for the horse to his wife, for which I took her receipt which I have kept and herewith present. I returned home the twenty-eighth day of January, 1776, but was not discharged until the first of May following. I, however, never took a discharge but received my pay for a year's service and considered myself as belonging to the army until that time.

The deponent further deposes and says that in the summer of 1776 an alarm was spread through the country for the militia to go to Sopus on the North River. Believes it is now called Newburgh. I was then a sergeant. The deponent did not mean to say he was a sergeant when he was at home and previous to his going to Newburgh or Sopus, but that by an order from the general I was placed in Capt. John King's company as a sergeant. I accordingly warned the men belonging to Capt. Jacob Cook's company according to his order, of whose company I was a corporal, and the company assembled at Captain Cook's house. All the officers refused to go above me in command, and there were none would go except some of the officers would go with them. I finally told the captain that if the fifer would play a tune, I would follow him and see how many would volunteer to go with me. We had no drums. The following-named persons volunteered and went with me to Sopus, to wit: Nathaniel Hubbard, Benjamin Baldwin, David Kibbe, Jr., Abijah Hubbard, John Kibbe, and Isaac Finch. We then fixed up and went on five or six miles before night. We went with all possible dispatch to Sopus aforesaid. The British did not land. They lay in sight of our army on the river. We stayed there two months or about that time. I served in Capt. John King's company. I cannot recollect the names of any other officers who commanded at that time. At the expiration of about two months the deponent returned home by order of the officer commanding, whose name he does not recollect. Did not take a discharge. I received the money at the time stated in the order herewith submitted and paid the same to the above-named persons.

JOSIAH SABIN *(1747–1833) was born at Fairfield, Connecticut, and resided at New Providence and Dalton, Massachusetts, at the time of military service. As one of Seth Warner's Green Mountain Boys, he was part of the reinforcement sent up the Lake Champlain corridor in early 1776 to assist Arnold in the vain effort to take Quebec.*

Smallpox decimated the besieging American army, and Sabin's account of his illicit inoculations shows the desperation of the troops in the face of the dreaded disease. His anecdote about Arnold's "woman hunting" is of more than prurient interest in that it was thought at the time that the smallpox was introduced to the American camp by infected women intentionally sent out of the city by the British.

Sabin moved to Stephentown, New York, Bennington, Vermont, and Otsego, Cazenovia, and Bath, New York, after the war. He applied successfully for a pension late in 1832, only months before his death.

That he enlisted on or about the first day of November in the year 1775, at New Providence, in the state of Massachusetts, where he then resided, under Capt. Reuben Hinman, Lieutenants Low and Blakesly (Christian names not recollected), regiment commanded by Col. Seth Warner and Maj. Jeremiah Cady; remained at Providence until the first of January, 1776. Commenced our march on that day to Lake Champlain, at Crown Point; thence to St. Johns, down the lake, on the ice; thence to Montreal, where we remained about two weeks on account of the badness of the weather; thence to Three Rivers; thence to Quebec, where we remained until about the eighth of May, 1776.

While at Quebec, this declarant had the smallpox. He inoculated himself; got the infection from the hospital. He also inoculated many of the soldiers, but as this was against orders, they were sent into his room blindfolded, were inoculated, and sent out in the same condition. Many lives were saved by this measure, as none thus inoculated died, while three out of four who took it the natural way died. He was reprieved by General Arnold, as he was suspected of inoculating, but his conduct was approved by his colonel (Warner), and when he was taken before

Der Americanische Gener: Arnold.

General Arnold, Colonel Warner went with him, and, after a considerable controversy and many sharp words between Colonel Warner and General Arnold, he was set at liberty without punishment.

The following incident took place while at Quebec. This declarant being on guard, General Arnold, who had been out woman hunting beyond the line of sentinels, late at night attempted to pass this declarant to come into quarters. This declarant ordered him to stand and to give the countersign. The latter he could not do, as he left his quarters before the countersign was given out. He was compelled to remain in this situation until the guard was relieved. General Arnold afterwards complimented this declarant for his faithful performance of duty.

Marched with the troops early in May 1776, about the sixth or eighth of the month, on their retreat to the Sorel River, thence up the Sorel River to St. Johns. At the falls of the Sorel, about fifteen miles from Three River Point, the boats were drawn about three miles by land round the falls. From St. Johns, passed up the river and into Lake Champlain, crossed over into the state of Vermont, thence to Providence, where we arrived sometime in June 1776, and about the last of June, same year, was personally discharged at Providence aforesaid, but said discharge has been lost. He has no evidence, documentary or otherwise, of said service.

This declarant further states that early in June 1777 he again entered the service as a militiaman at Dalton in the state of Massachusetts, where he then resided, under Capt. Zebulon Norton. Don't recollect the names of the other officers. This company marched to Bennington. Arrived there just after the battle at that place in 1777. Marched from thence to Fort Miller, thence to Fort Edward, thence to Fort George; removed the munitions of war and blowed up the magazine. Before we arrived at Fort George, an engagement took place between the Americans and the British at a place called, according to his recollection, Kingston Bridge, in which the British were driven. Thinks that General Schuyler commanded. Remembers that an officer had a horse shot under him, but his name he does not recollect. From Fort George, retreated to Fort Edward, thence to Fort Miller, thence to Saratoga, and "*yarded Burgoyne* at Stillwater."

This declarant was detached with others at Saratoga to go with the prisoners taken by Colonel Brown to Worcester. Went to Worcester with the prisoners and, while on our return to Saratoga, heard that Burgoyne was taken, and was honorably discharged at

Pittsfield, Massachusetts, somewhere about the latter part of October 1777, having performed a tour of about five months.

ABEL POTTER, *a volunteer for three tours of duty in the Rhode Island militia, provides a previously unknown narrative of one of the most daring exploits of the war. Under the command of Col. William Barton and Lt. James Potter, the pension applicant's brother, a force of thirty-four men quietly maneuvered their way past warships, landed on enemy-held Rhode Island, and captured Maj. Gen. Richard Prescott, the hated British commander. Barton later received a sword from Congress for the action. Prescott was exchanged for Gen. Charles Lee.*

Potter's narrative differs slightly from previously known accounts. The "keeper" of the house was named Overing, not Oberin; Mr. rather than Mrs. Overing is generally described as having first greeted the intruders. Such minor differences, however, demonstrate the originality of one of the most detailed of the few firsthand narratives of the event.

Abel Potter, like Colonel Barton, later moved to Vermont, and when he submitted this pension application in 1832, he resided in Jefferson County, New York.

In the year 1776 he resided in the town of West Greenwich, county of Kent, and state of Rhode Island, at which place he continued to reside during the three periods of service hereinafter mentioned.

He served the three following periods in the militia of Rhode Island during the Revolutionary War, to wit, one period of three months, one of nine months, and one of fifteen months.

In 1776 (being sixteen years of age) he volunteered and enlisted in the month of August (he thinks) and served three months under Captain Whitman, Lt. Joseph Kenyon, Ens. Thomas Sweet, 1st Sgt. Lorey Jenckes, as a private and carried a musket. He was enlisted by Lieutenant Kenyon, who lived in Coventry, a town joining West Greenwich. Captain Whitman was a stranger to the applicant until he enlisted and lived in Warwick. He does not recollect as he ever knew his (Captain Whitman's) Christian name. After enlisting as above, he marched (under Lieutenant Kenyon, as he belonged to his division) through East Greenwich to the seaside and there took a vessel (the whole company having united there) and went on together to Newport, on the island of Rhode Island, where the company was stationed two months until the British fleet came in, and then they crossed to the north end of the island and crossed by Howland's Ferry to the continent at Tiverton, where he was stationed one month and then discharged. He received four shillings New England currency per month. The company to which he belonged was a volunteer company if he recollects right. They were attached to no regiment or brigade as he can recollect. General Cornell and Colonel Barton were in command at the camp near Tiverton. During three weeks after returning to the mainland from the island, his company had no rations except one-half a sea biscuit, and fresh mutton without a particle of salt, which occasioned in camp distemper in the company, and many of them died. One of the company by the name of Ellis, a near neighbor of the applicant, died after being carried home.

In May in the year 1777, he enlisted as a volunteer for nine months under Captain Hoppin, Lt. George Tennant, Ens. Amos Frink, 1st Sgt. John Waterman, as a private soldier, but after four months he was chosen ensign. Captain Hoppin having died, Tennant was advanced to his post and Frink was chosen lieutenant. Being only seventeen years of age, it was a matter of some surprise to him to be elected ensign. The company did not know his age. He was vigorous and athletic in body and weighed 180 pounds and thinks he understood the military as well as any man on the ground or in the regiment. He lived when at home with his father during the services herein mentioned. When ten years old he was disciplined in the military art. He was the youngest of the family and had two older brothers in the service but not in the same company or regiment. They were in the regular service, James and William Potter, under Captain Olney and Colonel Olney of the Rhode Island line. James was a lieutenant in Captain Olney's company, and William was a sergeant. Claimant thinks (but cannot be positive) his brothers were in the regular service and in the Rhode Island line.

His field officers (in this nine-month service) were General Cornell, Colonel Toppin, Major Barton, and Adjutant Handy. The company to which he belonged met in Coventry after his enlistment and marched from there through Providence, thence to Tiverton at Howland's Ferry (the place at which he had been a short time the previous year), where he was stationed the whole nine months. They sometimes marched down to Fogland Ferry.

He served as adjutant while Adjutant Handy was sick a short time. He had an ensign's commission the last five months from the governor of the state and drew an ensign's pay.

He was one of the thirty-six volunteers who took General Prescott from his lodgings in the nighttime from the island of Rhode Island. Colonel Barton commanded at this adventure. His brother James Potter was second in command and he (this applicant) the third in command (don't recollect whether Barton was colonel or major at that time). His brother James, after the expedition had landed on the island, took the two first sentinels that they passed, and this claimant took the third and last one who stood at the door of General Prescott's quarters.

They went into the house and the Widow Oberin, who kept the house, cried, "Captain Potter, what's the matter?" His brother James had been a sea captain, the way he got the title, and was acquainted with the widow. He said, "You need not be scared, Mrs. Oberin. We are not agoing to hurt you. Where is the general?" She said he was upstairs.

He and his brother and Colonel Barton went up into the general's lodging room. He had raised up in his bed. He (General Prescott) spoke immediately and said "Gentlemen, your business requires haste, but do for God's sake let me get my clothes." Says Colonel Barton, "By God, it is no time for clothes."

They started him immediately and barelegged through a field of barley which pricked him some. They went quick to their boat, where a part of their party had remained, and with them went back to their camp. The enemy fired at them as they were crossing back. They saw the shot strike the water around them. None was hurt.

The three sentinels they took with them under guard. The mode in which he took the guard standing at the door was as follows. He answered as a "friend" and then stepped up to him to whisper the countersign in his ear and stooped forward to him, and as the sentinel inclined towards him he seized the sentinel's piece with his left hand and told him not to speak or he should die, the only words which this claimant spoke while on the island.

The sentinel answered "I won't," tremblingly. This same sentinel afterwards taught school in Pownal, Vermont, and claimant sent a member of his family to school to him. Leaving the island, claimant was the last of the party to get into the boat. They were in a great haste, and he waded to his breast after the boat as it started. After the expiration of the nine months, he was discharged and went home.

In the spring of 1778, there was sent to him at his residence with his father a lieutenant's commission from the governor of the state with orders to enlist a certain number of men and with money to pay them their bounty. He enlisted the number required in two days for a period of fifteen months and entered the service himself for that period and served it.

Commissions were sent to captains, lieutenants, and ensigns and orders for each of them to enlist a certain number of men, which being done, they met and formed a company. He did not apply for a commission and don't and never has known at whose instance it was sent to him. He met his captain at Providence (who had enlisted his share of the men), Captain Traffin, and from Providence they marched to Tiverton again (sometimes called Seaconnet), at Howland's Ferry, and was stationed there the whole fifteen months. In the last of July following his enlistment he was on the island at Sullivan's expedition. He was in the engagement. They came to bayonet. He was under General Cornell, Colonel Barton, the same men with whom he had waited upon General Prescott the previous year. Colonel Barton commanded the department to which he was attached in the action. He (the claimant) was wounded in this battle in his right thigh, by a bayonet as the doctor thought from an examination of the wound. The claimant did not discover his wound until his tuck leg boot was filled with blood. He was a lieutenant during the whole of this fifteen months' service. General Sullivan was commander-in-chief at this battle aforesaid. After the expiration of the fifteen months he was discharged. His commissions (after the war) were left with his mother in a trunk together with his father's commissions and papers, and his mother went to live with his brother in Herkimer County in New York State and carried the trunk, and, after his brother had built a new house, the trunk with its contents was burnt in the old house, as the claimant was informed thirteen years ago by his brother. His brothers are now dead. He moved into the state of Vermont from Rhode Island.

In the fifteen-months term, in the fall of 1778, he with two others went on to the island of Rhode Island to get apples. The island was in the possession of the British. They were overtaken suddenly by a scout and taken to the British camp. A lieutenant's commission was offered him (the claimant) by the British officers, which he spurned to accept. He told them he had a commission which suited him and which he intended to use again in a few days against them, as he expected to be exchanged. He, however, made his escape by getting his guard drunk and pretending to drink himself. He got outdoors to attend the call of nature, knocked down his guard, and made his escape fifty or sixty rods to floodwood on the shore, where he secreted himself till the first bustle was over (it was in the night) and then got onto a slab and swam across the channel towards his own camp. He almost perished with being chilled.

He was cordially received when he reached his quarters and called on General Cornell and told him he was at his mercy as he had crossed after apples against orders. General Cornell told him to go to his quarters, he should not break him, but should, if he went again, and added, "I knew you would be back again soon. I told 'em, they might as well undertake to keep the *devil* as to keep Potter."

He has had two severe fits of sickness which has impaired his memory some, the reason he cannot be more particular in mentioning his officers. He can only recollect things which made a deep impression on his mind at the time. He recollects a personal affray he had with his Captain Traffin, says he threatened to give him a whipping after their commissions should expire, but has never seen him since.

JEHU GRANT *was one of several dozen blacks who applied for Revolutionary pensions and one of hundreds who fought on the American side during the war. Rhode Island, a center of the colonial slave trade, had a relatively large black population compared with the other New England colonies. Both American and British forces, while in power, recruited considerable numbers.*

Grant, who escaped from a Tory master and served ten months in the wagon service, applied for a pension in 1832. Two full years later he was informed by the Pension Office in the Southern-dominated national capital that, because he had been a fugitive from his master, his service could not be counted. In 1836 he replied. His letter, written with eloquent, deeply felt irony, is probably the most uncompromising plea for black dignity left by a Revolutionary soldier.

After the war Grant managed, with the help of Joshua Swan, to purchase his freedom. He settled in Milton, Connecticut, married, had six children, and was blind in his later years. It appears that he was never granted a pension.

That he was a slave to Elihu Champlen who resided at Narragan-set, Rhode Island. At the time he left him his said master was called a Tory and in a secret manner furnished the enemy when shipping lay nearby with sheep, cattle, cheese, etc., and received goods from them. And this applicant being afraid his said master would send him to the British ships, ran away sometime in August 1777, as near as he can recollect, being the same summer that Danbury was burnt. That he went right to Danbury after he left his said master and enlisted to Capt. Giles Galer for eighteen months. That, according to the best of his memory, General Huntington and General Meigs's brigades, or a part of them, were at that place. That he, this applicant, was put to teaming with a team of horses and wagon, drawing provisions and various other loading for the army for three or four months until winter set in, then was taken as a servant to John Skidmore, wagon master general (as he was called), and served with him as his waiter until spring, when the said troops went to the Highlands or near that place on the Hudson River, a little above the British lines. That this applicant had charge of the team as wagoner and carried the said General Skidmore's baggage and continued with him and the said troops as his wagoner near the said lines until sometime in June, when his said master either sent or came, and this applicant was given up to his master again, and he returned, after having served nine or ten months.

Corroborating Letter of 1836

Hon. J. L. Edwards, Commissioner of Pensions:
Your servant
begs leave to state that he forwarded to the War Department a declaration founded on the Pension Act of June 1832 praying to be allowed a pension (if his memory serves him) for ten months' service in the American army of the Revolutionary War. That he enlisted as a soldier but was put to the service of a teamster in the summer and a waiter in the winter. In April 1834 I received a writing from Your Honor, informing me that my "services while a fugitive from my master's service was not embraced in said Act," and that my "papers were placed on file." In my said declaration, I just mentioned the cause of leaving my master, as may be seen by a reference thereunto, and I now pray that I may be permitted to express my feelings more fully on that part of my said declaration.

I was then grown to manhood, in the full vigor and strength of life, and heard much about the cruel and arbitrary things done by the British. Their ships lay within a few miles of my master's house, which stood near the shore, and I was confident that my master traded wtih them, and I suffered much from fear that I should be sent aboard a ship of war. This I disliked. But when I saw liberty poles and the people all engaged for the support of freedom, I could not but like and be pleased with such thing (God forgive me if I sinned in so feeling). And living on the borders of Rhode Island, where whole companies of colored people enlisted, it added to my fears and dread of being sold to the British. These considerations induced me to enlist into the American army, where I served faithful about ten months, when my master found and took me home. Had I been taught to read or understand the precepts of the Gospel, "Servants obey your masters," I might have done otherwise, notwithstanding the songs of liberty that saluted my ear, thrilled through my heart. But feeling conscious that I have since compensated my master for the injury he sustained by my enlisting, and that God has forgiven me for so doing, and that I served my country faithfully, and that they having enjoyed the benefits of my service to an equal degree for the length [of] time I served with those generally who are receiving the liberalities of the government, I cannot but feel it becoming me to pray Your Honor to review my declaration on file and the papers herewith amended.

A few years after the war, Joshua Swan, Esq., of Stonington purchased me of my master and agreed that after I had served him a length of time named faithfully, I should be free. I served to his satisfaction and so obtained my freedom. He moved into the town of Milton, where I now reside, about forty-eight years ago. After my time expired with Esq. Swan, I married a wife. We have raised six children. Five are still living. I must be upward of eighty years of age and have been blind for many years, and, notwithstanding the aid I received from the honest industry of my children, we are still very needy and in part are supported from the benevolence of our friends. With these statements and the testimony of my character herewith presented, I humbly set my claim upon the well-known liberality of government.

Most respectfully your humble servant

his
Jehu ✠ Grant
mark

RICHARD DURFEE *(1758–1845) was a lifelong resident of Tiverton, Rhode Island, a coastal town on the mainland, separated a mile from Rhode Island by Narraganset Bay. Except for one tour beyond the borders of the state to White Plains, his frequent terms of service were local, defending the shore around Tiverton from the numerous actual and threatened attacks of the British who occupied the island from December 1776 to autumn 1779.*

Wherever the British occupied territory for any length of time, civilian life for miles around was thrown into turmoil. For Durfee and his neighbors, as for people in the line of battle in any conflict, friends came to seem almost as troublesome as foes. War itself, with its social and economic destructiveness, became the primary enemy.

Richard Durfee applied for and received a pension in 1832.

In the year 1775, when the British troops under General Gage were in Boston and the English vessels of war *Rose, Kingfisher,* and *Glasgow,* under the command of the notorious Captain or Commodore Wallace, occupied the waters of Narraganset Bay and were harassing our shores and menacing with destruction the towns of Newport, Bristol, and other places in Rhode Island bordering on the shores of said bay, the militia, the only sort of defense that we then had, were called out to defend the most vulnerable points on the shores, to guard the towns, and watch the movements of said vessels of war. I then belonged to a company of militia in said Tiverton under the command of Capt. Benjamin Durfee. He was in the autumn of this year ordered into the public service and marched to Newport and attached to a regiment under the command of Colonel Babcock, of which he believes, and Richmond was lieutenant colonel. In this service he continued six weeks.

In December 1775 or in January 1776, he enlisted into Capt. Lorin Peck's company at Bristol, in Colonel Lippitt's regiment, for one year. In the early part of this service he was stationed at Bristol. From there, in the spring he, with the company to which he belonged, were marched to Bristol Ferry on the Portsmouth side of the ferry and worked for some time on the fort there, then marched to Newport and worked on the fort on Brenton's Point and other places in the vicinity of the town. There we stayed till sometime in August or September, when the regiment was ordered on to the westward. We crossed from Newport to the south ferry on Boston Neck and there by land through Newtown, New

Haven, etc., to Kingsbridge and Harlem, where we joined the American army under General Washington. Stayed there but a short time; we then retreated north to White Plains. He was in the action fought there. After the action, we retreated a short distance northerly, where he was encamped in the rear of the main army on a hill. We then marched to Peekskill, on the North River, where the army immediately prepared to cross over. Here he was taken sick and was no longer able to follow the army. After staying here some time, I sufficiently recovered my health to travel a short distance in a day, and when my time was about out I received my discharge and, through much suffering and distress and almost without shoes, money, or clothing, reached home after having been absent in the service a full year or more from the time he entered into Captain Peck's company as aforesaid.

After his return home and in the month of February, 1777, he was again enrolled in the militia company in Tiverton to which he belonged, then under the command of Capt. Jonathan DeVol. He was from that time till the month of December 1777 or January 1778 drafted from said company of militia at diverse times for one month at a time to guard the shores of Tiverton from the incursions of the enemy, who were now in possession of Rhode Island and the Narraganset Bay and who were waging a war of more than common vindictiveness of feeling against private property and the persons of all who were opposed to their royal master. Although he cannot now state with precision the number of times that he served during said period, yet he is conscious and always has been that he served in the militia in actual public service for one-half of the time. And he solemnly declares that, to the best of his knowledge and belief, he served as aforesaid for one-half of the time for the period aforesaid and in the manner aforesaid and for that time received pay therefor from the state. He was during this period, when in the service, under some of the officers of his own company attached to the regiment of Colonel Cook, but he thinks that Gen. Ezekiel Cornell, who then had the command at Howland's Ferry, had the main direction of the militia on this side of the bay.

In December 1777 or January 1778 he received a captain's commission over the third company of militia in said Tiverton, signed by William Greene, the governor of the state of Rhode Island. He, from this time until the British left Rhode Island in November 1779, commanded said company as captain and was continually in the public service, in the manner aforesaid, during said time. From the great length of time elapsed since these services were performed, he is unable to state exactly the number of times that he was called out into the public service, but he does declare that according to the best of his knowledge and belief, during the period last mentioned and while he was captain of said company, he was in actual military service doing duty in guarding the shores of Tiverton and the adjoining towns on the eastern shore of the bay for at least one-half of the time. The times were generally for a month, when the places of those in the service were supplied by others. These drafts took about half of the company. My company was small, having been much diminished in numbers by enlistments into the state service or flotilla service for the defense of Narraganset Bay or into the Continental line.

The fact was that many of the men belonging to the company under my command as well as other militia of the town who were under similar circumstances were compelled to enter the service to get a subsistence for themselves and families during the time the enemy held the possession of Rhode Island. During all this time the militia of Tiverton had to perform a duty more laborious and harassing than that performed by the men who were regular soldiers in the Continental line or state troops. This your declarant knows by experience, as he served in both capacities.

While the enemy were in possession of the island as aforesaid, the town of Tiverton was very little if any better than a military encampment. The want of men to do the work, who had mostly gone into the public service, was not the only or main difficulty in the way to the tillage of the earth. The beasts of the plow had been carried off by the enemy from the shores, or were removed back into the country out of their reach, or had been converted, for food, to the use of our own army. And if from some more favorable circumstances the farmer could plant his land, he was never sure of receiving his crop in the common and ordinary course of things, but was in constant jeopardy of losing it through the hostile attacks of the enemy on one side, who paid no respect to the common and legitimate usages of war, but whose principal aim appeared to be to distress the inhabitants as much as possible, and, on the other side, by the numerous wants and necessities of our own army, which lay encamped for the whole of said time in said town of Tiverton. These were among some of the causes that impelled so many of the male population of said town to enter into the regular army and to lessen the number of the militia, and consequently to throw a greater comparative amount of duty on those who remained.

It should be further remembered that said town had twelve

miles of shore to protect which lay contiguous to the island of Rhode Island while the enemy held it; that the strait or channel separating it from the main is sufficiently narrow to be within the range of musket shot at one place, and a cannon shot might reach across at almost any point in the whole distance. Thus situated as we were, under the very guns of an enemy of great force on the island and having also the complete command of the bay with their heavy ships, galleys, and barges, our own flotilla and two galleys being always obliged to keep along shore and in situations to be protected by the fortifications on the land when in the presence of the enemy, we were not only compelled to bear arms against the common enemy in actual military service, but we were at a given signal, as the firing of a gun, to assemble en masse at our post appointed to repel any sudden attack.

The Battle of Rhode Island

These occasions of sudden attacks by the enemy were numerous. Having the power to harass us, they did not scruple to use it to our great annoyance when it was of no possible advantage to them. He will mention a few occasions when the whole company were called out, that is, the part who were not on duty at the time were called out to assist in expelling the enemy: sometime in the year 1777, when the enemy attacked the village of Fall River and burnt some houses and the grist mill there; at another time, he thinks when they came up and took one of our galleys lying in the upper part of Mount Hope Bay between Swansea and Troy in Massachusetts. This happened within one-half a mile of his house. This was before Sullivan's expedition, he thinks in the spring of 1778; at another time, when the enemy planned an expedition against the boats in Kickemuet River that had been carried there for a place of safety after Spencer's expedition onto Rhode Island had been given up. This river or inlet from the northerly part of Mount Hope Bay is opposite to the location of the company at that time under my command. The enemy partially succeeded, and the boats were burned. This was a short time before Sullivan's expedition in August 1778.

At another time, a place just north of the north end of Rhode Island being left unguarded or not guarded sufficiently to repel an attack, and the enemy being apprised of the circumstance by their friends the Tories who were among us, they landed at this place and, from the secrecy and celerity of their movements, were enabled to carry off several of our near neighbors prisoners. This, he believes, was in the year 1779.

These were some of the times in which there was a general alarm as regarded his company, but they were not all. In fact, so completely had the military life absorbed the time of the whole militia, that the people were reduced to very great distress for want of food. It would now hardly be credited, but such was the fact that, at that time, some people were under the necessity of grinding flaxseed and cobs together to make bread, and of making potato bread, and of stewing down sweet apples and grinding cornstalks to obtain the juice to boil down as a substitute for molasses. During this said period of about three years, at diverse times but more particularly in the times of Spencer's and Sullivan's expeditions, our dwelling houses were converted into barracks by the American army, our gardens, meadows, and tilled fields (such as we had) hardly furnished the necessary forage for the horses of the troops of our own army, and this state of things drove away all the arts, occupations, and comforts of peace.

In the month of August, 1778, in one of the drafts aforesaid, he was ordered with a detachment of his company to a place called the "Four Corners" in said Tiverton. Here he stayed for a short time and was then ordered to cross over to Rhode Island under General Sullivan. He crossed over with his company from

[Sepowett] Neck, a place between Howland's Ferry and Fogland Ferry, and joined the main army at Butt's Hill. My company was at this time attached to Colonel Cook's regiment. We stayed on the island till the Americans retreated off, when we again took our stations in the guard duty on the shores in manner as before stated. My lieutenant in said company of militia was Humphrey Sherman, and Thomas Durfee was ensign. They both served in said company till after the British evacuated Rhode Island.

His company was attached to the regiment commanded by Col. John Cook and Lt. Col. Pardon Gray. He thinks also that he was sometimes under Col. Nathaniel Church of Little Compton. These being his superior officers, the orders to him were through them or some of them, though he understood at the time that Gen. Ezekiel Cornell of the state line or General Varnum, who was also at Howland's Ferry during a part or all of said time, had the command of the militia when called into the service the same as the other troops. In the guard service on the shores for a month at a time as aforesaid, the drafts were commanded more than half of this time by himself and the rest of the time by his said subaltern officers, Lieutenant Sherman or Ensign Durfee.

And your declarant avers and solemnly declares that, according to the best of his knowledge and belief, he served in Captain Peck's company as aforesaid for one year; as a private soldier in Captain DeVol's company of militia as aforesaid, for one-half of the time from February 1777 to December 1777 or January 1778, being five months as a private soldier; and from said last mentioned time till the month of November, 1779, as captain of said company of militia, in actual public service one-half of the time, being eleven and one-half months; and six weeks as a private soldier under Captain Durfee at Newport in the year 1775. All the above services he faithfully and truly performed in his country's defense in the war of the Revolution.

JOSEPH WOOD *(b. 1762) was born in Scituate, Rhode Island, and enlisted in the Continental army at age fourteen to serve as a waiter to Gen. Nathan Olney for one year. His parents moved to Colchester, Connecticut, farther from active hostilities, in 1778, and from there he served two year-long tours in the Connecticut militia.*

On 6 September 1781 Wood participated in the battle aptly called the Fort Griswold massacre. This previously unknown account is the only firsthand description of the murder of Col. William Ledyard, the American commander.

Modern historians tend to think that there was a misunderstanding of orders in the heat of battle. There has always been a question about who accepted Ledyard's sword and then killed him. Major Montgomery, field commander at the outset of the attack, was killed before the fort was entered. Neither Major Bromfield nor Captain Beckwith, one of whom has usually been blamed for the deed, was wounded or killed. If Wood's narrative is as credible as it seems, the perpetrator was probably one of the other British officers who himself fell a casualty of the battle.

After the war, Joseph Wood moved to Addison, Steuben County, New York, where he applied for and received a pension in 1848.

I was born in the town of Scituate in the county of Providence and state of Rhode Island on the first day of September, 1762, according to the family record of births kept by my father of the births of his several children. When I was fourteen years old (in my fifteenth year), I entered the service of the United States in the Revolutionary army as a waiter for Capt. Nathan Olney and continued in such service as waiter for Captain Olney one year. It was in the spring of the year I think when I so entered the service, but the month or the particular part of the spring it was when I so entered the service I cannot now state, for I do not recollect. From the time of my birth till I so entered the service, I resided in the said town of Scituate.

During the time while I so served as waiter for Captain Olney, I was stationed in Bristol in the state of Rhode Island. I think that there was only one regiment stationed at Bristol during the year while I was there and commanded by Colonel Angell, but I am not certain. I do not recollect how many companies there were in the said regiment, nor the names of the captains, except Captain Olney and one whose name was I think Knight, called Captain Knight. I do not now recollect the names of any of the members of Captain Olney's company except one, whose name was Thomas Eldredge, whom I knew in Scituate before I entered the service and who entered the service about the same time when I did, and I think it was in the spring of 1777 when I so entered the service. I enlisted at that time for one year and served faithfully that length of time as waiter for Captain Olney.

Before my time of service as waiter for Captain Olney had

expired, my father had removed with his family from the said town of Scituate to the town of Colchester in the county of New London and state of Connecticut. When my time of service as waiter for Captain Olney expired and when I was discharged therefrom in the spring of I think 1778, I went immediately to my father's in Colchester. I remained there at home with my father till the first of March, 1781, when I again entered the service of the United States in the Revolutionary army as a private in the company commanded by Capt. Simeon Allen and was stationed at Fort Griswold in the town of Groton in the state of Connecticut. Colonel Ledyard then commanded Fort Griswold. I remained in the service in the fort till the next September, when the fort was taken by the British.

At the time when the fort was taken, there were in the fort as I understood about seventy-five. I made my escape from the fort. A man by the name of Avery, whose Christian name I do not remember, also made his escape from the fort. I never heard of any others having made their escape from the fort at that time, but all who did not make their escape were put to death. Colonel Ledyard and Capt. Simeon Allen were killed.

When Colonel Ledyard found that he was not able to withstand the attack upon the fort, he opened the gate to surrender. As he did so, the British commander asked, "Who commands this fort?"

Colonel Ledyard answered, "I did, but you do now," and presented to the British commander his sword.

The British commander took the sword and thrust it through Colonel Ledyard. This I heard and saw. Upon that, Captain Allen, who was standing nearby in the act of presenting his sword to surrender, drew it back and thrust it through the British officer who had thus killed Colonel Ledyard. Captain Allen was then immediately killed by the British. This I also saw. I then leaped the walls and made my escape.

After I had made my escape from the fort, I met a fellow soldier by the name of Avery, but whose Christian name I do not remember, and who had also made his escape. Avery and myself traveled up the river together a short distance, I think about a mile, when we found a boat. We then got into the boat and rowed across to the other side of the river. We there met large numbers of the militia on their way to New London. We fell in with them and went down to New London. It was near night when we got to New London. It was before dark. When we got there, Arnold had burned the town and left with his forces.

I recollect that among those killed in Fort Griswold there were a number by the name of Avery, but how many there were of that name, or what were their Christian names, I do not now remember. I also recollect that a fellow soldier with whom I was well acquainted and whose name was Jehiel Judd was killed in the fort. I also recollect that a man by the name of Frink, another by the name of Allen, and another by the name of Miner were killed in the fort, but I cannot recollect either of their Christian names. There were two men in the fort by the name of Miner, one a drummer and the other a fifer, and I suppose they were both killed.

I stayed in New London overnight, and on the next morning I crossed over the river in a ferryboat and went to Fort Griswold. The dead were still lying in and about the fort, and the people were just then coming in to bury the dead. A man by the name of Ebenezer Averill went from New London across the river to the fort with me. We did not stay long at the fort. I did not then look about to ascertain whether I knew any of the dead. I felt much too sorrowful and gloomy to do so then. I showed Averill where I made my escape. After remaining at the fort a few minutes I, in company with Averill, crossed the river in the ferryboat back to New London. I left Averill in New London and went home to my father's in Colchester, where I arrived that night. I stayed at home that night, the next day, and the next night. On the next morning, Lieutenant Fox called for me to go with him to Fort Waterbury at Horseneck, and I went. I arrived at Fort Waterbury with Lieutenant Fox in some three or four days after we started from Colchester. When I arrived at Fort Waterbury, I entered the service in the company commanded by Capt. Charles Miles. General Waterbury commanded there. Mead was the colonel when I entered the service there, as I then understood.

I continued in the service the principal part of the time at Horseneck, where we built Fort Waterbury, till I was discharged about the first of March, 1783. After the close of the war, there was a man and fellow soldier who served with me during the whole of the last year named Willcox, his Christian name I cannot recollect, but I think it was John. One of our sergeants' name was Benedict, but I cannot now recollect his Christian name, nor from what place in Connecticut he came. There were in the company in which I served two brothers by the name of Gifford, but their Christian names I am not now able to recollect. I well recollect a soldier by the name of Dana, but his Christian name I do not now recollect, but I do recollect that he did not serve in the same company with me, but served in one of the other companies and I think in Captain Allen's. I recollect four of the captains in our regiment, viz., Captain Miles, who commanded our company, Captain Allen, Captain Stoddard, and Captain Granger. I recollect that during some part of the time Dana was engaged with the officers, but in what capacity I do not recollect. I recollect that after I went to Horseneck, and I think in the forepart of the year 1782, Major Humphrey left, and that, after he left, our major's name was Dana, but his Christian name I do not recollect.

I well recollect that, while I was at Horseneck, we had a great battle of snowballing. The men were regularly paraded on each side and had a regular fight of snowballing. I was engaged in the fight. The battle became very animated. The snow was wet and would pack very hard. Many of the soldiers got hurt, and the blood ran freely, and the battle became so warm and so much in earnest that the officers interposed and stopped it.

I also recollect well the man who was called "Potpie." He was called Potpie because he had, as it was said, stolen a potpie and been caught with it. I think the name by which I first knew him was Palmer. He deserted from our army and went over to the British. He, as I understood, deserted from the British, and while skulking about the country, was captured by our men and brought in and confined in prison. I was informed that he run the gauntlet, though I was absent on duty at the time and did not see it. I saw him receive three hundred lashes, one hundred each morning for three successive mornings. It was after that when he was sent away to prison.

I recollect that young Dana, Sergeant Benedict, and the two brothers Gifford served with me in the army during the last year. I would also name, among the many others who served with me, Bishop Tyler, Captain Miles's waiter, John Follet, William Brook, William Tuttle, Elijah Taylor, Daniel Thompson, Wilmot Tobias, and John Tobias, a man by the name of Babcock, and one by the name of Munroe, but I cannot recollect their Christian names. I recollect the surnames of many more. I recollect that young Dana was an active and smart young man and a good and courageous soldier.

I recollect that in February 1782, that one hundred of the British light horse came up to Palmer's Hill, a little east of Titus River, and had collected about one hundred head of cattle which they were about to drive off. We, while at the fort, heard of it, and

Ensign Allen with fifty men, myself among them, started, intending to intercept them at the bridge over Titus River which they had to cross. When we got to the bridge, we found that the British light horse had passed the bridge with the cattle. We pursued them and overtook them at the top of the hill where General Putnam rode down the steps. We attacked them there and they charged upon us, and we repulsed them and continued our attack. We followed them on about six miles to Byram River. Within that time and distance, the British light horse charged upon us twice more, and we each time repulsed them. We recovered the cattle, the last of them on the bridge over the Byram River. The British killed six of the cattle and cut many more of them. After the British passed the Byram River, they kept on and made no more defense. We took one horse from them, with the saddle, bridle, holster, and one pistol. The horse was wounded but recovered. I and two others shot at the man when the horse which we took fell.

I state this occurrence, believing that my companions, if any of them are still alive, will remember it. I cannot now recollect the names of any who were with me except Ensign Allen and a man by the name of Marshal and another by the name of Haskins. Marshal, Haskins, and myself were the three who shot at the British soldier whose horse we wounded and took.

After the first March, 1783, we were marched to Stamford and there discharged.

2

WAR AROUND MANHATTAN

*S*AMUEL *D*E*F*OREST *(1758–1837) was born in Stratford, Connecticut, and served six terms in the Connecticut militia. In response to a special appeal of Washington and Charles Lee, Samuel Blackman's company marched to New York and helped construct fascine batteries, which DeForest describes in amusing detail. On his second tour he again marched to New York, where he witnessed the Battle of Long Island. Uneducated but loquacious, Samuel DeForest provides a remarkable folk narrative of Revolutionary service.*

The reader should be warned that his last tale is not firsthand but is a description by the British prisoner Birk (or Burke?) of how he was captured at Princeton.

DeForest moved to Ballston, New York, in the mid-1780s, submitted this narrative, and was granted a pension in 1832.

In the fall in 1775, when the British evacuated Boston and went to Halifax and there wintered, General Lee, with direction from Washington, went to New York to advertise them to make preparation to receive them the next spring. On his way to New York, he gave notice to Connecticut that they would be invited to turn their strength towards New York. Capt. Samuel Blackman, an inhabitant of New Stratford, a parish of the town of old Stratford, [who] was captain of a company of light horse, made a declaration that he would not wait to be drafted, but would raise a company of volunteer infantry and would march on foot with them to New York. He raised the company at once. I enlisted in the company, and we commenced our march as well as I can remember about the first of November and passed old Fairfield, Norwalk, Middlesex, Stamford, Horseneck (the last town in Connecticut), (the first town in New York) Rye, New Rochelle, East Chester, Westchester, Kingsbridge, Harlem, New York.

Captain Blackman was introduced to the New York Committee, which was the highest authority in the country. Captain Blackman was the first company of volunteers of militia which had offered their service in fortifying New York. He proposed that we might soon set about it. The New York companies, by General Lee's orders, met us on the grand parade. It was on a cold day, and he was dressed with a coarse blue duffel overcoat. He gave us a short address. It was with pith and brevity. He went on to Philadelphia, where Congress then sat, from some authority.

We were sent up to Harlem swamps to make fascines. It was inquired, "For what use are they," and "How made?" Fascines are a substitute for stones to make walls or forts. They were used for those purposes long before the Christian era. History informs us that Julius Caesar, by setting a row of post in the ground and another row on the opposite side, and then by placing bunches of fascines on the inside of the two rows of post, and then casting in the center gravel or sand, this course will make a strong wall or a fort.

We ate breakfast early and traveled from seven to eight miles and did our stint, which was to make two bunches of fascines and return to our lodgings. A fascine must be about eight feet long, seven or eight inches thick, fastened with a withe at each end and a withe in the middle. The New York Committee employed carmen to convey the bunches of fascines where they were to be used for forts. When warm weather began to come on, we made a trial and proceeded well in making a fort with fascines, but by this time a new general presented himself to us. His name was Thomson [*sic*]. He was the first European who had presented himself before Congress with recommendatory documents for office under our new government. His personal appearance was elegant, and his address to his adopted country was eloquence. He left us that day and went to our northern army. Captain Blackman soon began [to] make arrangements to return home. There was an eastern man lay at the dock with a vessel. He hired him to take us to Fairfield or Norwalk, but he landed at Middlesex. I cannot tell nothing about the date, except the people were plowing and sowing grain. I had a short respite.

We began to hear from New York that the British army was fast assembling and pitching their tents on Staten Island and that General Washington was calling in the militia from all quarters, and, according to the best of my recollection, sometime about the first July, Colonel Lewis's regiment was called on to repair to New

York with his regiment. Captain Tomlinson of the parish of Ripton and Lt. Peter Curtis of the parish of New Stratford was to make out a company between them. I think we commenced our march not far from the first of July. I have some impression on my mind that Captain Tomlinson with most of his men went by water and that Lieutenant Curtis and myself, who was waiter to Lieutenant Curtis, and some other ones went by land.

Colonel Lewis had for his alarm post the Grand Battery, and at the beating of reveille every morning was with his regiment at his post. A rigid and strict discipline was observed through the army, and militia troops were flocking in from all parts of the country, and to quench the ardor of the British army and in some measure keep them at bay, all the commissaries and the stewards in the army were proclaiming almost continually that they issued more than one hundred thousand rations a day. Soon after we arrived in the city, the Declaration of Independence was read in general orders at the head of all the regiments. Major Generals Lord Stirling and Sullivan and several brigadier generals, with more than twenty thousand troops, went over to Long Island, and the British meanwhile were sending troops from Staten to Long Island.

On the twenty-eighth day of August, before Colonel Lewis had left his alarm post, we could see boats passing and repassing from Staten to Long Island loaded with men. After sunrise we returned to our quarters, and after breakfast Colonel Lewis, with some of his officers, among the rest Lieutenant Curtis (being his waiter, I was permitted to follow the company), [climbed] up several flights of stairs till we reached the top of the roof, from which we [could see] the British soldiers were landing at the foot of a road perhaps three-quarters of a mile south of Brooklyn Ferry. Leading an eastern direction, the road appeared about four rods wide, and the road was constantly filled with men. The road ascended gradually about forty rods and then lay on a level. The motion of the men's bodies while under march, which of course would give motion to their burnished arms which came in contact with the rays of a brilliant morning sun, . . . to the eye gleamed like sheets of fire. This road was filled with reinforcements from Staten Island for about six hours, and this time and much longer the battle was fighting.

About eleven o'clock, Colonel Lewis had orders to march his regiment along the dock opposite Brooklyn Ferry, and when there was an officer on horseback, we concluded he was one of the general's aides. He informed us that he was calling for volunteers to turn out and man every watercraft which lay along the dock. "All must know there was dreadful fighting, and if our men were driven to retreat we wish to be able to bring them over this side."

One Wells Judson and myself turned out. A periauger was committed to our charge, and we landed at Brooklyn Ferry about one o'clock. The thunder of the British artillery, the roaring of the small arms of both armies, was tremendous.

Judson and I walked up the ferry road and lay down under a shade, for it was very warm, and drank some cold water. While we lay under the board fence perhaps an hour, ruminating on the terrors of that day, we heard the tramping of men just over the knoll, but we [had] hardly time to think before they hove in sight, and the road was filled with redcoat regulars, and again we had hardly time for surprise before we saw they were prisoners, and they were hurried over the ferry and through the city and over the Hudson into Jerseys. We concluded there was between two or three hundred of them. The firing ceased a little before sundown, and a number of us got into a small boat and went back to our regiment. We learned soon that the flower of the army was killed and taken prisoners; that General Lord Stirling and General Sullivan and several brigadier generals and between nine and ten thousand soldiers were taken prisoners. The remaining of our army on Long Island retreated and pitched on the best and highest ground just back of Brooklyn and entrenched themselves as suddenly as well as they could. The British army left Flatbush, where the late and dreadful ill-fated battle had been lately fought, and were planting themselves alongside our troops in order soon to give the finishing stroke to Washington's army.

But shortly after, I do not remember how many days, a most wonderful thunderstorm took place. It commenced about one o'clock in the day. The thunder and the lightning was dreadful. The clouds run so low, that they seemed to break over the houses, and the water run in rivers. The darkness was so great that the two armies could not see each other, although within one hundred rods of each other. Through the whole of that stormy afternoon they were crossing as fast as possible, but they themselves did [not] know that they were retreating. They came over to get a little rest, and we [were] to go over and take their places. The sergeant major told us that Colonel Lewis told him we must be prepared to go over the next morning. In one hour after, the sergeant major come to Captain Tomlinson's quarters and warned us all forth to march up to the grand parade in order to pass a review and take further orders. The storm began at one, and it was now five o'clock. It now rained, but not so hard. The company would not turn out.

A Mr. Othniel French, a nice and good man, a friend and neighbor to my father, he says to me, "The men will not turn out Samuel. You are a minuteman. Will you turn out with me and go up to the grand parade and see what is going to be done?" I says, "Yes, Mr. French, I will go with you."

There was a few in other companies belonging to Colonel Lewis's regiment fell in, and we marched up to the grand parade, and we found three or four hundred men.

There was an officer there who says to us, "Come, my brave boys, I am glad you are not afraid of a few drops of water." By this time the rain had subsided. It appeared to be turned into mist and fog. "A picket guard is to be set tonight a little this side [of] Bunker Hill on the Bowery."

Mr. French says to me again, "Samuel, keep close to me."

"I will, sir," and we marched on, and we come to the house where the picket was to be kept, and the sergeants began to distribute the sentinels.

Mr. French says to the sergeant, "I wish you would be so good as to let this young lad stand next to me, for there is none that either of us are acquainted with," and the sergeant placed me close to the guardhouse and Mr. French next. I found out the whole of three or four hundred men who marched with us was to form a line of sentries from the North River to the East River, once in forty feet.

As soon as the sentries were set, an officer on horseback, he rid close to me and says to me, "Let no man pass you this night. Take no countersign nor watchword. If any man come to you, see that he is put under guard. You must keep your station here till morning." There was no more through the night. The fog thickened, and all was silent as death. At about twelve o'clock and so on, the dogs began to bark, the cattle to low, the Indians to howl and yell. All these noises was from Long Island, by reason of the thick and heavy fog, and all the other dense qualities which conspired to tune the air like an organ. We supposed that the barking of the dogs and the lowing of the cattle and the howling of the Indians was two miles from us. It was said afterwards that perhaps there was three or four hundred Indians attached to our army on Long Island. They made as much noise as the yelling of a thousand under other circumstances. It was said that the Indians was set to yelling that night by the counsel of General Putnam's.

About day, the noise was all still, and about sun an hour high, the fog began to go off. At this instant a man in the appearance of an officer came up to the guardhouse. One of the officers asked him where he was from. He replied, "From Long Island, Sir."

"What's the word from there?"

"Our army has all came off the night past."

The officer says, "Gentleman, this man ought to be put under guard."

The gentleman who had just came up said, "You can put me under guard if you please, sir, but I presume that in less than forty minutes, you will find what I tell you is true."

The officer of the guard now says, "Gentleman, if this is true, we shall be all sacrificed. What can hinder the whole British army now on Long Island? Flushed with conquest, thirty or forty thousand can march their army up the island till they get opposite to Kingsbridge in four hours, and their fleet can send them the boats which we see them cross their army from Staten Island to Long Island in as short a time."

By this time, Mr. French and I began to think about hunting up our courageous comrades and to learn whether they had kept themselves dry through the storm. I have but a confused recollection of what passed after this scene—all bustle and preparation to retreat out of the city as soon as possible. Mr. French and I, after the fatigue of the stormy day and standing sentry all night in our wet clothes, was quite sick, and preparations was to leave the city next morning, and he saw a man with a wagon that night from New Rochelle, and he hired him to carry us both to his house. We got our pass and went on, and stopped and recruited, and went as I could. I reached home about the last of September and soon listed under Lt. Isaac Burr of old Fairfield into the Black Rock battery service, according to best my memory for one year.

Black Rock rock or battery lay on the top of a rock alongside of a narrow and crooked channel environed on every side with rocks, which made it dangerous for vessels unacquainted with the channel to enter. I cannot remember how many cannon was placed on the platform. I think six or eight. It belonged to the town of Fairfield and lay about half a mile east of the courthouse and jail. I believe the fortification was kept up till peace. I have forgotten how many men was supported for its defense, whether thirty or forty, I cannot [remember]. There was no particular occurrence took place of notice until about the close of the year 1776.

Near the last of December, Colonel Abel, a patriot and prominent character in the town and county, early in the morning he sent his waiter, a colored man by the name of Bill Molat, with a message to Lieutenant Burr. When Molat had reached within perhaps fifteen rods of the barracks, he began to shout and holler, "Huzzah, huzzah, huzzah!" He jumped up, knocked his heels together, and shouted, "Colonel Abel has news from Washington, and he had taken the whole Hessian army!" Lieutenant Burr haloed for Molat to come to the barracks, and when he came, he presented a short, brief statement in print stating that Washington, agreeable to a preconcerted plan, commenced his march at dark through rain, hail, and sleet on Christmas Day evening. He arrived at Trenton the next morning before daylight and, as they had been holding Christmas frolic, drove them out of their bunks and took them all prisoners. Thus the setting sun of the dreadful summer of 1776 sheds some rays of light on her horizon and was presageful of better days, and in fact this event was the dayspring to those better days, and the news flew swift through the land. In three days after, we had news that while twelve thousand British soldiers was racing after Washington's whole army of less than two thousand, while Lord Cornwallis was in pursuit of Washington and his little army, the British army halted on a hill and pitched there in encampment at night. Washington halted on a hill in sight and pitched his encampment and began to set fires at dark, and left men enough to recruit them with rails through the night and commenced his march with his little army of less than two thousand twenty miles. Reached Princeton College in a dark, foggy morning, where there were three regiments of British regulars encamped, and them he made prisoners, and the fifth day after, at night, were marched to old Fairfield under a guard of Maj. Joseph Hoyt.

The next morning, Colonel Abel sent a written request by his waiter, Bill Molat, for Lieutenant Burr to send two of his men to come to town and take charge of two of the prisoners Major Hoyt had left behind and go on with them to Hartford, the place of their destination. As Major Hoyt had but a small guard with him, Lieutenant Burr says, "John Parent and Samuel DeForest, be you willing to go on to Hartford with the prisoners?" We both answered we were. Went over to town at once. Colonel Abel committed them to our charge. Major Hoyt had been gone about two hours. One of the prisoners' name was Birk, Sergeant Birk, a smart, intelligent, likely young man. I do not remember the other's name. This was an interesting and joyous scene when contrasted with the dreadful scenes which flashed in our eye and stoned our ears in New York. The wrecks of three British regiments of prisoners had just passed the doors of a people whose hearts palpitated with joy, and would come into the streets to meet us with greetings and grateful salutations to heaven for such a sudden and such an unexpected deliverance. As we passed through old Stratford and Milford, gentlemen, yea and men of every grade, would almost block up the path we traveled. Major Hoyt and his prisoners were billeted among the citizens, the same as they had been in Fairfield. This was in New Haven. John Parent and I was taken to Mr. Elias Beers's, where we were treated with all the kind civilities we could wish. This was the happiest enterprise I was engaged in. We reached Wallingford the next day. We reached the pretty little city of Middletown the next day. The fourth and last day, we arrived at Hartford.

Before I dismiss this subject, I will relate a little short narrative give us on our way from Fairfield to New Haven. Sergeant Burk [or Birk] said, after General Washington had made such a sudden and successful assault in taking three or four regiments of Hessians at Trenton, and as many as twelve thousand of their best troops was in full pursuit of him, and it was thought they would most assuredly get hold of him, and the last accounts was our army had come up with him: "When we were taken, it was a warm, very foggy morning. We had eaten our breakfast and were in the college yard, stripped, with our coats and hats off, playing ball, and as to having any fear about an enemy, we felt as safe as if we had been in the kingdom of heaven. But at once we heard the sound of men's feet tramping, and I stooped down and looked under the fog, and I could see their legs as high as their hips, not more than six rods from us. Not a moment was left to look for our coats and hats. I run for the [pair?] of [bars?]. They were pretty high. I sprung and threw my breast across the top rail. At that instant, a ball from a fieldpiece struck in the middle of the rail. I was at one end and another man at the other end of the rail. The ball took the rail in two in the middle, and I was cast to the ground swift, and gave me such a jar, I thought myself mortally wounded, and, to sum it up, you see we are all prisoners."

The events of two weeks appears to have rolled on a pivot which has sealed and gave a stamp to the destiny of America. . . .

MICHAEL GRAHAM *(1758–1834) was born in Paxton Township, Lancaster County, Pennsylvania, and, as a six-month volunteer in Pennsylvania's Flying Camp, participated in the American defeat at Long Island on 27 August 1776. His account of the American rout captures all the panic and confusion of the day.*

On completing his tour of duty, he joined his brother, Rev. William Graham, who had taken charge of Liberty Hall Academy (now Washington and Lee) in Rockbridge County, Virginia. He served twice in the county militia, moved to Bedford County in 1789, and received a pension in 1832.

About the last of May or first of June, 1776, being then a little turned of eighteen years of age, I turned out a volunteer in a company commanded by Capt. I. Collier (pronounced Colyer). We composed a part of the corps denominated the Flying Camp. We marched by Lancaster, Philadelphia, Trenton, Princeton, Brunswick, Amboy, Elizabethtown, and Newark to New York, where we joined the main army.

After continuing some time at New York, we were taken to Long Island and stationed at Brooklyn. There is a high ridge running from the Narrows across the island. Below this ridge the British army lay and the Americans above. There is a road leading across the ridge at Flatbush to Brooklyn. The day before the battle, eight men were taken from the company to which I belonged on picket guard and posted near this pass, and I was one of that number.

On the next morning, the battle commenced about the break of day or perhaps a little before. At the Narrows, where Lord Stirling commanded, there was a pretty heavy cannonading kept up and occasionally the firing of small arms, and from the sound appeared to be moving slowly towards Brooklyn. This continued for hours. At length the firing commenced above us and kept spreading until it became general almost in every direction.

We continued at our post until I think about twelve o'clock, when an officer came and told us to make our escape, for we were surrounded. We immediately retreated towards our camp. We had went but a small distance before we saw the enemy paraded in the road before us. We turned to the left and posted ourselves behind a stone fence; from the movements of the enemy, we had soon to move from this position. Here we got parted, and I neither saw officers or men belonging to our party (with the exception of one

man) during the balance of that day. I had went but a small distance before I came to a party of our men making a bold stand. I stopped and took one fire at the enemy, but they came on with such rapidity that I retreated back into the woods. Here I met Colonel Miles, a regular officer from Pennsylvania, and Lieutenant Sloan, a full cousin of my own. As soon as I had loaded my gun, I left them (Colonel Miles was taken prisoner and Lieutenant Sloan killed), as the firing had ceased where I had retreated from. I returned to near the same place. I had not been at this place I think more than one minute before the British came in a different direction from where they were when I retreated, firing platoons as they marched. I turned and took one fire at them and then made my escape as fast as I could. By this time our troops were routed in every direction.

It is impossible for me to describe the confusion and horror of the scene that ensued: the artillery flying with the chains over the horses' backs, our men running in almost every direction, and run which way they would, they were almost sure to meet the British or Hessians. And the enemy huzzahing when they took prisoners made it truly a day of distress to the Americans. I escaped by getting behind the British that had been engaged with Lord Stirling and entered a swamp or marsh through which a great many of our men were retreating. Some of them were mired and crying to their fellows for God's sake to help them out; but every man was intent on his own safety and no assistance was rendered. At the side of the marsh there was a pond which I took to be a millpond. Numbers, as they came to this pond, jumped in, and some were drowned. Soon after I entered the marsh, a cannonading commenced from our batteries on the British, and they retreated, and I got safely into camp. Out of the eight men that were taken from the company to which I belonged the day before the battle on guard, I only escaped. The others were either killed or taken prisoners.

At the time, I could not account for how it was that our troops were so completely surrounded but have since understood there was another road across the ridge several miles above Flatbush that was left unoccupied by our troops. Here the British passed and got betwixt them and Brooklyn unobserved. This accounts for the disaster of that day.

The night after the battle, as well as [I] recollect, a heavy rain commenced and rained incessantly nearly all the time we were on the island. We were at length marched off in the night behind fires made along our entrenchments to the East River. Here boats were ready to receive us, and we were landed in New York a little before the break of day.

We continued but a short time in New York. We were then marched in the night over Kingsbridge and encamped several miles to the east or northeast of this bridge. We continued here I think about two months or upwards. While we lay at this place, nothing important transpired in which we were engaged except some little skirmishing with the Hessians. At length the British made their appearance near a place called Westchester. Here some cannonading and skirmishing took place. We then retreated to the White Plains. With the main army here we halted, threw up entrenchments, and waited the approach of the enemy. Here an engagement took place betwixt part [of] our troops and the British, and everything seemed to indicate a general engagement, but the British declined attacking us. From this place we retreated a few miles farther up the country. Here we continued some time.

At length we were taken over the North River and encamped at a village called Spangtown. While we lay at this place, Fort Washington was taken. We could distinctly hear the firing. From Spangtown we commenced our retreat through the Jerseys, passing through Elizabethtown to Brunswick. Soon after we crossed the Raritan, the British came in sight. Here some maneuvering and cannonading took place, but it is believed without effect on either side. This was the last sight I saw of the British that campaign. From Brunswick we marched through Princeton to Trenton. This as well as I recollect was about the first of December. Our time had now expired. We were discharged, and I returned home. This was a tour of six months.

During my absence, my father sold his plantation with an intention of removing to the state of North Carolina, and, my oldest brother having removed to Virginia and settled in Rockbridge County and was then rector of Liberty Hall Academy, in the spring of the year 1777 I came to Virginia and lived several years with him. In the month of July, as well as I recollect in 1781, being then a resident of Rockbridge County, I was drafted as a militiaman and went under the command of Capt. James Gilmour. The subalterns were Samuel McCampbell and John Kilpatrick; our field officers were Col. Samuel Lewis and Major Long. We marched by the way of Richmond, and after many marches and countermarches Cornwallis at length posted himself in York. From this time to the arrival of General Washington, we encamped betwixt Williamsburg and York. Soon after his arrival we were marched down to the investment of York and encamped below the town. Here we continued until about four or five days before the surrender of Cornwallis. Our time had now expired, and we were discharged. This was a three-months tour.

In the month of February, 1786, I married in Rockbridge

County, and the fall of the year 1787 I removed with my family to Bedford County, where I have resided from that time to the present. I rendered nine months' active service to my country during the Revolutionary War, having never failed in a single instance to perform the duties required as far as I can now recollect from sickness or any other cause. The secretary of war requires applicants to give the names of the field officers under whom they served. I would here observe that the recollection of names was the first and is yet the principal thing in which I have found my memory to fail me. The field officers under whom I served in the year 1776 I had never seen before that campaign, nor have I seen them since. As well as I can recollect, the colonel's name was Clendenan, but [I] cannot be positive. One thing I distinctly recollect, that part of the time we were under command of Colonel or General Hand. He was styled by the troops "General."

THOMAS CRAIGE *(b. 1754) was born in Boston and lived at Worcester and Northampton, Massachusetts, from which he enlisted for a five-month tour. He was obviously popular and a leader of young men of his age. He was appointed a sergeant and employed in recruiting.*

Craige had little ambition or sense of responsibility, but he had the sort of reckless courage that can make a good soldier. His description of the Battle of White Plains is the best to be found in the pension files.

He served one further tour at the time of Burgoyne's defeat. After the war he moved to Westminster and then to Windsor, Vermont. He applied for a pension in 1833.

At Northampton, in the state of Massachusetts, on some day (not recollected) in the month of June, 1776, there came a requisition for men of the militia to join the army near New York, and the declarant was told by some of the leading men of the town that, if he would enlist, other young men would be thereby induced to enlist. Whereupon the declarant did persuade ten or twelve of his companions to pledge themselves to enter the service on said condition and with them did enlist for a term of five months into the company of Captain Wales of West Hampton, in the regiment commanded by Colonel Mosely, Lieutenant Colonel Wells, and Major May. The company did not march for a period of about four weeks, but the declarant immediately abandoned his civil employment and was at once placed under the orders of his captain and put on duty of one kind or another, in which time (of four weeks) he was engaged in recruiting, although not constantly, and recollects that once he was sent by the captain to Colonel Mosely, who then lived in Westfield as he believes.

On some one of the very first days of August after his enlistment, the company marched, passing through Suffield in the state of Connecticut to Norwalk in that state. Here he strongly believes he tarried some time, for what reason he does not remember, nor can he say how long. Soon after marching (a few days only), at some place in Connecticut he was appointed an orderly sergeant and as such acted until the close of his service. From Norwalk he marched to Kingsbridge, New York, thence to Westchester, where, and at Frog's Point, he was stationed some time. From thence he was sent out to East Chester and other places.

At this time a guard was every [day] detailed in charge of General Washington's quarters. On this duty, the declarant went twice in his turn. Afterwards General Washington sent to Colonel Mosely to have detailed and continued steadily on guard at his quarters a certain sergeant (describing him) who had been in that duty before. Captain Wales came to the declarant and proposed to him to go, but whether he was or was not the one the general desired, he does not know. The declarant endeavored to get off, but the colonel came and said he *must* go, and he went. When General Washington went out to reconnoiter, his guard went with him. In this duty the declarant remained until the enemy made preparations to march to White Plains.

Then his regiment marched from Valentine's Hill something like a mile out in front, there opened to the right and left, and stood until the army marched through, and then fell in the rear. The army marched in almost perfect silence all night (except a few minutes during which they lay down to rest), no one being allowed to speak above a whisper. The British marched by the right-hand road, the Americans by the left, both roads uniting at a point near the Plains. The American army reached there a little before the British, and just at sunrise the American rear flank guard was in the same field where the enemy's front flank guard was. The front of our army had (as the declarant learned) reached the Plains in the night, and when his regiment marched up they went into entrenchments already to some extent prepared and immediately began to extend them.

The position taken up by the Americans left a gulf, or ravine, between them and the enemy. There was an orchard in front of the American line which the men immediately cut down and made into pickets for the entrenchments. On higher ground, back, our army had some redoubts. The British came up to the opposite side of the ravine and in the afternoon opened a cannonade. The Americans tore down a large house which stood in the way of their extending the entrenchments. A road, the same into which the two roads by which the armies marched united, came across just upon the American right. General Washington came in the rear, to the right, and ordered the men to dig a new entrenchment between the road and the place occupied by the two armies, extending right out to front from the right so as to take the British line lengthwise. Whether the men that dug that entrenchment were of Brook's regiment, of McDougall's, or some other corps, the declarant is not certain, but it was soon done, and then Brook's regiment, with some other troops, went into it. Brook's regiment was next to us.

Then the British sent infantry forward, down into the ravine, or hollow way, who then turned to their left and came up to storm the entrenchment last mentioned. The Americans twice repulsed the enemy's infantry back into the hollow. While they were rallying, the Highlanders came down, stacked their arms, drew their broadswords, and formed in rear of the infantry. Then they all came up. Our men opened their fire as before, and soon the enemy's infantry opened, and the Highlanders marched into our entrenchments, and the Americans retreated down the hill westwardly. After the enemy got that entrenchment, our guns in the redoubts were brought to bear lengthwise of the entrenchment with grape, and the enemy left it pretty soon and did not enter it again, but the cannonade was kept up till after dark. Next morning the British moved a large column to their left as if they would come round and attempt to turn our right, and we expected a hot time of it, but they did not come within the reach of small arms, for so soon as they came within cannon shot, some large guns placed beyond our right, which I had not before seen, now opened upon the enemy, cut lanes through 'em, and broke them up, and in a short time, they marched back. The night following, the Americans lay all night upon their arms. At break of day the enemy had moved off. We pursued them to North River, and just as we reached the river the last of the British was crossing into the Jerseys.

We were then ordered back to the Plains and there and in the vicinity remained until after snow came, after which the declarant once went on parade in his bare feet when the snow was four or five inches deep, not because he hadn't shoes, but to show the men it wasn't so great hardship, as they complained of their shoes. From the Plains, the troops moved back easterly (as he thinks) to a place, the name of which he has forgotten, where [he] was discharged; but whether he received a written discharge or not he is unable to recollect. The declarant has always confidently believed that he was discharged on some one of the first three or four days in December, but having seen that his witnesses fix the discharge in November, he is induced to distrust his own recollection in this particular. Of this, however, he is perfectly confident—that, if not in December, it was in the very last of November. He is equally confident that he served his full term of five months, at the expiration of which he assisted the adjutant in making out the payroll.

The said Thomas Craige further declares that, at Northampton, aforesaid, the first part of June, 1777, and immediately on arrival of the intelligence that "the Ti" was given up, he volunteered into a company that was marched off under a Lieutenant Stearns, but was afterwards under command of a captain whose name was (as he believes) Clapp, and on the tenth day of June, 1777, the declarant marched from Northampton to Stillwater, New York, and thinks he went by White Creek. From Stillwater he was marched to Fort Edward and lay near the fort, hard by where Moore's Creek emptied into North River.

From this post he was often sent out with scouting parties and was engaged in skirmishes with the Indians acting under Burgoyne, was of a party that went out to surprise and capture a large company of British officers assembled to sup at a house near their (the enemy's) lines. At this time the American party succeeded in reaching the front yard to the house without being discovered, but as they rushed in the enemy party left the house by the opposite side, their tables standing and provisions prepared.

As the British approached Fort Edward, his regiment, or the corps in which he then was (for he was often transferred for a short time), moved to Schuyler's Meadow and there remained until Burgoyne's army came pretty near them, when the army moved away to Stillwater, from which place he was sent away to assist in removing the hospital to Albany. Then he returned to Stillwater and rejoined the army. In the first part of August he was discharged and sent home in care of a number of sick of the volunteers and reached Northampton on the thirteenth day of August, having been out two months and three days. During this term he acted as sergeant. He was so frequently detached and transferred from one party to another, often finding his company now in this place and now in that on returning from the scouts, etc., that he cannot recollect the names of the officers under whom he served through his various changes of place and duty. He recollects that, of his regiment proper, Murray of Hatfield, Massachusetts, was then major or adjutant.

ALPHEUS PARKHURST *(1760–1842) was born in Holliston and enlisted at Brookfield, Massachusetts, for two three-month tours. In 1778 he guarded prisoners from the Convention army at the Rutland, Vermont, prison camp, and in 1780 he served at West Point.*

No event, except perhaps the Yorktown surrender, made as sharp and lasting impression on the common soldier as Arnold's treason. Parkhurst had been selected as one of the general's life guard, and he was close enough at the time of Arnold's departure to give an accurate description of the dramatic moment.

In one particular, and in this he was joined by many other reminiscing soldiers, he was wrong. André had never visited Arnold's headquarters before his capture.

After the war Parkhurst removed from Brookfield, Massachusetts, to Bennington, Vermont, and finally to Little Falls, New York, where he applied with this narrative for a pension in 1832.

He entered the service of the United States in the Revolutionary War in the state of Massachusetts when he was eighteen years of age in the year 1778, in the spring of the year after the surrender of Burgoyne and in the latter part of the month of March or first of April of said year 1778. He went to Roxbury to muster. He listed into the service into the Massachusetts state troops. The company to which he belonged was commanded by Capt. Thomas Whipple. The orderly sergeant was a Mr. Bellows, and he cannot recollect the other officers of the company. The company belonged to a regiment of which Nathaniel Reed, he believes, was the major and Colonel Rand was colonel.

There was many other companies at Roxbury, but Captain Whipple's company did not long remain there but were sent with Captain Harrington's company to Rutland, near Worcester, to guard the prisoners taken the winter before from Burgoyne, and he, Parkhurst, was with Whipple's company in this service. He believes there were three or four thousand British prisoners at Rutland at this time. The prisoners were all confined in a large piece of ground with high, strong pickets round it so that they could not escape, and this space was occupied by barracks. The business of Parkhurst and the others of the two companies was to stand guard by turns around this picketed enclosure. He continued in this employment for three months, the time for which he listed, and he well recollects the day he was discharged, it being the very day that the wife and two of Burgoyne's men who had escaped were hung for the murder of a Mr. Spooner at Worcester. He did not receive a written discharge. After his discharge he returned home to Brookfield in Worcester County, and it was in the forepart of the month of July. At the time he and his company were discharged, another company came and took their place in the same service.

In the year 1780, and at any rate the same year that General Arnold deserted and in the latter part of the month of July of that year, he listed again for three months in Brookfield, and when the company got together they all went down to West Point with a large body of troops. His company was commanded by Captain Pike, but he cannot now name the other officers. He cannot remember the general officers that accompanied the troops to West Point. On their way to that place, they stopped at Claverack below Albany and waited as much as two weeks, waiting for orders, as he was informed. They went by land all the way to West Point and did not cross the river until they arrived at West Point. When they got at that place, they crossed the river in boats onto the point.

When they had been there three or four days, a draft was made of two men out of each company to form General Arnold's life guard, and he (Parkhurst) and one William Bragg were drawn out of Captain Pike's company for that purpose and went into that service. General Arnold was at that time on the east side of the river, two miles below the point, at a place called in those days Robinson's Farms. General Arnold, he recollects, was a lame man, having been wounded in his ankle, and on that foot he wore a large red shoe. He was a smart-looking man about middling size. His life guard consisted of one hundred men. Arnold lived in Robinson's house and his guard in tents and barracks around it. Their business was to stand guard and sentry around the house and to go on errands to different places and was all the time under arms.

He was present when the Traitor went off. He went from the house of this Robinson, and Parkhurst saw him go. The first he saw of the transaction was the aide-de-camp rode up in great haste, and the general came to the door, and the aide-de-camp ordered the general's horse to be brought as quick as it could be done. The horse was brought out, and he recollects it was a bay horse. The house stands about two hundred or three hundred rods from the bank of the river. The general and his aide started off together for the river, and the aide soon returned and brought back the general's horse. He saw the general dismount, step into a barge that lay there, and draw his sword, and the barge started off in great speed. He saw the barge till it had proceeded near a mile down the river, and the general was sitting down. Three or four British vessels lay down the river, and the *Vulture* lay the nearest, and he always understood that the general went on board that vessel.

He saw Major André at the general's camp several times, dressed in blue citizen's clothes, before Arnold went off. Arnold had a wife at Robinson's house, and he recollects that as Arnold stepped to the door, when his aide rode up, he turned to his wife and said, as near as Parkhurst can recollect, "Something has come to light and I must bid you good-bye forever," and then mounted his steed and galloped away. He recollects that his wife had fits and appeared to be in great distress of mind, and he stood at the door and saw her, and she was in great affliction for several days while Parkhurst remained there.

General Arnold had not been gone over forty or fifty minutes when Parkhurst heard a great rumbling and trampling of horses and, looking round, saw a great smoke of dust, the weather being dry, and in a few moments General Washington with 160 horse rode up, but, as all was then confusion, he did not hear what was said by him. Washington did not stay long, but went back in about fifteen minutes toward West Point, and this was the first knowledge that Parkhurst received of the design of Arnold to turn traitor. The guard did not stay more than an hour at Robinson's Farms after Washington went off but marched directly to West Point. When he got to West Point, he saw General Washington and Major André with him, and he was then dressed in blue citizen's clothes. André's arms were pinioned back, but he rode on horseback. General [Washington] went the same night with all his horse to Poughkeepsie and took André with him. The object, as Parkhurst understood, was to keep that place from being taken, as the general was afraid of some attack at that place, and the general came back early the next morning. He recollects that André was tried before General Greene at West Point, but Washington was not there at the trial.

He (Parkhurst) remained at West Point for two or three weeks after André was hung, which he thinks was in the forepart of October 1780 (but he was not hung at West Point), when his time was out and he was dismissed. He and a great many others with him, among whom was Captain Pike, all in company returned to Brookfield. Here his services as a Revolutionary soldier were ended.

Capture of Andre.

ELI JACOBS *(1762–1839) was born in Killingly, Connecticut, and served three tours of duty in the Massachusetts line and numerous short militia tours from Athol. He was fourteen at the time of his first service, and after quarreling with his stepmother in the spring of 1780 he was almost continuously in service until after Yorktown. Jacobs was chosen to guard André on the day of his execution, and his pension application provides one of the most intimate of the narratives left by the thousands of men who witnessed the event.*

After the war, Jacobs lived successively in New Hampshire, Chester, Vermont, Sempronius, New York, and Almond, New York, and he died in Moravia, New York. He received a pension in 1832.

He entered the service of the United States at the age of fourteen years at the town of Athol, in the county of Worcester, in the state of Massachusetts, as a substitute for Shoda Bates for the term of six months and, according to his best recollection, in the militia of Massachusetts (of this, however, he cannot now be confident) under the following-named officers and served as herein stated, to wit: Capt. Oliver Holmes, Lieutenant Graves, and in a regiment commanded, he thinks, by Colonel Brown on or about the sixth day of April, 1776, and marched immediately to Worcester, and from thence to Roxbury, and remained there in guarding the shore and in drilling and disciplining until on or about the sixth day of October, 1776, when he received an honorable discharge signed by Capt. Oliver Holmes, making a term of service as a substitute, aforesaid, of six months according to the best recollection of this applicant.

That he again entered the service of the United States at Athol, aforesaid, by enlisting on or about the first of April, 1780, for the term of nine months and he thinks in the Continental establishment, but of this he cannot be positive, under the following-named officers: Captain Miller or Mills, cannot now recollect which; cannot recollect the lieutenant's name; Col. Joseph Vose; adjutant's name was Bowles. Marched immediately to Springfield and remained there until officers came after us and then marched to Litchfield and from thence to Danbury and from thence to Robinson's Farms on the east side of Hudson River and then crossed the Hudson River and joined the American troops at West Point, some being assigned to one regiment and some to another, the purpose of our enlistment being to fill up the Continental regiments, as this applicant was informed. Remained at West Point some few days and then marched to Tappan and remained here a short time and scouted and marched and coutermarched and from thence marched to Morristown, from thence to Totaway, and from thence to Crompond, and while we lay here an express came that we must march immediately to West Point, and on our arrival at West Point was the first that this applicant learned that General Arnold had deserted and that Major André was taken. Remained here a short time and then marched to

Crompond and remained there until the second day of October, 1780, when this applicant was on the guard at the execution of Major André.

We took Major André from a stone house in which he was confined, and he walked between two of the American officers, arm in arm, and when he suddenly came in sight of the gallows, he started backward, but on something being said by some one of the American officers, this applicant distinctly heard André say, "I detest the mode." When things were ready, André stepped into a wagon and, after he was fairly under the gallows, took from his pocket two white handkerchiefs, with one of which the marshal pinioned André's arms, and the other André hoodwinked his own eyes with and put the noose of the rope round his own neck. After this, Colonel Scammell told André he might speak to the spectators, at which André raised the handkerchief from his eyes and said, "Bear me witness that I meet my fate like a brave man," and then the wagon was immediately moved from under him and he expired. His body was placed in a coffin, dressed in his royal regimentals, and buried at the foot of the gallows. Soon after the execution of André, marched to West Point and there remained on duty until on or about the first of January, 1781, when the nine months for which this applicant enlisted had expired, and he was honorably discharged by Colonel Vose, he thinks, in writing, making a term of service under the enlistment, aforesaid, of nine months according to the best recollection of this applicant.

That he again entered the service of the United States as a volunteer at Athol, aforesaid, for three months in the militia of the state of Massachusetts under Captain Sibley of the town of Royalston, thinks Lieutenant Works, cannot recollect the colonel's name, on or about the first of August, 1781, and marched immediately to Springfield, from thence to Litchfield, from thence to Danbury, from thence to Fishkill, and from thence to West Point, and there was detached and sent to Crom Elbow on the west side of the Hudson River and there put to chopping wood for the army and garrison at West Point, and our daily task was a cord of wood a day. We remained here until about a week previous to the expiration of the three months for which he volunteered and then returned back to West Point and remained there until on or about the first of October, 1781, when he was dismissed, making a term of service of three months as a volunteer, aforesaid, according to the best recollection of this applicant.

That he entered the service of the United States at several other times not mentioned above as a volunteer and drafted and served sometimes a month, and two months, and ten days, and twenty days, but from the elapse of time, and the change of officers, and the confusion that the frequent depredations of the British and Tories occasioned, he cannot recollect the particular times nor the names of officers but will venture to say that all of his services in the war of the Revolution amounted to more than three years.

JAMES HAWKINS *of Frederick (now Putnam), New York, was drafted for a five-month tour in 1775, in which he was primarily occupied in building Fort Defiance near Kingsbridge. He served a nine-month tour at Kingsbridge as a substitute in 1777 and was a minuteman at Frederick from 1778 until the close of the war.*

While at Kingsbridge, he had a personal interview with the commander-in-chief. Hawkins's narrative delineates a side of Washington that appears over and over in the pension narratives but has been essentially lost in later histories. Instead of the stiff, cold, aloof figure of Stuart portraits and the presidential years, Washington was, to his common soldiers, a warm, fatherly figure. In the dozens of pension narratives that describe personal encounters with the general, he comes off in every instance as an approachable, athletic younger man. Literally thousands of men, especially in the dark winter of 1776 and 1777, when he made personal appeals for units to remain beyond their discharges, saw their service as a personal favor to their friend General Washington.

James Hawkins moved to Reading, New York, after the war. He applied for and received a pension in 1832.

Sometime in June 1775, being then a resident of the town of Frederick (now called Putnam), in the county of Dutchess, in the state of New York, he was drafted from a company of militia commanded by one Consider Cushman for the term of five months. That the recruits thus raised by draft were organized into a company commanded by one Comfort Luddington, or Littleton, and attached to the regiment of our Colonel Swartwout, whose Christian name is not remembered, but who resided in the town of Fishkill in the same county. In eight or ten days after he was drafted, he marched with his company as a private to Peekskill on the North River. Having remained there five or six days, he marched to Tarrytown, thence to Tuckahoe, where the company with the regiment and brigade remained about a month, after which he marched to near Kingsbridge and labored there in building a fort called Fort Defiance. After serving about two or three months, the said James Hawkins was taken sick with what was called the camp distemper, and, being unable to do duty, his brother David Hawkins obtained permission to take him home on condition that he, the said David, would during his sickness take his place in the army. He, counseling to do so, took him home, where he remained about one month, at the expiration of which time he, the said James, so far regained his health as to enable him to return to his post at Fort Defiance, where he continued to serve until the expiration of his aforesaid term of five months and was duly discharged, which discharge has, however, long since been lost or destroyed.

In the spring or summer of 1777, according to the best of his recollection as to time, one Solomon Nixon, a resident of the same town of Frederick above mentioned, was drafted for nine months. In this company of nine-months men commanded by Elijah Townsend, the said James Hawkins enlisted as a substitute for the said Nixon and performed the whole term of service, principally near Kingsbridge. The names of his officers during this tour of duty, according to his best recollection and belief, were the following: Capt. Elijah Townsend, above mentioned, commanded his company in the regiment of Colonel Graham (Christian name not remembered) in General Putnam's brigade or division.

During a part of this time, General Washington, on his way to the South as the said James understood, was in command, and he well recollects a personal interview with him under the following circumstances. He, the said James, and a soldier by the name of Elijah Morehouse, a tent mate of his, being barefooted and having made fruitless applications to their under-officers for a furlough to enable them to procure shoes, applied to the commander-in-chief at his quarters. Having been conducted into his presence by a file of soldiers, they found the general surrounded by officers, who rose, and, pointing them to seats, he himself took a chair and with the utmost condescension and kindness of manners listened to the story of their sufferings. The good general, after a pause of a few moments, replied, "My brave fellows, you see the condition in which I am placed. Yonder upon the East River is the enemy. Should they advance, and we expect them every moment, I shall need every man of you. My soldiers are my life. Should they retire, call again, and you shall have your furlough." The said

James from this service also was duly discharged, but the discharge is believed lost or destroyed.

Wahrhafte Abbildung der Soldaten des Congreßes in Nordamericka, nach der Zeich=
nung eines Deutſchen Officiers. Die Mütze iſt von Leder, mit der Aufschrift Congreß. die
gantze Kleidung von Zwillich überall mit weiſſen Franzen beſetzt, die Beinkleider gehen bis
auf die Knöchel herunter. Die Meiſten laufen barfuß. Ihre Feuer-gewehr ſind mit ſehr langen
Payonets verſehen, welche Sie auch ſtat eines ſeiten gewehrs gebrauchen

After this service, the said James returned home to Frederick, where he continued to reside until the close of the war, acting as a minuteman, turning out from time to time when the alarm was given, by day and by night, sometimes once or twice a week, sometimes longer, and at other times yet shorter. And the said James Hawkins further says that, in view of this service last mentioned, he verily believes it did amount in all to at least one year.

JOSEPH RUNDEL *(b. 1762) of New Fairfield, Connecticut, enlisted in February 1778 in the Continental service. General Israel Putnam took him from the ranks as a waiter. In the general's personal service he participated in one of the memorable events of the war. The true story of Putnam's famous ride down the stone steps near the Greenwich meetinghouse on 26 February 1779 is told for the first time in this previously unknown account.*

Israel Putnam, or "Old Put" as he was affectionately called, was quite a character. He had had an adventuresome career as an Indian fighter in the French and Indian War. He possessed a ready wit, the appearance of hoary wisdom, and a remarkable presence. He was something of a folk hero in his own time, and he played upon this with skillful brilliance. No Revolutionary officer except Washington so thoroughly captured the affection of the common soldier. David Humphreys published an anecdotal biography in 1788 that went through edition after edition.

The stone steps incident had been the talk of the army at the time. The Putnam Hill chapter of the DAR erected a monument in 1900 to commemorate the feat. The fact is, as this account convincingly states, that Old Put dismounted a fifth of the way down and led his horse the rest of the way. If it appeared more spectacular than that to those who watched him descend from the top, the general would have been the last person to contradict the impression.

Rundel was captured after his own escape down the famous steps, was lodged in one of the notorious Sugar House prisons, and staged an escape remarkable for a sixteen-year-old boy. He returned and served with the army until Putnam's retirement. He received a discharge for reasons of health.

After the war, Rundel drifted from town to town for the rest of his long life: Oblong, New York; Cairo, New York; Schoharie, New York; Davenport, New York; Marietta, Ohio; Oxford, New York; Andes, New York; Colchester, New York; Sandford, New York; Menomonie, Wisconsin; and Medina, Ohio. His 1832 application, which included this narrative, was turned down because he had served as a waiter, not as a regular soldier.

I enlisted at Horseneck in the town of Greenwich, state of Connecticut, on Long Island Sound, on or about the first day of February (the day I cannot recollect), 1778, for the term of three years in the Continental service. I was thus enlisted by Charles Bush, a Continental recruiting officer. He was called Captain Bush. I never joined any company or regiment and cannot tell in what company or regiment I did enlist, not being able to recollect. The reason is this. On the day or day after I enlisted, General

Putnam, whose headquarters were at Reading, Connecticut, was visiting Horseneck, one of his outposts. He saw me at that place, at what was called the Picket Fort. He told me I looked too young (I was then in my sixteenth year) to go into the line and said he would take me as his waiter. I told him I should like it. He took me with him to Bush, the person who enlisted me, and told him he should take me as his waiter. I then went into his service in that capacity.

A few days after I enlisted, the British, being a part of General Tryon's forces, I believe, attacked our men. Our men had stationed near the meetinghouse a cannon or two, which fired upon the enemy till they approached in so great force and so near that General Putnam ordered his men to retreat and save themselves the best they could. He also retreated on his horse at full speed, pursued closely by the British horse. He made down a flight of stone steps, the top of which were about sixty rods (I should think) from the meetinghouse. He did not ride down more than fifteen or twenty of them (there being, I think, about one hundred of them in the whole). He then dismounted and led down the horse as fast as possible. I was at the bottom of the steps as soon as he was. He then mounted his horse, told me to make my escape to a swamp not far off, and he rode off.

PUTNAM'S ESCAPE AT HORSE-NECK.

By the time the British horse, who had gone around the hill by the usually traveled road, come in tight pursuit, I run towards the swamp. One of the dragoons (I think there were six who come round the hill) took after me. As I was getting over a stone wall, he overtook me. He halloed, "Stop, you little devil, or I'll take your head off." In attempting to get over the wall, my foot slipped. He struck my left arm with his cutlass and inflicted a wound, the scar of which is still visible. I surrendered. He took me to Kingsbridge near New York City. From there I was sent with other prisoners to the Sugar House in the city of New York and there confined. I remained there about three months.

As I was young and small of my age, they permitted me in the daytime to be out, and I was sent to bring water and do chores about the yard. Some others of the prisoners were also permitted to be out. It was the custom at night to lock us up. The names were called over, and care taken to see all were in. I had gained the confidence of a Hessian soldier named Michael Hilderbrand. He could speak broken English. He was one of our guard at the Sugar House. I proposed to him to go off with me. He at first declined, saying that they would catch and shoot him. He finally consented, and we agreed upon a plan. When he stood sentinel, it being dusk, when our names were called over to go in and be locked up, he secreted me under his watch cloak. When my name was called, he said that I had gone in.

After dark, we started from the Sugar House and went with all haste out of the city about three miles on the Hudson River. We then made a float of some posts we procured from the fence and some slabs and boards and got over the river on the Jersey side. We slept in the bushes. Early next morning we went to a house. They asked us to come in. We declined, as we were lousy. They brought us out some victuals. We then made our way to West Point, where we arrived the next day about dark. The name of the person to whose house we stopped as above was Ephraim Darby. I have known him since. He lived in Cairo, Greene County, New York, and died there about twenty years since. I stayed at West Point two days. They gave myself and Hilderbrand some new clothes. From West Point, I went with Hilderbrand to Horseneck and there again went into General Putnam's service as waiter. I stayed there about five weeks. General Putnam then went to West Point. I went there also on one of the baggage wagons.

I continued at West Point as such waiter till I was discharged, which was in December 1779, the last of the month I think. At the time of my discharge, General Putnam had been gone some weeks from West Point to Connecticut and was there taken sick, as I was informed, and did not again join the army. Previous to my discharge, I was sick and unfit for duty for about six weeks. My brother-in-law Thomas Johnson, who was then in the service at West Point, wrote to my father, informing him of my sickness. Soon after, my father came to West Point with my discharge, which he had procured from General Putnam, he then being in Connecticut. The discharge was signed by Israel Putnam and I think by some other officer. I kept it until my father's house was destroyed by fire, in Cairo, Greene County, New York, about twenty years since. My discharge was burned at the same time in the house.

JOSEPH PARKER *(b. 1760) was born in Groton, Connecticut, and moved to Keene, New Hampshire, where he was drafted to guard prisoners for one month in the spring of 1777. He volunteered in November of that year as an artificer to make shoes, and in April 1778 he transferred to the Connecticut line. Captured by the cowboys near Horseneck in April 1779, he was one of many American soldiers who enlisted in the British army, preferring such service to imprisonment and figuring that a chance for escape would come. Temporarily taking up arms of the enemy, certainly treasonable in more formal armies than that of Revolutionary America, was common. It was rarely censured, provided escape was successfully carried out.*

Parker had a very casual attitude toward his service, and after returning to the American lines he removed to Swanzey, New Hampshire, and never reported back to his unit. He later moved to Windsor, Vermont, applied for a pension in 1832, and finally received sixty dollars a month in 1842.

At Keene, in the state of New Hampshire, where he then resided, in the spring of 1777 he was placed on guard over a party of Tories there taken, but how long he is unable to state. In June next after, an alarm was made and a call for men on account of the British coming up Lake Champlain. He thereupon volunteered, took his gun and pack, and with others went hastily onto the lake without any particular order to reach the scene of action as soon as they could. A little beyond Castleton, Vermont, he met our troops retreating from "the Ti" and turned and went home. He cannot say precisely how long he was engaged in the foregoing services but thinks it was not far from one month.

The said Joseph Parker further declares that at Keene, aforesaid, either the last of October or the first of November, 1777, he enlisted as an artificer (shoemaker) for three years or "during the war," and he cannot say which, in Capt. Gamaliel Painter's company of artificers.

Upon his enlistment, he was marched to Bethel, a parish set off from Danbury in Connecticut, where he remained until (to the best of his recollection) the last part of April, 1778, when by the assent of his officers given he enlisted into Colonel Meigs's regiment of the Connecticut troops in the company of Captain Mansfield. Lieutenant Potter was of the company. He enlisted at Robinson's Farms, going to that place from Bethel for the purpose of so enlisting. He supposes that it was only transferring, as he cannot recollect that any writing was done about it. Soon after this change, the regiment marched to White Plains, making stops by the way, and he remained at the Plains the principal part of the summer, doing scout duty occasionally round Horseneck and its vicinity. Late in the fall he was selected with others to go on a party consisting of two hundred or more who went out to repair the road from the Plains up towards Bull's ironworks near Litchfield, Connecticut, preparatory, as he understood, to the moving the artillery to that place. On his return from this duty, he was seized with the putrid fever and remembered nothing of what passed for two months or more after this except his being carried into the hospital, a Quaker meetinghouse at Quaker Hill, so called. After he got some better, he was transported to a hospital in Danbury, Connecticut. Remained there some time, and by kindness and attention of the inhabitants there, among whom he wandered, he gained some strength, and in March after (1779), so nearly as he can recollect, he joined the company again at Reading, Connecticut, but did not do much duty, as he thinks he was on guard but once.

He thinks it was in April after this (1779) there was a detachment of men to go down upon the line,.and he (though still out of health) was of that detachment. They went to Horseneck and thence to White Plains, where they continued scouting and watching for some time. After this they marched back to Horseneck. Here, another (a young man) and myself went out to get us some fresh provisions, and a party of cowboys took us up and carried us to Kingsbridge. While on the way to Kingsbridge, the cowboys told us that they had a guinea a head for all they took up and brought in, and that we would have to go on board of a guard ship. He thought it would be dangerous in his poor health to go to the guard ship, and he offered to, and did, enlist with the British, intending to escape from them as soon as he could. After he enlisted with the British, he remained with them at Kingsbridge a short time, during which he was three or four days so sick that he could not set up. After he had there been with them nearly or quite three weeks, he drawed a suit of clothes and a gun. A few days after this, he moved to Valentine's Hill.

During this time, thirteen of the men, one an "old countryman" and twelve Americans, agreed to come off, and if they could not get off any other way, were to fight their way through. They lay at Valentine's Hill but a little time before four of them (of whom he was one) had a chance to come off. The way they got away was this. The ensign had been out into the country, and when he came back he said he wanted some of the American boys to go and get some pigs which he had seen and told us where he had seen them. The declarant then told the ensign, what was not true, that he knew the place where the ensign said the pigs were.

After dark, the "old countryman," two others, and himself (the four above spoken of) set out. The night was rainy and dark. Before they went, someone said that the ensign told him that he (the ensign) was going on the outpost that night and they could go by. They started, and on coming to the sentry, he hailed them. They answered and said they were going after the pigs, and he replied to them in nearly these words, "Go and prosper." They passed, and finding that they could not tell the way, the night was so dark, they called up a man and inquired the way to Valentine's Hill, and then they went the opposite way and just at daybreak got onto the Plains. Here they found a man plowing, who told them where the nearest guard of the American troops was, and they marched nearly two miles to said guard. The guard gave them breakfast and sent them to the commanding officer at Horseneck. He asked them a few questions, and the declarant asked him for a pass, and he gave him one, and he came to Swanzey, New Hampshire, where his mother lived.

When he got home, his friends told him that his brother Amasa, who was in service, had written home that he had been over to see the declarant, but he was lost, and they supposed him dead. On this the declarant procured a man to write his brother Amasa, giving an account of his adventure and requesting him to see his officers and let them know about it. To this Amasa replied, saying that he had been to see the officers, and they said they should be glad to have him come back and join the company. He did not go back. The reason was, that if he went back and the British took him, it would be death for his deserting them, and he has always supposed this was the reason his officers never sent for him again nor said any more about it. He reached home in June 1779. He knows that at Hatfield and other towns on Connecticut River they had just begun haying. His health remained very poor for a long time after he reached home. He has no documentary evidence of any of his services; he never received any written discharge.

WILLIAM PATCHIN *(b. 1760) was born in Weston, Connecticut, and served three terms in the state militia from Ridgefield and Wilton. Southwestern Connecticut and the entire shoreline on Long Island Sound were, from 1776 until 1783, within striking distance of British-held territory. Armed parties on both sides initiated numerous raids: British soldiers and Tory cowboys attacked through Westchester County, New York, into Fairfield County, Connecticut, and Americans attacked in the other direction; whaleboat raids were launched on both sides between Long Island and the Connecticut shore. William Patchin saw his full share of this guerrilla warfare, and he described various incidents on the mainland and on Long Island with remarkable clarity and detail.*

For Patchin and his fellow soldiers who were to confide so much in pension narratives dictated fifty years after the events, Revolutionary service was the primary act of their lives. Patchin was a millwright by profession but apparently was not very successful. After the war he moved ten times, from town to town in Connecticut and New York. By the time he got around to applying for his pension in 1846, his contemporaries were mostly gone and acquaintances were several towns behind him. His name does not appear in the standard (though incomplete) list of Connecticut soldiers, but internal evidence strongly supports the authenticity and general accuracy of his narrative.

I was born on the sixteenth day of December, 1760, at the town of Weston, county of Fairfield, and state of Connecticut, and was in my fifteenth year when the war of the Revolution broke out. I went in my sixteenth year to learn my trade (that of a millwright) at Ridgefield, Fairfield County, Connecticut. Ridgefield was not far from Fairfield, the county seat of Fairfield County, and during my apprenticeship I often attended on duty to guard the courthouse during the sessions of the court to guard against the incursions of the enemy, bodies of whom were then stationed at Huntington, Lloyd's Neck, on Long Island. I recollect once, while on guard, one Squires, an artilleryman (I think his name was Daniel), had his hands shot off while ramming down a cartridge with an iron ramrod.

Fairfield County lay on the sound and was subject to incursions from the British and Tories from time to time. In 1779 a body of state guards was formed in the county of Fairfield. Early in 1779, and I think in the month of April, I enlisted in Captain Hull's company belonging to this regiment, which was composed of cavalry, for nine months. Mr. Hoyt (I do not recollect his given name) was the first lieutenant of our company; Mr. Husted (I do [not] recollect his Christian name), coronet; Corporal Lockwood (his Christian name I cannot recollect), who was afterwards promoted to be a captain. I do not remember the other corporals' names.

As soon as we made up our company, which was rising [?] of a hundred, we went to Greenwich. Met in Greenwich. One Colonel Delancey, a British officer who commanded a regiment of Tories, had come up to Greenwich on a plundering and marauding expedition, and our company went to defend the town. We met at Greenwich and went on duty there. Greenwich lay on the sound and was the most southwestern town in the county of Fairfield. Our duty there was to divide into scout patrols and scatter through the country and, if we found a party of the enemy, to give notice to the militia to rally. The county was infested with marauding parties of British and Tories.

I recollect that in the month, I think, of August, 1779, I was out on one of these scouting parties to reconnoiter the enemy. We were about a hundred and perhaps more in all, part of whom were from our company and part from the neighboring towns, Danvers, New Milford, Stratford, and other neighboring places. We marched to New Rochelle in Westchester County in the state of New York, near the Saw Pits, where we met a detachment of the enemy of about an equal force sometime in the afternoon of the day in the month of August, as nearly as I can recollect the month. We met on four corners. Major Tallmadge, who belonged to Colonel Sheldon's regiment, commanded our party. He was a large, strong, and powerful man and rode a large bay horse which he took from the British. He was a brave officer, and there was no flinch in him. He was a man of few words, but decided and energetic, and what he said was to the purpose. We blocked the corners by forming in close column and waited for the enemy to come up. They formed as they came up. We had an engagement with them which lasted half an hour, if not more, when they sounded a retreat. They were all mounted men, light horse. They retreated, and we followed, killing some and making some prisoners, the number I did not know. I was in the right part of the line, and early in the engagement one of the enemy, a strong and good-looking fellow, rode up, spurred up to me, and said, "Get back, you damned rebel."

I said to him, "Keep your place." He then made a pass at me, cut through my cap, and wounded me slightly on the forehead, and the scar now remains. I then made a pass at him and so used my sword that he fell from his horse, and, although I do not know the final result, I have no doubt he never afterwards raised the battle cry of King George and his herd of cattle-stealing Tories. Major Tallmadge saw it and shouted, "Thank God Almighty. Give them another."

We made it our headquarters at Greenwich during all of the time I served in the guards. I enlisted in this troop of horse for nine months, and we lay at Greenwich on service during the whole nine months, off and on, and served during that time according to my enlistment. My time was out in the winter of 1779–80, which was a hard winter, and the sound was frozen over and the snow fell deep. I served and ranked as a private and acted as a pilot or guide.

In the spring of 1780, and to the best of my recollection in the month of April (it was after the snow had gone off and before the leaves were out on the trees), I enlisted in the regiment of foot, comprising a part of the Connecticut state guards, for nine months. The officers of our regiment were Col. Samuel Canfield of New Milford, Major Smith (his Christian name I cannot remember). The officers of the company in which I served were Capt. Hanford Hoyt of the town of Stamford, First Lieutenant Raymond (his Christian name I do not recollect), Ensign Raymond (I do not recollect his Christian name, they were brothers), Joseph Patchin, a first cousin of mine, was orderly sergeant, and Jacob Richards, second sergeant. There were two more sergeants, but their names I do not remember. Moses Gates was first corporal, and the names of the others have escaped my memory. Gideon Weed was our steward. Our company was stationed at North Street in Greenwich. Our duty was to separate

Tisdale del et sc.

BRITISH HEROISM.

into scouting parties to protect the country from marauding expeditions of the enemy.

There was a man named Frink, a notorious cowboy, a refugee who had held the rank of major in the American service, who kept his headquarters at Morrisania, near New York, who commanded some seventy-five Tories who came out to Greenwich on a plundering expedition about the latter part of April or first of May in the year 1780, shortly after we went on duty. He came with a detachment of about fifty Tories and came up to reconnoiter our position. We were then lying about five miles from Greenwich meetinghouse. He came up in a field to the west of us. We exchanged shots with him. They were mounted and on horses I have no doubt they stole from the Whigs. Colonel Wells commanded our party. After Frink had retreated a short distance, he shouted to his men: "Come," said he, "let's give Colonel Wells another shot before we go." They did form, and we exchanged shots, and a young man who had shortly before been discharged from the regular army, the Continental service, a fine young fellow of our party, was killed and was the only one of our party who was injured. They then retreated, and we saw them no more at that time.

In August 1780 I heard that Frink was down at Pecksland and told all of our company who were willing to go out with me to follow. A party of about one hundred was raised, and we came up with Frink's party on the main road from Boston to New York. When we came up, Frink's party ran, but Frink remained. I fired at him and cut his coat under his arm, and he then turned and retreated. They left their cattle, which were returned to their owners. During this occurrence, I was out in a party of about thirty volunteers who had requested me to act for them as guide. We stopped at a schoolhouse some half a mile from Greenwich meetinghouse to refresh ourselves, where we were surprised by a party of the enemy mounted. Our party foolishly rushed out and were all cut down except myself and one Blackman. I stove out the back window with the butt of my musket, and myself and Blackman leaped out and ran through an orchard, running from one tree to another and followed by two of the enemy, mounted, who said, "Give up, you damned rebels." I shot one of them and Blackman the other, and we jumped over a fence nearby and escaped.

In the latter part of August we had another engagement with Frink in the town of Rye, about eight or ten miles from Greenwich meetinghouse. There were about eighty in our party and some seventy in Frink's. We defeated his detachment, killing and wounding several in this engagement, which lasted about three-fourths of an hour and in which I was wounded a little below the right knee. The engagement took place near a large stone house about a half a mile from a Mr. Budd's tide mill on the sound, about eight o'clock in the morning. One Ensign Hoyt commanded our party. Frink came up in an orchard just above the stone house. We formed behind a stone fence and were ready to receive them. During the action one Sergeant Brown was wounded, but not mortally. During the action Ensign Hoyt said to me, "Pilot, what do you think of a charge?"

"Short meter," I replied, and we sprang over the fence and went at them, and they immediately retreated. Near the close of this action I received the above-mentioned wound, a little below the right knee, by a musket ball and was laid up, disabled about a fortnight. Our officers were kind to us.

Sometime in the latter part of August or first of September, 1780, a party of some fifty or sixty British and Tories came over from Long Island in seven whaleboats who landed on the west side of Horseneck. I had been down two or three days before and ascertained they were coming. We met them with a party of four or five hundred and took them all prisoners and took their boats. We had other engagements and skirmishes between our scouting party and those of the enemy from time to time. I served in the foot my whole time of enlistment in the year 1780 nine months. I served as a private and was detailed as a pilot or guide.

In the spring of 1781 I again enlisted for nine months at Wilton in Fairfield County. Col. Samuel Canfield was colonel of our regiment. Capt. Hanford Hoyt was captain of our company. The names of the other officers I cannot recollect. I was detached from the company a good part of the time, acting under Capt. Ebenezer Couch of New Milford. My duty this year also was that of a pilot or guide. I enlisted as a private and served as such until about the middle of the summer, when I was appointed sergeant major of the regiment and held that office until the close of the period of my enlistment. We were engaged in reconnoitering from time to time. We were stationed in the middle road between the North River and Boston Road. Our regiment went down into Westchester County, New York, during the forepart of the summer. Washington and his army were there. It was before he went south to take Cornwallis. Our company was there, and I was also there. I recollect that a body of about thirty of the enemy were at one time firing at Washington's life guards when some eighty of us, under the command of Captain Couch, attacked them and defeated them. They retreated, and we returned to camp.

During this year, but at what particular time my memory will not enable me to state, Major Tallmadge took five hundred men to take Fort Slongo on Long Island. My best recollection as to the time is that it was about the first of July. We crossed the sound in the evening and got there about midnight. The fort was occupied by about three hundred of the enemy. We surrounded the fort, and, on being hailed by the sentinel, the words, "Groton, goddamn you," rang all around our lines, alluding to the taking of Fort Griswold. I never saw fellows more frightened. They cried "Quarters! gentlemen, quarters!" and immediately surrendered.

In the summer, and I think in the forepart of the summer, of one of the years during my service and which I have forgotten and cannot recall it, the British sloop of war *Shuldham* of eight guns lay off Belden's Neck. Lieutenant Deforest of the Continentals raised a party to take her and came to me, and I joined them. We muffled our oars and dropped down to them in the evening, and some ten or eleven o'clock P.M. we boarded her. They retreated to the cabin and bolted the door against us. We turned one of the pieces, a six-pounder, and threatened to put a ball among them. They then surrendered. We took the sloop to Norwalk, and she was afterwards used as a privateer.

Cornwallis was taken in the fall of the last year of my service as above stated, and we had no engagements of consequence afterwards. In the fall our regiment returned into the west part of Stamford and threw up what we called a fort and erected barracks. I served out my time, nine months. We were paid for services in Continental bills, but after the French came we had some silver. The whole period of my service in the state guards of Connecticut was twenty-seven months.

JONATHAN NICKERSON *(1762–1840) was born in Ridgefield, Connecticut, and served from there. He volunteered at age fourteen and served one year as an artificer in the Continental army in 1776. He joined the militia at the time Danbury was burned, volunteered in the state militia in the spring of 1780, and served as a substitute in the New York line for six months in 1782.*

A considerable portion of Westchester County, New York, was virtually uninhabitable during much of the war, with bands of Tories, British soldiers, and Americans roving through the countryside, foraging, looting, reconnoitering, and attacking enemy patrols on similar missions. Nickerson's narrative gives readers a sense of what this no-man's-land was like. He was wounded and captured by James Delancey's notorious cowboys, a highly effective Tory unit, and was luckier than many who met that fate and were either killed or sent to the terrible prisons of New York.

Nickerson moved from Ridgefield to Cairo, New York, in 1784. He submitted this narrative in 1832 and was granted a pension.

In February or March 1776 he entered the service by enlistment in the quartermaster's department in the town of Danbury, county of Fairfield, state of Connecticut, as an artificer for the term of one year under Captain Clark, who kept the office of the department at that time. Maj. Ezra Starr was assistant quartermaster general. He (the applicant) worked the first part of the time at building barracks and workshops, the latter part of the time at building wagons and carriages, ironing them, and at other smith's work. He was informed that the department was under the Continental establishment, and as there were large stores deposited in this town, there was a commissary and paymaster who acted in the department and gave him his rations and pay. The commissary's name he believes was Edwards, and the paymaster's, Everett. He (the applicant) quartered in the barracks and served out the full period of his enlistment.

He further says that in April 1777 he was informed that a British force had landed and was proceeding towards Danbury. He volunteered and proceeded to said Danbury, where he found the British in possession of the same and the stores. The stores were burnt by the British, consisting, as was said, of 1,800 barrels of beef and pork, 800 of flour, 2,000 bushels of grain, clothing for one regiment, 100 hogsheads of rum, 1,790 tents. He pursued the enemy under General Wooster to Ridgefield, where he (Gen. W.) was wounded. They pursued them to their ships, when he (applicant) returned.

And he (the applicant) further says that in the month of February or March 1780 or 1781, then living in the town of Ridgefield, Fairfield County, state of Connecticut, a detachment of the militia was called out to proceed to the lines then kept at or near Horse-

David Wooster. Esq.r
Comand.r bey der Provinc.al Armee in America

neck, state of Connecticut. He volunteered his services with others, as was said, for thirty days. He was marched to Horseneck and there joined a company commanded by Capt. Richard Shute, name of lieutenant, Frisby, at first commanded by Col. John Mead, afterwards by Colonel Canfield. After being there a short time, he (the applicant) enlisted to serve nine months. A Sergeant Little had orders to recruit, with whom he enlisted. Served in the same company and under the same officers.

After he had served under his enlistment for two or three months, his regiment was ordered on a scout, by order as was said of General Waterbury. Marched to or near White Plains and made a halt, as was supposed for the night. After calling out the guard, there were ordered two scouts to be taken, consisting of one sergeant, one corporal, and twelve privates each, and the say was, "Who will volunteer?" Sergeant Little, he (the applicant), and several others belonging to the same company volunteered. The sergeant being unacquainted with the scout, he was directed to proceed. A pilot was procured for his party. This party of Sergeant Little's, of which the applicant was one, left the regiment and proceeded down towards the British lines for several miles till very late in the night. Made no discoveries; put up at a house where the people had fled and left empty, between the lines, and refreshed themselves and stayed till near daylight. Then proceeded on towards the British lines kept, as they were informed, at Frog's Neck.

They proceeded down to within two or three miles of the British encampment, when they discovered a number of horses in a meadow near a house; went to the house, found two armed men watching the horses, disarmed and examined them; said they and five others turned out the horses to feed, did not know where the others had gone. After some threats, showed them where the saddles and bridles were. Caught the eight horses and took the two men prisoners and commenced returning to the regiment.

Had gone about four miles on their return when they discovered a drove of cattle, forty-four head, driven towards the British lines. Came near enough to discover nine armed men with the cattle. Held a council and concluded to attack them. Rushed upon them, dismounted, and turned the horses loose into the drove. Several shots fired, and one of their men fell. The rest ran. None hurt on the American side. In the bustle, the two prisoners escaped. The man wounded had his thigh shot through and bone fractured; left him and requested a family nearby to take care of him. In the skirmish, the cattle and horses ran into a grove nearby. Collected them together and proceeded on. Sent forward to find the regiment; found they had moved, where, they did not know.

A little distance below and east of White Plains they were overtaken by a party of British horse, seventy or eighty in number, said to belong to Colonel Delancey's corps. The horse came upon the party full speed and were in the midst of the cattle and horses before the party could move through the drove, calling out, "Surrender, you damned rebels, surrender!" Several of the party were struck down, when he (the said applicant) presented his musket to surrender. Instead of receiving it, he was struck down to the ground, his skull fractured, and cut through the bone for four inches or more and, while lying on the ground, was rode over and struck four strokes in the head and several in the body with a cutlass. No one of the party escaped except the pilot (Honam) to carry the news to camp. One of the party, after the British left, was alive and was brought in by the inhabitants to the house where he (the applicant) was.

After he (the applicant) had been stripped of his neckcloth and silver shoe buckles and his pockets searched by the British, they discovered that he was not dead, for he had lain perfectly still before plundered. The captain then asked him to what troops he belonged and how many there were of the party, which he told him. Captain said one had escaped and asked him if he could ride with them to the British lines. He answered he could not tell, as he did not know how bad his wounds were. He was then put onto a horse and told that he must try to ride. He rode on with them perhaps half or three-quarters of a mile, when he grew faint with the loss of blood and clung down by the horse's mane in the road and told them that he could go no farther with them.

Someone asked, "Shall we kill him?" The captain said, "No, let him alone. He will die soon himself."

He (applicant) asked captain to tell the people in the next house to come and bring him in. Said he would, and presumed he did, for in about half an hour a number of the inhabitants living between the lines came and carried him (applicant) into the house of one Joseph Hart in a blanket. They also brought one more of the party belonging to the same company by the name of O'Brien who died in about an hour. The next morning two doctors, belonging as they said to the Continental line, having been down to the British lines with a flag of truce, called and cleaned and dressed his wounds.

He (the deponent) remained at Hart's for fourteen days. During that time, had not been dressed, undressed, or out of the couch on which he was first laid. Late in the night of the fourteenth day, a detachment of British horse and foot commanded by the captain who made him prisoner came and put up to the house where he lay. He said it was more than he expected to find me alive and said something must be done or he would soon be off and fighting them again. Said he would put deponent under parole and wrote two. Each took one, the words of which deponent well remembers. They were these, "I, Jonathan Nickerson, acknowledge myself a prisoner to the British army and do pledge my faith, word, and honour that I will not say or do any thing prejudicial to the British army until exchanged and that I will come into the British lines as soon as able," signed by both. Captain signed "Frederick Williams, Capt. Comdr., Frog's Neck." The same morning the British marched off towards the American lines.

About ten o'clock of the same day, a party of militia commanded by Capt. Ichabod Doolittle, of twenty-five or thirty men, and a company of Continental troops commanded by Captain Fog, belonging to New Hampshire, it was said, came to Hart's house. He showed them his parole. They said they came purposely for him, and he must go with them. They took and put him on a led horse and brought him to the American lines and from thence home to Ridgefield. He, deponent, further says that he had not his own arms and accoutrements when taken and had to acccount for those taken. And he, deponent, further says that soon after this he requested Ezra Nickerson to go to the lines and bring his equipments and clothing home and inquire of General Waterbury what he should do about answering his parole when able. Ezra told him that General Waterbury said he need not answer his parole, that he, General Waterbury, would see him exchanged soon, and that the deponent need not return for the remainder of his time. Received no written discharge.

And he, deponent, further says that in the month of March, 1782, he entered into the service as a substitute for one John Barber, hired by him, and subscribed his name to the roll for nine months and was accepted by Capt. Henry Pawling. Then lived at Ridgefield, Connecticut. Joined the company and regiment at Marbletown, Ulster County, New York. Regiment commanded by Col. Frederick Wisenfelt; company in which he served commanded by said Captain Pawling. Regiment was stationed by companies on the frontiers to protect against the Indians. Captain

Pawling's company was stationed at Saugerties, Ulster County, New York. Served out the full period of the enlistment, nine months, and was discharged at Kingston, Ulster County. Received no written discharge; were called New York levies.

BENJAMIN JONES *(b. 1764) was born at White Plains, New York, and moved with his family to Horseneck, Connecticut, in 1769 and to Norwalk in 1776, from which place he served a one-month and two two-week tours at Horseneck in 1780. He joined the Connecticut line for a one-year term as a substitute in May 1781.*

Benjamin Jones was obviously a great storyteller, and the lack of documentation on many skirmishes that occurred between the lines around occupied New York makes it difficult to corroborate or disprove his account. His service is clearly documented in existing Connecticut muster rolls of 1781, and Waterbury's regiment was indeed stationed in Westchester County in the summer of 1781. A Maj. Mansfield Bearmore commanded the Loyal Westchester Refugees, but he had been killed in November 1780 at Pine Bridge, more than twenty miles north of Byram Bridge. Jones may have relied on the notoriously bad "camp news" for the identity of the cavalryman who was shot, or there may have been more than one Tory with the same name. Whatever the case may be, he left us one of the most exciting personal narratives of the war.

Benjamin Jones left Norwalk in 1789, and over the next fifty years he moved nine times in Connecticut and New York. He made this declaration of service in 1832 and was granted a pension.

He was born at the White Plains, state of New York, in the year 1764. That he has no record of his enlistment. That on the fifteenth day of May, 1781, he entered the service as a substitute for Jonathan Taylor in the town of Branford, state of Connecticut, under Capt. Nathaniel Edwards of the town of Waterbury and state aforesaid in the regiment commanded by David Waterbury of Stamford, and that he joined the regiment at Greenwich, in the state of Connecticut, and stayed there till June and then marched to White Plains and remained there till November. His service was keeping guard and scouting.

The French light horse during the time lay at White Plains. The French used the password "France." Saw the French light horse have a battle with the Tory horse at Morrisania, near Rochelle, not far from White Plains. This was the time that Waterbury was ordered down to Frog's Neck to dislodge a regiment of Tories. He was in the battle on the island. This was in August, about harvest. A part of the Tories were driven aboard the British vessels and a part killed and some taken prisoners of war. Their fieldpieces were dislodged and broken and thrown into the creek. Destroyed their provisions and liquor.

He was a scout before the last-mentioned battle and went to New Rochelle and came out onto the main road from New York to Boston about eight o'clock A.M., thinks in the month of July. His officer made a halt. They had been out all night, and while halting a gentleman rode up and asked where the commander of the scout or party was.

Ensign Smith, who had the command, said, "I am here."

He said, "You have got sixty light horse in a quarter of a mile of you."

Smith said, "I care not for that."

The man rode away. Smith ordered the men to ready, and you saw the light horse coming in sight on full speed. The scouting party struck across the fields, and the light followed, and they formed into a hollow square. They formed around his party, there being only twenty-seven of his party. The commanding officer of the horse told Smith if he would resign himself up he should be used like a prisoner or he would parole him and his men. Smith told him he should not do it.

The officer of the horse said, "If we have to fight and take you, we shall cut you into inch pieces."

Smith said, "You must take us first."

The officer said he would give five minutes to surrender.

Smith said, "Charge and be damned."

Every man was ordered on his right knee and the britch of his gun on the ground, and Smith stood in the center and told his men the first that gave back he would cut his head off with his sword. Then one-quarter of the horse charged on them, and their horses were pricked, and one of the horses was thrown, and the rider fell over into the hollow square. And Smith put his foot onto the horseman's sword and said, "I have got one. I want some more. Charge again."

The horse made another charge and were repulsed. And the third charge was made and repulsed again, and our party took a prisoner and killed a horse, and one of his own men's arm was broken and bayonet was broken. And the horse rode off and formed, and our men all raised on their feet and rested, and the prisoners sat in the center.

Smith then ordered one of the soldiers to take the commander off of the horse as he was parading his men. The soldier drew up and shot him, and he, the officer, fell dead. Then another officer took the command, and he was ordered to be shot, which was done. And the third took command and rode out from the horse and said to Smith, "If you will give up, it shall be well. If not, we will send for 100 more horse, and have you, we will."

Smith told him to "send and be damned. I want to manure the ground with the Tories, so that it should bear something after the war."

Two of the horse were dispatched immediately. Smith ordered his men into rank and file at two paces distance in front, and rear opposite to the spaces so as to fire through them. Smith ordered the front rank to begin a scattering fire on the right and to fire to the left and then the rear to do the same from the left to right, and every man to take good aim, which was done, which drove the horse off. There were but twenty-four left [on] the field beside the two that had been sent away. The rest were taken or killed or wounded, and their scout went home to their own party.

Also he was at Byram Bridge in June, same year, just before he went to White Plains. They heard news the Tory horse were coming down that night upon the guard. The commander ordered the applicant to stand at the butment of the bridge and acted as sentry, and a guard lay behind the butment of the bridge in a garden. And the lieutenant stood near the bridge and said he must not hail till they struck the bridge, and a sentry was placed below the bridge a quarter of a mile on the York side. In the night, about midnight, he heard the sentry hail below.

They answered, "A friend."

Sentry asked, "To whom?"

They said, "To America."

The sentry told them to stand and advance and give the countersign, and [a horseman] advanced and said he had not got the countersign, but was a scout of the American horse which had been out, intending to stay at the guard that night. The sentry let them go. On they came, and as the first horse struck the bridge, the applicant hailed. They made no answer, and they came on. He hailed a second time. No reply, but they came on. And as he hailed the third time, he fired, and the forward man fell, who was discovered to be one Nathaniel Bearmore, captain of the Tory horse whom the applicant had before known. He jumped, as he was ordered, over the wall and over the guard which lay behind it and ran to the guardhouse, and the guard rushed on the Tories and broke them to pieces. And the Tories rode before the guardhouse and formed, and our men, one-half went up under the wall, leaving a space between the two parties of the guard, and as the horse returned towards the bridge, they came between the two parties and were fired upon both ways, and twenty-six were killed and wounded out of the sixty. About the first of November, he went to North Stamford. There was a redoubt built there. Stayed there all winter and was discharged in May, about the middle. Had a written discharge signed by Waterbury, which is lost. He served one year. Before the above-stated service, when he was sixteen years of age, about the month of May in year 1780, he volunteered to keep guard at Horseneck under Captain Sellick of Norwalk. Stayed two weeks and was dismissed. About middle July, volunteered; went again under Lieutenant Comstock. Thinks his captain was from Wilton or Norwalk; does not recollect his name. Stayed at Horseneck two weeks and was discharged. And in the month of October, same year, he volunteered to guard the shore of Norwalk to keep the Tories and British from coming over to get provision. He was under Captain Scofield; served one month and was discharged. Has no documentary evidences of his service.

3
COUNTERING BURGOYNE

DAVID HOLBROOK *(b. 1760), born in Sturbridge, Massachusetts, volunteered at age sixteen for six months' service in the Rhode Island militia. He later served one term in the Continental army and four in the Massachusetts militia of Berkshire County. His father saw active duty as a commissary, his older brother was a surgeon, and much of Holbrook's service was in supporting capacities as well: guard of munitions and stores, wagoner, surgeon's steward, and on his last term, August to December 1781, simultaneously adjutant, quartermaster, and quartermaster sergeant for a battalion. He commanded a company in the hard-fought Battle of Johnstown on 25 October 1781.*

It is his description of the Battle of Bennington, one of the decisive American victories, but one very poorly documented, that makes this a highly important record, particularly of the second battle with Breymann's reinforcements. The heroic "old man," seen by Holbrook as almost a supernatural figure, must have been an officer of Seth Warner's regiment. Warner's arrival in midbattle was largely responsible for the final victory.

Holbrook's family had moved to East Hoosac, Massachusetts, in 1776, and after the war he moved to several New York towns, settling for good at Lafayette, Onondaga County, in 1802. He submitted this narrative in 1832 and was granted a pension.

That he entered the service of the United States under the following-named officers and served as herein stated. That he entered the service, aforesaid, about the first of December, 1776, at Providence, in the state of Rhode Island, in the company under the command of Captain Mason and Lt. Benjamin Freeman, in the regiment of militia commanded by Colonel Holman, as a private soldier and continued in said company little over two months. Then said Freeman gave him the command of a guard of twelve or fourteen men and sent them to Rehoboth in the state of Massachusetts to guard an old ashery in which was said to be ten tons of powder. That he stayed and guarded said powder fifty-three days and was then relieved and went home near the last day of March, 1777.

That at the time of entering the service aforesaid this declarer resided with his father at Sturbridge, Worcester County, Massachusetts. That when he returned from the service aforesaid, his father had sold his farm and immediately thereafter removed to East Hoosac, Berkshire County, in the state last aforesaid, when on the third day of June, 1777, the declarer enlisted or volunteered under Lt. William White, a militia officer, to serve until duly discharged, and went to Bennington in the state of Vermont, where said lieutenant with his men, twenty-eight or thirty in number, stopped and guarded the storehouses a short time and then went to Manchester in the same state and then halted and remained waiting orders two or three weeks. From thence, pursuant to orders, went to Willard's Tavern in the town of Pawlet, where were some military arms which they guarded until the sixth day of July, 1777, when they were joined by a Continental captain with twenty-four or twenty-five men and sixty or seventy head of cattle for the army and went to Skenesborough, where they were met by a number of invalid soldiers who had escaped from Ticonderoga, which had been attacked by the British army under the command of Burgoyne and which was evacuated by General St. Clair. The cattle were then driven back to Pawlet and thence to Manchester, and this declarer, with a sergeant of the Continental troops and about twenty-eight or thirty men, went on and very soon met the vanguard of the British army and had a little skirmish, and while this declarer was intent upon firing upon the enemy, the sergeant and all the men except three had left him, and the British had got between, when this declarer and his three companions made their escape by running across Wood Creek upon some trees that fortunately had fallen across it. But a sergeant of the enemy pursued, and as the two hindmost of this declarer's companions were crossing on the log, he cried out to them to surrender, whereupon this declarer fired upon him, and he fell. This declarer and his three companions, after remaining in the woods all night, started in pursuit of their company and overtook them at Allen's Tavern in Pawlet, aforesaid, and went on to Willard's Tavern, aforesaid, and waited there ten or twelve days until the stores were removed and thence went on to Manchester and there remained until about the first of August, when, this declarer being sick and his father's team having come to bring a load of provisions for the army, he obtained a furlough and went home.

That he remained at home at East Hoosac aforesaid (now Adams) until the fourteenth of August. In the morning, having regained his health, and hearing the alarm that the enemy were about to attack Bennington, this declarer started immediately and got to Bennington the same night, and next morning went to the lines of the enemy and remained there watching their movements that day. And, the next day being the sixteenth of August, Capt. Enos Parker, Lieutenants Kilborn and Cook of the Massachusetts militia, belonging to Colonel Simon's regiment, selected a company of sixty or seventy men from the men who had promiscuously come together, of which this declarer was one, and marched them across the river by a circuitous route of five or six miles, mostly through woods, with all possible silence and brought them up in a piece of woods at the enemy's rear, where a line was formed and the company aforesaid formed on the right, and there, pursuant to orders, sat in silence until a signal (the firing of two muskets) was given, when the American army, upon three sides of the British encampment, made a simultaneous attack, the American army under the command of General Stark and the British army under the command of General Baum. The American army made a rush upon the British entrenchments, which being received by the British with boldness, the battle became general and desperate immediately and continued about two hours close combat without form or regularity, each American fighting according to his own discretion until the entrenchments were completely routed, and those who had not been killed and had not escaped surrendered at discretion. General Baum, being wounded, was among the prisoners.

About the time of the general rout of the British army, and [while] some of them were running to escape, Colonel Herrick of the Green Mountain Rangers rode along near where the declarer was and cried out, "Boys, follow me." And this declarer with one other ran after him about two miles to Ramplar Mills, where he stopped his horse, and drew up his piece, and fired, and then wheeled his horse and said there was a reinforcement of British coming, which was soon discovered to be from nine hundred to twelve hundred British soldiers with a nine- and six-pounder and a band of music. Colonel Herrick ran his horse to give intelligence to General Stark, and this declarer and his companion, having got out of breath, ran behind a haystack and rested till the British army came along and then went out from behind the stack and discharged their pieces at the enemy and ran. The enemy returned the fire by the discharge of a six-pounder, which gave general alarm. The Americans then ran together and formed about a mile southwesterly from the entrenchments which had been occupied by General Baum and headed the reinforcements, which was under the command of Colonel Breymann and Major Skene of Skenesborough, but the Americans, in pursuing those who escaped from the entrenchments, had got scattered and fatigued, and but few assembled at first, but kept falling in continually until a line was formed along a fence on the northeast side of the meadow in which was the haystack, aforesaid, in the edge of a piece of woods. And the British army formed a line in the meadow and extended across the road. And the firing commenced as soon as they came within musket shot, but the Americans, not being sufficiently strong to keep the ground, retreated from tree to tree, firing as they left the trees, until they came to a ravine where was a log fence, then made a halt, and held the ground. The British came up within about sixteen rods and stood. The firing then continued some time without cessation, when Colonel Warner, with the remains of his regiment, came up, and some of his men, understanding the artillery exercise, took one of the fieldpieces taken in the first engagement and formed at the right of the party in which was this declarer.

And, about the same time, an old man, with an old Queen Anne's iron sword and mounted upon an old black mare, with about ninety robust men following him in files two deep, came up and filed in in front of the company commanded by Captain Parker, in which this declarer then was. And, just as the old man had got his men to the spot and halted, his mare fell, and he jumped upon a large white oak stump and gave the command. Captain Parker, seeing the old man's company between him and the enemy, ordered his men to file in between their files, which were some distance apart, and which was immediately done, and the battle then became desperate. And immediately this declarer heard a tremendous crash up in the woods at the right wing of the American troops, which was seconded by a yell, the most terrible that he ever heard. Then he heard the voice of Colonel Warner, like thunder, "Fix bayonets. Charge."

Then the old man on the stump cried out, "Charge, boys," and jumped from the stump and ran towards the enemy. His men, some with, and some without bayonets, followed suit and rushed upon the enemy with all their might, who seeing us coming, took to their heels and were completely routed. As we came up to the enemy's lines, their fieldpieces being charged, a Sergeant Luttington knocked down the man with the port fire and caught hold of the limber and whirled about the piece and fired it at the enemy, and the blaze overtook them before they had got ten rods and mowed down a large number of them. Those of the Americans who had not got too much fatigued pursued and killed and took a number of the enemy (British). The Indians that survived the slaughter escaped.

This declarer, in the scaling of the breastwork of the enemy in the first engagement, put his right hand upon the top of the breastwork and threw his feet over, but his right leg was met by a British bayonet which held it fast, and he pitched headfirst into the entrenchment, and the soldier hit him a thump upon the head. But he was dispatched by the next man that came up, and this declarer was thereby relieved, and in the heat of feeling forgot his wounds. But when the enemy fled in the second engagement, he found himself exhausted and could not pursue, the blow upon his head and the wound in his leg having occasioned the loss of considerable blood. He found himself unable to walk and was put upon a horse and carried back to Bennington, where he remained ten or twelve days, until he got sufficiently recovered from his wounds to march, when Lieutenant White, with whom this declarer enlisted, came on, and he went with him to Manchester, soon after which this declarer was taken with a fever and was sent home, where he remained sick a number of months. And on twelfth February, 1778, Lieutenant White came to this declarer's father's and gave this declarer a discharge, he being then very sick and not expected to recover, and was not able to do duty during the whole of the year 1778. . . .

THOMAS WOOD *(b. 1756) was born in Rehoboth, Massachusetts. He enlisted in the Massachusetts line in June 1775 and served six months on garrison duty at Crown Point and Ticonderoga, returning to his home in Pownal, Vermont, after completing his term of service.*

The Burgoyne expedition, commencing favorably with the hard-fought victory at Hubbardton and the capture of Ticonderoga, began to falter with the defeat at Bennington on 16 August 1777. British supplies were running short, the terrain was rugged, and the American militia from throughout New England, sensing Burgoyne's vulnerability, were gathering for the kill.

By early September it was clear that Burgoyne was aiming for Albany, toward Gates's army. His only options were to push south or to retreat by way of Lake George, Ticonderoga, and Lake Champlain to Canada. Gen. Benjamin Lincoln, stationed at Pawlet and relieved of possible direct attack by the British force, moved quickly to cut off Burgoyne's line of supply, communication, and possible escape. On 13 September Col. John Brown, at Poltney, received orders to attack the British garrisons on Lake George and Lake Champlain. Colonel Herrick's men, Thomas Wood among them, marched by way of Castleton to Cold Spring, on the east side of Wood Creek, where they crossed in boats captured by Colonel Woodbridge at Skenesborough. By the seventeenth, Colonel Brown and his militia had arrived on the heights near Mount Defiance, unnoticed by the British General Powell. On the eighteenth they captured the landing at the head of Lake George, a guard unit stationed on Mount Defiance, and the blockhouse at the mill. They then crossed the bridge to the west side of the outlet and captured a barn and a storehouse.

The British were able to withstand an ineffectual siege upon Fort Ticonderoga and Mount Independence, and on 22 September Brown set off with captured vessels and cannon to obtain British stores on Diamond Island at the southern end of Lake George. The British garrison there under General Aubrey had been warned by an American deserter, and the American bombardment failed. Brown burned his vessels on the east side of Wood Creek and marched to Skenesborough.

Simultaneous to Brown's activities, Burgoyne had been brought to battle at Freeman's Farm on the nineteenth. The brief campaign Wood participated in with Colonel Brown had not been a complete military success, but it had helped tighten the noose around the British army. Burgoyne surrendered on 17 October. The British evacuated Fort Ticonderoga and Mount Independence on 8 November.

Thomas Wood served two more brief, uneventful tours of duty in 1778. He moved to New York State after the war and was living in Groton, Tompkins County, in 1833 when he successfully applied for a pension with this deposition.

He enlisted at Williamstown in the state of Massachusetts in June 1775 as a volunteer in the Massachusetts line under Captain Stewart, Sergeant Childs (does not recollect the names of his other company officers), in Colonel Easton's regiment as a private for the term of six months and served his term out. He marched with the company immediately after enlisting to Crown Point on Lake Champlain, passed through Bennington and Manchester to Skenesborough (now Whitehall) at the head of said Lake Champlain. Here the company took boats and went by water to said Crown Point. This place had a short time previous been taken by our troops from the enemy. The upper part of the fort had been burnt, the magazine blown up. He says our people took a great quantity of lead out of the magazine. His duty while here was garrison duty. Towards the latter part of this six months, some part of the troops at the said station of Crown Point were ordered, including the company to which he belonged, to Ticonderoga on said lake, where they were stationed in the fort. Here his duty as before was garrison duty. When his said turn expired, he was regularly discharged and returned immediately home to Pownal in the state of Vermont.

He next enlisted as a ranger in July 1777, at Bennington in the state of Vermont, for six months under Capt. John Warner and Lieutenant Easton. The company, as was then said, consisted of three hundred rangers, which was soon augmented by two hundred militia from Stockbridge in Massachusetts. Under the said captain and lieutenant last named, they marched from Bennington aforesaid through Manchester, Rutland, to Castleton, where the company halted three days. From thence they marched by the direction of a pilot through the woods to Cold Spring on the east side of said lake. During this march, Col. James Herrick took the command of the troops, and while they lay at Castleton, Colonel Herrick sent to Skenesborough a number of soldiers who made arrangements for a number of boats to meet the company at said Cold Spring and then returned to Castleton loaded with pork for the use of the company. Each soldier was then furnished with nine days' provisions.

When they arrived at Cold Spring, it was about three o'clock in the morning. The route was rough and fatiguing. They halted at a little distance from the said spring in a hollow, and while the men were cooking some victuals, their officers went down to the spring to drink, after which they concealed themselves in ambush near the shore of the lake, and while so lying they discovered a boat with five of the British regulars coming down the lake. They came ashore and made directly for the spring, and after drinking, and when returning to their boat, our officers arose upon them and captured them and their boat. These regulars, as they confessed, were going to Skenesborough to get the pork which our troops had just obtained and then had in their knapsacks as above stated. This was while it was yet dark, and soon after the boats expected from Skenesborough arrived while the troops were busily engaged in eating. They were ordered to march. They were accordingly immediately embarked on board the boats and by nine o'clock A.M. were all safely landed on the west side of said lake and immediately marched up the lake in the woods. During this march they were ordered to make no unnecessary noise and at night forbid to make any fire or to speak a loud word. They were two days and two nights on this march and halted at Fort George landing. This was at break of day. Colonel Herrick ordered an immediate attack upon the enemy's fortifications. They captured them without resistance, consisting of five hundred.

They were immediately ordered to attack the enemy at Mount Hope, and in the meantime Captain Allen, one of the American officers, was ordered by Colonel Herrick to attack a captain's guard stationed on Mount Defiance and who had charge of a brass eighteen-pounder, a part of whom he captured and a part escaped and fled to Fort Ticonderoga. The troops marched up and came upon the enemy at Mount Hope on surprise and captured the blockhouse and a gristmill, both of which were occupied by the enemy as fortifications. Also at this time our troops captured a number of cattle and horses. At the landing, aforesaid, were five hundred American prisoners, previously captured by the British at Hubbardton, [who] were recaptured by our men. The scene was now reversed: the five hundred British in their turn became prisoners, disarmed, and put under the care of the aforesaid five hundred American prisoners and ordered to march for Bennington aforesaid.

Immediately our troops were ordered to cross the bridge over the outlet of Lake George. This was promptly done, and our troops marched up and captured a house and a barn (and the troops within), which were surrounded with tents and filled with the enemy. They then marched directly into the breastwork of Fort Ticonderoga. Here they found our cannon, which had been left by our troops when they retreated, which they found spiked. Our commanding officer ordered these cannon put in order, which being done, they, together [with] the aforesaid eighteen-pounder, were turned upon the enemy within the said fort. At this time the enemy held possession of Forts Ticonderoga and Independence and also had a number of vessels on the lake. On the shore of Champlain, near the fort, was a storehouse in which our troops discovered a large quantity of European goods which we captured and loaded three boats therewith and in the night were sent to Skenesborough. Every precaution was taken to guard against giving alarm. A guard was sent along shore, of which this deponent was one, to defend the boats, but they passed in safety to the place of their destination. And he further saith that our troops captured a sloop and a number of boats from the enemy at the landing aforesaid.

After remaining a short time at Fort Ticonderoga, aforesaid, Colonel Herrick ordered the troops to take the aforesaid cannon from Fort Ticonderoga and the said eighteen-pounder on Mount Defiance, put [them] on board the said sloop, which being done, the troops embarked for Diamond Island, where it was reported Burgoyne had deposited large sums of money designed for the payment of the British troops. This island is in Lake George. They moved up the lake to said island and made an attack upon the enemy. This engagement was with cannon and a very severe one. A considerable number of our men were killed and the said colonel ordered a retreat, the sloop being very much disabled by the shots of the enemy. Our vessels moved down the outlet of Lake George into a bay, on the south side, where they were burnt. They then marched through the woods to Fort Ann, and from thence to Skenesborough, and from thence to Pawlet in Vermont. The aforesaid goods was sent from Skenesborough to Pawlet and deposited in a house owned by one Wilson. Here deponent was discharged.

In the month of June, 1778, he again entered the service at Bennington aforesaid as a ranger under Captain Seeley, Ens. Daniel Welch, and Sergeant Wright. Does not recollect any other company officer's name. They marched under said officers to Saratoga, and from thence to Fort Edward, and from thence to Jessup's Patent. This service was three weeks, and was then discharged. In the month of July, 1778, he volunteered under the said Captain Seeley and Lt. Solomon Wright to guard the military stores at Pownal, Vermont. This service was two months, according to the best of his recollection.

RICHARD WALLACE *(b. 1753) was born in Nova Scotia, moved with his family to Thetford, Vermont, and in 1775 was sent to school in Exeter, Connecticut. He volunteered in February 1775 and served with the Con-*

necticut troops near Boston until the British evacuation. He returned to Thetford and had begun clearing a new farm when "the great Burgoyne alarm," as he called it, brought him back into military service as a ranger for a month in the spring of 1777 and again from July 1777 to January 1778.

Wallace, like Thomas Wood, was attached to Colonel Herrick's regiment and served under Colonel John Brown on his expedition against Ticonderoga. As noted in the introduction to Wood's narrative, Brown was on the peninsula between Lake George and Wood Creek on 17 September. A small British fleet lay in front of Ticonderoga, and a separate American militia force under Gen. Jonathan Warner was on the east side of Wood Creek, ready to attack the British post on Mount Independence. Wallace and his companion Webster were chosen by Colonel Brown to carry a message to Warner, coordinating their attacks. It is almost certain that Wallace's swim took place at dusk on 17 September. They would have walked from Brown's camp, a few miles south of Mount Defiance, to the western shore of Wood Creek. They swam to the eastern side, slightly below Mount Independence.

The water of Lake Champlain is frigid in mid-September, and the swim deserves to be considered one of the greater athletic feats of the Revolution. Wallace's memory and his description are vivid, although he is off by about two weeks on the date of the expedition. On the eighteenth, attacks were made on both sides of the lake, though success was achieved only to the west.

Wallace returned to Thetford, Vermont, after the war, farmed there throughout his life, and submitted this narrative in 1832.

In the month of February, 1776, about the first as near as I can recollect, I enlisted into Captain Mason's company of Lebanon, in the state of Connecticut, for the term of two months, one Chamberlain being the lieutenant and one Abbott being the ensign of said company, which is all that I can recollect about the officers of the army at this time. But I can well remember the service I performed. I was among those who went onto the Dorchester Heights near Boston the first night to build the two forts which we completed by daylight. I was drafted to go into Boston to cleanse the town from the smallpox and guard the town, where I remained a number of days and saw the Castle blow up. When the British troops were gone, the two-months men were dismissed without pay in the month of April, about the first as near as I can recollect, at which time I left the service by parole permission, having served out my term and returned to Thetford, where I did then and do still reside, and commenced a settlement on a new farm about six miles from Connecticut River in the west part of the town and moved my family into said farm in the spring of 1777. Shortly after my removal, the great Burgoyne alarm, as it was called, was given, when it was said that General Burgoyne had planned to send three detachments to distress and destroy the habitants on Connecticut River from Newbury to Brattleborough in Vermont and Charlestown, New Hampshire. This design was discovered by our scouts taking one of the British scouts or spies who had orders to the Tories to be ready for the massacre. Of the statement I am certain, for I saw the orders and heard them read at Charlestown, New Hampshire. At the alarm, the people west fled to the river, where the inhabitants were more numerous, to save their lives and property. I, among others, left my farm and volunteered as a ranger and followed scouting up and down Connecticut River from Newbury to Charlestown and to the west. In this service I continued about one month. I am certain that it was more than three weeks.

I further declare that on the fifteenth day of July of the same year, 1777, I enlisted as a private for six months as an Indian spy in Capt. Elisha Benton's company and Colonel Herrick's regiment, then called rangers, John Powell being lieutenant of said company. We marched to Manches[ter] in Vermont and then to Pawlet, where our business was to scout in various places and to guard the frontiers. In this train we continued until the last of September or first of October, when General Burgoyne was so hemmed in and surrounded by General Gates's army that he could not escape, only by forcing his way to Lake George and there taking shipping to Lake Champlain and proceeding on to Canada. To prevent this, General Gates contrived to cut off the British watercraft on Lake George, and for that purpose sent two detachments of five hundred men each, one on the west side of the lake to the south side of the mountains that lie south of Ticonderoga, where our troops were ordered to halt. I belonged to this detachment.

Directly after halting, Colonel Brown came to me and inquired if I could swim. I told him I was not a great swimmer. He said he wanted me to swim a little way but did not then tell me where or for what purpose. After excusing myself a little, I agreed to swim, [as] he was exceedingly earnest to have me engage. He then said he wanted a man to go with me and enquired who would volunteer in the service. A man by the name of Samuel Webster offered himself and said he was a great swimmer. Colonel Brown engaged him to go with me. This done, Colonel Brown called several officers and some soldiers, and we all set off together and traveled up the mountain a few miles until we came in full view of the British encampment, and, after reconnoitering the mountain east and west for about three miles and taking observations, the officers arranged all things for an attack at break of day the next morning. Colonel Brown then called Webster and myself and told us of "the little way" he wished us to swim, which was nothing less than across Lake Champlain, then in view about five miles distant. He accordingly gave us our instructions, both verbal and written, and we made our [way] over rocky mountains and through hurricanes of fallen trees to the lake, where we arrived a little before sunset, so near the enemy's ships that we could see them walk on their decks and hear them talk, and had they seen us they might have reached us with their grapeshot.

With deep anxiety for the event, we undressed, bound our clothes upon our backs, drank a little ginger and water, and entered the cold waters of the lake, here about a mile in width. Webster went forward, and I followed. After proceeding a few rods, I was on the point of turning about. The water was so chilling I thought I could never reach the opposite shore, but when I reflected that the lives of many of my countrymen might depend upon the success of my effort, I resolved at every hazard to go forward, and if I perished I should die in the best of causes. When we had got into the middle of the lake, the wind blew and dashed the water onto our bundles of clothes and wet them and made them very heavy. And the garter with which I bound on my bundle swelled and got across my throat and choked me and exceedingly embarrassed me. When we had swam about two-thirds across, I found myself almost exhausted and thought I could not proceed further. But at the instant I was about giving up, the Lord seemed to give me new courage and strength, and, shifting my manner of swimming a little, I went forward and soon discovered a tree directly before, about twenty rods from the shore. This tree I reached with a struggle and thought I could not have obtained the shore if it had been to gain the world. The tree was large, and I made out to get onto it and adjust my bundle.

At this instant Webster, who was about twelve rods north of me, cried out, "For God's sake, Wallace, help me, for I am adrowning!" The cry of my companion in distress gave me a fresh impulse. I swam to the shore, ran opposite to him, and directly found there poles, which had been washed upon the beach, about twelve or fifteen feet long. I flung one toward him, but it did not reach him. I flung the second without success. The third I pushed toward him until the further end reached him; he seized it and sunk to the bottom. I then exerted myself with all my might and drew him out, I hardly know how. As soon as he came to a little and could speak, he cried out, "O Lord God, Wallace, if it had not been for you, I should have been in the eternal world." I told him not to make any noise, as the enemy might be watching us in ambush.

I then wrung his clothes and dressed him and put on my own, and we set out to find the American encampment. But it soon became so dark that we lost our way, and in a short time we found ourselves in an open field near the enemy's guard. We then returned into the woods and remained in a secure place until the moon rose, which appeared to rise directly in the west. I, however, told Webster the moon must be right, and we traveled on until we came to the road that led north and south, just as the enemy fired their nine o'clock gun. But we did not know whether to go north or south. Our object was to find General Warner's encampment and deliver our express to him. But we were not certain whether he was north or south of us, and we might fall into the enemy's hands, let us go which way we would, and the whole plan of our officers fail of success. In this trying dilemma, we agreed that one should go north, followed by the other at few rods distant, and risk his life to the best advantage, and if taken by the enemy, the hind one should go south and deliver the express. It fell to my lot to go forward, and, after I had traveled about an hour, I came to a sentry who hailed me and said, "Who comes there?"

I answered, "A friend."

He asked, "A friend to whom?"

I asked him whose friend he was.

He then said, "Advance and give the countersign."

This I could not do, as I did not know the countersign of this detachment. I knew the sentry was an American from his voice, yet he might be a Tory in the British service. I then asked him in a pleasant voice if there was another sentry near and if he would call him. He did so, and to my great joy, I knew the man and informed them at once that I was a friend to America and had brought an express to their commander and requested to be conducted to him immediately, and, calling Webster, who was a few rods behind, we were conducted by an officer and file of men to General

Warner's quarters and delivered our message, both written and verbal. I also informed General Warner that the British were much nearer than he imagined, and that unless everything was kept still in the camp, the plan would yet fail. He then ordered all lights to be extinguished and no noise to be made. We then retired a little into the woods and lay down cold and wet in blankets furnished us by the commissary, and when we awoke in the morning all our troops destined to this service on both sides of the lake were in motion. The Indian spies took possession of all the watercraft belonging to the British on Lake George, and about five hundred prisoners were taken. After this I continued the scouting service in the vicinity of Ticonderoga until about the first of January, as near as I can recollect, and then returned to Pawlet in Rutland County, Vermont, and was then dismissed, having served out my term of six months to the acceptance of my officers.

SAMUEL WOODRUFF *(1760–1850) was born in Southington, Connecticut. He served as a substitute for his brother in Westchester County in 1776; served two tours with the militia in 1777; and served ten days at New Haven in July 1779 at the time of the Tryon raid.*

The high point of Woodruff's military career was his participation in the second Battle of Freeman's Farm, 7 October 1777. His description of the event, obviously based in part on after-the-fact knowledge of the enemy's movements and perhaps on historical reading, also contains detail that could only have been related by an observant participant.

Woodruff moved to Windsor, Connecticut, after the war. He prepared this narrative in 1832 and was granted a pension.

On or about the fifteenth day of August, 1776, according to his recollection and belief, his brother Jason Woodruff, then of said Southington and then belonging to a militia troop of horse, was drafted for an unlimited tour of military service to be performed at White Plains and its vicinity. That this applicant was accepted as a substitute for said Jason and performed the service of that tour at White Plains, East and West Chester, and Mamaroneck and continued in that service to the fifteenth or sixteenth day of November than following. Colonel Trout, he believes, commanded the regiment; the name of the officer commanding the company not remembered. During the continuance of this term of service, no battle of importance was fought in that section of country excepting that at White Plains, about the twenty-eighth of October, in which he was not engaged, and respecting which he is unable, from his own personal knowledge, to state any particulars. He has no documentary or other positive evidence that Colonel Trout commanded the regiment in which he served, but distinctly remembers that once or twice while on this service he performed the duty of sergeant of the grand rounds with that officer in the night, visiting the sentinels and guards at the various posts and giving them the countersign. He remembers also that, for the first time, he had the pleasure to see Generals Washington and Fayette at White Plains.

That on or about the twenty-sixth day of April, 1777, he volunteered his service as a private soldier in a military company which marched from said Southington under Capt. Asa Bray of said Southington, since deceased, to perform a tour of military duty at Danbury at the time the British troops under the command of General Tryon burned the public stores and several private buildings at that place. That in this service he was absent from home twelve days. While at Danbury, he, together with Whitehead Howd, Daniel Sloper, and Mark Newell, all of said Southington and belonging to said company, but now deceased, went into a house where they found several of the family ill with the smallpox. They immediately withdrew from the house but, having been exposed to the disease, were advised by the officers of the company to be inoculated without delay. All of us except Howd, who had a numerous family of children, complied and were inoculated. That about eight or ten days after our return home, said Howd broke out with the smallpox in the natural way. We went into the town hospital together, where this applicant was confined by said disease thirty-five days. The physician's bill and all other attending expenses were paid by his father.

Respecting this tour of service, the applicant would state the following reminiscences. The different bodies of the American troops were commanded by Generals Wooster and Arnold of New Haven and General Silliman of Fairfield. General Wooster was mortally wounded, and General Arnold's horse was killed under him in a battle with the enemy between Danbury and Norwalk. Dr. Atwater of New Haven was also killed by a musket shot through his head while firing upon the enemy from behind a stone wall.

This applicant further declares that on or about the tenth day of August, 1777, he was enrolled as a volunteer soldier in a military company under the command of said Capt. Asa Bray at said Southington and marched with them through Albany to Saratoga, where on or about the twentieth day of October, three days after the surrender of General Burgoyne with his army, our company was disbanded, and he returned home about the first or second day of November following. He would further state that while in this service at Saratoga he was engaged in the battle fought by the hostile armies on the seventh of October, the following particulars of which, together with many others which might be related, he distinctly remembers: viz., that about eleven o'clock in the forenoon of that day, the British troops advanced under the command of General Fraser, who led up the grenadiers, drove in our pickets and advanced guards, and made several unsuccessful charges with fixed bayonets upon the line of the Continental troops at the American redoubts on Bemis Heights, near the headquarters of General Gates. But meeting a repulse at this point of attack, the grenadiers commenced a slow but orderly retreat, still keeping up a brisk fire. After falling back two or three hundred yards, this part of the hostile army met and joined with the main body of the royal troops commanded by Lord Balcarres and General Riedesel. Here, on a level piece of ground of considerable extent called Freeman's Farms, thinly covered with yellow pines, the royal army formed an extensive line with the principal part of their artillery in front. By this time the American line was formed, consisting of Continentals, state troops, and militia. The fire immediately became general through the line with renewed spirit, and nearly the whole force on both sides was brought into action. General Fraser, mounted on a gray horse a little to the right of their center and greatly distinguishing himself by his activity, received a rifle shot through his body (supposed to be from one of Colonel Morgan's sharpshooters), of which he died the next morning at eight o'clock at the Smith house, then the headquarters of General Burgoyne. Soon after this occurrence, the British grenadiers began reluctantly to give ground, and their whole line, within a few minutes, appeared broken. Still, they kept up a respectable fire, both of artillery and musketry.

At about this stage in the action, General Arnold, while galloping up and down our line upon a small brown horse which he had that day borrowed of his friend Leonard Chester of Wethersfield, received a musket ball which broke his leg and killed the horse under him. He was at that moment about forty yards distant from this applicant and in fair view. Isaac Newell of said Southington, since deceased, and one or two others assisted this applicant to extricate Arnold from his fallen horse, placed him on a litter, and sent him back to the headquarters of General Gates.

A regiment of the royal grenadiers, with the brave Major Ackland at their head, in conducting the retreat came to a small cultivated field enclosed by a fence. Here they halted, formed, and made a stand, apparently determined to retrieve what they had lost by their repulse at the redoubts in the commencement of the action. They placed in their center and at each flank a strong battery of brass fieldpieces. The carnage became frightful, but the conflict was of short duration. Their gallant major received a musket ball through both legs, which placed him hors de combat. Retreat immediately ensued, leaving their killed and some of their wounded with two brass fieldpieces on the ground. Ackland, leaning upon a stump of a tree in the corner of the fence, was made prisoner by Adjutant General Wilkinson and his servant, who were passing by. They dismounted from their horses and, placing the major on the servant's horse, sent him to General Gates's headquarters to have his wounds dressed.

The retreat, pursuit, and firing continued till eight o'clock. It was then dark. The royal army continued their retreat about a mile further and there bivouacked for the night. Ours returned to camp, where we arrived between nine and ten o'clock in the evening. About two hundred of our wounded men, during the afternoon, and by that time in the evening, were brought from the field of battle in wagons, and for want of tents, sheds, or any kind of buildings to receive and cover them, were placed in a circular row on the naked ground. It was a clear, but cold and frosty, night. The sufferings of the wounded were extreme, having neither beds under them nor any kind of bed clothing to cover them. Several surgeons were busily employed during the night extracting bullets and performing other surgical operations. This applicant, though greatly fatigued by the exercise of the day, felt no inclination to sleep, but with several others spent the whole night carrying water and administering what other comforts were in our power to the sufferers, about seventy of whom died of their wounds during the night.

The next day (October 8th), this applicant was detached from our company to assist others detached from other companies in burying the dead remaining on the field of battle. This was a sad and laborious day's work. On the cleared field already mentioned and within the compass of a quarter of an acre of ground we found and assisted to bury between twenty and thirty dead bodies of the royal grenadiers. The brigade in which this term of service was performed was commanded by Gen. Oliver Wolcott of Litchfield, former governor of Connecticut.

That on or about the fifth day of July, 1779, when a body of British troops under the command of General Tryon came to New Haven, this applicant was called out by alarm, and, as a volunteer, went to New Haven and West Haven with a military company from said Southington and placed himself under the command of Gen. Andrew Ward of Guilford and was absent from home in this tour of duty ten days, making in the whole of the different terms of his military service, including the time he was in the hospital with the smallpox, seven months and twenty days.

SIMEON ALEXANDER *(b. 1757), a lifelong resident of Northfield, Massachusetts, served three terms in the Massachusetts militia. He was in the American camp around Boston at the time Washington took command, at Saratoga when Burgoyne capitulated, and on a brief, unproductive march into New Hampshire in 1780. If his camp intelligence can be believed, Burgoyne came close to losing his life to an American cannonball the day before his surrender.*

Simeon Alexander successfully applied for a pension in 1832.

About the last day of May, A.D. 1775, one Elihu Lyman, who had the rank of ensign, came to Northfield from the army then lying at Cambridge and told us that men were wanted in the army. I, together with a number of others, agreed to go down, and we left home either the very last of May or the first of June (I cannot be sure of which, but I think the first of June) and went down and joined the army. I enlisted in the company of Captain Smith of Hadley, a town near Northfield, as soon as I arrived at the army, which was not more than four days after I left home, but I cannot fix in my mind upon the very day on which I enlisted. I enlisted for eight months, though I believe it was called the nine months' service. The company officers were Captain Smith, First Lieutenant Kellogg, Second Lieutenant E. Lyman. I think Captain Smith died while I was with the army, and Lieutenant Kellogg was promoted. I remember the names of only two other captains in my regiment, Captains Hubbard and Millins. My regimental officers were: Ward, colonel, and Majors Bigelow and Barnes.

Major General Ward was in command of the army at the time I enlisted. Soon after, General Washington came and took the command. General Lee came with Washington, I believe. I remember him well; he was a small man, and the soldiers used to laugh about his great nose. Morgan came with his regiment of riflemen either with Washington or soon after his arrival. The uniform of Morgan's regiment was a short frock made of pepper-and-salt colored cotton cloth like a common working frock worn by our country people, except that it was short and open before, to be tied with strings, pantaloons of the same fabric and color, and some kind of a cap, but I do not now remember its form. This was their summer dress. They were stationed at Roxbury. Generals Warren and Sullivan were also with the army and General Putnam. I remember his looks well. He was not a tall man, but very stout and strongly built, and he had a remarkable head of white bushy hair. My impression is that Generals Gates and Montgomery were also with the army. I do not remember that my regiment was numbered or had any particular name, except Colonel Ward's regiment. We were stationed east of the colleges, on a hill, at a work called Fort No. 2. We were there on the seventeenth June when the Battle of Bunker Hill was fought.

Major General Putnam.

During all the early part of the battle we were kept under arms and ready to march, and towards the last of the battle orders came for the regiment to move, and it marched onto the hill, but I believe was not engaged. I say I believe, for I did not march with the regiment. My orders were to stay in the fort, which I did. I was told at the time that they met the American troops retreating and

An idealized view of one of Morgan's riflemen

came back. Some were wounded, but I believe none were killed. Sometime after the battle, my regiment was ordered to Dorchester. We were billeted about at different houses. Captain Smith's company was quartered at the house of a Colonel Clapp, where I remained till the middle of September, when I was taken sick and got leave to go home and came home. I had a written permit signed by Colonel Ward. I kept it for many years, but I have now lost it, I do not know how. I came home and did not return.

In the month of July, 1777, Colonel Williams of Warwick, a town adjoining to Northfield, who commanded the militia regiment in which I was then enrolled, sent to Captain Hunt of Northfield information that men were wanted in our northern army which then lay at Ticonderoga. The company in Northfield were called together, and I was among those who volunteered to go. The volunteers from Northfield and Warwick united and formed a company. The company officers were Captain Proctor and Lieutenants James and King. Colonel Williams and Major Locke were our regimental officers. The only other officer in my regiment whose name I now remember was Captain Sweetser. I cannot tell the very day we left home, but it was not far from the fifth of July. We marched through the western part of Massachusetts and thence to the Hudson River, which we came to a little above Troy. We thence marched up the river to Fort Miller, where we met the advanced guard of our army. The main body were lying at Fort Edward. We were attached either to the brigade of a French general (whose name I cannot spell, but we called him General Pouroi) or to the brigade of General Poor, I do not remember which. General Schuyler was then commander-in-chief, and General St. Clair was also with the army. I recollect also Colonel Scammell and Major Hull. The army was retreating, but we were sometimes stationary for several days at a time.

While the army was lying in Saratoga Meadows, orders came for a small party to go to the rear to a place called McKneel's Ferry. I was among those detached to join this party, which was commanded by Major Hull and numbered about one hundred men. Captains Hutchins and Murray were also with the party. We marched about three miles to the rear and arrived at the ferry about ten o'clock A.M. Here we were told that scouts were wanted and that they who would go out scouting should be excused from standing sentry, a duty we were very glad to escape from, for the Indians were all around us in the woods and frequently shot down our sentries while on duty. I volunteered to go out as a scout and was absent all day but returned to the party in the evening without seeing the enemy. In the course of the evening, Major Whitcomb of the rangers, who had been out with a party which had been attacked and dispersed by the enemy, came to our party and told Major Hull that the British were near us in great force. Major Hull said he would send and see, and Adjutant Howe, who belonged to our party, volunteered to go. He went, accompanied by a soldier, and in a short time they returned and reported that a very large body of troops, apparently the whole British army, were lying on the plain at the distance of about half a mile. Major Hull sent notice to General Schuyler of the position of the enemy and asked for a reinforcement. The answer was an order for us to do our duty. We remained under arms all night, expecting the enemy. About eleven o'clock A.M. a party of British troops, about two hundred in number, appeared, descending a hill about thirty rods off. At the bottom of the hill they displayed and fired a volley, when we were ordered to retreat. We fell back about sixty rods to a piece of woods, which we had hardly entered when the Indians rose up from the bushes on each side of us and fired upon our party. Each man then made his escape in the best way he could, and about one-half of our number were killed or taken. I escaped without a wound.

Soon after this time, I left the army and returned home, the time for which I had engaged being expired, but I do not recollect how long I was with the army at this time nor at what date I set out on my return. I had no written discharge. I came directly home, where I had been, I think, only a day or two, certainly not more than a week, when, hearing that our services were much wanted, forty or fifty of my townsmen, and I among the number, enrolled ourselves into a company under Captain Merriman and marched back to the army. I am not certain whose regiment my company was attached to at this time, but I think it was Colonel Williams's of Vermont. I did not cross the river, and General Bailey was the only general officer on the east side of the river whom I remember. He commanded on that side. On the day in which the Battle of Bemis's Heights was fought, I was stationed at a place called Schneider's Mills on the Battenkill River, very near the place where the river emptied into the Hudson. Being on guard in the night of that day, I heard some persons approaching, challenged them, and called the officer of the guard. He came, and two men on horseback were brought in who, being carried before Captain Merriman and examined, proved to be the bearers of orders from General Gates to General Bailey to march up the river and cut off General Burgoyne's retreat in that quarter. The men were suffered to proceed, and early in the morning we received orders to march and moved up the river about seven miles to an old fort whose name I have forgotten. Here we were higher up than Burgoyne's army, and here we found a very large body of militia.

We were soon after marched down the river to a place opposite to where Burgoyne lay, and, while there, a circumstance occurred which I will relate. There was a small red house on the other side of the river, situated on a side hill near a little river called by us Schuyler's River. This house was just out of musket shot from our position, and an officer one day observed, "Who knows but Burgoyne is in that house?"

"We will try it and see," said another. So they brought a gun to bear on the house and fired. We heard the cannonball strike the house, and immediately a number of men, who we thought were officers, ran out of it. During the following night there was a cessation of arms agreed upon, and the next day some of the British soldiers came over into our camp, and one of them told me that Burgoyne and his officers were holding a council of war in that house at the time the ball passed through it.

Soon after this time Burgoyne surrendered, and a few days after his surrender we were dismissed and came home. It was the month of October when we were dismissed, and I think a little past the middle of the month, but I cannot be sure of the day. I am certain that from the time I left home in July to the time I returned in October, which I did directly after being discharged, was more than three months, deducting my intervening absence, but I cannot tell the exact time. I received no written discharge.

Sometime in the year 1780 a company from Northfield volunteered to go against the enemy who had just burned Royalton, Vermont. I was among the number. We marched to Oxford, New Hampshire, under the command of Capt. Elisha Hunt, but, learning that the enemy had retired, we returned. I think I was absent from home at this time about three weeks.

At each of these periods of service I was a volunteer. I never was drafted, nor was I ever a substitute. I never had any documentary evidence of service except the written permit, which I have mentioned above and which I have now lost. I never was in a battle other than the skirmish above mentioned, nor have I ever been wounded. My brother, Elisha Alexander, knows of my having been out, and I can procure his testimony to the fact.

4
NEW JERSEY MOBILIZED

MICHAEL SMITH *(1760–1842) was born in New York City and volunteered to guard the city's defenses in April 1775. When the British fleet arrived in March 1776, his regiment volunteered as a unit in the Continental army. Smith's company was provided with a gunboat and ordered across the Hudson to Smith's Ferry, near Bergen Point, to guard the inhabitants from British foraging parties sent ashore from the vessels in the harbor.*

Smith, with two other men, manned a six-pounder, fired upon a British tender, and drove it from shore, killing seven and wounding nine. Although the heroic action brought him temporary fame and a captain's commission, Smith refused the honor and slipped back into obscurity as a private soldier. He participated in the battles of Long Island, Harlem Heights, and White Plains. After the British occupation of New York, he moved to Tappan, then New Windsor, serving several short tours of duty and working on the chevaux-de-frise at Nicholl's Point.

He resided at Cornwall, New York, when applying for the pension in 1832 and was granted $101 a year.

Deponent entered the service in the month of April in the year 1775, in the city of New York, in a company of volunteer militia commanded by Capt. Theophilus Beekman as a sergeant and served in the same as sergeant until the month of March following. Said company belonged to the regiment of Col. John Lasher. We were volunteers and were to serve in the city, aforesaid, exclusively.

The Tories had been in the habit for some time of spiking our cannon on the battery and elsewhere. This occasioned their removal by us to Valentine's Hill at the eighteen-mile stone. The Tories, who seemed to be mightily afraid of the touchholes of our cannon, came down to Valentine's Hill and began again to spike them. To prevent this foul play, a detachment of our company was sent in succession to stand guard over the cannon. I took my regular tour with my company.

In the month of March, 1776, about the time the British fleet lay at the Narrows near Staten Island, our whole regiment volunteered to serve in the regular Continental army for nine months under the same officers. In the month of April, Gen. George Washington ordered a detachment from our regiment under command of Lt. Ralph Thurman with a boat and fieldpiece and twenty-four men to keep guard and prevent the enemy from harassing the inhabitants on the Jersey shore. I was orderly sergeant of the said company, and one of the detachment, John Garret, whose affidavit is hereunto annexed and who had joined the said company at its first organization in April 1775 and had continued to serve in it ever since, was also along. We were stationed up the Kills at Smith's Ferry near Bergen Point.

We had been cruising about this place three days when an enemy's vessel was seen to approach us under a press of sail. It was an armed square-rigged vessel and full of men and seemed to be particularly desirous of a more intimate acquaintance. As we did not feel ourselves honored by their visit, we run our boat, which was flat, on the shore in order to give them a better reception. No sooner had the boat landed than Lieutenant Thurman and all the party except John Garret, one Cannon, one Young, and myself ran off to their quarters, treating our visitors with the utmost neglect. As I was now commander-in-chief, I ordered my company of three men to assist me in throwing over our six-pounder and the carriage. We had just got it placed in a conspicuous situation on the bank when the enemy approached within speaking distance and commenced firing at us without effect. We had plenty of shot, both round and grape, and fired several times with round shot, but they passed over them. The enemy seemed to tantalize us for our random shots, and we resolved to give them an assortment, so we loaded our piece with grape. She had anchored. Just at the instant she had swung round so as to present her whole length to us, we gave her a raking fire which swept the deck from stem to stern. The enemy immediately slipped her cable and made off with as much speed as possible. They seemed to be in great hurry and confusion. No sooner had they got under way than Lieutenant Thurman and his party made their appearance. We drew our piece about three miles.

Next morning I returned with the three men before named, against the remonstrance of the lieutenant, to endeavor to secure our boat. We found two British tenders lying near her. Whilst we were near them, we saw three British soldiers approaching us, and, on halting them, they said they were friends to Congress. They proved to be deserters from a party who had landed in the night for the purpose of cutting off our retreat. They informed us that our last shot had killed the captain and six men and wounded nine others. We dragged our cannon to Paulus Hook and crossed, but the news of our victory preceded us and occasioned considerable excitement in the city. Lieutenant Thurman immediately resigned, and Congress, without my solicitation, sent me a captain's commission; but, having a grandmother, mother, and sister to support who lived in the city, I at their earnest solicitation declined accepting it.

In the month of May next thereafter, our regiment was ordered on Long Island and continued there on duty until the twenty-ninth day of August, when, according to the best of deponent's recollection, the army retreated. At the Battle of Flatbush I was one of the picket guard. We were drove in and retreated according to orders to General Washington's headquarters at Brooklyn. General Greene, Lord Stirling, and General Sullivan are the regular officers deponent recollects at that battle. Smallwood's regiment of regulars, part of Paulding's regiment, Drake's regiment of militia, and also Lasher's regiment were present. Sullivan and Stirling were taken prisoners.

From New York our brigade, under the command of General Scott, which deponent thinks had all been at the battle on Long Island, retreated on Sunday the fifteenth day of September to Harlem Heights. On Monday thereafter we had a skirmish with the enemy. Captain Willcox commanded our party. General Washington viewed the encounter from Harlem Heights. Our brigade lay on their arms the night following. From thence we retreated to Kingsbridge and lay there in tents and barracks until after the British landed at Frog's Neck. Then we retreated to White Plains. I was in that battle, which was fought the latter part of November in the year 1776. Our brigade, under the command of General Scott, formed the center of the line. Generals George and James Clinton were present, as I have been informed and believe, and Paulding and Drake's regiments of militia.

McDougall commanded. The attack of the British was on the right and center of our line. They made a feint on the center and reinforced on the right. Both armies encamped that night after the battle on the battleground. It was a dark and rainy night. We distinctly saw the light of their fires and could hear the confused noise of their camp occasionally break through the silent gloom which reigned throughout the field of battle. Washington had determined on renewing the engagement the next morning, and to prevent surprise we slept by our arms. By dawn of day next morning the army was drawn out in line of battle at beat of reveille, when, on examination, the British army were gone. They had retreated to Dobbs Ferry and crossed. We were ordered to march immediately for King's Ferry and head them. Next day we crossed the ferry to King's Ferry to Stony Point. The time of our regiment had expired, and we were left at Haverstraw until paid and were then discharged. I received a written discharge sometime in the month of December, but it is now lost. John Garret, whose affidavit is annexed, served with me in the same company from the beginning of my service in 1775 until I was discharged as aforesaid and received his discharge on the same day.

After the British took possession of New York, my mother removed to Tappan. Before I had returned home, I heard that the British had burnt Tappan Village. I turned out as volunteer under Captain Blauvelt, and we followed them as far as Hackensack. I was gone one day.

In the year 1777 I removed to New Windsor, then Ulster, now Orange County, and joined the company of Capt. Christian VanDuzer as a militiaman. The company was divided into detachments. There were several redoubts erected extending from West Point to the Forest of Dean, numbered 1, 2, 3, 4. In the beginning of summer, as deponent thinks from the circumstance of cutting weeds for a bed, I was ordered with a detachment to Redoubt No. 1 in the mountains. I was in this service one fortnight and was then relieved. Henry VanDuzer of the town of Cornwall was there with deponent.

In the spring of the year 1777 I commenced working on the chevaux-de-frise at Nicholl's Point and continued to work about one year until they were finished, but I was still liable to military duty. Was ordered out to train as usual and was several times during that period ordered down to Fort Constitution and West Point as a soldier on alarm and went accordingly.

A chevaux-de-frise

JOHN ADLUM *(1759–1836) was born and raised in York, Pennsylvania, and volunteered in one of four local militia units that, except for the oldest members, became part of the famous Pennsylvania Flying Camp and joined Washington's army at New York. Adlum was a corporal. The unit was detailed to erect Fort Lee, and Adlum, along with many of his fellow Pennsylvanians, was captured at Fort Washington in November 1776.*

John Adlum was quite a character, and his anecdote about meeting Gen. Nathanael Greene is but one of many incidents as soldier and prisoner that he set down in a manuscript memoir, edited by Howard H. Peckham and published in 1968.

After being paroled by the British, he removed to Northumberland County, Pennsylvania, in 1798 to Havre de Grace, Maryland, and then to Washington, D.C. At his home at Washington, he maintained an orchard and published two pioneering works on wine making. He submitted this narrative in 1833 and was granted a pension.

Interrogatories, with answers:
FIRST: Where and in what year was you born?
ANSWER: I was born in the town of York in Pennsylvania on the twenty-ninth day of April, in the year of 1759.
SECOND: Have you any record of your age, and, if so, where is it?
ANSWER: The time of my birth is written in my late father's Bible, where I remember to have often seen it. This Bible is, I presume, either in the hands of my brothers or sisters, now living in Muncy

Township, or its neighborhood in Lycoming County in Pennsylvania.

THIRD AND FOURTH: Where were you living when called into service? Where have you lived since the Revolutionary War, and where do you now live? How were you called into service? Were you drafted, did you volunteer, or were you a substitute, and for whom?

ANSWER: I was living with my father at York Town, above mentioned, when I volunteered to go with the militia to camp. Independence was declared on the fourth day of July, 1776, and on the evening of the sixth of July following, the Honorable James Smith, our neighbor (and one of the signers of the said Declaration), with Capt. Francis Wade and a Dr. Young, arrived at York Town to see how the good people of the town and its vicinity relished the said Declaration. Accordingly, on the morning of the seventh day of July, the four companies of the town militia was paraded (Mr. Smith was the colonel of the militia regiment), when the Declaration of Independence was read. Mr. Smith made a speech, as did Captain Wade and Dr. Young, pointing out the advantages that it would be of to our country, etc. Mr. Smith made a short concluding speech and then threw up his hat and hurrahed for liberty and independence. The militia on parade and others attending followed their example.

There was then a proposition of "who will go to camp," when I believe everyone on parade without an exception volunteered to go, and of which I was one, but it was thought prudent to retain and keep those at home that was more than forty years old to take care of and guard the town. And on the eleventh day of July we marched for camp. The four companies of the town were commanded by Capt. Charles Lukens, the sheriff of York County (and to which I belonged), Capt. William Bailey, a respectable man, a coppersmith, Capt. Rudolph Spangler, a silversmith, and Capt. Michael Hahn. I am not certain as to his occupation, but I believe it was a smith, and it was generally believed that he was the most sensible and smartest man of these four captains.

Lt. Col. Joseph Donaldson and Maj. Michael Swope commanded the militia of York Town and its vicinity on their way to camp and while at camp until what was called the Flying Camp was formed. Mr. Smith, the colonel, was then a member of Congress. Major Swope was then appointed the colonel, Robert Stevenson, the lieutenant colonel, and Capt. William Bailey was appointed the major of our regiment. Colonel Watts of Cumberland County was appointed the colonel of the regiment from said county, and William Montgomery, Esq., was appointed the colonel of the regiment from Chester County. I do not recollect who was the lieutenant colonel of Watts's regiment, but his major's name was Galbraith and who had, as I stood informed, about 140 men of the regiment with him on the day we were taken prisoners, but, being a prudent man, he kept them out of harm's way, except a few of his men without orders ran to where the fighting was and acted like men and soldiers, and no doubt they all would have done so if their officers had led them on. Lieutenant Colonel Bull commanded Colonel Montgomery's regiment from Chester County. I do not recollect of seeing Colonel Montgomery at camp. Colonel Bull was a Quaker gentleman and as brave a man as was in the army. I saw him ride along the whole front of a British regiment within eighty yards of them when they were firing briskly, and it appeared to me that he done it to show the men whom Colonel Swope and others were rallying that the firing of the enemy was not so dangerous as might be apprehended. These three regiments were commanded by Brig. Gen. John or James Ewing of York County, Pennsylvania.

As to where I was born and my marching with the militia, is answered above. But I was a corporal in Captain Stake's company of the Flying Camp and generally done the duty of a sergeant when on guard. Our adjutant, who on the parade acted in the place of our brigade major, Lieutenant Sherriff, generally placed me when on the parade on the right of the sergeants and gave me a separate command, and sometimes I was sent a considerable distance on command for several days. On the sixteenth day of November, 1776, I was taken prisoner at Fort Washington and taken into New York, and sometime in the month of February 1777 I got a parole to go home. But, being a prisoner, I did not get a commission of ensign as I expected, and most of all the officers, with scarcely an exception, were superseded. I stayed at York Town with my father until April 1781, when I went to Fredericktown, Maryland, where I resided until after peace was proclaimed . . . .

Question Five: State the names of the regular officers who were with the troops where you were, such Continental and militia regiments as you can recollect, and the general circumstances of your service.

Answer: At this distance of time I cannot recollect the names of many of our own officers, even in the regiment I served in, which

I suppose is owing to their having seldom appeared on parade. Of our regiment, there was Captain Stake, to whose company I attached myself. His subalterns were: Lieutenant Sherriff, who was appointed brigade major and who had been a schoolmaster in York Town; Lieutenant Holtzinger, a brother-in-law to Colonel Hartly, who commanded one of the Continental regiments during the Revolution. Holtzinger was fellow prentice with Simon Snyder, afterwards governor of Pennsylvania, to Michael Doudle, a tanner. Captain Smyser. I only recollect of Lt. Zachary Shugart, his first lieutenant. I do not recollect of any of Captain Nelson's subalterns, and of Captain Trett's company I only recollect Ensign Myers, a blacksmith, and who was the most uncouth-looking man in the army and one of the greatest dunces. Ens. Jacob Barnitz of Stake's company was shot through both legs and lay on the field of battle all night naked, having been stripped by the Hessians or their trulls. He was taken up the next day after the battle by those appointed to bury the dead and carried to the hospital in New York, where one leg was cured, and he would not suffer the British surgeons to amputate the other. He carried the ball a little below his knee for thirty-two years, when it became so painful, he was obliged to have his leg amputated above his knee. In our brigade the sergeants, etc., with but few exceptions, were the most talented and efficient officers in the brigade.

Before New York was evacuated by our troops, our brigade was sent up the North River, where we began to erect Fort Lee. Colonel Putnam, who I believe was a nephew to Gen. Israel Putnam, was the engineer who laid it out. I think this was towards the last of the month of September, and after the battle of the White Plains General Greene assumed the command, and, if my memory is correct, he brought two or a part of two brigades with him of the New England troops. I think one was called Glover's, and I recollect a Colonel Meigs. I do not recollect the names of any of the other officers of these brigades.

When General Greene assumed the command of the troops at Fort Lee, I was out on command about twenty miles from the camp at a bridge over Hackensack River, where there was a commissary's store, and to intercept deserters from our camp. And while I was there, and before I had ever seen General Greene, an Irishman named Kilpatrick, and who had been in the British service and who came over to us while our troops lay before the city of Boston,* was the sentry on the bridge. General Greene, with

*When any of the British deserted and joined our army, which they generally

another gentleman, was passing that way, when Kilpatrick stopped him and called for me. I went to the bridge. Kilpatrick observed, "Here is a gentleman who says he is General Greene, and your orders to me is not to let anyone pass into the country that had the appearance of a soldier, etc." I felt very much confused, not to say frightened, but I handed him my orders, which was written by Brigadier Ewing and endorsed from one sergeant to another. General Greene read them and then handed me a letter from General Putnam introducing him to a gentleman in the country a few miles from the bridge. I told the sentry to let him pass. After he had passed the bridge, I told Kilpatrick that he had got me into a pretty hobble, as I was afraid the general might not be pleased with my conduct or at being stopped. But Kilpatrick answered, "This will be the making of your fortune. You may depend on it that the general will rather approve of, than censure you," and he added, "now we must be prepared to receive him on his return in the best manner we can."

We accordingly dressed ourselves as well as circumstances would admit of, and as we saw the general returning we formed, and when he came up to us, we presented our arms. He told me to bring the men to an order. He then asked me a number of questions as to whether any disaffected people were in that neighborhood, and what supplies might be got on an emergency, etc., to all which I could give him tolerably satisfactory answers. There was an intelligent farmer who lived within forty or fifty rods from the bridge who was in the habit of coming and sitting with me in the evenings, and he gave me a history of the neighborhood for several miles round, with the real or supposed disaffected, with its resources, a thing which I probably should not have thought of inquiring after if this old gentleman had not communicated them to me. This command always lasted for a week. General Greene after this always took notice of and frequently spoke to me when I chanced to meet him in camp or otherwise.

Question Sixth: Did you ever receive a discharge from the service and, if so, by whom was it given, and what has become of it?

Answer: I was taken prisoner at Fort Washington on the sixteenth day of November, 1776, and I got a parole to go home in the month of February following. And I was not notified to do militia duty until sometime in the year 1780. I went and mustered once, and I then desired the captain to inform me what evidence

---

did, it was called "coming over to us," as it was considered a great insult to ask them if they deserted.

he had of my being exchanged. He said he had none, but that he supposed from the time elapsed since the capture of Fort Washington, he thought it was very probable that an exchange of prisoners had taken place. I told him that whenever he could satisfy me that I was exchanged, I would be ready to perform militia duty, and, until he could do that, I would not again attend parade. And I never was again called on to do militia duty.

. . . I expected to receive an ensign's commission on the first day of January, 1777, as I understood that on that day the Seventh Pennsylvania Regiment was to be organized and to be commanded by Captain Magaw, who at that time commanded the Fourth Pennsylvania Regiment, and the times of service of the men of the said regiment as I understood expired on the first day of January, 1777, and of course to be discharged except the reenlisted, when twelve regiments were to be raised in Pennsylvania and to be newly organized on that day. But the unfortunate affair at Fort Washington deranged the whole business, and the Council of Safety of Philadelphia superseded and appointed officers in the place of almost all those that had the misfortune to be prisoners to the enemy. I know of but one exception, and that was Maj. Otho Holland Williams, afterwards General Williams, but there may have been others that I did not know of.

Colonel Rawlings, who was colonel of the Maryland rifle regiment and Major Williams's superior, was superseded. Colonel Rawlings was one of the handsomest as well as one of the bravest officers in the army, for he, with Major Williams, with 309 men of their regiment, a picket guard of 100, and a captain's guard of 40 men, repulsed near ten times their number at least twice, and the enemy acknowledged the loss of 600 men and, if it had not been for the British light infantry, who formed in the rear of the Hessians and drove them on our troops with their bayonets, would have been beat to a certainty. This I mention with some hesitation, as Major Williams did not attend to it or know anything about the British that charged on the Hessians, and I was within less than five yards of him when he was wounded. I saw Dr. Wm. [James] McHenry (afterward secretary of war) cut out the ball with which Major Williams was wounded as he was sitting on a rock, exposed to all the fire of the enemy and but a few minutes before the British charged bayonet on the Hessians.

WILLIAM LLOYD *(1757–1837) was a resident of Upper Freehold, New Jersey, throughout his life. New Jersey instituted a system of militia service whereby males above sixteen, unless serving in the Continental army or sea service, were on active call in alternate months. For those unable or unwilling to pay a substitute, civil life was severely disrupted, and many young men, serving in place of gainfully employed fathers or brothers in off months, saw almost full-time militia duty.*

William Lloyd was a rather carefree, undisciplined youth of nineteen when he began serving in the summer of 1776, and his account of six years' service has the credible, human quality so lacking in most records of the war. Just before the Battle of Monmouth, he recklessly broke from his company to take a shot at General Clinton and barely returned with his life. Desiring a close look at the enemy near Freehold, he boldly asked Washington to lend him his spyglass. He mentions slipping from the ranks on a night march for a nap under the porch of a nearby house and describes the diversions improvised by the soldiers at Tinton Falls and Shark River to dispel the tedium of guard duty.

Lloyd submitted this deposition and was granted a pension in 1832.

That he entered the service of the United States as a militiaman in Upper Freehold in the month of July or August, 1776, according to the best of his recollection under some of the following officers (but which of them I have forgotten, but remember that the service was performed in the township of Freehold). I think at this time the regiment of Upper Freehold militia where I lived then consisted, in that part, of Col. Samuel Forman, Elisha Lawrence, Maj. William Montgomery, Gesbert Guisebertson, Joseph Copperthwaite, Nathaniel Polhemus, Peter Wikoff, John Coward; Capts. James Brewer, William Perrine, Gilbert Longstreet, Jonathan Pitman; lieutenants and inferior officers I cannot name with certainty; neither am I sure that I am correct in naming the others, there were so many changes took place shortly after the first organization of the militia in the year 1775, and continued to change till the end of the war.

I recollect serving monthly tours in particular places in Middletown and Shrewsbury for several months under Capt. Nathaniel Polhemus, Capt. William Montgomery, Capt. Joseph Copperthwaite, Capt. Jonathan Pitman, but [it was] in Freehold, Monmouth Courthouse, where a constant guard was kept and much the greater part of my services were performed. I cannot distinctly remember the company officers I served under except Capt. David Baird and Lieutenant Longstreet. The field officers I served under I believe were Maj. Thomas Seabrooks at Middletown and Col. Samuel Forman and Col. Auke Wikoff in the early part of the war, but after the winter of 1777 I think Gen. David Forman commanded the militia in Freehold until the termination of the war. He had also under his command at the same place three or four companies of enlisted men; the names of the captains were John Burrows, William Wikoff, and one other, from Maryland as I understood, his name not remembered; also Captain Huddy, who had a small company of artillery, but whether they were enlisted or not is to deponent unknown.

Deponent knew of the Continental officers of the Jersey line: General Maxwell, Maj. David Rhea, Capts. Wm. Barton, Ten Broeck Stout, and Moses Sprawls, subalterns. Knew several of the officers in the Congress regiment commanded by Col. Moses Hazen, namely Lieutenant Colonel Antill, Major Reed, Captains Munson, Saterly, Duncan, Lt. William Hurst, and others. Capt. Richard Lloyd of the same regiment was my brother. He entered as such at the organization of the regiment and continued in it during the continuance of the war, and after peace he was appointed agent of the regiment to settle with Pierce, paymaster general, and received the dues of the regiment in certificates and continued I believe a year or nearly before he accomplished that service. Deponent is his representative, as eldest brother, in the Cincinnati Society of New Jersey. He has been dead many years.

From the time the British army appeared off Sandy Hook in June 1776, or thereabouts, I believe the Monmouth militia were called out, one-half monthly to the end of the war, and on this point reference may be had to the corroborating testimony of the many applicants of the Monmouth militia for pensions. From the time of my first entrance in the service, I continued to serve, in monthly alternations, to the end of the war when called upon (with the exception of the year 1778, being exempted that year on account of other employments, I went out on special and emergent cases).

Besides, I very frequently turned out when not on monthly service on special occasions when the enemy were committing depredations in places not sufficiently protected on the shores in the county and once marched sixty miles to Egg Harbor in Burlington County under Maj. Elisha Lawrence and oftentimes after refugees that secreted themselves in the adjacent pines in the daytime and would come out at night to steal horses (and take them to the British by the way of Sandy Hook) and rob the houses of the inhabitants of the neighborhood where I lived. And in one instance they broke in the house of one of my near neighbors and killed the man and his wife and wounded another of the family. I was generally called upon and went out on all such occasions, both night and day, and at all seasons. I was once called upon by Captain Nixon of the Brunswick light horse to go with him in pursuit of refugees in the pines. Traveled night and day through a deep snow and piercing winter's cold. We took several prisoners, and he took them to General Putnam, then at Princeton, in compliance of the instructions given from the War Department.

I will state a few out of many dangers I encountered. In June 1778, on hearing that the British army had crossed the Delaware from Philadelphia and were approaching towards Monmouth, I went as a volunteer to General Maxwell's headquarters then at Crosswicks. The British were then at the Black Horse, better than twenty miles from Philadelphia. Their van, two or three miles in advance, were posted on a high ground at the house of one Curtis near the highway. I went the same day with about one hundred footmen and perhaps twenty militia horsemen under the command of Maj. David Rhea of the Jersey line to reconnoiter the enemy. When we had approached within about a mile of the enemy, he halted the foot, and the horsemen advanced further, but did not go far when they all fell back, except one horseman and myself went near to them, and, seeing a gap in the fence upon our right, we turned through it, descended two or three hundred yards over a rough piece of ground to a tree that stood in a field within gunshot of the enemy and in open view to them. My companion dismounted whilst I held his bridle and rested his gun against the tree and fired at them. He then mounted his horse, held mine by the bridle while I did the same. He then gave me my bridle, rode off in haste, and left me alone. A troop of British light horse were then advancing in full speed towards the gap through which I had to pass. My situation at this crisis seemed inauspicious. I had a hill to rise, and the ground uneven, having been ridged with a plough, I on my feet, and the enemy not having much further to go than I had to make the gap. I might have taken a different way, but, being a stranger to the ground and not knowing what obstructions would be in my way, I thought it best to make an effort for the gap. I mounted my horse, and the first jump he made, my saddle girth broke. I instantly seized hold of the horse's mane and held the gun and bridle with one hand and with the other reached back and took hold of the saddle, which I could not release from the horse for he held the crupper with his tail. I then slipped on the horse's bare back, put my horse to his full speed, and hopped through the gap twenty or thirty yards before them. They pursued no further. Had I fallen off when the girth broke, I should probably [have] been killed by them, or had they pursued my chance would have been little better, for my horse being pushed so hard up the hill had put him very much out of wind. A soldier that was taken prisoner told me a few days after that one of the shots we had made came very near to General Clinton.

General Maxwell gave me a letter to take to Colonel Nelson of the Middlesex militia of Allentown, and after my departure the British drove him out [of] the village of Crosswicks over the bridge. They then proceeded to Allentown, west about two miles further, and encamped. I then met with Colonel Morgan and his rifle company. He drove a party of the enemy out of Allentown. I pursued after [and] came near a light horseman. He advanced towards me. I fired at him. He ran and was too near their main body to pursue him.

A day or two after this, being with Colonel Morgan on his march near the pines, about a mile south of the route the British took, I rode in company with a militia horseman about a mile distant from Colonel Morgan. Met with two horsemen of the enemy armed. I supposed them to be refugees. They saw us first, turned out in the woods, and I did not discover them until I heard the rustling of the leaves made by their horses. I called upon my companion in arms to pursue them with me. He refused. It was my lot again to act alone. I pursued them myself a considerable distance, came within about sixty or seventy yards of them, checked my horse in order to fire at them, but before I could be ready they took themselves behind the trees and escaped. I searched about the woods some time but could not find them.

The next morning I heard firing of cannon and small arms at Freehold. I rode immediately that way, came on the battleground, was near the center of our troops that were engaged. The balls flew thick around me. I was there when the enemy advanced with charged bayonets and Colonel Monckton, their commander, was killed. I saw him as he lay lifeless on the ground. The enemy then retreated precipitately, throwing away many of their guns. I was, I believe, the foremost in following, got as many of their guns as I could conveniently manage on my horse, with their bayonets fixed upon them. Gave them to the soldiers as they stood in rank. They threw away their French pieces, preferring the British. I remember at the time one of the officers gave me his canteen of grog to take a drink. It was the most delicious to my taste of any I ever drank. I was thirsty, the day extremely hot, and no water to be got handy but warm brook water.

At another time, when on monthly duty at Freehold, the militia I believe were generally called to General Washington's headquarters on Steel's Mountain. The British army, or part of them, had marched out of Brunswick to Somerset Courthouse. I went with the militia, then on duty I believe under the command of Lt. Gilbert Longstreet. He was the only officer that I can remember with us from Upper Freehold. We marched by the way of Princeton to Sowerland Mountain. Met with General Sullivan and his command there. About sundown he ordered a fire to be made upon the mountain, and as an answering one as I supposed appearing on Steel's Mountain, we were ordered to march. We continued marching all night (excepting a little before day, being very tired, I slipped out of my place by a house, with one or two more lay under the piazza, and went on early in the morning). I believe the others reached the mountain before they halted. About the second day after we arrived at headquarters, the British commenced a retreat from the aforesaid courthouse. I saw General Washington view them striking their tents, and by his permission I looked at them through his spyglass, and I heard him say that if he had some men near them, their baggage might be taken from them.

The next morning I volunteered to go with a larger party of militia and I believe some regulars towards Woodbridge on the left flank of the British army as they were then on their retreat from Brunswick and on their way to Amboy. We continued our march until we came opposite to the rear of the enemy within about a mile of them. They were posted on a hill said to be called Strawberry Hill (not far from Woodbridge or Amboy I believe) behind a piece [of] woods thinly timbered. The main body halted (I mean of our men), and I volunteered again with about two hundred men to make nearer recog[nizance] of the enemy, and when we came to the woods within about three hundred yards of them, as near as I can calculate the distance, they opened their fire upon us with two fieldpieces. The first shot cut the bayonet off of one of the men's gun. We marched under their fire directly towards them, but before we got out of the woods they made a hasty retreat. The officers that commanded us, who were said to be Virginia officers, estimated the number of the British to be about a thousand men and said that if they had known our small number, they would have taken us all prisoners. I suffered much fatigue, hunger, as well as danger. I had but one meal of victuals for two or three days, and that was with Captain Lloyd, my brother, on Steel's Mountain. My fare was small apples not larger than a hickory nut.

Those services that I have previously stated to have performed under the several officers named in Middletown and Shrewsbury were accompanied by particular circumstances that gave them a more definitive and lasting impression. At one time the Negro refugees fired upon a sentinel, and we pursued after them near to a place called Jumping Point on Shrewsbury. Went into the river with one of the men. He got tired a considerable distance from the land and could swim no further. I swam to him, suffered him to take me by the hips, and swam to the shore with, and saved his life.

At another [time] of service, pursuing some refugees in company of three other militiamen, I, being foremost in the pursuit, was fired at by one of them from behind a tree a short distance off and at Shark River; another time of service, recollect being stationed on monthly service at Tinton Falls by the circumstance of diverting ourselves by riding horses in the millpond there and sliding off of them and taking them by the tails, and they would draw us after them. And at the time at Shark River, we dug the inlet through the beach that had been stopped up for some time in order to let the salt water into the river to make the oysters better. I recollect being quartered two months while on duty at a particular private house and near the courthouse and at another time at another private house, same village, and served another month as a light horseman at a private house near a mile from the courthouse and under the immediate command of General Forman. During that month I was sent with three or four others to Egg Harbor for a particular purpose and was once sent express with a letter to General Washington at his headquarters near Chatham in Morris County. My other service was principally performed at the courthouse, where General Forman kept his headquarters; I mean he kept his headquarters at a house near the courthouse and the militia quartered in taverns in part and in private houses.

There was such a sameness in the duty we had to do here for many months that I cannot recollect the routine of these nor the officers of the companies under which I served in a single instance of all of those last-enumerated tours. It seems strange to me that they should be as entirely obliterated from my memory, and yet perhaps it is not less strange that I can recollect so much at this length of time in looking back through the waste of time. The years and months and events seem to blend together so much, the mind becomes in a measure lost and bewildered to such a degree, that I rely more upon a general than particular recollection upon the whole. Upon a full consideration of all, I feel confident that I have been in the service more than two years and think and believe that I am justly entitled to a full pension from the time I first entered the service as a militia soldier. To the close of the war I was neither fined, drafted, or hired a substitute to my knowledge, but always performed my tours of duty personally and voluntarily. I never received a commission or discharge.

SAMUEL SHELLEY *(b. 1760) was born at Hempstead Plains, Long Island, and was serving as an indentured servant in New York City. His father was a ship's carpenter who escaped from forced labor with the British army. The family's property was confiscated, and they had to take refuge in New Jersey.*

Samuel Shelley was an acknowledged draft dodger, claiming, on the basis of his youthful appearance, to be twelve years old "for a good many years" until discovered and forced into service. He participated in only one skirmish, but his narrative of camp life is composed with a charming, intimate style.

He moved from Canoe Brook to Newark and New York after the war and finally settled in Wantage Township, Sussex County, New Jersey. He did not apply for a pension until 1851, at age ninety-one, and, although he never received one, his narrative appears to be honest and accurate.

I entered the service of the United States during the "hard winter" of 1779–80. I think it was between the sixteenth and eighteenth of March of the year 1780. I entered under Captain Reeves of the New Jersey brigade, Colonels Dickinson and Ogden. I continued to serve until a few days before the first day of January, A.D. 1781. I was discharged between Christmas and New Year's Day. I received my certificate of discharge at Morristown from Colonel Dickinson, Colonel Ogden being at the same time present. I surrendered my accoutrements at Morristown and returned home, having been in actual service nine months and some odd days. I entered the service for the term of nine months. I was at that time a resident of Canoe Brook, about twelve miles from the city of Newark in the county of Essex and state of New Jersey.

I enlisted under the following circumstances. There were two American officers came to my father's at Canoe Brook and desired a conveyance to Green Brook. My father sent me with them. This was in the month of March. I traveled in a sleigh across the fields and over the fences. One of these officers was named Brennan or Brainard and acted as major in the regiment in which I afterwards served. When we arrived at Green Brook, I was asked concerning my age. I told them I was twelve. They let me pass, and I returned home. When I reached home, one James Ballard, an orderly sergeant in the army, came and inquired my age. I told him the same thing. He then went to an old aunt of mine who was ignorant of his purpose, and from her he learned the truth. He then said to me, "My fine fellow, I will take care of you. Do you not know that there is a heavy fine if you do not join the army when you get to your age?" I told him I did not. He then carried me off to Green Brook in a sleigh. When there, they tried to persuade me to enlist during the war. I did not like to do it. Then Colonel Dickinson and Captain Reeves told me I had better enlist for nine months and then they would give me clear, and I accordingly did so.

I was enrolled in Captain Reeves's company. My lieutenant was named Parcell. Brainard or Brennan was one of the majors. In our mess one Burrill was cook, and Stephen Tichenor was one of my messmates. There was one Townley and one Mount who were in the service at the same time. The names of the others I cannot now recall. One Thomas Trusdall was our "fife major."

We laid at Green Brook until in May, and the soldiers having then recovered from the effects of the hard winter, we were marched to Baskingridge. Word came that the British, five thousand strong, with cannon and a troop of horse and large supplies, had crossed over from Staten Island to Elizabethtown Point. We were immediately set in motion to meet them, but before we had arrived at Connecticut Farms, they were burned to the ground. The British began their retreat. General Greene rode up and ordered the Jersey Brigade to take the Vauxhall Road and follow it on until we met a regiment which had marched by another road at a place where the roads came together. When we reached this point, we found the other regiment engaged with the enemy. The skirmish was short. The British retreated, and we followed on until we saw them cross at Elizabethtown Point. Captain Reeves was badly wounded at the point where the roads come near together. The ball entered his side and passed upwards, coming out near the breastbone. He recovered of his wound but died sometime afterwards from the effect of it.

After the British crossed to Staten Island, we were marched around for some days until we reached Chatham. We there encamped. General Washington was there with us. His quarters were in a house below the academy. We were on the high ground beyond. We continued there until the twenty-second or -third of June, and then we heard the alarm guns fired, first one, then another, and again the third. We were all immediately aroused and busy. General Greene ordered the Jersey Brigade to Springfield. We marched to Springfield. Before we arrived, the Rhode Island troops had been engaged at the bridge near the meetinghouse and had been almost all cut off. Our colonel (Dickinson) rode up and ordered forty or fifty of the *spryest* to go and cut off the British light horse. We ran across to a place where the road ran near a stone fence overgrown with sumac bushes. We concealed ourselves and fired upon the stragglers as they passed towards Day's Hill. Many were killed. The British again retreated, and we again followed them to Elizabethtown Point. In the pursuit, they left their cattle near where Governor Livingston used to live. He, with his troop of horse, also pursued them and hurried them, so that they outran the Jersey Brigade. Just as they crossed in their boats, Washington descended the hill on one side and Greene, with his troops, on the other. Washington fired upon them with his cannon. It was his purpose to cut them off but was too late. Greene, fearing that some of the British might have gone up the creek to attack our rear, ordered a flank movement, and I was marched up the river. This was in the night. In the morning the British had disappeared. We were then marched back by easy marches, halting wherever we could find provisions. We remained a short time at a place called the Short Hills. We had occasional alarms but no more skirmishes.

In the fall, when the cold weather began to set in, we were marched to Morristown to take up winter quarters. We were encamped on a ridge where the army had been before. We fixed up the cabins they had left. General Washington was at times in the Freeman house, and sometimes he was in the house of one Ford,

Judge Ford I think. I remained there until between Christmas and New Year's. A short time before I left, the Pennsylvania troops came in. Whilst laying there, I remember one Stoneburgher had charge of the Continental teams. He collected provisions for us. Between Christmas and New Year's, I got my lieutenant to calculate the time of my service. He did so and told me my time was up. I asked him how I could get my discharge by applying to the colonel. I asked him to do so for me, and he did. Colonel Dickinson, in a day or so afterwards, handed me a paper with a large seal upon it and some "sage leaf" money, wishing me at the same time good luck, for I had been a faithful boy. I could not read at that time, and I do not know what the contents of the paper were. It has been lost or destroyed for many years.

I then returned to Newark and enrolled myself in a company of horse commanded by one Captain Condit. I remained in Newark until the British left New York. . . .

Interrogatories

Question: Where and when were you born, and where did you reside before your enlistment?

I was born in Hempstead Plains on Long Island on the second day of August, 1760, according to the best of my information and belief. I was serving my time in New York City when the British took that place. I remained in that city until the British compelled my mother to leave Long Island. They stole everything she had. My father was a rebel and by trade a ship carpenter. The British had tried to get him on board their ships, and he was obliged to skulk. They at last caught him and placed him on board a coaster vessel. The vessel met with an accident somewhere on the coast, and he was sent in the woods to score timber for repairs. He watched his opportunity and escaped. He found his way to a place near Newark and there concealed himself for some time. When it became safe for him to appear, he got word to my mother, who escaped from the island in a coaster commanded by my uncle with such things as she had been able to save in a hogshead buried in the cellar. She carried me with her. Here they sent me to New York again, where I stayed until my boss got killed by an accident. I then got back to Newark and was in that neighborhood until I entered the service.

Question: How did you get over from New York to Newark?

In my uncle's vessel. He was an Englishman and married my father's sister. He was allowed to pass by the British. He found me

idling about the city after my boss was killed, and he told me I had better go home.
QUESTION: What business was your father engaged in when you arrived home?

He was building a sloop on the Newark River for someone. He returned home to Canoe Brook, a distance of twelve miles, every Saturday night on horseback. I stayed around home for a time, getting wood for the family. Then a man named Baldwin employed me to work in his tanyard at Orange. I remained there for a short time. When the fall before the hard winter set in, I left, intending to go to Albany. I stayed around home whilst my mother was making me some clothing, and then the cold weather set in, and I could not go, and that's the way that the sergeant caught me. I was twelve years old for a good many years. I was always very small in stature.
QUESTION: What had the two officers whom you took to Green Brook been doing at Canoe Brook? How long had they been there, and what were their names and rank?

They came to my father's house about the time [of] the heavy fall of snow and stayed there until in February. I suppose they were on furlough, I don't know, though they were great gentlemen, and I never had any conversation with them. Brennan or Brainard was afterwards my major. I cannot tell the name or rank of the other, and I never saw him after I left him at Green Brook.
QUESTION: How long were you in driving from Canoe Brook to Green Brook, and mention the incidents of your drive.

We started from home in the morning and reached the army in the afternoon. The major spoke to the sentinels, and they let us pass. We drove up to a house a little distance from the army, and I tied my horses by the door and went in. I found the room full of officers. They were common officers and seated around the fire, some of them wrapped up in blankets smoking their pipes. They told me to come to the fire, but there was but little there. All the higher officers were in another part of the house. There was no place to put up my horses, so I concluded I would go to Springfield that night. I went out and found one of my blankets taken off the horses. An officer came out and inquired after the blanket. The sentry said that the one who had been there before him had taken it off. The officer sent for him. He came up shivering with the cold with my blanket around him. I told him to keep it, and I went home without it. I was told, when I met the first sentry I must say "fight," to the next, "let him go," and to the last, "good-bye." It was all new to me, and I have always remembered them words. I reached Springfield that night, and next day I got home. I traveled a straight course on the crust, over fences and everything. This was in February.

QUESTION: What was the name of the officer who compelled you to enter the army, and what do you know of him?

His name was Ballard, Jim Ballard, and his folks lived near my father's. He learned my real age from an old aunt, and then he told me he was going to carry me off. I remember he had a large cloak on. I do not know whether he had a uniform on or not. I think he was an orderly sergeant. He kept fetching in the new recruits all the time. He one day brought an old acquaintance from Orange. His name was Tichenor, I think it was Stephen Tichenor. When he was taking me to Green Brook, he picked up another man on the road.

QUESTION: When he took you to Green Brook, what did they do with you?

I told them to take me to Captain Reeves. He had lived close by my father's, and I knew him well. They wanted me to join the Continental service. I would not. Then Colonel Dickinson, who lived about four miles from my father, came up and said to me, "Sam, join us for nine months and then maybe the war will be over." So I joined them, and I was placed in a tent where there was six more. Burrill, the cook, and Tichenor afterwards was in the same mess. The next day after I arrived in camp, they gave me a musket and bayonet, a knapsack and canteen, a cartridge box and an old rug to sleep on. They then began to learn me the exercise, and they found me a green hand, for I had never fired off a gun.

QUESTION: Who taught you the exercise?

Sometimes one man and sometimes another. They called him a "fugleman."

QUESTION: Who were your superior officers?

My ensign I cannot now remember. He had a crooked Dutch name. My lieutenant was named Parcell. Captain Reeves commanded the company. Then there was Colonel Ogden and Colonel Dickinson. Colonel Dickinson seemed to be superior to Ogden. He was a very high officer, and I always looked up to him because I had know him before. He might have been a general, but I think that he was called colonel, though maybe I have forgot. General Greene always had command of us on general parades, and after I had been in the army a few days General Washington reviewed us. He rode past the lines with his hat in his hand, although it was very cold. It was the first time I ever saw him.

QUESTION: Can you remember the names of any other of the officers?

I cannot. There is our major, whose name I have mentioned: Ballard. It runs in my mind that there was a General or Colonel Mexel or Matsell. He was some high officer and was over us. Then there was another officer named Angel, Colonel Angel I think. I remember him in the Battle of Springfield. He did not belong to our brigade. I was so often detached from the main body and marched around through the hills for provisions, that I hardly knew to what brigade I belonged.

QUESTION: Was there a village called Green Brook?

There was no village and but very few houses. We were encamped very near a large swamp where there was wood to be had. As the snow sunk away, it left the stumps of the trees standing ten or twelve feet high.

QUESTION: Where was the first place you encamped after leaving Green Brook?

We encamped a few days at a small village a short distance from Green Brook. The soldiers' feet were so sore that they could not march far at a time. There we broke up our quarters again and got as far as Baskingridge, where we remained until the word came that the British had come over. If I recollect, a gentleman brought a letter to Washington. I think I was told so at the time. There was no firing of alarm guns as before the Battle of Springfield.

QUESTION: How far is it from Baskingridge to the Connecticut Farms, and how long were you marching there?

I do not rightly know the distance. It took us some time to get there. Major Lee with the horse made more speed. When we got there, it was all on fire. The horse had been there, and the British were gone. We were ordered to take the Vauxhall Road to keep them from going to Springfield. We marched along the road until we came to a place where there was two roads approached. Over in the other road there was skirmishing, and we fired on the British. Here is where my captain was wounded. At the time he received the wound, he was a little way off from the rest of us reconnoitering, and he was fired on and badly wounded.

QUESTION: Did Captain Reeves ever do duty after that?

He did not. At Springfield battle, Lieutenant Parcell was our commander.

QUESTION: Did the British retreat, and where did they go?

They did, and we followed them till they crossed. I did not say I saw them cross, but they escaped us.

QUESTION: Where was Washington that day?

I do not know. I did not see him.

QUESTION: Where did you go after returning from the pursuit?

We lingered along in the little villages until we got to Chatham, and there we took up our quarters, thinking that the fighting was over.

QUESTION: Can you describe your encampment at Chatham?

We were scattered around on the rising ground, and Washington was down below us beyond the academy or schoolhouse. It was whilst we laid here that the alarm guns fired.

QUESTION: Where were these guns fired?

Off towards Elizabethtown.

QUESTION: What occurred when the guns fired.?

The first one we paid no attention to. The second made us prick up our ears, and when the third one was heard we were all as busy as bees. We were ordered to Springfield and two or three other regiments or brigades with us. Here is where I first recollect Angel or Hangel. As we came near Springfield, we saw the church on fire. It appeared that before we came there had been a smart action by one of the bridges between the Rhode Islanders and the British horse. The Rhode Islanders fired away all their ammunition and then fixed their bayonets, but the horse were too much for them and drove them back, crossed the bridge, and the foot followed. This was before we got there. When we came in sight, the streets of Springfield were full of redcoats. They had got past the meetinghouse and were firing the last house. The horse were ahead. When they got the last house burning, they then aimed for Day's Hill, a village nearby. We were ordered to cut them off. Two or three hundred marched up, and a few were stationed behind a stone wall, maybe fifty of us. The road ran near the river, and the scattered horsemen had to pass us. We dropped them as they came along. Some had two or three balls in them. We killed all that passed except a little Irishman, and his horse was killed under him and he taken prisoner. He it was who told us they were going to burn Day's Hill.

When the pursuit began, we had one cannon with us. They rigged up an old horse to it and followed on after the British. He would ride up and pour it in on them, and Lee was there too, and they were mightily harried. We could not get anywhere near them. All this while we saw nothing of Washington until we came

to Elizabethtown Point, and then he hove in sight.
QUESTION: Did you have any more skirmishes during your term of service?

This was the last. This occurred in June, I think, and I knew it was in the middle of the same month that we had the skirmish at the Connecticut. I am positive it was in June from the appearance of a cornfield through which we ran when we were going to cut off the British.

QUESTION: How much money did Dickinson give you at the time you left the service, and have you ever received any other pay or emolument?

It was but a small sum, two or three bills. I suppose it was to pay my expenses home, and it is all that I have ever received either in pay, bounty, and/or pension.

THOMAS BROWN *(b. 1760) was born in New Jersey and was living at Forked River, Monmouth County, New Jersey, when he enlisted in the militia in October 1776. The swamplands and pine barrens of the middle and upper New Jersey coast were infested with bands of marauding Tories who had water communication with British-occupied New York, and militia duty was hazardous and demanding.*

Samuel Brown, father of the applicant, was captain of the company formed at Forked River. He was a shipbuilder and many of the men were watermen; to combat the Tories more easily, the company built a gunboat that they named The Civil Usage. *Thomas Brown had briefly volunteered as a hand on Capt. Joshua Studson's whaleboat for an abortive cruise into Amboy Bay, and when* The Civil Usage *was launched in May 1777, he became a crewman, guarding Barnegat Bay. For the rest of the war the vessel, active in the summer months, was used to capture several Tory vessels, and in the spring of 1781 it participated in a sea engagement that cleared the Tories out of Clam Town, now Tuckerton, New Jersey.*

Brown's family home was destroyed by Tories in 1778, and he moved to Woodbridge, later to Mannahawkin, New Egypt, Chesterfield Township, in Burlington County, and finally Bordentown, where he made this deposition in 1832.

This deponent is the son of Samuel Brown, who resided at the time of the commencement of the Revolutionary War at Forked River, in the township of Dover (according to the present bounds of the township so designated), in the county of Monmouth and state of New Jersey, aforesaid, which river empties into Barnegat Bay; was navigable for boats and galleys of not more than three feet draught of water and with which there was a communication from the Atlantic Ocean through Barnegat Bay and Barnegat Inlet. That those parts of the said counties of Monmouth and Burlington either bordering upon the sea or upon the bays and rivers immediately communicating therewith, and which were separated from the improved and cultivated parts of the said state by an immense tract of uncultivated and uninhabited land covered with forests and swamps, in many parts almost impassable, were taken possession of by that portion of the inhabitants of the state who had abandoned the standard of their country and flown to the British for refuge from their justly incensed countrymen, the forests and swamps furnishing fastnesses from which it was difficult to dislodge them. And from their retreats they made incursions into the cultivated parts of the state, committed every species of depredations, carried the plunder seized in these incursions into the woods, from which they could conveniently transport it by water on board the British vessels.

In this state of things, it became necessary for the Whigs inhabiting those parts of the said counties to associate themselves together for self-defense, and at Forked River a company of about thirty men was formed who chose the said Samuel Brown as their captain, Joseph Bell, lieutenant, and William Holmes, ensign. This company were called minutemen, their duty being understood to be to hold themselves continually in readiness to turn out at a moment's warning to resist the depredations of the Tories and refugees in whatever place their services might be required. The said Samuel Brown received a commission under the authority of the state of New Jersey to act as captain of this company. This deponent, being then between the age of sixteen and seventeen years, entered as a volunteer in the said company, and his name was the first inscribed on the list of the privates of the said company. From the time of the organization of the said company until the month of October of the same year, the company was stationed at the mouth of Forked River, about one mile and an half from the residence of the said Samuel Brown, in order to watch the motions of the enemy, during which period the said Samuel Brown commenced building a heavy gunboat on the said river and no more than a mile from the place where the said company was stationed. This boat was intended to be used for the annoyance of the enemy, and a part of the duty assigned to the privates of the said company while so stationed at the mouth of Forked River was, by turns, to aid in the construction of the said boat and watch over her safety.

In the said month of October a certain John Morris, a native of the said countycounty

In the said month of October a certain John Morris, a native of the said county of Monmouth, a Tory and refugee who was reputed to have received a commission to act as colonel in the British service, marched from Shrewsbury in the said county of Monmouth at the head of three hundred Tories and refugees and stationed himself and his men at Toms River, about twelve miles from the place where the said company was stationed, and the station of the said company was thereupon immediately changed to a cedar swamp between where the said boat was building and said Toms River, and at a place where the main road from Toms River to Mannahawkin crosses the middle branch of Forked River, in order more effectually to check the measures of Colonel Morris and his refugees, who having learnt the position of the company, and being aware of the advantages of their situation, did not venture to approach them, but remained quietly at Toms River until the month of January following, when he returned with his force to Shrewsbury, having done nothing during his three months' stay at Toms River but to invite the inhabitants of the surrounding country to come in and receive British protection. The said company remained on guard in the said cedar swamp during the whole of this period.

After the said John Morris had retired, the company returned to their original station at the mouth of Forked River and there remained until the spring of the year 1777, when Capt. Joshua Studson, who then acted as the captain of a gunboat in the service of the United States, arrived at Forked River in a whaleboat then used as a gunboat in search of men to complete the crew of his boat, she being then five deficient of the complement necessary to work and fight her to advantage. And, the Tories and refugees having then retired from the vicinity, five of the said company, by and with the assent of the said Samuel Brown, their captain, volunteered to serve on board the said boat under the said Capt. Joshua Studson, of which five this deponent was one. The said five volunteers having entered on board the said boat, she immediately afterwards, this deponent thinks about the first of April in the year last aforesaid, proceeded in the night to sea through

Barnegat Inlet and reached Sandy Hook, passed the *Roebuck* man-of-war then lying there, and in Amboy Bay boarded a British schooner, captured her, and took her into Middletown Creek in the county of Monmouth, where we were shortly afterwards blockaded by British vessels, from which a force superior to ours was landed who attacked us in the night, retook the schooner, and, after a short contest, burnt our boat, burnt Captain Burrough's mills at Middletown Point in the said county of Monmouth, and then returned to their vessels.

This deponent with the rest of the crew of the boat then returned to Forked River in the same month of April, when this deponent and the other members of Capt. Samuel Brown's company who volunteered to complete the crew of Captain Studson's boat returned to the performance of their duties in the said company. At this time, the boat which the said Samuel Brown had commenced building on Forked River, as herein before stated, was nearly completed. She was called *The Civil Usage* and was launched sometime in the month of May in the year last named. She was armed with one long six-pounder, four swivels, and two walepieces, and muskets for each of the crew. The said Capt. Samuel Brown took command of the said boat, and this deponent and the other members of the said company entered on board the said boat under the command of the said Captain Brown and constituted the larger part of the crew, the whole crew consisting of from thirty-six to forty men. The duty assigned to the said gunboat, after she was so armed, equipped, and manned, was to guard Barnegat Bay and Inlet and prevent, as far as practicable, aggressions of the enemy through these sources. The crew drew their rations from John Richardson, who acted as commissary under the authority of the state of New Jersey and was stationed at Toms River. Asher Holmes, stationed at Middletown in the said county of Monmouth, acted under the same authority as paymaster.

Shortly after the said gunboat was so armed, equipped, and manned, and during the early part of the summer of the year 1777, while cruising in the said gunboat off Barnegat Inlet, we captured a British brig from the West Indies bound to New York loaded with rum, sugar, molasses, and limes, and carried her into Toms River. We continued to cruise in the said gunboat on the same station until the fall of the same year, and a little while before the severely cold weather set in, we run the said gunboat up Oyster Creek into a cedar swamp and placed her in the best situation we could select in the said creek to protect her through the winter from the attacks of the Tories and refugees who had at that time collected in considerable bodies in the vicinity and laid concealed in different parts of the cedar swamps and pine forests between the bay shore and the cultivated and inhabited parts of the interior. During the following winter, the crew of the said boat, this deponent among the rest, kept such watch as they could to guard the said boat, themselves, and the property of the Whigs in the neighborhood generally from the depredations of the enemy, sometimes passing their nights in houses and sometimes in the adjoining woods and swamps.

In the following spring, in the year 1778, Capt. Samuel Brown, with the whole of his company except about twelve, left that station and marched to join General Morgan, who commanded a regiment of riflemen in the Continental army under General Washington, General Morgan being at the time stationed somewhere in the state of Pennsylvania. The twelve members of the company who were left behind, and of whom this deponent was one, remained under the command of William Holmes, ensign of the company, having the said gunboat in charge, and being instructed generally to act according to their best judgment in guarding as they had power the persons and property of the Whigs from the depredations of the enemy. We remained at that station, and the said gunboat continued in Oyster Creek, where we had placed her for safety, until after the Battle of Monmouth.

After the Battle of Monmouth, Capt. Samuel Brown returned and again manned and took the command of the said gunboat, and during the same summer, whilst on a cruise, succeeded in capturing a boat of the enemy engaged in trading with loyalists resident at a village then called Clam Town (now Tuckerton) in the township of Little Egg Harbor in the said county of Burlington. During the following winter, Captain Brown and his company occupied their station at Forked River, where the said gunboat laid during that winter. In the following spring, in the year 1779, Captain Brown and his said company again manned and resumed cruising in the said gunboat, and to the southward of Barnegat descried, engaged, and captured a gunboat belonging to the refugees under the command, according to this deponent's present recollection, of a Captain Whiley, armed with four swivels and a walepiece and with a crew of from twenty-five to thirty men.

After the capture of the refugee gunboat, we continued to cruise for some time, when, in the latter part of June or the beginning of July of the same year, having discovered that our gunboat required repair, we run her into harbor at Toms River for that purpose. Being about twelve miles from Captain Brown's house, where his wife and family were, while the boat was repairing Captain Brown and this deponent paid a visit to their family, leaving the rest of the company with the boat. We arrived at home a little while before dark and slept there. The next morning, as the sun was rising, we were alarmed by the dog barking fiercely, and, immediately running to the window, this deponent saw a large number of men whom he supposed to be refugees engaged in fording a creek about thirty paces from the house. This deponent immediately informed his father, Captain Brown, of what he saw, and he and this deponent, feeling their danger, immediately left the house and, with all the speed they had, made for the woods. They were under the necessity, in making their escape, to pass through a cleared level field of thirty acres, and no obstructions intervened between this field and the position occupied by the refugees but a slight fence. Captain Brown and this deponent left the house with no other garments than their shirts and, though fired at by the whole body of the refugees, were so fortunate as to reach their gunboat at Toms River unhurt.

When we reached our boat, we learnt that the refugees who had attacked us were bodies of men under two refugee captains, known as Captain Davenport and Captain Roch, who were supposed to have come up the bay in two boats from Clam Town, and information was brought to us that they designed to pass out to sea through Barnegat Inlet and go to New York. Their number was estimated at 160 men. The repairs of our boat being then completed, we immediately put to sea to watch them and, if possible, to attack and capture them. Capt. Andrew Brown and Capt. Joshua Studson being then at Toms River, and each in command of an armed boat and tendering us their aid, we stationed our boats between Cranberry Inlet and Sandy Hook and there watched for the refugee boats. But we watched in vain. The refugees, a few days after their attack upon Captain Brown and this deponent, taking advantage of our absence and having probably learnt the position of our boats and that it would be dangerous for them to attempt to reach New York, returned to Forked River, and, finding Captain Brown's house without other guard than his wife and younger children, they robbed it of everything of value that it contained, forced his wife and children to leave it, and then burnt the house, barn, shop, and other outbuildings to ashes. And at the same time they burnt a valuable schooner belonging to Captain Brown of forty or fifty tons burthen then lying in Forked River. After this occurrence, we continued to cruise in our gunboat on the same station till the fall of the same year, when this deponent accompanied his father, the said Captain Brown, to Woodbridge in the county of Middlesex, to which place he removed his family and took up his residence, leaving the remainder of his said company in charge of the said gunboat. We remained at Woodbridge during the following winter, this deponent keeping guard occasionally during that time at the mouth of Raritan River under the command of William Ross, a captain of the New Jersey militia. During the same fall that Captain Brown removed to Woodbridge, Dr. Aaron Swain, under his direction, took command of the said gunboat, *The Civil Usage,* and took her round to Crow's Ferry, above Amboy in the Raritan River, where she remained during the following winter.

In the following spring, in the year 1780, and as this deponent now thinks in the month of March of that year, the said Dr. Aaron Swain entered on board the said gunboat, *The Civil Usage,* as captain, and this deponent as lieutenant, by virtue of commissions under the authority of the state of New Jersey handed to them by General Heard of the New Jersey militia. And from the period in which this deponent so received his commission as lieutenant until the close of the Revolutionary War, this deponent served on board the said gunboat, *The Civil Usage,* as her lieutenant and was the chief in command of the said gunboat for more than half that period, Captain Swain being frequently absent from his command and for periods of a considerable length of time. The boat was employed from the time this deponent had become her lieutenant until the spring of the year 1781 in cruising along the coast from Raritan River to Shrewsbury River as a check upon the refugees and traders with the enemy, Captain Samuel Brown continuing to act during that period as adviser to the officers and crew of the said gunboat and in part directing her proceedings.

In the fall of the year 1780, a considerable body of refugees and Tories being located at Clam Town in the township of Little Egg Harbor, before mentioned, parties of them were dispatched from thence to penetrate into and commit depredations in the cultivated parts of the counties of Burlington and of Monmouth. By these marauding parties, Clayton Newbold, John Black, and Caleb Shreve of the county of Burlington, and John Holmes of the county of Monmouth were robbed of large quantities of silver plate, money, clothing, and other articles, and of a number of Negroes. The marauders took their booty to Clam Town and put the same on board a lumber sloop lying there under the control of the refugees, to be transported to New York as soon as the navigation should open in the spring. Captain Swain, the captain of the said gunboat, being in the interior of the county of Burlington at the time these robberies were committed and by that means becoming informed of the same, conceived the idea of intercepting the booty in its passage to New York. He rejoined his crew and ordered his gunboat to Shrewsbury Inlet to watch the motions of the enemy. Early in the spring following, in the year 1781, we proceeded to Barnegat Inlet, and on our way we fell in with and captured the schooner containing the booty which had been taken by the refugees in the previous fall as before set forth and had the satisfaction of restoring the same to its owners.

Immediately after the capture of the schooner, we fell in with a Captain Gray from Rhode Island commanding an American privateer. With him we concerted the plan of dispersing the refugees established at Clam Town. It was agreed that he should approach Clam Town from the sea through Egg Harbor Inlet and decoy them out to sea in their boats, and that we should approach the same inlet through the bay, keeping ourselves concealed, and in case he should succeed in decoying them out, we were to follow and support him in the engagement, placing the enemy between two fires. Captain Gray accordingly approached within sight with covered guns, putting about as soon as he perceived he was observed by the enemy, affecting to fly with all the sail he could make. The ruse succeeded. The refugees pursued in their galley commanded by Captain Davenport. When they were out at sea, Captain Gray hove about and stood for them. The vessels engaged. Captain Davenport and eight or nine of his men were killed by the first broadside from the privateer, when the galley of the refugees struck and was immediately taken possession of by Captain Gray and sunk. The survivors of the galley's crew were received on board the privateer and from thence sent to the gaol of Burlington County. After this defeat, the refugees and Tories broke up their establishment at Clam Town, and we returned with our gunboat to the Raritan River. In the same year we were joined by Capt. John Storey, commander of another gunboat, and, in a thick fog in the fall of that year, the two gunboats, Captain Storey's and *The Civil Usage,* boarded and captured the British guard galley that lay in Prince's Bay and sent her into New

Brunswick. After this occurrence, we continued with our boat on the same station in service until peace was proclaimed.

5
THE PHILADELPHIA THEATER

WILLIAM HUTCHINSON *(b. 1759), born and raised in London Britain Township, Chester County, Pennsylvania, served six terms in the Chester County militia and one year, July 1780 to July 1781, in the Second Delaware Regiment. He participated in the battles of Trenton, Brandywine, and Germantown, and his description of a survivor of the Paoli massacre and of a camp hospital are memorable. Contrary to his statement in the last paragraph, the British did not evacuate New York until 1782, but the account as a whole, where it can be checked, is factually accurate.*

After the war he resided in various places in Chester County, Pennsylvania, Cecil County, Maryland, and New Castle County, Delaware. A letter accompanying his 1836 application mentioned that Hutchinson was "wretchedly poor" and his sons and sons-in-law "worthless and dissolute." He was granted forty dollars a year.

That he entered the service of the United States under the following-named officers and served as herein stated. First, on the twentieth day of October, 1776, being not yet eighteen years of age, I joined a volunteer company of infantry commanded by Capt. Samuel Evans of Chester County, marched in a few days afterward, rendezvoused in Wilmington, Delaware, marched from Wilmington through Chester and Darby to Philadelphia, where our company was attached to a regiment commanded by Lieutenant Colonel Montgomery, who was also of Chester County. Our company was detailed to mount guard and patrol the streets of the city at night and continued in that service under the command of Captain Evans for two months, at which time his tour of service expired and he retired to his home. The tour of a number of our men had also expired, and they too returned home, which was (as well as this declarant can recollect) on or about the twenty-fifth of December in the same year.

Second, at which time Lieutenant Hops of Captain Evans's company appeared at Colonel Montgomery's quarters, bringing with him nine or ten men belonging to Captain Evans's company who ought to have marched with us in October but did not, and, being young and in love with the cause, I again joined the squad brought up by Lieutenant Hops. And we were all attached to a company commanded by Capt. James McDowell, who with his company had a few days before joined Colonel Montgomery's regiment, who still remained in command, and rendezvoused in Philadelphia. I cannot recollect who was the general in command in Philadelphia at this time, but after we had heard of the Hessians being taken, we were reviewed by General Putnam on foot, who addressed us as he walked close along the line. And as he came opposite to this declarant and a youthful fellow soldier who stood by his side and who in the struggle for Independence filled the grave of a brave man, the general, observing our youthful appearance, turned to us and laid his hand on the shoulder of each of us and remarked that he liked to see such young men turn out and that they would make men when their beards grew. He then took off his hat and showed us his head, which had been scalped by the Indians.

That same evening we were ordered to march from Philadelphia. Our company and the whole regiment were conveyed up the Delaware in shallops to Bristol and from thence across the river to Burlington, and from thence we marched to Bordentown and to Crosswicks, where we lay two days. And on the night of the third day, we were marched to Trenton, where we arrived on the morning of the battle of that place, in which this declarant partook with all the patriotic glow and ardor of a freeman fighting for the liberties of his country and aided in the slaughter and defeat of the body of Hessians which had been sent from the main body of the enemy to force the bridge by which we had made a stand. They were driven back with great slaughter occasioned by the well-directed fire of our artillery, and in the afterpart of the same day a certain Hugh Coppell and myself passed over the ground which they had occupied during the battle and their attacks upon us. Their dead bodies lay thicker and closer together for a space than I ever beheld sheaves of wheat lying in a field over which the reapers had just passed.

On the next day, Captain McDowell's command was ordered to take charge of the baggage train, which we did and with it marched to Burlington, thence back through Bordentown to

Trenton again, thence to Princeton, and while our company was traveling about the country with the baggage, the Battle of Princeton was fought. And, in consequence of the duty in which we were engaged, we were prevented from participating therein. We then went on through Brunswick to Morristown and done duty in traversing that section of country from place to place till we were finally discharged at Morristown, previous to which we were addressed by General Mifflin, giving us great applause for our patience and fortitude and anxiously desiring us to remain in service until other troops would arrive to take our place. Captain McDowell and his company were discharged by order of General Mifflin at Morristown after continuing in the field for two months and a half.

Third, in the month of July, 1777, and near the latter end of the month, I again joined the army as a volunteer in a company commanded by Capt. Allen Cunningham of New London Crossroads, Chester County, which was about to take the field. We marched the first day to Wilmington, Delaware, and were lodged that night in the academy. Next morning, proceeded to Chester, at which place our company was lodged in the courthouse and continued there until the main army under the command of General Washington came from Philadelphia on their march to meet the enemy, who it was understood had made a landing at Turkey Point on the Chesapeake. Next day, after the main army passed through Chester, our captain with his command, agreeably to orders, marched back to Wilmington. Our company were then ordered to work on a hill in the rear of the town in the construction of a fascine battery, at which we continued to work for either three or four days and were then ordered to the banks of Red Clay Creek and were employed in cutting timber to create all possible obstructions in the public roads and highways for the purpose of preventing the passage of the enemy in their march to Philadelphia, which it was generally understood was their design and destination.* From Red Clay Creek we passed through Chester County by a circuitous route to a place then called the Turk's Head, now known as West Chester, the seat of justice of this county. From West Chester we marched to Downingtown, where we were joined by several other companies of volunteers and

*I frequently saw . . . also the Marquis Lafayette and by him we had the honor of being reviewed on Quaker Hill at Wilmington, Delaware, while we were at work erecting the battery I have before spoken of and were there addressed by him. He was with us both on horseback and on foot.

General Lafayette

militia but cannot now recollect that they were under the command of any field officer but distinctly recollects to see Maj. Patterson Bell with the troops at that time. We went from Downingtown to McClellan's Tavern, where we lay doing camp duty for several days.

On the morning of the Battle of Brandywine, we were marched down the west side of the creek near the Chad's Fording and ordered to cross to the east side of the creek, which we did by wading, and marched up the stream about half a mile, where we lay upon a bottom, then clothed with woods, between the hill and the creek. During the battle we were frequently fired upon by the enemy, both by artillery and infantry, and with all good will we returned their fire with our small arms, which was all we had at command. During the battle we saw no field officers except such as came in battle haste to our captain with orders, and the declarant does not recollect to have ever heard the names of any of them and saw no general officer during the battle. Our captain was a gallant man, and we had full confidence both in his skill and courage.

After the battle, we continued on the ground for some time and for several days kept near the same spot, but every day in motion and every night in camping in a different place, sometimes in a house or barn and sometimes in the woods. During this time, the sad and heartrending massacre committed by the infamous General Grey upon our troops which lay near the General Paoli under the command of the gallant Wayne took place. During our perambulations at this time through Chester County, we took up I think about 150 deserters (Americans) who had fled from their colors and were making for home. Most of them were Marylanders. General Smallwood had given Capt. Allen Cunningham information that a great many of the Maryland men had fled and particularly desired him to keep a sharp lookout for them, with orders to bring every one he could take up to headquarters. Our company at this time were stationed at McClellan's Tavern in the Great Valley, where we had before laid for a few days at the commencement of our tour.

The second morning after the Paoli massacre, and whilst we were at McClellan's, a circumstance took place which the declarant asks permission to relate, as it has not yet formed any part of the history of the period to which he is alluding. A Quaker, a stranger, came to our quarters and brought with him a man which he said he had found lying in the woods whose clothes, coat, vest, and trousers were stiff with gore. And declarant believes they would have stood alone when taken off him. He was a Virginian and had shared in the consequences of the massacre; had been singled out at the close thereof as a special subject for the exercise of the savage cruelty of the British soldiers. He told us that more than a dozen soldiers had with fixed bayonets formed a cordon round him, and that every one of them in sport had indulged their brutal ferocity by stabbing him in different parts of his body and limbs, and that by a last desperate effort, he got without their circle and fled. And as he rushed out, one of the soldiers struck at him to knock him down as the finis to the catastrophe, in which only the front of the bayonet reached his head and laid it open with a gash as if it had been cut with a knife. He made, however, his escape, and when brought to our captain, he had laid in the woods twenty-four hours. He had neither hat, shoes, nor stockings, and his legs and feet were covered with mud and sand which had been fastened to his skin by mixing with his own blood as it ran down his limbs.

Our captain immediately dispatched his lieutenant for a physician, who, when he returned, was so fortunate as to bring two with him. We then procured the means of washing and cleansing the wounded man, and upon examining him there was found, as our captain afterwards announced to the men, forty-six distinct bayonet wounds in different parts of his body, either of which were deep and sufficiently large to have been fatal if they had been in vital parts. But they were mostly flesh wounds, and every one of them had bled profusely, and many of them commenced bleeding again upon being washed. His wounds were dressed, his bloody garments were burned, and by orders of our captain, he was waited upon with strict attention until he was able to walk, and then was by Lieutenant Corry (our lieutenant) taken somewhere not distant to an hospital, and declarant heard no more of him.

In a short time we received orders to march and join the army in the vicinity of Philadelphia, by which time the enemy had got possession of that city. We joined the army under the commander-in-chief near Germantown, was in that battle, and had the honor of firing many rounds at the enemy entrenched in Chew's house, at which time declarant was wounded in the right arm by a musket ball from the enemy while his arm was elevated in ramming down a charge in his own gun, the mark of which yet distinctly remains to be seen.

After the Battle of Germantown, the declarant had occasion to enter the apartment called the hospital, in which the wounded were dressing and where the necessary surgical operations were performing and there beheld a most horrid sight. The floor was covered with human blood; amputated arms and legs lay in different places in appalling array, the mournful memorials of an unfortunate and fatal battle, which indeed it truly was. From Germantown we were marched by White Marsh to Chestnut Hill and in eight or ten days afterwards were discharged after having served two months and one week.

Fourth, in the month of October on the same year (1777) this declarant, after having been but a few days at home, again entered the service in a company commanded by Capt. John McGee of Chester County as a substitute for his father, who had been drafted to perform a tour of service. Rendezvoused at New London Crossroads, where we mustered for three or four days, from which place we were marched to Cochran's Tavern at a place now known by the name of Cochranville. Stayed one night, and from thence to McClellan's Tavern in the Great Valley. Encamped there about one week; thence marched by the Swedes Ford on Schuylkill to Graeme Park in Montgomery or Philadelphia County. Lay there two weeks. Then marched to Neshaminy in Bucks County, thence to Smithfield in Philadelphia County, and there our company was placed under the command of Gen. John Lacy of Jersey, and from there we were dispatched to Pennypack Mills and ordered to destroy them so far as to prevent the enemy from having any use of them, which orders were punctually and effectually obeyed. From thence we marched back to Smithfield, about which time the enemy made prisoners of a body of tailors who were peaceably engaged at Newtown, Bucks County, in providing clothing to a great amount for the American army and with them captured the whole of their work and materials. The time for which my father was drafted soon after expired, and Captain McGee and his men were marched to White Marsh and were discharged in this tour. I served two months; this was near the latter end of the year 1777.

Fifth, after the expiration of my tour as a substitute for my father under the command of Captain McGee, I did not return home but remained at Doylestown, where the public armory was kept, and in a few days Capt. Samuel Evans (the same captain under whom my first tour of duty was served) appeared at Doylestown with his company to draw their arms for another campaign. This was near the commencement of the year 1778, and I again joined his company. From Doylestown we were marched to Graeme Park, to Pennypack, to Bustletown, to Smithfield, and many other places, frequently over the same ground. The enemy were at this time in possession of the city of Philadelphia, and our service was to watch and harass them on every occasion that might offer.

We were at this time under the command of General Potter and acting always on the alert and appearing suddenly everywhere, as our commander kept us and himself almost constantly in motion everywhere almost night and day so that the direction in which we were marching one day gave no evidence of the course we might be pursuing the next. We continued in this kind of service for the period of two months and were marched to Doylestown, where Captain Evans and his company gave up their arms to the military storekeeper and were discharged, and the next day, on their march home, upwards of twenty of the command and part of our company and all the baggage fell into the hands of the enemy, and some of them afterwards died in prison, and some of them died soon after their return to their families in consequence of the hardships they had to endure from cold and hunger while in the enemy's prisons.

Sixth, in the month of February, 1778, I again entered the service as a volunteer in a company commanded by Capt. John Taylor, who with his command came from someplace up the Juniata River and rendezvoused at Doylestown for the equipment of his men. At that place I entered his command, and from thence we were ordered to a place called the Crooked Billet, now known as Hatborough, and from thence to and through the various towns and places in Philadelphia, Montgomery, and Bucks counties, constantly performing the same kind of service in which I had been engaged in my tour preceding this with Captain Evans for the purpose of preventing the enemy from foraging in that district of country and also of preventing the disaffected of the vicinity from having any intercourse with the enemy, in which we were very industrious and successful too. We were still under the command of General Potter. I think there was a colonel with or near us, but his name has escaped the memory of the declarant. Recollects, however, that Major Bell of Kennett Square (not the same Major Bell before mentioned) was occasionally with us. Also recollects that General Wayne was frequently at General Potter's quarters, and that he and General Potter and Major Bell had on these times many jovial nights.

The Honᵇˡᵉ ANTHONY WAYNE, Esqʳ
Major General in the American Army
J Nor Sc.

In this way the services of Captain Taylor and all his volunteers, of which the declarant was one, continued for the term of four months, although the drafted men he brought out with him returned to their homes at the end of two months. We were at the end of four months discharged. The British having evacuated the city, we were marched from Pennypack into Philadelphia, where we found and received from 100 to 150 deserters from the ranks of the enemy, finding them concealed in cellars and hogsheads and in various other places.

And further, this deponent declares that he enlisted in the army of the United States at Newport, Delaware, in the latter end of the month of July, 1780, with Captain Robinson and served in the Second Delaware Regiment of the line under the following-named officers. Declarant and four others, his companions all from Chester County, were at the same time enlisted by the said Capt. William Robinson at Newport in the state of Delaware and engaged to serve for the term of one year unless sooner discharged. That he and his companions each received four silver dollars and with them some Continental money, the amount not now recollected, bounty. That he and his comrades, under the command of Capt. William McClements of Dover, were marched from Newport to Wilmington and were there registered and sized, and in Wilmington was appointed orderly sergeant. From thence were transported by water to Philadelphia, where we drew our arms and whole military clothing and equipments, joined a regiment, and under the command of Captain McClements we were transported by water to Trenton. Our regiment was commanded by Col. Henry Neale, and we had one major, viz., Maj. James Mitchell of Dagsborough, Sussex, Delaware. From Trenton we were marched to Princeton and rested in the academy one night, to Brunswick, to Troytown, to Morristown, to Hackensack, and lay there some days; afterwards to several other towns and finally to a place called Dobbs Ferry, thirty miles east of New York, at which place the different companies composing our regiment were collected and encamped but had no increase of field officers. At Dobbs Ferry, was detailed to aid the surgeon of the regiment. Our main army at this time lay at Tappan.

While we lay there, the enemy were in possession of the city of New York, and their gunboats almost daily came up the river and fired upon us, but the men never ventured to come on shore. Lay at Dobbs Ferry all the fall season and until Christmas, doing nothing but camp duty. We were then ordered to Morristown and from thence to Princeton, thence to Trenton, and from thence we were transported by water to Philadelphia, thence by water to Wilmington, Delaware. At Wilmington we lay about three weeks.

About this time news of the cessation of hostilities between America and her enemy was spoken of and probably proclaimed, and also we heard of a part of the army having been disbanded, and our regiment were dismissed upon parole or furlough with orders for every man to hold himself in readiness to march at a minute's warning. And about the same time we heard of the enemy having vacated New York. This was in the year 1781. After this we were never called upon and received no discharge.

JOHN MCCASLAND *(b. 1750), a native of Cumberland County, Pennsylvania, volunteered in the Pennsylvania militia and served three months at Perth Amboy and on Long Island, where he participated in the battle of 27 August 1776. He was drafted in January 1778 and served until March at Valley Forge, primarily engaged in scouting. A frontiersman by birth, McCasland was an excellent marksman, and his account of picking off a Hessian looter and capturing him and his companions is graphic.*

He moved to Kentucky in April 1780 and served in two expeditions of Gen. George Rogers Clark. He later participated in and escaped from St. Clair's defeat of 1791. He left Kentucky for Davidson County, Tennessee, in 1801, submitted this deposition in 1832, and received a pension.

That he was born on the first day of June in the year 1750 in Cumberland County, in the state of Pennsylvania, and entered the service of the United States sometime in the month of August, 1776, in Capt. Thomas Campbell's company of volunteers of the Seventh Regiment Pennsylvania militia (as he believes) commanded by Colonel Brown. That he was a volunteer, and after the company was made up, the officers were elected, and that he was elected an ensign.

That the company was made up in Cumberland County, Pennsylvania, and marched to Philadelphia and then went by water to Trenton, and from Trenton they marched to Perth Amboy, and while at Amboy the British lay on Staten Island. And there was occasional cannonading, but the distance was so far that no damage was done, after which time two British men-of-war went up the North River by breaking a chevaux-de-frise which had been stretched across the river to prevent their passing up the North River. Said vessels were said to be laden with provisions and munitions of war. And from Perth Amboy, went to Long Island under the command of General Putnam. We found troops on Long

Island (American troops), and soon after our arrival an engagement took place with the British, who I think were commanded by General Howe. We were defeated with a considerable number killed and a number taken prisoners, and among the number taken prisoners by the British was Captain Campbell. We then marched to Philadelphia, were paid off and discharged, and allowed a penny a mile to take us home. We then returned home the same route we went. I do not recollect the time we were absent, but we volunteered for three months. This deponent states that he got a discharge in Philadelphia which was signed by his lieutenant, Samuel McHatton, and Colonel Brown.

This deponent states that the next tour he served was in January 1778, when he was drafted in Cumberland County, Pennsylvania, in Capt. Joseph Culbertson's company of the regiment commanded by Col. Samuel Culbertson and was an orderly sergeant in said company. That the company marched to Valley Forge, where General Washington had his headquarters. That this was the first and last time he ever saw General Washington. That he was under the command of General Lacey, who commanded the militia. The British lay in Philadelphia this winter, and the American troops lay at Valley Forge. We had no fighting, but we had to scour the country to prevent the Hessians from plundering and destroying property, who generally [went] out in small gangs. And at different times we took Hessians prisoners and delivered them to General Washington at Valley Forge.

And on one occasion, sixteen of us were ranging about hunting Hessians, and we suspected Hessians to be at a large and handsome mansion house in Bucks County, Pennsylvania, about sixteen miles from Philadelphia. We approached near the house and discovered a large Hessian standing in the yard with his gun, as a sentinel we supposed, and by a unanimous vote of the company present it was agreed on that Major McCorman or myself, who were good marksmen, should shoot him (McCorman was then a private). We cast lots, and it fell to my lot to shoot the Hessian. I did not like to shoot a man down in cold blood. The company present knew I was a good marksman, and I concluded to break his thigh. I shot with a rifle and aimed at his hip. He had a large iron tobacco box in his breeches pocket, and I hit the box, the ball glanced, and it entered his thigh and scaled the bone of the thigh on the outside. He fell and then rose. We scaled the yard fence and surrounded the house. They saw their situation and were evidently disposed to surrender. They could not speak English, and we could not understand their language. At length one of the Hessians came out of the cellar with a large bottle of rum and advanced with it at arm's length as a flag of truce. The family had abandoned the house, and the Hessians had possession. They were twelve in number. We took them prisoners and carried them to Valley Forge and delivered them up to General Washington. We were drafted for two months on the twenty-second of January and was discharged about the twenty-second of March at Valley Forge, and from Valley Forge we marched home the same route we came, and I got a discharge at Valley Forge.

In April 1780 I moved from Cumberland County, Pennsylvania, to the neighborhood of the falls of Ohio in the state of Kentucky and landed at the falls of Ohio, April 16th, 1780. The Indians were very troublesome, and in the afterpart of the summer of 1780 I went out as a volunteer under General Clark as a private against the Shawnee Indians and marched up the Ohio River on the southern side and crossed it at the mouth of the Miami River, thence to Chillicothe, and at Chillicothe we had an engagement with the Indians. We defeated and routed them, cut their corn down, and burnt their houses and then returned home the same route after an absence of about six weeks. I went out under Captain McClure and was paid by the United States at the falls of the Ohio and was discharged there. That no discharges were given to the volunteers.

This deponent further states that he went out another tour of duty, in 1782, against the Shawnee Indians as a private and as a volunteer under the command of General Clark in Capt. Jacob Vanmeter's company. Crossed the Ohio River at the mouth of Licking River, built a blockhouse where Cincinnati now stands, and left fifteen or twenty invalids at the blockhouse to take care of such military stores as we could not take with us. We proceeded up the Miami River to the Shawnee towns, five days' march. The Indians discovered us about two miles from the towns and made their escape. We burnt their corn, which was gathered, and burnt as many as seven little towns, took five Indians (women and children) prisoners, and killed five or six warriors who were scouting about. We then returned home the same route after an absence of something less than two months to the falls of the Ohio, where we were paid off. And I am of the opinion that none of us got a discharge.

HENRY YEAGER *(b. 1763) of Philadelphia enlisted at age thirteen and served as a drummer in Pennsylvania and in Philadelphia militia companies for eleven short tours of duty from December 1776 through July 1778. In late 1777, while the British held Philadelphia, he and a friend went into town to see their families and were taken prisoner, convicted as spies, and at least ostensibly sentenced to hang. It seems probable that Provost Marshal Cunningham intended only to give his two prisoners, the older only fourteen, a good scare, but the drama was carried to the last degree. Yeager was released after eight weeks' imprisonment, and upon evacuation of the British, he promptly enlisted as a private in an artillery company stationed at Fort Mifflin and served for two years. He signed on board a privateer, then on the merchantman* Franklin, *and was captured.*

He spent two years imprisoned at Plymouth, England, returning in 1783 to lifelong residence in Philadelphia. He submitted this deposition in 1837, but, as with many drummers who were under sixteen, he was never given a pension.

He was a resident of Philadelphia when he volunteered as a drummer in a company commanded by Captain Weed towards the close of October or beginning of November, 1776. The regiment to which his company was attached was commanded by Colonel Ayres or Eyre, and Major Boyd, in his rank as major, was attached to the same regiment. The regiment went up the River Delaware in boats from Philadelphia to Trenton, where they encamped. General Washington, with the army, was on towards Princeton, and Colonel Ayres's or Eyre's regiment had drawn three days' provision and raised their tents to march onward in pursuance of orders, when they were directed to retire to Philadelphia, General Washington having determined to retreat in consequence of the British, in a large force under Cornwallis, marching upon him from New Brunswick. Colonel Ayres or Eyre with his regiment therefore retired to Philadelphia in boats and encamped in the district of Kensington, in the county of Philadelphia, where they remained under orders for about ten days, when they were dismissed in December, about the middle of the month, 1776. In this tour declarant served not less than six weeks. Upon Washington's retreat, as herein mentioned, he crossed the Delaware from New Jersey and destroyed the bridges and removed all boats to prevent the British, who were very close upon him, from following.

Declarant again entered the service of the United States and volunteered as a drummer in Philadelphia in a company commanded by Captain Ashton in the month of February, as near as he can state, 1777. He went with the company to the fort at Billingsport, in the state of New Jersey, in a sloop from Philadelphia. He does not recollect the name of the officer who then commanded the fort. He remained there two months, when, his term having expired, he returned to Philadelphia.

Immediately after his return, he volunteered again as a drummer in the company commanded by Captain Eastburn, or Isburne, attached to the Second (as he thinks) Regiment, Pennsylvania Volunteers. He again went to the fort at Billingsport with this company. At this time Colonel Bradford commanded the fort. He remained there two months, when, his term having expired, he returned to Philadelphia.

Immediately after his return, he volunteered again as a drummer in the company commanded by Captain Eastburn, or Isburne, attached to the Second (as he thinks) Regiment, Pennsylvania Volunteers. He again went to the fort at Billingsport with this company. At this time Colonel Bradford commanded the fort. He remained there two months, when, his term having expired, he returned to Philadelphia.

In a few days after his return, he volunteered again as a drummer in a company commanded by Captain Esler. He went again to the fort at Billingsport with this company and remained two months with Captain Esler, who at the expiration of that time returned to the city with his company, their term having expired. But declarant remained at the fort and volunteered as a drummer in the relieving company which arrived there at that time commanded by Captain Peale. Colonel Will of the Third (he thinks) Regiment, Pennsylvania Volunteers, then commanded the fort. Sometime after he had joined Captain Peale, a superior British force from below that point approached the fort to attack it, and Colonel Will retreated, having first spiked the cannon. The troops under Colonel Will went over to Fort Mifflin from Billingsport, but they could not be, or at all events were not, received there. They then crossed to Red Bank in Gloucester County, New Jersey, and from thence marched up through New Jersey as far as Burlington, Burlington County, in the last-named state, where they encamped. They had been there but a short time when information of hostilities at Germantown was received, and they immediately marched under Colonel Will towards that point for the purpose of joining the army there; but on their way they were met by some scattered portions of the American troops, who informed them of the unfortunate termination of the battle at the last-named place. Colonel Will therefore marched his troops on to White Marsh, in the county of Montgomery, Pennsylvania, where they encamped for about ten days or two weeks, when, their term having expired, they were dismissed. In this tour, as in the previous ones, declarant served two months. His service at Billingsport all together, including the time occupied going and returning from there, amounted to more than eight months.

Upon being discharged as above stated, the declarant, in company with one George Lechler, who was also in Colonel Will's regiment when it was dismissed at White Marsh, returned to Philadelphia. They had been at home in Philadelphia but a few days when they were both arrested by British authority (the British then being in possession of Philadelphia) and taken to General Howe's quarters in Second Street below Spruce, opposite Little Dock Street in Philadelphia. Declarant was accompanied by his mother, and when they arrived at the general's quarters, a Major Bedford asked her if declarant was her son, and being answered affirmatively, he remarked that declarant would be hanged. Declarant was put in a guardhouse at the corner of Second and Little Dock Streets. Lechler was confined separately in another in Little Dock Street.

The next day they were taken to the house at the northwest corner of Second and Spruce streets for trial. Declarant was taken before the judges first. He was charged with having brought letters from the American army, and he was asked if it was true. He answered in the negative. He was asked if he belonged to the rebel army. He answered that he belonged to Washington's army. He was then charged with having come to the city as a spy and was asked if such was not the fact. He answered no, but that he came to see his parents. He was examined for a length of time upon similar matters without eliciting more than is herein stated. After a short conference, one of the judges asked him his name, and, upon declarant giving it, the former said to him, "You are to be hanged by the neck until you are dead, dead, dead." Declarant was then conducted from the room. In the entry or hall, he met Lechler, who inquired what had taken place, and declarant informed him that he was to be hanged. Lechler was then conducted before the judges, and declarant was afterwards informed by him that similar proceedings occurred, and a like sentence was pronounced on him.

They were then both taken to the Walnut Street prison. Soon after they had been there, Provost Marshal Cunningham, in the hearing of declarant, directed the "spies" to be brought before him. Declarant and Lechler were accordingly conducted to him, when he said to them, "I'll give you half an hour and no longer," and ordered them to be confined in separate dungeons. At the expiration of the half hour (to declarant a very short one), they were again taken before Provost Marshal Cunningham, who ordered a Negro to bring two halters. The marshal asked who was the oldest. Lechler answered that he was the youngest. The marshal then directed that all the other prisoners should quit the yard and the gates be closed. He directed the Negro to place one halter on Lechler's neck, and the other on claimant's, to back both against the gate, and to draw the ropes through the top of it, which was done. At this moment, a man came in and gave a paper to the marshal, who read it and then ordered the ropes to be loosed from the gate and wound round prisoners' bodies. Declarant and Lechler were then ordered to their dungeons, where they were taken. The next morning they were brought to the marshal's room, when the ropes were taken off them and they put into the yard among the other prisoners. After this, declarant remained in prison eight weeks and three days before he was released.

Soon after the British evacuated Philadelphia, to wit, in the month of June or July (according to the best of declarant's memory), 1778, he, declarant, volunteered again as a private, in Philadelphia, in the seventh company of an artillery regiment. He cannot now recollect the name of the colonel who commanded the regiment, but the company to which declarant was attached was commanded by Capt. Samuel Neeves, or Neebs, who, being intemperate, was deprived of his command and succeeded by Capt. Andrew Boyd. Mr. Walters was first lieutenant, and Mr. Wetherill second lieutenant in this company. Part of the regiment was stationed at Fort Mifflin and part at Billingsport, according to the best of declarant's recollection, and the remainder was left at Philadelphia as relief. The company to which declarant was attached was stationed at Fort Mifflin, where he served under the officers above named four terms of more than two months each term. Declarant belonged and remained attached to this company more than two years, and during that period, when not serving at the fort, was with the relief on duty at Philadelphia, attending muster and drill regularly.

From the time that declarant first volunteered in Captain Weed's company until and including his last-named service under Captain Boyd, he served, as hereinbefore stated, two years and eleven months or thereabouts, and also served on other occasions which he cannot at this time recollect with sufficient accuracy to describe. Soon after leaving the artillery regiment, above mentioned, declarant shipped in Philadelphia on board the privateer ship *Rising Sun,* Capt. Samuel Carson. They sailed on a cruise which was to have been for six months, but at the expiration of about five months, having taken several valuable prizes, the captain broke it up and returned home. During the cruise they captured the British privateer brig *Rattlesnake.* Not long after he returned from this voyage, declarant shipped in the merchant ship *Franklin,* Capt. John Angus, freighted with five hundred hogsheads of tobacco bound to a port in France. The ship carried twenty-two long nines. On the voyage they took an English brig, but about a week afterwards the *Franklin* and her prize were captured by the English frigate *New Adventure.* Declarant, with the others on board, were taken to Weymouth, England, from thence to Portsmouth, and thence to Plymouth in the *Dublin,* seventy-four, and were imprisoned there nearly two years until exchanged about six weeks after peace in 1783.

DANIEL MORRIS *(b. 1756) was born in Scotland. His family emigrated to America in 1770, and Morris was sold by his father as an indentured servant to a Quaker, John Garrett of Philadelphia (now Montgomery) County. Morris's narrative of the ordeal he went through to join the army, twice escaping his master, gives us a rare glimpse of the vulnerability of children and servants, particularly immigrants, in early America.*

Morris eventually managed to join Flower's regiment of artificers, a rather remarkable unit scattered in several Pennsylvania towns, which supplied the American army with armaments and accoutrements. Morris himself made leather goods: belts, shoes, and cartridge boxes.

He submitted this narrative in 1846 at age ninety, but either because of death or from lack of proof, he never received a pension.

My father removed from Scotland with me and the rest of his family when I was about fourteen years of age, in the [year] 1770, to the best of my knowledge. We landed at Philadelphia, in the state of Pennsylvania, in the autumn of the same year, and, my father not being able to pay for my passage, I was sold to one John

Garrett, a farmer who lived about twelve miles from Philadelphia in Upper Dublin Township.

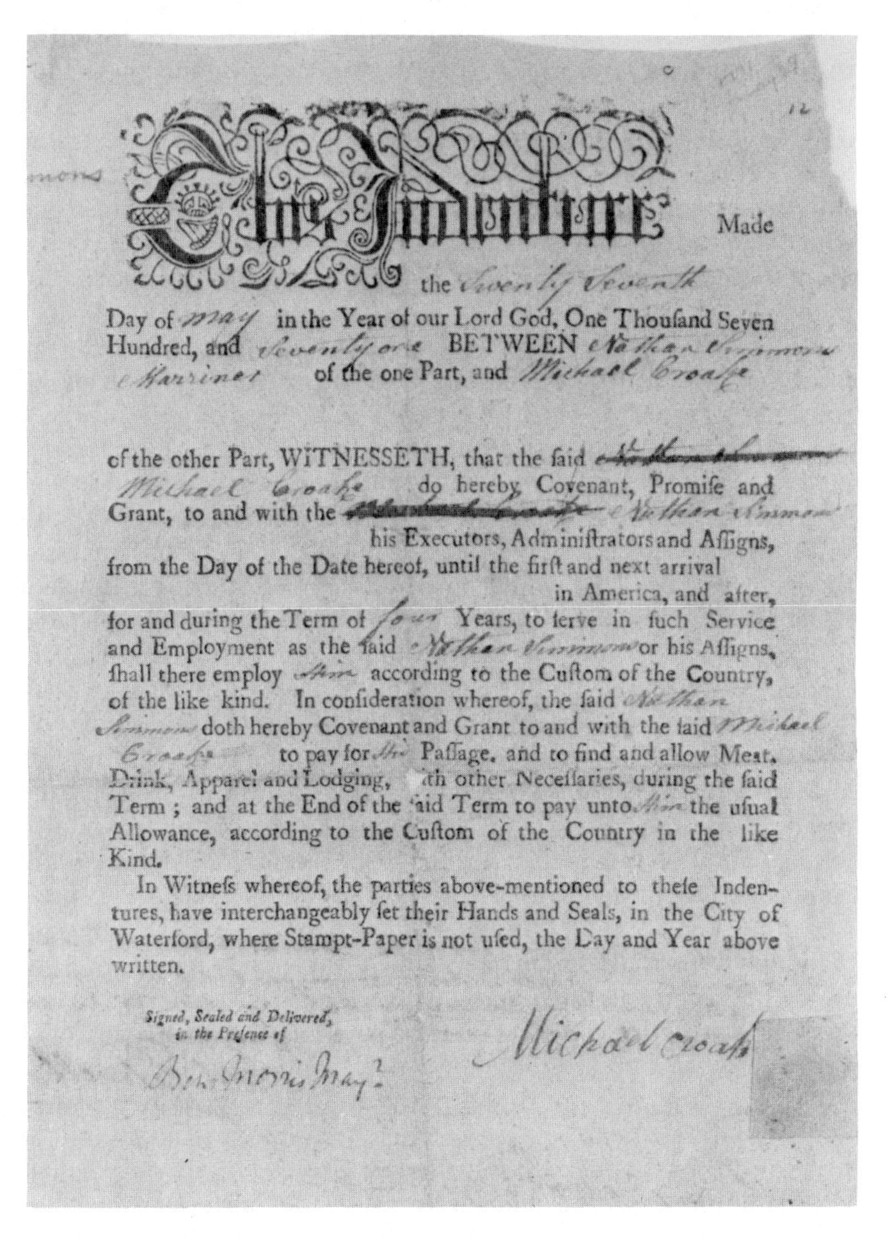

This Indenture Made the Seventy Seventh Day of may in the Year of our Lord God, One Thousand Seven Hundred, and Seventy one BETWEEN Nathan Simmons Marriner of the one Part, and Michael Croake of the other Part, WITNESSETH, that the said Michael Croake do hereby Covenant, Promise and Grant, to and with the Nathan Simmons his Executors, Administrators and Assigns, from the Day of the Date hereof, until the first and next arrival in America, and after, for and during the Term of four Years, to serve in such Service and Employment as the said Nathan Simmons or his Assigns, shall there employ him according to the Custom of the Country, of the like kind. In consideration whereof, the said Nathan Simmons doth hereby Covenant and Grant to and with the said Michael Croake to pay for his Passage, and to find and allow Meat, Drink, Apparel and Lodging, with other Necessaries, during the said Term; and at the End of the said Term to pay unto him the usual Allowance, according to the Custom of the Country in the like Kind.

In Witness whereof, the parties above-mentioned to these Indentures, have interchangeably set their Hands and Seals, in the City of Waterford, where Stampt-Paper is not used, the Day and Year above written.

Signed, Sealed and Delivered, in the Presence of

Ben Morris Mayr

Michael Croake

A colonial indenture

I lived with him until the time that General Washington was crossing the Schuylkill, about the time the British left Philadelphia, when one Isaac Tyson told me that the American army was pressing all the horses and wagons they could find to take their baggage across the Schuylkill. When I went to the house, I told my master, who was a Quaker, of it. He said, "Does thee not wish that they would come and press my horses and wagon and press thee to drive it?" I told him I did. I had a whip in my hand which he took from me and gave me several lashes with it and said, "Thee Scotch rebel, thou was a rebel in thine own country, and now thou has come here to rebel." So I was determined to leave him, which I did in about a week from the time he struck me, and then I enlisted in Colonel Preston's artillery, in Captain Rice's company.

I was there about three weeks, when one John Naylor, who lived in Philadelphia, a relation of my mistress, requested me to come along home with him and see where he lived, and he allowed, then, I could come and see him whenever I had time. He appeared so very friendly, that I did not think but his intention was to betray me. So I agreed to go along with him. I asked my captain leave, which he granted, but he gave me orders to be back against the roll was called. So John Naylor and myself set off, and when we arrived at the place where he lived, they had the constable waiting for me, who took me into his custody, and I thought he would take me back to the barracks, but instead of that, he took me to jail. And when we had got to the jail door, I thought it was time to make my escape to the barracks, but the turnkey flung his key, which struck me on the back of my head and knocked me down. Then they put me in jail, where I was confined about a week, when I was taken home to my master again. My mistress still continued to call me a rebel.

I stayed at home about a week, when I started off again, determined to go in the main army which was then lying at Trenton. But, when I came to the ferry, the ferryman accused me of being a runaway. I told him that I was. He asked me what I run off for. I told him that my real mother was dead, and that my father had married again, and that my stepmother was so very cross to me, that I could not bear her any longer. This line just happened to suit, for one of the men that assisted with the boat said that he had left his home upon the same account, so they agreed to take me over. But they had not went far, when they were hailed from a sloop that was fishing up stone out of the river for ballast. The captain of the sloop asked them who they were taking over, and they told him they were taking over a man who was going to join the army. He asked what countryman I was. They told him I was a Scotchman. He said I had better come along with him to see his father, for he was Scotchman too. So I agreed to go with him. And so I went to Philadelphia with him. And when we got there, the captain went on shore and told me to stay in the cabin. But the captain had not been long away, when I came out of the cabin and saw Matthew Tyson, a neighbor of my master, on the shore looking to our vessel, so I went down again into the cabin and stayed there until the captain came back. So I told the captain that I had saw one of my master's neighbors standing on the wharf, so he loosed the vessel from the wharf and went to his father, who lived near Dover in Delaware, where I resided for between three and four weeks. The captain's name was Joseph Campbell.

Then I came up to Philadelphia and enlisted in Colonel Flower's regiment of artificers in Captain Parker's company. I served under him until he was broke of his commission, and he was succeeded by Sir Robert Dow, who was the first lieutenant of the company before he was appointed captain. But before Captain Parker was broke of his commission, my master came after me, and my colonel sent for me, and when I came he told me that my master had been there. So he asked me if I had received my bounty money or not? I told him that I had not, and then he told me that was all my master could get. And then he took me before a magistrate by the name of Little, as near as I recollect, and I was sworn in, and my master gave up my indenture to the colonel. The first six months I billeted at the widow Flower's, who had four sons in the army. Her son Edward was one of the fifers to our company. And two years I billeted at Thomas Foster's, who was our sergeant, and six months at one Stroud's at the Sign of the Limekiln in Fourth Street, and that made up the three years, which time I was engaged in making scabbard belts, shoes, and covering cartridge boxes, and after I left the army I went privateering in the brig *Enterprize* and served under Captain Gardner for six months.

SAMUEL LOCKWOOD *(1755–1834) was born in Worcester County, Maryland, moved with his family to Sussex County, Delaware, in 1761, and offered himself in 1776 and 1777 as a volunteer in the Delaware militia. He was a member of a company assigned to shore duty on Delaware Bay, stationed at Lewes and at Cape Henlopen.*

The company to which he belonged was occupied in building a fort at Lewes during much of 1776. In 1777 Captain William Peery took charge of the defensive force. Two row galleys were sent in 1777, and Lockwood, with fellow militiamen, joined their crews and participated in several skirmishes. On 11 April 1777 he witnessed the encounter between the Roebuck, *the* Perseus, *and U.S.S.* Morris. *Capt. James Anderson did indeed blow up the ship and lose his life.*

Lockwood moved to Kentucky in 1791 and later became a licensed minister in the Methodist Episcopal church. He submitted this statement in 1833 and was granted a pension.

He entered voluntarily into the militia of the state of Delaware and in the Delaware regiment. He first joined at Lewestown, Sussex County, state of Delaware, early in the beginning of the year 1776, the precise day nor month not now recollected but thinks it must have been in January or February of that year and served under Capt. David Hall, afterwards Colonel Hall; First Lieutenant Harney; 2d Lt. John Learmouth, and Ens. Cord Hazzard, with Colonel Haslet, Lieutenant Colonel Bedford, and Major McDonough, who was said to have been after this time wounded in the knee at the Battle of White Plains above New York.

He served under the above officers as a private soldier for about three or four months, alternately guarding at the lighthouse which was on Cape Henlopen (about the distance of one mile from Lewestown) and working on the fort at Lewestown. That is to say, a portion of the troops was at stated times detailed from their usual duties in the camp and taken on what was called fatigue duty, which was to work as aforesaid and any other work which was necessary to put the country along the shore of the bay in a state of defense. He continued engaged as before stated and under the officers before named until about May or June, the month not now precisely recollected, when he was transferred to the company of Westley with the lieutenants and ensign before stated. Or, the said Captain Westley was transferred to our company—which, he does not now recollect. But be it which way it may, he never knew the cause of the arrangement unless his former captain was promoted, which it is likely was the case. However, be the cause as it may, in a week or two all the field officers before spoken of and many of the officers of the line, together with nearly all or quite all of the companies of the aforesaid regiment, marched off for Long Island in the state of New York, leaving none but the company to which he belonged, unless indeed he had been transferred to another regiment. At any rate, he never after this time served with and in company of a regiment but always with the single company to which he belonged except when there was an alarm such as to draw together the troops (for the moment) from the different stations along the shore in the state of Delaware, which seldom happened. He believes most, if not all, of the stations before spoken of was occupied by one company only.

This whole year was occupied by the company to which he belonged by guarding at the lighthouse and working as aforesaid, always taking their muskets, etc., with them. And whenever they heard two cannons (which was the signal), they laid by their laboring tools, seized their arms, and repaired to the point where there was danger apprehended and again, when the alarm was over, returned to their work unless the time for their relief had arrived. About the close of this year or the beginning of the year 1777, the different works of defense which he had been engaged at work on was completed, or so far advanced that nearly all the year 1777 he was confined to the lighthouse as a station and marching about, guarding the coast and observing the enemy's shipping, which was frequently this year in the bay, the fort at Lewestown being principally confided to the care of the citizens thereof, who was all minutemen.

But this year he was transferred to a new set of officers altogether, to wit: Capt. William Peery, 1st Lt. John Westley, 2d Lt. William Hazzard, and Ens. William Hall. During this whole year there was not any field officers with us, and our operations before spoken of was confined principally to five or six miles each way up and down the shore from the lighthouse on Cape Henlopen.

Sometime in the spring or beginning of the summer of this year, Congress, or someone having the authority, sent to the lighthouse two row galleys to be used in the neighborhood, and they were but about half manned, and his captain permitted the declarant and nineteen others to go on them, where they stayed about three or four weeks and then returned to their company again. One of these galleys was commanded by one Lawrence, and the other (the one on which this declarant went on) was commanded by Daniel Murphey.

And during his stay on board of said row galley and while cruising up and down near the shore, she, one night while the tide was up, run on a sandbar at the mouth of Lewes Creek and about two miles from the lighthouse. And the next morning the tide had left us, and we were out of water. There was at that time a British sloop of war lying off in the bay (she was said to be from New York). Early in the morning, the sloop was seen moving towards us, towed by three or four barges, when we held a consultation and determined to fight her, as we could retreat in the event of our being too weak and in no event lose more than our galley which would be lost if we left her at first. As soon as we had come to the determination to fight the British vessel, we went to work and prized up our galley and fixed skids under her so as to turn her about with tolerable convenience and in that way bring our gun to bear on her so soon as the enemy came in what they thought a convenient distance of us. They opened on us a fire and continued to fire on us about one half hour, but they could not bring their guns properly to bear on us, while on our side we, after the second or third fire, caused every shot to take effect, which in the course of the action very much cut her hull and damaged the barges. When they left us and when the tide again came in, we got off our galley. In this action we lost no men, killed or wounded.

At another time (the time exactly not recollected), about three-quarters of a mile from the lighthouse, there was a trading schooner loaded with tar, pitch, and other articles from North Carolina pursued by the enemy's barges so closely that she was run on shore (a British man-of-war at that time lying off in the bay and in full view). And the crew of the schooner abandoned her, when the enemy set fire to her. But we came upon them at that instant, and they could receive no assistance from the man-of-war, and, we being too strong for them, they in turn was compelled to put out for their shipping. And we very nearly saved all of the hull of the schooner and the principal part of her cargo by cutting a hole in her keel and shoving her off so as to sink her low enough to put out the fire, the cargo being of articles that the water would not injure.

At another time, and after he had left the row galley before spoken of and in the same year, but the particular time of said year he cannot now recollect, he was near and in sight of a battle in which two British ships (the *Roebuck* and another, name not known) and an American or French ship was engaged. He does not know whether the last ship was American or French, but it was in the American service and was loaded with clothing and arms for the American army, with, as he understood, dispatches on board from Dr. Benjamin Franklin, who was the agent or minister either at the court of France or some other government.

As he was then young and paid but little attention to the reports of the day, he may not in consequence of the distance of time which have intervened recollect the minutiae correctly of the day. But it was a hard battle, and when the officer who commanded the American or French ship saw that he could not hold out against the two British ships, he run his ship ashore, and after his men got on land, the ship was blown up. The arms, a great many of them, was gotten possession of by us, and they were sent to the army to be refitted up for use, they having been much burnt and otherwise injured. There was about one hundred or more men on board who was Frenchmen and Americans. He at this time thinks that he then understood that the American ship was commanded by one Anderson but will not be positive. At any rate, he does not recollect to have seen the captain of said ship. The report in camp was that as soon as the captain got his men on shore, he himself applied the match, as it was believed, and blew up the ship rather than it should fall into the hands of the enemy. This, however, was camp news, upon which at no time much reliance can be placed. He is not certain that his recollection is correct in relation to the name of the captain of the ship.

His service during this year, to wit, 1777, continued throughout as before stated, guarding along the Delaware shores, and when not moving about, stationed at the lighthouse on Cape Henlopen. He does not now recollect any other incidents worthy of note during the balance of his service.

He served as aforesaid until the close of the year 1777, or until the beginning of the year 1778, and until he had completed his two years' service, when he was discharged and at the same [time] received said discharge in writing, in the body of which he was styled a private in the Delaware regiment of volunteer militia, and it also gave him credit for two years' service, and it was signed by Capt. William Peery, who was at that time his captain and had been for about one year.

CHARLES CONAWAY *(b. 1752) was a native of Kent County, Maryland. He served a total of six months' duty in the Queen Anne County militia between September 1777 and April 1779.*

The Delmarva Peninsula, particularly the remote central portions of

Kent and Sussex counties, Delaware, and the neighboring areas of Maryland, were a stronghold of loyalism and indifference. The population was largely illiterate, poor, and far removed from the intellectual and economic currents that brought on the Revolution.

Many of the residents resented political domination from New Castle County, Philadelphia, and the Western Shore of Maryland as much as British claims of sovereignty, and this hindered American recruitment efforts. The arrival of Howe's army at Philadelphia in September 1777 emboldened the loyalists, and in April 1778 several hundred, under the leadership of Cheney Clow, built and manned the fort that Conaway refers to near present-day Kenton, Delaware. The British withdrawal from Philadelphia in May 1778 left identifiable Tories defenseless. Clow's fort was abandoned, and brazen loyalism throughout the section disappeared.

Conaway's narrative is of interest for conveying not facts, but feelings. His conception of an almost supernatural Washington was shared by many Americans, in and out of the army. This implicit faith in the commander-in-chief was a primary factor in maintaining American morale throughout the long and often discouraging war.

Conaway moved to Fayette County, Pennsylvania, in 1787 and to Adams County, Ohio, in 1817. He submitted an application in 1832 and a revised version (published here with a footnote taken from the first appplication) shorty afterward, and he was granted a pension.

I was born in Kent County, state of Maryland, June 30th, 1752. My father died before I was two years old. My mother moved into Queen Anne's County, in the same state, when I was about sixteen years of age, when she bound me out to learn the carpenter's and joiner's trade. My freedom took place about two years before the Revolutionary War commenced.

In the spring of 1775, orders were given to enroll for mustering to prepare for the war. My brother Samuel and I joined the first company raised in our county under Dr. Samuel Thompson. In June the same year, a regiment of volunteers were called under the name of Flying Camp from the peninsula where we lived. I stepped forward to join the company. My brother thought my health was not sufficient for to stand the fatigues. As we could not both leave our mother, he went and stood his five months' tour and returned safe; he then joined with me to work at my trade till August 1777.

The British fleet came up Chesapeake to make their way to Philadelphia and landed at the Head of Elk and cut off our communication. The militia called for to join the army to meet the enemy at Brandywine, the greater part of them refused to go and fled into the woods, took up arms to defend themselves, which throwed our country into great confusion and distress. The officers consulted Washington about what was to be done. He knew the situation and state of our country. The Chesaspeake was on the west, the Delaware on the east, the ocean on the south, and he knew the minds of the people: that through fear they became disaffected; that they would not take up arms against the British. He directed or advised the officers to try if they could raise volunteers to protect and defend that section of country, and they should have it for their station, exempt from all other service or from sending any men to the army. A company of volunteers was raised under Capt. James Kent. My brother and I both joined them about the seventh or eighth of September, 1777. We marched in pursuit of them. In the first attack we had, my horse threw me, and I lost my gun and saddle but made my escape. Our troubles continued till sometime in December we had our last skermage [skirmish]. We took one prisoner, and I got my gun, for he had it. Here is three months for 1777.

We was at rest till the first of March, 1778. Undiscovered and unsuspected, the Tories had increased their number more than threefold and had got arms and ammunition from the British and had erected themselves a fort for to defend themselves. We were now all called immediately, but our volunteers' numbers were but small. Colonel Henry thought that he could attack the fort safely, but he found his mistake, for he was soon defeated, which throwed the whole into great confusion and trouble. It was then thought best to fix guards and to cut off the communication, to keep them in the fort, which brought on skirmishes almost every day. A little time before the British left Philadelphia, which was sometime in June, they stole out of the fort, as we supposed in small parties, and left the fort vacant, and as there was some of the British vessels lying in the bay, they was pursued, but they made their escape to them and stole some of our trading shallops and manned them with refugees and so fell to plundering.* Here we

*At a place called Jordan's Branch, a fort was built by the Tories in March 1778, where it was said there were a thousand Tories stationed. This applicant, with a strong force of other volunteers under the command of Colonels Fauntleroy amd Wilmer, were stationed from March 1778 till June the following in the vicinity of said fort to cut off the communication of the Tories with [the] British and starve them out. In or about June, the Tories were dispersed and

have three months in 1778 and three months in 1777, making six months. Here the volunteers in the lower counties were called to arms, where they had to continue till the spring of 1779, but we in the three upper counties, Queen Anne's, Kent, and Cecil, was never called upon for any services after June 1778 till the spring of 1780, when six men out of every company were sent for by choosing, which was done with pleasure. So the applicant conceives that he is entitled to the benefit of the act of 1832.

driven off, some to Canada and some to the British, and others secreted themselves.

His Ex.cy George Washington Esq.
Captain General of all the American Forces

6
WAR IN THE CAROLINAS

JOSIAH CULBERTSON *(b. ca. 1748) was a resident of Ninety Six, South Carolina, and served numerous tours of duty, totaling more than three years, in various South Carolina military units. He participated in the battles of the Cowpens, Ramsour's Mill, Kings Mountain, and Charleston, but by 1832 his memory was poor.*

One incident, certainly one of the more remarkable of the war, was permanently engraved on Culbertson's memory. In 1776, with the sole support of his mother-in-law, he successfully held off a party of 150 Tories and saved a cache of ammunition that was later used at Gen. Thomas Sumter's victory at Hanging Rock.

Culbertson resided in Greenville District until 1810 and was residing in Davis County, Indiana, when awarded a pension.

The first service that this deponent engaged in was as a volunteer in a company commanded by Capt. John Thomas, Jr., the regiment commanded by his father, Col. John Thomas, and the whole commanded by General Mason. This was, as near as deponent now recollects, in the fall of 1775. Deponent served six weeks. It was what was known in South Carolina as the Snow Camp campaign.

In June 1776 he started again as a volunteer in the company commanded by Capt. John Thomas, Jr., and Colonel Thomas, colonel of the regiment, the whole commanded by General Mason, on a tour of fourteen weeks against the Cherokee Indians who were committing depredations on the frontiers of South Carolina. That he was drafted and went out under the command of the same captain and colonel at the time Savannah was besieged and was absent on this tour doing duty for three months. That he was out as volunteer in several campaigns from 1775 to 1780 against the Indians, Tories, and British, most generally under the same officers, the particulars of which or the length of time he served at each he cannot now exactly recollect. The camp to which he was attached, from its frequency of movement and action being known and designated as the Flying Camp, during which they had several engagements with Colonel Ferguson's men, the Tories, and Indians. That he was out in all more than three years in service, adding up the whole time he was engaged in the service. That he was in the Battle of Cowpens, Ramsour's, and Kings Mountain and in various smaller engagements with the enemy. He served with the regular troops at the time General Lincoln and Morgan commanded them. The names of the other regular officers who were commanders of regiments and companies of the regular troops he does not now recollect. The captain of his company at the Battle of the Cowpens and Kings Mountain was Roebuck.

That he cannot in consequence of his advanced age and the consequent loss of his memory now give the particulars of all the various engagements and combats he was in during the Revolution, but as one event is connected with the history of the times and well known in his native state, South Carolina, he will briefly refer to it. In 1776, Governor Rutledge sent up ammunition to the Whigs in the district of Ninety Six, where deponent resided, to keep the Tories in awe, who were plenty enough in that section and continued to do more mischief than even the British. A part of this ammunition was deposited at the house of Col. John Thomas before mentioned. In the spring of 1780, while the British besieged Charleston, this ammunition, which was all important to the American cause, was guarded by the deponent and twenty-five men. The success of the British inspirited the Tories, and a Colonel Moore with about 150 men determined to attack the house in which the ammunition was lodged and destroy it. Moore with his men approached. The guard, being fearful of such odds, retreated, although strongly remonstrated with by this deponent, leaving no one to defend the house but deponent and his mother-in-law, Mrs. Thomas. The house was a log house, and the rest of the guard having retreated, he determined, great as the hazard was, rather than give it up, to defend it himself against the besiegers. He accordingly loaded his guns and, while his mother-in-law was employed in running him a supply of bullets, kept up such a fire upon the Tories from the house that they, believing the whole guard there, then retreated, leaving himself, his mother-in-law, and the ammunition safe. The destruction of this

ammunition would have been a serious loss to the Americans, and the same was afterwards made use of by Sumter at his fight on the Rocky Mountain and at the Battle of the Hanging Rock.

The Hon.le B. LINCOLN, Esq
Major General in the American Arm

JAMES FERGUS *(1756–1837), of Scotch-Irish background, was born in Chester County, Pennsylvania. He resided in Sherman's Valley, Cumberland County, when he first volunteered in 1776. After a brief residence in the Shenandoah Valley, Virginia, he moved to near Camden, South Carolina, in the fall of 1778.*

He volunteered twice in the Pennsylvania militia, serving at Staten Island at the time of the Battle of Long Island. He was at the Battle of Princeton. After moving to South Carolina, he went out against a Tory company under Captain Coleman, and in 1779 he volunteered for the campaign against British-held Savannah, serving with two hundred horsemen for scouting and reconnaissance duty. He was present at the American rout at Briar Creek, and, like most of the dozens of pensioners who had been there, he was highly critical of General Ashe, the American commander. Fergus later was at Charleston and kept a journal that he reproduced in the pension narrative. He took sick, was treated in Charleston by Dr. David Ramsay, and was fortunate enough to be sent home before the British capture of the city.

The first half of his narrative, covering his tours of duty in the North, has been omitted here because of its length. In 1794 Fergus moved to Kentucky, and in 1832, he moved to Carroll County, Tennessee, from which place he successfully applied for a pension with this deposition.

In the autumn of the year 1778 my father moved to South Carolina and settled in what is now York County, then called New Acquisition, Camden District. Late in the season the Tories, hearing of the British coming to Savannah, rose in a place called Thicketty, south of Broad River, and embodied under a Tory Captain Coleman. A Whig Colonel Brennan in Fair Forest Settlement collected a company to oppose Coleman, but unfortunately Brennan was surprised in his camp by the Tories and defeated with the loss of four men killed. As soon as we heard of this defeat, about three hundred of us collected under the command of Capt. Andrew Love, to whose company I was attached, and marched to support Colonel Brennan. On the way, before we got to Broad River, we met Colonel Brennan with about twenty men flying from the enemy, and all the art of Captain Love could not prevail with the colonel to turn back with us and pursue the Tories; nor did he, but went on over the Catawba River into North Carolina before he halted. We pursued on over Broad River to Thicketty and Fair Forest but found Coleman and his Tories had gone off to join the British in Georgia and was got too far ahead for us to overtake them, as we were not prepared for a long march. After burning a number of the Tories' houses that were gone, we returned home.

In January 1779 there was a call for men to go to Georgia to assist that state against the English, who had got possession of Savannah, and to suppress the Tories who were joining them there. Colonel Neal, Lieutenant Colonel Watson, and Maj. Francis Ross were the field officers who commanded the regiment of militia at this time to which I belonged. Mounted men to scour the country and reconnoiter was the kind of troops called for; two hundred men were quickly enrolled for marching. In this company I went a volunteer. Whether any was drafted or not, I do not now recollect. This detachment was commanded by Lieutenant Colonel Watson and Major Ross. Capt. James Martin was my company officer. There were besides the mounted men a number of foot with wagons loaded with provision and baggage. It was a very wet winter, the roads exceedingly deep. We had two hundred miles from where we started to Augusta, where we were to join General Williamson. We had a very uncomfortable march and a tedious time on the road. I think there was eight days on the way the sun never appeared to us; it sometimes rained incessantly, and frequently showery. This I can well remember—all that time, the clothes on my back was not dry, nor had I them off, for we had generally to encamp in the woods and always to take care of our horses. What time we got there, I cannot now recollect. However, General Williamson sent us on from Augusta to join General Ashe at Briar Creek time enough to get defeated.

Some days after we got there, we got intelligence of the English coming up the opposite side of the creek from Ebenezer, where they lay between us and Savannah. The river was very full by reason of the late rains; the backwater extended up the creek twelve miles at least to where it was fordable from where we lay. To ascertain the truth of this report, forty of us were ordered up the creek to reconnoiter. With this party I went. We set out late in the evening with a guide. About midnight we came to a house where was a woman and children. We pretended to be a party of loyalists from North Carolina coming to join the British and wished to know if she could inform us where they lay and how we could get to them. The woman seemed delighted and told us they were encamped about a half a mile from us on the bank of the creek; that they were on their way to drive the rebels out of the forks and would make us very welcome; her husband was then with them at the creek; that it would be best to wait till morning before we joined them, or at least till her husband came home, for fear they might mistake us for rebels. From her we got all the intelligence we wanted, and after giving our horses plenty of oats we returned to camp the next day and gave General Ashe the above account, and that we might expect them on us the next day at farthest.

Notwithstanding this, General Ashe the next morning ordered the balance of our detachment that had not been out the day before, consisting of 160 men under Major Ross, to cross the creek and proceed towards Ebenezer to make what discoveries they could. A bridge was repairing but not finished. Ross and the men swam their horses over and went on. Two young men was likewise sent off with an express to General Williamson at the same time with an old man that had liberty to return home. By this time the British had got into the road between us and Augusta and was coming down on us, when they met our men that carried the express and took them prisoners. The old man that was with them, being some distance behind and riding a swift mare, escaped and came back to camp with the information that the enemy was coming on us. It appeared that General Ashe took no notice of this, nor was there any preparation made for action till the British vanguard was fired on by our sentries.

What of us that belonged to Major Ross's detachment that had been on the scout up the creek and was left in camp lay about a quarter off from the main camp to take care of our horses in an old field. [We] had orders sent us to get our horses, mount them, and come into camp. This we did. The line was just formed as we arrived to the left wing commanded by Colonel Elbert, who had a company of Georgia regulars. We rode close along the rear of the line, when the first general fire was made; as we were on lower ground than the enemy, it passed chiefly over our heads. We had got to the extremity of the right wing where General Ashe commanded by the time the second fire was made. This was our post, but we had not time to give more than one fire, when the general wheeled and fled and the whole wing with him. He was gone 150 yards or more before our little party followed. The British left wing was advancing rapidly, and, as Colonel Elbert afterwards informed me, he knew not that the right wing was gone till he found the enemy in his rear, killing his men. Of course he and all his men that escaped death were made prisoners. (It was after Colonel Elbert was released that I met him in Virginia, and he gave this account and added that he fully believed General Ashe betrayed us to the British, and declared that if he ever met with him, one of them should die before they parted.)

LIEUT COL JOHN BAPTIST ASHE.
Member of the Continental Congress.

John Baptist Ashe

General Ashe rode a good horse, left his men, and got round the enemy and made to a ferry above, crossed, and escaped, while the rest of us were drove into the swamp between the creek and the river. There was several cuts or lagoons that crossed between the creek and the river. The banks of these were so steep and deep that the horses that went in could not get out again, and some men would have been drowned had not canes been put into their hands and helped them out. Here I left my horse and furniture, threw off my coat, and swam. We now got into a thick canebreak, and the enemy pursued us no farther. This was late in the evening. Twelve of us got together, and, as it was moonlight in the night, we formed a small raft of driftwood in the mouth of a lagoon, on which three of us with danger and much difficulty got over the river, after being carried above a mile down before we landed.

We got out of the bottom and wandered up the river till daylight, and fortunately, in the mouth of a branch, we found a large periauger loaded with corn in the ear. Opposite to us on the other bank we discovered a great number of the North Carolina men. We quickly rowed over and took in as many as the boat would bear and caused them to throw out the corn while we crossed back. By this means we got all our men that were there off before the enemy came down to the river. Major Ross, who had crossed the morning before, came in the night to the camp, not knowing of the defeat. They were fired on and drove back over the creek, passed to the river below the mouth of the creek, and there crossed at a ferry, and the next day the remains of our detachment got together and moved up the river to General Williamson's camp and joined the troops there. Many of our men were half-naked, having stripped to swim the river. The third of March we were defeated, and that night there was a light frost, and many suffered with the cold, having nothing on but a shirt or breeches. Here we lay, I know not how long. Here I had the command of a brigade of twelve wagons given me and was sent with them to Saluda for flour, which I brought to camp.

About this time a party of our men with Major Ross crossed the river above Augusta in pursuit of some Indians and came up [on] them; had a small skirmish in which the major received a mortal wound, was brought into camp, and died in a few days. Shortly after this we were discharged and returned home under the command of Lieutenant Colonel Watson, I think in the beginning of April. When we returned, we found a part of our regiment under the command of Colonel Neal was called out and gone on what was called the Stono campaign. As soon as I got clothed for the summer campaign, I volunteered again with a few others and followed on to Orangeburg and fell in with our regiment under Colonel Neal there. Colonels Wynn and Brown and some others were there with their men, all under the command of Colonel Senf, a foreign officer who it was said was sent out to discipline our southern men.

While we lay here, Colonel Senf laid off the ground for a fort and employed our men in cutting turf and working on it until we heard that the British had crossed Savannah River and got to Purysburg. I now, for the first time, began to keep a small journal in a memorandum book, which I continued until I was taken with the fever and carried into Charleston.

On the first day of May, 1778, we received intelligence that the enemy had got possession of Purysburg.

2d of May: Preparation for marching to meet the enemy was made, to set out on the following morning. Toward evening, twenty-eight or twenty-nine wagons from Charleston arrived, loaded with arms, ammunition, entrenching tools, two howitzers, shells, and cannonballs, etc., etc. Governor Rutledge arrived also.

3d: The general "alarm" was beat early this morning and orders given for marching at a minute's warning. Preparations for marching completed. In the evening, the governor reviewed us.

4th: Paraded and marched off early this morning. Took with us a great number of Tory prisoners and some of the Queen's Rangers that were taken in Georgia and sent here. There were about three hundred of us commanded by the governor and Colonel Senf. Went about ten miles and encamped.

5th: Marched to a place belonging to the governor on Edisto River, crossed it there, and encamped on the bank.

6th: Went down Edisto about fifteen miles to the sawmills and crossed the river back again, finding that the enemy were likely to get between us and Charleston on this route. Cooked fresh beef and rice, ate, and moved on in the evening across the country and marched all night. Three of the prisoners made their escape; one was a lieutenant of the Queen's Rangers (who came and gave himself up to us the next day).

7th: About nine o'clock, halted and took breakfast; moved on to the Four Hole's Bridge. The carriage of the fieldpiece broke down. The piece was hid in the swamp. This evening, the artillery that was with us left us and pushed on for town, fearing the enemy might get before them. Note: they were part of the Charleston train.

I pass over the eighth and ninth days; on the tenth we got into town and hoped to have a night's rest after our fatiguing march, but an alarm took place, and we had to lie on the lines all night.

May 11th: This day Count Pulaski with his troop of horse arrived. And in the evening the enemy came before the lines, after they had driven in our picket guard and Pulaski's horse together with a company of light infantry, who had a severe skirmish with the van of the British army, in which it was said we lost of horse and foot about eighty-five men. At night, a little after dark, a party of our men went out to set fire to tar barrels that were placed in front of our lines to give light during the night. At this time an alarm was given, and heavy firing of cannon and small arms took place on the lines from one river to the other; also from the armed vessels in Cooper and Ashley rivers. This was unfortunate for the party out firing the tar barrels. Major Huger and two others, I think, were killed and several wounded by our firing.

12th: Flags of truce passed between us and the enemy the chief of this day; nothing done. Four men, two white and a mulatto and Negro, were taken outside the lines and brought in, supposed to be deserting to the enemy. The governor, coming by at the time, was asked what should be done with them. He said, "Hang them up to the beam of the gate," by which they were standing. This was immediately done, and there they hung all day.

13th: Last night, the enemy retreated silently and crossed Ashley before morning. Our light horse brought in a number of deserters and some prisoners that were straggling behind this day. From this time to the twenty-first of this month we lay here and kept guard on the lines and then marched off to join General Lincoln, which we did on the twenty-third at Dorchester.

May 24th: This morning, perhaps two hours before day, I joined a regular company of forty men who went as the advance guard of the army. The army followed in the morning. In the evening we got to the church at Bacon's Bridge, the plank of which was taken off. Drove the British picket from the opposite shore; kept under arms all night.

25th: This morning, a party from our army with a fieldpiece came down and repaired the bridge, returned back, and we, the advanced guard, passed over to the side next the British camp, set out sentries, and remained there till evening, when Pulaski with his horse came over with forty foot who joined us. The light horse passed us on the road leading to the British camp. We quickly formed and run after them, till the British picket fired on them and killed one of Pulaski's men. He charged on them and killed four of the guard and drove them in. At this time we were formed in his rear to cover his retreat, and he came slowly back by us, and we wheeled about and followed after. Before we got to the bridge, we found our army had passed it and was formed in an old field on our right. The British, however, did not choose to quit their entrenchments but laid still. We did not stop or join the army, but marched by and kept marching and countermarching all night, often formed in line, and again moving on till near daylight, when we came to our army drawn up in a line of battle in front of the British entrenchments. We were then formed with the line on the extremity of the right wing and had liberty to sit down. At this time General Lincoln was examining the situation of the British, and it no doubt appeared to him that they were too strongly posted for him to force their works without losing too many men or perhaps failing altogether, and so he moved back over the bridge to the old camp early in the morning. This was the third day from [when] we left Dorchester before day and had no sleep or rest, drinking bad water and enduring the scorching sun by day and the chilling dews by night.

26th: This day, in the evening, I was taken with a high fever and was carried over the river to our baggage wagons by Capt. Andrew Love and his brother.

May 27th, 1779: Here ends my journal.

I sent into Charleston to Dr. David Ramsay, who I understood was principal of the hospital in the city, for some medicine. He sent it, but advised me to be brought into the hospital. I replied I had seen the hospitals in Philadelphia, Princeton, and Newark and would prefer dying in the open air of the woods rather [than] be stifled to death in a crowded hospital.

I had a relation living in the city who, hearing of me, sent for me to be brought to his house to lie there. I was taken there in a wagon, and by the time I got in I was partly insensible. My friend brought the doctor to see me, and he ordered what he thought proper and called duly morning and evening to see me until the fever was broke. How long that was, I know not now. It appears like a dream to me now. To the great care and attention of the humane and kindhearted Dr. Ramsay, under God, I am indebted for my being a living, though infirm, old man at this day.

The fever was broke on me at the time there was a sham burying of Count Pulaski with the honors of war in this city, for I can recollect the firing of cannon all day, and what it was for as I was told. I continued in a convalescent state a long time. I left the city sometime in the winter to go to see my parents in the upper part of the state and was told afterwards that the British landed about a week after I left it. Thus I have given in detail an account of the four tours I served in the army regularly. After the fall of Charleston, to the end of the war, I did duty as a partisan under General Sumter and others in the upper part of the state, dispersing and keeping down the Tories. Of the time I spent in this way, I am now unable to give a particular account. It was a perilous time, and we were in a continual state of warfare until after Cornwallis surrendered, in which warfare I had my share.

WILLIAM GIPSON *(1753–1835) was born at Moncks Corner, South Carolina. He volunteered five times between 1777 and 1781 in North Carolina military units for a total of two years' service.*

The Revolution in South Carolina and central North Carolina, inflamed by ethnic differences, British occupation, and a large and active Tory population, exhibited a vicious brutality matched in no other part of the country. Gipson made occasional contact with the main army under Greene, but he largely served with small companies roving the country, searching for Tories and meting out justice as they saw fit. The company headed by Colonel Moore, on Gipson's third tour of duty, executed one prisoner and tortured another by "spiketing," a brutal backwoods version of "picketing" (the spike was supposed to merely touch the foot, not be driven through it, as was the case here), an antiquated form of discipline occasionally used in both the American and the British armies. Gipson's narrative was included here because it demonstrates the harsh aspects of the war that are often forgotten in accounts of battlefield heroism.

In other places, Gipson's account is faulty, although it appears to have been the result not of intentional deception but of failing memory as to dates and officers. The Battle of Briar Creek occurred in March 1779, long before Greene was in the South and a year and a half before Gipson's dating of the event. The Roebuck, *on which he claims to have been imprisoned in Savannah, did not arrive in the South until early 1780, making a March 1779 capture improbable. There was an engagement at Deep River, North Carolina, on 29 July 1781, where a Colonel Alston and twenty-odd men were killed or taken, but this took place far north of Briar Creek. One can only guess about the engagement, place, and time when Gipson was actually captured by the British.*

After the war Gipson moved to Virginia, North Carolina, Kentucky, and finally Boone County, Indiana, where he successfully applied for a pension in 1832.

In June or July in the year 1777, he volunteered and entered the company of Capt. James Armstrong in Rowan County, North Carolina. Besides Capt. James Armstrong, his company was officered as follows: one Sharp was lieutenant, one Irvin was ensign, and this applicant was first sergeant; the company belonged to Col. William Armstrong's regiment. His company volunteered to go down into the lower counties of North Carolina in order to drive out and disperse the Tories collecting under one Eli Branson. His company rendezvoused at Salisbury Courthouse, otherwise Rowan Courthouse, two days, when they marched. No other company went with them, but Gen. Francis Locke and the said Col. William Armstrong went in company with them. This applicant, with the company, marched from Rowan Courthouse to Randolph Courthouse, thence to Hillsboro, thence to Chatham County, thence up Deep River to the Sand Hills. At the latter place the company took several Scots Tories and there hung one of them, thence proceeded up Deep River into Moore County, where they met with Colonel Philip Alston's regiment and marched with his regiment about fifteen miles to the Colonel Alston's plantation. He recollects there was one Capt. John Carrall and one Major Irvin belonging to Alston's regiment. At Alston's plantation they left his regiment, and applicant's company proceeded low down on the Big Pee Dee River, about the swamps on that river, where his company dispersed a collection of Tories.

He then, with his company, marched up that river to the Grassy Islands, where the company halted, and his captain took out about thirty men, among which number this applicant was one, and went to the lower end of Randolph County to take or disperse one Hugh McPherson and his associates, Tories, who were there collected and forming into a band to commit depredations. This force of thirty men ranged through the lower part of Randolph and Rockingham counties and went to a Quaker meetinghouse in the latter county, where they took one Campbell, a lieutenant in McPherson's company, and from thence immediately started to meet the balance of his company left in command of Colonel Armstrong (General Locke having returned home when the company were at Randolph County on their march out), and they proceeded on their journey about four days, when at night some disaffected persons in the detachment, as it was supposed, turned Campbell loose, and he made his escape. The company then proceeded and joined Colonel Armstrong in the lower end of Rowan County, on the Yadkin River, and then proceeded home, where he arrived about the last of November or first of December to the best of his recollection, making a campaign of about six months, the term for which he volunteered. During his absence, his mother, a widow woman, was tied up and whipped by the Tories, her house burned, and property all destroyed.

This applicant would now set forth his second tour of duty as a soldier of the Revolution. In the month of March or April, but the precise month not now recollected, in the year 1778, General Locke ordered Colonel Armstrong with the same company, or detachment, to march to the upper parts of South Carolina, on the waters of the Pee Dee River, to disperse certain Tories then in that neighborhood collected. This applicant, with his company under the same colonel, captain, and other company officers (except he declined serving as sergeant), in pursuance of the general's order, in the year and one of the months last above stated, met at General Locke's, the above place of destination being about sixty or seventy miles from Rowan Courthouse. That he thinks sometime in the month of May, but is not certain, he and his companions in arms on some small branch of the Pee Dee or Yadkin engaged with a number of Tories, and in the engagement Colonel Armstrong received a shot in the hips which penetrated through and through. In this engagement, there were three of his company wounded and several killed to the best of his recollection. The Tories were driven and a number killed and wounded. They were commanded, to the best [of] his recollection, by one Bryan, and [he] is certain the Tory company were a squadron of Bryan's men. Colonel Armstrong was taken home, where he shortly after, to the best of his recollection, died with his wounds above described, and after the engagement above related, this applicant and his company in about three weeks returned home nearly direct from near a little town in South Carolina called Charlotte. The company marched to General Locke's in Rowan County, and there this applicant received a discharge from the general including his first term of service of six months and the last tour of duty, three months, which was certified in the same discharge. The last campaign he thinks terminated in the months of July or August and made nine months which he had then served his country in the cause of independence. But the discharge showing these two terms of service, this applicant regrets to say, were not esteemed as valuable as the prosperity of his country and the gratitude of the present generation have since made it, and he in a short time afterwards lost or mislaid the same and has no knowledge at this time of its existence.

Sometime in the winter of 1779, this applicant's family having suffered greatly by the disaffected party called Tories, his home and patrimony having been almost entirely destroyed in consequence of the attachment of himself and brother to the cause of independence, he joined a very small party of Whigs who had been more or less harassed and inspired by the disaffected, which party were headed by one Risdel Moore (colonel), Capt. John Haley, Lt. Elijah Charles, Ens. Elisha Charles, and others of Guilford County, North Carolina. This party ranged through Guilford, Randolph, and Surry counties.

That sometime in the summer of 1779, at one Wm. Brazleton's in Guilford county, he and his party were in the house, when suddenly two armed men stood at the door. They, seeing the party within, immediately wheeled, and Colonel Moore knocked down one of the men, who proved to be the notorious Hugh McPherson, a Tory. His party soon took the other one, who proved to be one Campbell and brother to the Campbell taken prisoner and made his escape during the first campaign above related. His party took both of these Tories to Guilford Courthouse, about fifteen miles from the place of capturing them. There, a court-martial was held, composed of the officers of his

Pay-Table Office, Decemr 16th — 1783

SIR,

PLEASE to fecure to Mr Lewis Hurd
the Payment of Thirty pounds four shillings and four pence

being the Balance found due to him
for Service in the Continental Army, in the Year 1780
Agreeable to Act of Affembly---and Charge the State.

£·30..4..4

[illegible] } Committee.

JOHN LAWRENCE, Efq; Treafurer.

party, and McPherson was condemned and shot in the presence of this applicant. And Campbell was condemned *to be spicketed,* that is, he was placed with one foot upon a sharp pin drove in a block, and was turned round by one Thomas Archer, to the best of his recollection, until the pin run through his foot. Then he was turned loose. This applicant cannot forbear to relate that as cruel as this punishment might seem to be to those who never witnessed the unrelenting cruelties of the Tories of that day, yet he viewed the punishment of those two men with no little satisfaction, as they were then supposed to belong to the identical band who inhumanly inflicted corporal punishment upon his helpless parent, who had committed no other offense than that of earnestly exhorting her sons to be true to the cause of American liberty. So notorious was the conduct of this applicant and his party towards the Tories of that neighborhood, that they were compelled to range the country, not daring to return home to stay anytime or separate until about Christmas 1779, when he separated from his party, where he stayed for the most part of his time until about October or November 1780.

In the months of October or November, 1780, there was, to the best of applicant's recollection, a call for a regiment of men in the counties of Guilford, Randolph, and Moore, and Colonel Philip Alston and Captain Carrall wrote from Moore County, where they resided, to Guilford County, where he resided, requesting him to join their regiment to go to the southward. And this applicant, upon receiving this letter, went without delay to Colonel Alston's, and in about two weeks after his arrival the regiment was made up, and on or about the first of November, 1780, the regiment marched, as it was then said, to join General Greene's army. They crossed the Pee Dee at the Grassy Islands, thence towards Columbia, South Carolina, and within a short distance of that place had a slight brush with the enemy. Thence they marched towards Camden, crossed the Wateree River above Camden, thence towards the Congaree, where his regiment joined General Pickens's regiment, who took command, crossed this stream below Columbia, South Carolina, thence they marched towards Savannah, crossed Briar Creek, and within a few miles of the crossing of that creek they joined the main army commanded by General Greene, thence down to the mouth of Briar Creek, where the American army halted and the British army came up and gave battle. This applicant was [in the] engagement. He was close by Colonel Alston when he hoisted a white handkerchief upon the hilt of his sword as a signal of his surrender, and this applicant, with twenty or thirty of the regiment, including Colonel Alston, were taken prisoners, and a great number, but how many he does not recollect, were taken prisoners from other regiments.

The prisoners in a few days were marched towards Savannah,

and this applicant with the rest were there confined in an old ship called "the old *Roebuck,*" which was placed at a considerable distance out in the bay. He thinks about five hundred prisoners were in the ship, including what were in before with the number captured at the mouth of Briar Creek. This applicant well remembers the severity of this imprisonment. He and his fellow sufferers were daily tempted to enlist into the king's army by gold and promise. A great many listed, and many died with disease.

After he had endured for better than a month his imprisonment, Colonel Alston proposed to him and several others, particular and personal friends, to make their escape from the ship by throwing certain scantling out of the portholes. This project was accordingly, about ten or eleven o'clock that night, put in execution by the colonel by throwing a few pieces of scantling out as proposed. The colonel got out, and this applicant alone followed him, the others not venturing the hazardous enterprise. This applicant, placing himself upon a piece of scantling, followed his brave colonel and, together with him, as a good Providence would have it, this applicant was after some little effort and the aid of the tide, which was then favorable, carried to land safe. He and the colonel entered a swamp, and where they wandered that night. At daylight they were directed by the sound of an ax to a Negro man who was boating wood, or rather towing it out with a canoe. The colonel soon made an agreement with the Negro to set him and this applicant upon a certain point, not now recollected, and the colonel was to carry the Negro to the British and set him free as a reward for his services, and they were accordingly taken to the place. They then left the canoe in the care of the Negro, promising him to return soon and fulfill the agreement. That day, after the Negro landed them, they lazed about plantations, then being in an enemy's country, until night, when the colonel left the applicant and went to a house where he procured a piece of meat and returned. They attempted, dark as it was, to travel on towards the upper part of South Carolina. After several days, they arrived at one Hughes's, an acquaintance of the colonel. He furnished the colonel with a Negro, a horse, money, and clothes, and with this applicant proceeded to the Waxhaws settlement to the widow Jackson's, mother of the now venerable president of the United States, to the best of this applicant's present belief. At the widow Jackson's they stayed two days. There, at the hands of the old lady, they both received a suit of clothes, and the colonel was furnished also by her with a horse to ride home.

They arrived at the colonel's residence in Moore County late in the winter of 1780. There, the colonel gave this applicant a discharge, and he thinks the last of February, 1781, making about four months. This discharge he also shortly after lost. He returned home to Guilford County and there stayed a few days, but such was the notoriety of his sentiments and feelings and attachment to the cause of liberty among the Tories that he did not feel safe to continue there but for a few days.

And about the first of March, 1781, with one Capt. Thomas Hamilton with about fourteen or fifteen others, volunteered to go and meet the main army under General Greene, then retreating before the British. They met the main army at Charlotte, North Carolina. Their little squad kept along near the main army for several days, until they arrived at Salisbury, and continued on in the same manner until they arrived at the Moravian towns, and thence through Guilford County, crossed Haw River at the High Rock Ford, thence to Halifax Old Town in the state of Virginia, where Greene's army was reinforced. And the British retreated, and the American army following, recrossed the Haw River at the same place where the British burned their wagons, but this applicant's party arrived on the ground before they were entirely burned. Next morning, Captain Hamilton of this applicant's party had a little engagement with the flanks of the British, and this applicant had his horse shot from under him, lost his pistols, sword, and cap, and made his escape back to the main army. Captain Hamilton procured a horse and equipment for this applicant, and he was again mounted; thence they proceeded to Guilford Courthouse and the British to Deep River Meeting House, and at these two places the two armies lay preparing for battle several days.

The fourteenth of March, to the best of his recollection, Captain Hamilton advised his party to join Colonel Little's company, and the party accordingly fell in upon the left wing of Little's regiment. And on the fifteenth he was engaged in the battle at Guilford Courthouse. With army, retreated to Troublesome Ironworks on the waters of [Troublesome] River, where they rendezvoused for one day with the main army, when, with Captain Hamilton's squad, they again returned to near Guilford Courthouse and there discovered the British to be upon the move. They returned back to the main army but found them just ready to proceed after the British. His party continued to follow the main army, camped with it (if not out at night) for several days, when

Greene turned again for South Carolina. Hamilton, with his party, left the main army and went down into North Carolina, to one Colonel Crump's, who commanded a regiment of militia, where this applicant with Hamilton's party stayed some days, perhaps a week.

Then they crossed the Pee Dee in South Carolina, joined a party commanded by one Marion, with whom they stayed about two weeks, caught one Tory, who was left with Marion to deal with. Then Hamilton's party went again to General Greene's army, laying between the Wateree and Congaree. When they came to the army, they were preparing to march to the Eutaw Springs, where the British army then lay. The day after they arrived, the army moved towards the springs. Hamilton's party continued to flank the main army until the day before the engagement at the springs, when they attached themselves to [Colonel] Washington's corps of horse and entered into the engagement with the corps. The horse broke through the brush breastworks enclosing the springs. Washington was taken prisoner, and they retreated back about five miles upon the same road upon which they had marched to the engagement. There the party under Hamilton again left the main army and went back towards the springs to take observations of the enemy, whom they found retreating, and they returned again towards Greene's army and found him advancing again towards the springs. They proceeded, with the Americans harassing the British until the latter took shelter in Charleston. Greene marched then up to what was called "the Four Holes" to winter, and a short time after this, going into winter quarters, the army had cause to celebrate and rejoice at the fall of Lord Cornwallis, and, soon after this memorable event, this applicant took sick, went about four miles from the main army, and lay at a private house all winter sick, and in the meantime his party under Hamilton returned to North Carolina.

In March or April he went into camp, where he found that Hamilton had left a discharge with one Colonel [blank] of the regular army and a recommendation or paper certifying the good conduct of this applicant, both of which this applicant lost or mislaid in a very few years. He returned home the summer of 1782 on foot, having, the winter before, lost his horse.

GARRET WATTS *(1756–1838) was born in Caroline County, Virginia, and moved with his family to Surry County, North Carolina, in 1768. He served three times in the North Carolina militia from Surry and from Caswell counties. He is slightly confused in his dates, but he served in the battles of Camden and Guilford Courthouse.*

Watts's narrative is one of the most remarkable we have, because he freely admits to being among the first to run from the field at Camden. He describes his fear in detail and objectively tries to analyze its cause.

Watts was a drifter after the war, moving to Georgia, South Carolina, Tennessee, and finally Alabama, and it seems likely that a sense of guilt haunted him throughout life. No other explanation adequately accounts for his unnecessary confession, fifty-four years after the event. He was granted a pension.

To the best of my recollection, in the fall of the year 1779 as a private I entered the service of the United States. It was a company of cavalry that I first entered under the command of Capt. Minor Smith. This company composed a part of a regiment of cavalry (the number of which I cannot remember). The major of the regiment was Charles Polk (called "Devil Charley") of Mecklenburg County of North Carolina. The colonel who commanded this regiment was also called Colonel Smith. I do not know his given name. I lived in Surry County of North Carolina at that time and believe it was in October of the year above stated that I entered. My term of service was for three months as follows.

I well remember that at this time Lords Rawdon and Cornwallis were said to be in Wilmington, and the Tories had become greatly encouraged down in that quarter. We first proceeded from Surry County to Salem, from ten to fifteen miles, thence in the direction of Wilmington, a distance of perhaps near two hundred miles. Information was received by our officers from a Colonel Leonard who resided in the neighborhood which was called the "truce ground" that there was to be a large assemblage of the Tories in his neighborhood. We passed near Wilmington. After much fatigue and hardship in crossing swamps, lakes, etc., we approached the place at which the Tories were to assemble by two different routes and from opposite directions. Whether our arrival was too early or had been suspected by the Tories it is uncertain. We found but seven men at the place, all of whom were killed. There was a great multitude of women there. We moved a few miles from that place and encamped during the night, which was dark and rainy. We were attacked suddenly by a large body of

Tories, and we were warmly engaged for a short time. After the first confusion was over, we were ordered to charge, dark as it was except the light of the guns. We were successful in driving them back. A few were killed and wounded on both sides. We lost some of our horses but succeeded in recovering most of them next day. We also killed one or two of the enemy next day. This was near a lake, which was called Waccamaw, which we swam several times. I think I was now near twenty-three years old. What I have above stated is the principal part of my service that was important during my first three months' service. Our return was by way of Fayetteville, then called Cross Creek. At this place we were discharged. It is rather my belief that I had a written discharge. If I had, I have lost it and know not how.

Four or five months after my first term expired, I was again, and after I had moved to Caswell County in the same state, called into service as a private in the North Carolina militia, a foot soldier. The lieutenant of the company to which I belonged was named [Borneau?]. The captain was named Odom. The name of the colonel of the regiment to which I now belonged I do not remember, for we marched in a single company from Caswell County. I marched from the upper part of North Carolina down to Fayetteville. At this place we were put under the command of General Butler. This was a distance of sixty or eighty miles. We were thence marched to Charlotte in North Carolina, a distance by the route of march one hundred miles. We here joined the command of General Gates, a regular officer, also of General Dickson. De Kalb also had command here of the regular soldiers. We next marched to Rugeley's Mills (the name of a notorious old Tory colonel) in South Carolina, perhaps a distance of seventy or eighty miles, from Rugeley's Mills, five or six miles further to a place called Sutton's (as well as I remember). This was not far from Camden, where the British were under Rawdon and Cornwallis.

The two armies came near each other at Sutton's about twelve or one o'clock in the night (this was in the year 1780). The pickets fired several rounds before day. I well remember everything that occurred the next morning: I remember that I was among the nearest to the enemy; that a man named John Summers was my file leader; that we had orders to wait for the word to commence firing; that the militia were in front and in a feeble condition at that time. They were fatigued. The weather was warm excessively. They had been fed a short time previously on molasses entirely. I can state on oath that I believe my gun was the first gun fired, notwithstanding the orders, for we were close to the enemy, who appeared to maneuver in contempt of us, and I fired without thinking except that I might prevent the man opposite from killing me. The discharge and loud roar soon became general from one end of the lines to the other. Amongst other things, I confess I was amongst the first that fled. The cause of that I cannot tell, except that everyone I saw was about to do the same. It was instantaneous. There was no effort to rally, no encouragement to fight. Officers and men joined in the flight. I threw away my gun, and, reflecting I might be punished for being found without arms, I picked up a drum, which gave forth such sounds when touched by the twigs I cast it away. When we had gone, we heard the roar of guns still, but we knew not why. Had we known, we might have returned. It was that portion of the army commanded by de Kalb fighting still. De Kalb was killed. General Dickson was wounded in the neck and a great many killed and wounded even on the first firing. After this defeat, many of the dispersed troops proceeded to Hillsboro in North Carolina. I obtained a furlough from General Dickson and had permission to return home a short time. This last tour was for the space of three months and truly laborious.

Not long after the defeat of General Gates at Camden, I think near three months, General Greene, a regular officer, came from towards the north. This was also, as well as I remember, in 1780. I entered the service again under Captain Odom, being again drafted. I do not know what the colonel's name was, I think Colonel Moore however, and was placed under the command of General Greene. I was at the Battle of Guilford Courthouse under General Greene. This was fought at some old fields turned out and surrounded by broken fences. General Greene having divided his army into three divisions, behind one of these fences [he] placed first a division of select riflemen; second, the militia were stationed in the rear in the woods; last, and still further in their rear to prevent a retreat like General Gates's, were placed the regulars. This was a great battle. Both sides fought until they were willing to cease, but we had the advantage, for the last division were just beginning to bear heavy on them, and the British had to give back. These were times of great suffering. We had but little to eat, as little to wear, feeble and worn down.

I was also during this term of my service with General Greene at the battle at Camden, or near it. Through carelessness or otherwise, the tired soldiers were suffered to loiter and wash at the River Wateree, and in the meantime a drummer belonging to some of the regiments under General Greene deserted, entered Camden, and let the British know our condition. They came out upon us, and we had to fight hard and finally were compelled to give way. Shortly after this, my last term of service expired. To the best of my recollection, I served and was subject to constant service for nine months if not more. If I ever had written discharges, I have lost them, but my recollection is indistinct as to that. I never did receive the amount of pay I was entitled to. The small amount I did receive was in Continental money, which turned out to be of no value. I served as a private the whole time. I have no documentary evidence of my service. I know of no person now living whose testimony I can procure or who can testify as to my service.

MOSES HALL *(b. 1760) was born in Rowan County, North Carolina, and served nine tours of duty of from one to three months in 1780 and 1781. His description of the Battle of Haw River, 23 February 1781, where Colonel John Pyle's Tory force was defeated, is superb, but it is his account of the murder of six prisoners after the battle that is exceptionally important.*

In many areas of the Carolinas, loyalists were as numerous as Whigs. Deep hatreds translated themselves into atrocities on and off the battlefield. A remarkable feature of Hall's narrative is that he records his own radicalization. The horror of senseless bloodshed can be seen transforming a sensitive young man of twenty-one into a hardened soldier, anxious to commit equally brutal acts himself.

Hall moved to Kentucky in 1788 and to Monroe County, Indiana, in 1830. He submitted his application in 1835 and was granted a pension.

He entered the service of the United States in the militia of the state of North Carolina (then living in the said county of Rowan) as a private soldier and volunteer in the company of infantry commanded by Capt. David Caldwell in the regiment commanded by Col. William Davidson. He thinks he was then colonel; he might have been general. He, said Davidson, if not general then, was afterwards. He, this declarant, entered the service for no particular period but to serve in an expedition against the Indians and Tories. He was rendezvoused at Beattie's Ford on the Catawba

River. He entered the service in this tour as near as he feels safe to state in the year 1777 or 1778.

He was marched in said company about sixty or seventy miles from home at the furthest point, reconnoitering the country in various and circuitous routes for the purpose of discovery and guarding the inhabitants. Upon our advancing toward their haunts, the Tories and Indians dispersed. According to the best of his recollection, he served at least six weeks in said tour. During this said tour, the main body of the troops in which he served remained nearly or entirely stationary whilst small detachments scouted around. In said expedition, he crossed the main Catawba, the south fork, and less streams. He was dismissed in the fork of the Catawba. Some of the troops with him, in returning home, crossing at Beattie's Ford, some at Cowan's, some at Sherrill's, some at the Island Ford. He crossed at the latter. He did not receive any written discharge for said tour, nor did any of his comrades that he knew of. He served faithfully in said service to the acceptance of his officers in regularly organized and embodied corps in the war of the Revolution.

In the same season in which he performed his said first tour (it is his best impression), he again and for a second tour entered the service of the United States in the militia of North Carolina as a private volunteer soldier in the company commanded by Capt. David Caldwell, in the regiment commanded by Col. Francis Locke, in the brigade commanded by General Rutherford, his first name forgotten. He entered the service in said tour for no particular period now recollected but to serve in an expedition to Ramsour's Mills. He was rendezvoused in said company, being infantry, he thinks at Charlotte. He was then living in said county of Rowan in said state of North Carolina. He, with said troops, marched through a part of Rowan County, Mecklenburg, Lincoln, and to Ramsour's Mills. The battle at that place was over as was said about two hours before this applicant and troops arrived on the ground. After being upon and about the battleground for a short time, he was dismissed. He served in this expedition up to the time of his dismissal at least four weeks. He returned home one night or evening, and an express arriving by his brother, James Hall, giving information of the celebrated Tory Col. Samuel Bryan having collected a considerable force in the forks of the Yadkin, he again entered the service the next morning.

He entered for a third tour in the militia of North Carolina as a volunteer private soldier in the company of infantry commanded by Capt. David Caldwell, then living in the county aforesaid. He rendezvoused at Bryan's Hill on Little Dutchman Creek. After continuing there for some days for their numbers to increase sufficiently, they marched in pursuit of said Colonel Bryan, who with his force was making for the British. We crossed the Yadkin and other less streams on this expedition. In this tour he served at least two months. He does not recollect where he was dismissed if at any place of note. He does not recollect whether Colonel Locke and General Rutherford were along with his troops in this expedition or not. Maj. Joseph Dixon, he well recollects, was. After this, for a short time his Tory neighbors were thought to be pretty well subdued. The time of entering this third tour was the next morning after returning from his said second tour, and his return was without any delay. He was in said service in embodied corps.

About three or four weeks after his dismissal from said third tour, he again and for a fourth tour entered the said service in the militia of North Carolina, then living at the county aforesaid as a volunteer private soldier in the company of rangers or mounted infantry made up and commanded by (the said) Capt. David Caldwell. A few footmen belonged to said company. Said company was detached and not joined to any other troops. He, with said company, ranged in the forks of the Yadkin and on the east side of said river. He served in said ranging service at least three months. Said company was marched back to Captain Caldwell's residence. Immediately and without going home, he was employed to make up a team out of the public horses and haul a load of public flour to Major Dixon's. On the way, his wagon was broken, and he had to take out a horse and ride to Major Dixon's for help, who sent his son and wagon for that purpose. He had been employed in hauling five or six days and returned to Captain Caldwell's said residence. Upon his return to said Captain Caldwell's, he, said captain, was mustering a company to march down to Mecklenburg for to join General Greene. He entered said company and service, without going home, for the following fifth tour.

He entered said militia of North Carolina for a fifth tour as a private volunteer soldier in said company commanded by said Capt. David Caldwell and joined and was under the command of Colonel Davie. He joined with said company [under] the command of said colonel at some noted old field, the name of which he has forgotten, between Salisbury and Charlotte. He and said troops marched down to Mecklenburg by way of [blank] to Charlotte. He with said troops was stationed near Charlotte and reconnoitered the country around them. He was marched once to Waxhaw. Whilst there, the British came into Charlotte, and a skirmish took place between Colonel Davie and the enemy, when the main body of which came up, we had to give way. Our small scouting parties frequently fired at the British as they passed about in large foraging parties. He served at least three months in this tour, probably longer. Some of those who served in said campaign, he is informed, say they served longer. Our object in this tour was to annoy the enemy and to impress them with our intention to resist them to the last. After some time, they (the British) moved off from Charlotte southward, and I was dismissed. I cannot recollect at what place; it was not one of notoriety. There was neither form nor regularity in disbanding said troops. He served faithfully and to the satisfaction of his officers in said service and in a corps regularly embodied in the war of the Revolution.

Not more than ten days or two weeks after this last-named tour or expedition to Mecklenburg, he again, for a sixth tour, entered the service in the militia of said state of North Carolina in the company of mounted infantry commanded by the same Capt. David Caldwell. He did not enter said service in said expedition for any particular period of service. The object of such expedition was to go into the forks of the Yadkin against the Tories and for the purpose of collecting provisions for the main army. He does not recollect all the circumstances of this expedition. He, with said company, marched into the forks of the Yadkin and without any serious obstacles succeeded in the purposes of the expedition. Said company was not attached to any other troops or higher command. During said expedition he was in the said service at least six weeks. Said company was a regularly authorized and embodied corps. He served said tour six weeks faithfully and to the acceptance of his officers in the war of the Revolution.

A very short time after the said expedition into the forks of the Yadkin to collect provisions for the main army, hearing that a number of persons were going through the country administering oaths of allegiance to [the] British cause, about twenty, including this applicant, organized themselves under the command of said Capt. David Caldwell and pursued said persons or agents of the British and Tories as far as Salem, or Moravian Town, but never overtook them. In this expedition he served at least ten days. In this, his seventh tour, he was a volunteer private soldier in the militia of said state of North Carolina. Said detachment was infantry. During said tour, he was with said company the same way embodied and was raised by competent authority.

After the last-named expedition against the said British and Tory emissaries, I entered into a contract with and at the request of said Capt. David Caldwell and said Maj. Joseph Dixon to go to Chiswell's lead mines and haul a wagonload of lead from said mines to the residence of said Captain Caldwell. According to said contract and promise of said officers, I was to have credit for, and said hauling was to count, one tour of three months. I, with other teamsters under the command of a wagon master, proceeded to said mines and hauled and delivered a good full load of lead to said Capt. David Caldwell at his residence. In this, my eighth expedition, I was at considerable trouble and expense and risk of life. I would much have preferred to have been in the lines with my gun and knapsack or mounted in a company of horse. Every principle of justice would sanction an allowance for this tour. Not only his life, as in other tours, but his property in addition was risked.

After this expedition after lead, how long he cannot state, he entered the service for the following tour. To the best of his recollection it was in the year 1779 or 1780, he thinks in the fall season of the year. Then living in said county of Rowan in the said state of North Carolina, he entered the service in the militia of said state in the company of mounted men or mounted infantry commanded by Hugh Hall. He thinks said Hall's commission was that of lieutenant, but commanded said company on account of, and in the absence of Capt. David Caldwell. They, this applicant and said company, marched in an expedition to and through the counties of Wilkes and Surry in said state against the Tories. They dispersed before we reached their resorting places.

We turned and, without going home, marched down by Moravian Town, or Salem, through Guilford County, Hawfields, and in pursuit of Cornwallis. We were marched in circuitous routes around and about Hillsboro and that part of the state. A little after a skirmish on the Alamance, and not far from Haw River, we were joined by Colonel Lee and his light horse. I was on picket guard at the time. Our said company belonged to and was joined to a higher, their captain's command. They were (our said company) commanded by Maj. Joseph Dixon. Whether he had a battalion, or owing to the absence of a colonel had commanded a regiment, I cannot now state.

When I ordered those in front of Colonel Lee's troops to halt and give the countersign, they were unable to do so, and I proposed to Colonel Lee, not being certain who they were, whether friends or foes, that I would send my comrade who was standing guard next to me and one of his men in to Major Dixon whilst the Colonel Lee should stand with me, which was done. During this time, perhaps half an hour or more, I had the satisfaction of an intimate and familiar conversation with Colonel Lee. He was one of the finest looking men and best riders on horseback. Shortly after this, and during my said tour, a body of Tories had raised, as were then informed, with the view of reinforcing Colonel Tarleton.

Our troops and this body of Tories and Colonel Tarleton all being in the same neighborhood, our troops on the march met said body of Tories at a place called the Race Paths, and, mistaking our troops for Tarleton's, Colonel Lee and officers kept up the deception, and Colonel Lee and his light horse marching in one column or line, and Major or Colonel Dixon's command in another, some interval apart, the Tories passed into this interval between our lines. Or, perhaps which is the fact, the Tories having halted, our lines passed one on each side of them whilst marching along to cover them so as to place them between our said lines. They frequently uttered salutations of a friendly kind, believing us to be British. Colonel Lee knew what he was about and so did Major Dixon. But I recollect that my Captain Hall, perceiving they were Tories and thinking that Colonel Lee did not know it and was imposed upon by their cries of friendship and misunderstood them to be our friends instead of the British, he called to Colonel Lee across the Tories' line and told him, "Colonel Lee, they are every blood of them Tories!" Colonel Lee gave him a sign to proceed on with the execution of the command, which was to march on until a different command was given. In a few minutes or less time, and at the instant they, the Tories, were completely covered by our lines upon both flanks, or front and rear as the case may have been, the bugle sounded to attack, and the slaughter began, the Tories crying out, "Your own men, your own men, as good subjects of His Majesty as in America." It was said that upwards of two hundred of these Tories were slain on the ground. They were, I think, headed by a Colonel Pyle or Pyles. Tarleton at this time was in a few miles of us, and in pursuing him next morning we found he had encamped in four or five miles of the said Race Paths (where we met the Tories under Colonel Pyle) the night after that affair.

The evening after our battle with the Tories, we having a considerable number of prisoners, I recollect a scene which made a lasting impression upon my mind. I was invited by some of my comrades to go and see some of the prisoners. We went to where six were standing together. Some discussion taking place, I heard some of our men cry out, "Remember Buford," and the prisoners were immediately hewed to pieces with broadswords. At first I bore the scene without any emotion, but upon a moment's reflection, I felt such horror as I never did before nor have since, and, returning to my quarters and throwing myself upon my blanket, I contemplated the cruelties of war until overcome and unmanned by a distressing gloom from which I was not relieved until commencing our march next morning before day by moonlight. I came to Tarleton's camp, which he had just abandoned leaving lively rail fires. Being on the left of the road as we marched along, I discovered lying upon the ground something with appearance of a man. Upon approaching him, he proved to be a youth about sixteen who, having come out to view the British through curiosity, for fear he might give information to our troops, they had run him through with a bayonet and left him for dead. Though able to speak, he was mortally wounded. The sight of this unoffending boy, butchered rather than be encumbered in the [illegible] on the march, I assume, relieved me of my distressful feelings for the slaughter of the Tories, and I desired nothing so much as the opportunity of participating in their destruction.

We pursued Tarleton across Haw River, after which crossing Colonel Dixon took eighteen men, including this applicant, and went in advance of the main body (many of whose horses were tired) for the purpose of discovering Tarleton's position or intentions. Finding that he had marched toward Hillsboro, we remained nearly stationary for some time, that is, the main body of our troops. A short time after becoming thus stationary, and whilst this applicant and a party of our troops were out hunting provisions, Tarleton, having got a reinforcement at Hillsboro, returned and drove the main body of our troops eight or ten miles and until night stopped the pursuit. This applicant, after this retreat, during the same night with his party, having found our main body of troops and having been put on picket guard a half mile or more out, and our troops again shifting ground, the same night removed so suddenly that when I received orders by a messenger for such purpose, the main body under Colonels Lee and Dixon had left the camp and were some distance on the march. And the British pursuing Colonels Lee and Dixon, myself and another sentinel with difficulty had to guess at our way in the dark under the fearful apprehension that the British were between us and our troops. Whilst in this hazardous search for our troops, I recollect that I directed my comrade to ride about forty yards behind, upon the account of his horse being not so swift as mine, expecting any moment to meet with some of the enemy. Groping our way, in returning to our troops before the above circumstance, on the same night I met Col. Meshack or Micajah Lewis. I knew him by his bald or white-faced horse. He was a noble soldier, spying to ascertain the position of the enemy. After he left me about forty rods, I heard the firing of the gun by the soldiers of the British, which killed him, as I was afterward informed. No engagement ensued. About and after this time, recruits coming in every day and it being expected that Greene would arrive, and the troops to which I belonged having been a long time from home, the company to which I belonged was permitted to return home. I served I believe four months in this tour, but at least three months. . . . Although his memory has failed greatly, he is clear and positive that he served as much as he has stated.

He has not been as circumstantial in the details relating to his services as perhaps upon reflection he might. . . . At the affair with the Tories under Colonel Pyle, as mentioned in one of his foregoing tours, I came in contact with a man of large stature with an uncommon large horse and large rifle which he swung by means of a leather strap. He attempted the turning of his horse and then his gun towards me to shoot, but, being unwieldy, and I with my gun presented (it was empty but he did not know it), he surrendered and gave up his gun. A blackjack having previously deprived me of my hat, I thought I would take the first I found. I first picked one up off the ground by a dead man, but blood being in the crown of it, I threw it down again and took the hat off this large Tory and put it on my head. And, after going some distance, this Robert Luckie, a friend with whom I was intimate, came toward me in great hustle and cautioned me that my hat had a Tory sign on it and to take it off. It was a red strap passing over the crown. It would probably have caused me to be shot by the first of our troops who should have met me who were not acquainted with my person, and I was perhaps very fortunate in not suffering such a consequence before my friend Luckie cautioned me to remove the Tory sign from the hat. . . .

One thing omitted to be stated in describing the affair with the Tories at the Race Paths: sixteen, I think, of Dixon's and as many of Lee's dragoons were dispatched, being an advance guard to keep Tarleton in play whilst the Tories were engaged by our main body of troops in case he should be near, and it was after the main body came up, being of the advanced guard, that I witnessed the scene of hewing the six prisoners. In hauling said load of lead, he furnished his father's wagon and team. It was difficult to procure hauling, and he was unwilling and went only at the earnest solicitation of Captain Caldwell and Major Dixon. Where he has stated in his declaration that he entered again into the service in a short time after the end of a preceding tour, he means a few days or weeks. He does not, to the best of his recollection, remember being at home or out of the service from the beginning of his first tour to the close of the services for which he has claimed more than a few weeks or at most, say, a month.

JOHN TAYLOR *(1756–1837) was born in Virginia and lived in Mecklenburg County until he moved with his family to Granville, North Carolina, in 1777. He resided there for the rest of his life and served four tours in the North Carolina state troops as private, captain, and commissary. His memory was failing when he submitted this narrative in 1832, but his honesty about what he forgets makes what he remembers all the more credible.*

Taylor describes his fortuitous escape from the Briar Creek massacre, his conversation with William Davie, and an encounter with a Tory recognizance party. He was forced to cooperate with Malmedy and de Globack, but, like most American soldiers, he had little respect or affection for his French allies.

Taylor was granted a pension in 1832.

In the year 1778 a company was raised in the county of Granville and was marched to the defense of South Carolina and Georgia. I am told that my brother Richard Taylor was the captain of this company, but of this fact I have no recollection. The wife of my brother Richard had had no intelligence of her husband in some time and in consequence expressed uneasiness upon the subject in my presence. To this I replied that, as I had no family, I would go and, if permitted, serve out his time as a substitute. Accordingly, I soon set out with two young men of my acquaintance, Solomon Walker and Solomon Mitchel, to join the American army. We reached the army then stationed on the north side of Savannah River opposite to the town of Augusta, which was then in possession of the British army. Here I learned that my brother Richard had returned home, for what cause or under what circumstances I have no recollection, but I have recently been informed and believe that by reason of pique or disappointment in not being raised to the grade of major he had resigned his commission and left the service. We were gladly received into the service, and I was a considerable time in the early part of my tour in the family and marquee of Colonel Lytle.

A detachment under the command of General Ashe, having been ordered across the river, were directed to take their station at the point where Briar Creek empties into the Savannah River. At this time I belonged to the company of which Lt. Pleasant Henderson had in part the command, and I believe I was of the same mess with him. This company belonged to the detachment under General Ashe. How long we remained on duty at the post on Briar Creek I am unable to state, but a few days before the attack on our detachment which proved so fatal to it, General Ashe sent Lieutenant Henderson with dispatches to the general commanding at Purysburg (I believe it was General Lincoln), and

I was selected to accompany him. On the instant of our departure, Lieutenant Henderson, seeing I had not my saddlebags, insisted that I should return and get them. I replied it would be unnecessary, as we should be back again in a few days, but the solicitation being repeated, I did return to my quarters and get them. We mounted our horses and had not traveled far before Henderson remarked to me that he had a particular reason for insisting on my taking my saddlebags.

"You nor I," says he, "will ever see this place again. There will be a battle here before we return." In due time we arrived at Purysburg. Here we remained perhaps three or four days, when we set out to return to our station. On our return we met the stragglers of our party flying from the battleground at Briar Creek, and I recollect of giving away to them all the clothes in my saddlebags. I have no recollection at this time but presume we returned and joined the army at Purysburg. Nor do I recollect where we were discharged. I have ever thought, and I now believe, that I joined the army in so short a time after the commencement of the term of service, that I was received for the whole tour, though it was at the same time impressed upon my mind that the term of service was but for five months. I have, however, recently been informed that the term of service was for six months after being mustered at Charlotte, and it may be that I have confounded the time I actually served with the length of the whole term of service. I am satisfied I served at least five months.

In the month of August, 1780, a regiment of volunteers was mustered into service at Oxford in the county of Granville under the command of Col. Phil. Taylor, of which regiment I was a member, and although subject at all times to the military duty of a soldier, was frequently engaged in doing the duties of commissary. The regiment marched through Hillsboro, Salisbury, and Charlotte and finally to the Catawba River. At Salisbury the regiment was placed under the command of Colonel Davie. I have not a recollection of many events which occurred during this tour, perhaps of none which are known at the Department of War, nor are the above facts stated as of my own knowledge or recollection. I recollect of encamping at Harrisburg, near Oxford, I suppose soon after the forming of the regiment, perhaps while it was organizing; of passing through Charlotte and being much annoyed by the fumes of beef in marching through a recent encampment of the British army; of purchasing on one occasion a large quantity of flour for the use of the army. Also, on one occasion our regiment, being aware of its liability to be attacked, laid down to sleep upon our arms. In the course of the night we were waked with as little noise as possible and changed our ground. I think it was afterwards said that in a short time after our leaving it, the ground was covered by the dragoons of Tarleton, who would, but for our timely notice of his approach, have cut us to pieces.

At the Waxhaws, I remember of being in company with General Davie when the latter pointed out to me a meetinghouse and remarked that he was educated by his uncle to succeed him as the pastor of that house. I particularly recollect of being much affected by the solemn spectacle of the tombstones in the surrounding churchyard. I have no recollection of the length of this tour but have been informed and believe it was for four months; nor do I remember where we were discharged. I have no recollection of serving a less period than the whole term and believe that I did serve out the whole term.

Shortly after the expiration of this tour of duty, a regiment of mounted volunteers was raised in North Carolina and placed under the command of Colonel Malmedy and Maj. Pleasant Henderson. One company was raised in my neighborhood. Among other persons composing the company were James Lyne, James Lewis, Joseph P. Davis, John Farrar, James Minge Burton, two of my brothers, Lewis and Edmund Taylor, the one older and the other younger than myself, and Robert Goodloe Harper, who has since been distinguished in the public councils of his country. When the company met at Oxford, in consequence I suppose of my having seen some service in the tours above recited, they were pleased to elect me their captain. I think we marched from Oxford to Hillsboro, but my only reason for thinking so is that Hillsboro was a common place of meeting on such occasions.

I, however, distinctly recollect that after we joined with Malmedy and the other companies of the regiment, and within seven miles of Guilford Courthouse, while at breakfast we heard the report of the artillery in the battle which had just commenced. Malmedy, guided by the report of the artillery, attempted to reach the battleground by marching through the woods instead of the more circuitous route along the road, but the ground became so rocky and uneven that we had finally to retrace our steps to the road we had left. Here we met hundreds of our men flying from the battleground. They could give us no information as to the issue of the engagement, and we pursued our march until we arrived in sight of the ground. This we found in the possession of the enemy. I think it was now about night. I recollect of seeing the guns of the enemy stacked around their fires and that a council of officers was held to consult on the propriety of attacking their camp, and I think further that the measure was opposed only by Malmedy himself.

I suppose we, of course, after this followed on after General Greene, though if we joined him (and it is my impression we were with him for about half a day) it was for a very short time, for Malmedy was ordered to pursue Cornwallis after the latter had left Guilford Courthouse. In the course of the pursuit, I was ordered to find out the position of the British army, with the permission to take with me as many men as I pleased. I selected seven; among them were Benjamin Hester, James Minge Burton, and Robert Goodloe Harper. My instructions were that I should find Colonel Malmedy on such a day at such a place, and on such another day, at such another place, etc. After I think two or three days' search, we obtained information of the situation of the main body of the British army and also that on another road the enemy were driving three hundred beeves, and that they would be compelled to march fifteen miles before they would meet the main body.

Soon after this discovery, I believe it was in a few hours and while in the immediate neighborhood of the enemy, so much did our company and our horses require refreshment, that we were tempted to halt at a cabin and turn our horses into a wheat lot near the house and to partake of breakfast, which was promised us by the woman of the house. While the woman was frying our hominy, for it was all she could offer us, I went out on the eastern side of the cabin in company with the rest of my men, except James M. Burton, who remained in the house. The morning being cool, we went out to bask in the sun, leaving our arms within. In a few minutes I heard a voice inquire for the man of the house, when on looking round, I saw the front part of the cabin surrounded by seven or eight armed men on horseback. I whispered my party to follow me, who readily obeyed, and I walked into the cabin, parting as I went two horses on which were mounted as many men armed with rifles. The enemy not knowing whether we were friends or enemies, or perhaps from pure cowardice, made no attempt at resisting our progress. After getting into the house, I ordered my men to get their guns and, drawing my sword, presented myself at the door and inquired of them who they were for. Having been satisfied, from signs of confusion among them, that they were enemies, perhaps it was by a motion among them to retreat, I ordered my men to fire. They did so, but it was in such a hurried manner that it was without much effect, although the enemy had to march single file through a small gate in front of the house. One man, however, I observed put his hand to his back, and at the same time his hat dropped from his head, and I afterwards understood it was one Captain Dark of the British army, who died of a wound he at that instant received. The wound was well understood to have been given by Robert Harper.

No sooner had the enemy departed, than we became much alarmed for the danger we had passed, and catching up our horses we set out on our return to our regiment. Malmedy was not at the place he had appointed to be at on that day. Where that place was, I do not recollect, nor do I remember where we joined him nor how long I was in search of him, but I remember it was esteemed particularly a matter of regret that we had lost the opportunity of taking the beeves, as it would have been so easy a conquest.

Soon afterwards, I have been informed it was while Cornwallis was at Ramsay's Mills, Colonel Malmedy ordered an attack on Tarleton's dragoons in order to draw them out in pursuit, that Maj. Pleasant Henderson, with a detachment placed in ambush, might attack them when then drawn out. The command of this attack I have recently been informed was given to de Globack, a young Frenchman, though I had always believed he was subordinate to myself. The necessary preparations having been made, de Globack and myself set out at the head of a company ordered to make the attack, consisting I think of about forty men. Riding side by side, de Globack remarked to me that one or the other of us would in all probability be killed, to which I replied, if they kept double pickets, perhaps we both would be. In a little time, accordingly, we saw two pickets. After getting within about forty yards, they fired at us, and we rushed forward at full speed. The pickets ran a short distance, when they joined twenty or thirty more of their fellows who had been stationed as sentries to the main body. The whole of them then ran in the direction of the main body, which was perhaps two or three hundred yards further on, but they were overtaken by us and three of them taken prisoners. While our attention and operations were thus directed to the guard, before we were aware of it, we were nearly surrounded by about four hundred Hessians, and, being unable to return in the direction in which we had made the attack, were compelled to retreat in a different direction. Although the enemy assailed us with a shower of shot, we sustained not the least injury and brought off our prisoners.

In conversation with Maj. P. Henderson afterwards, he said he thought 3,000 shot had been fired at us. I have understood that Tarleton refused to pursue us, suspecting that it was a decoy of General Greene. The prisoners were ordered by de Globack to be executed, on the pretense that the enemy would pursue us, but this order was countermanded by me. James Lyne, one of my nearest neighbors, brought off a Hessian rifle which he took home with him. When Cornwallis left Ramsay's Mills for Wilmington, Colonel Malmedy was ordered to pursue him for the purpose of protecting the intermediate country from his ravages. My impressions as to the length of this term have always been that it was for two months. I have recently understood that it was rated for three months by reason of our finding horses.

Besides the military tours above recited, I was employed by General Davie as an assistant in his commissary department on the following occasions, the precise date of either of which I have forgotten. I have no documentary evidence on the subject, nor can I find any persons who has any other than a vague and indefinite recollection of the subject. I believe, however, that the most if not the whole of the service was rendered after the termination of my last military campaign. The first occasion on which I was called to act was to go into the lower counties of the state for the purpose of receiving from the sheriffs or collectors of the public monies the sums they may have collected and to pay them over to General Davie. I recollect of receiving sums to a very considerable amount and of suffering some uneasiness upon my neglecting to take a receipt from General Davie. I think I was about two months on this duty.

On another occasion I was ordered to follow the track of the American army and to find out the situation and in whose possession were the cowhides belonging to the public for the supply of the public tanneries. In the performance of this duty, I went to the South Carolina line. I do not distinctly recollect the time I was employed in this service but suppose it must have been three months. I was again employed to find and engage beef to be delivered at different points for the use of the army. This service took and required a long time, but how long I am unable to state. I am satisfied, however, that I was a year or more, probably eighteen months, engaged by General Davie on these several occasions. I have no documentary evidence of any service which I rendered in the war of the Revolution.

GUILFORD DUDLEY *(1756–1833) was born in Caroline County, Virginia, but moved with his parents to Halifax County, North Carolina, in 1763 and served in the North Carolina militia from there during the war. In the spring of 1774 he joined a volunteer company at Hillsboro, and he answered the call for minutemen from Halifax County to oppose the British at Great Bridge, near Norfolk, Virginia, in December 1775. In all, he served five terms, rising to major of the First Battalion, North Carolina militia, then lieutenant colonel while serving with Greene's army, and colonel of a regiment of light horse raised to oppose David Fanning in May 1781. In August 1781 he was put in command of a recognizance force by the governor to keep track of Cornwallis's movements. In spite of ponderous sentences and tortuous grammar, he had a gift for historical narrative, best demonstrated in the accounts of the Battle of Hobkirk's or Hobkick's Hill (24 April 1781) and a breakfast meeting with General Greene.*

Unlike many officers, who achieved economic advantages and political prominence on the basis of their military service, Dudley was not very successful after the war. He moved from Halifax County to Fayetteville in 1785, then to Roanoke, to Prince Edward County, Virginia, back to Roanoke, and to Williamson County, Tennessee, in 1807. He submitted this deposition in 1832 but died the following year.

In the summer of 1775, North Carolina having raised some regiments of minutemen, a species of regular troops at that day but enrolled without receiving any bounty, I entered into the one raised in Halifax, my own district, composed of six large counties, commanded by Col. Nicholas Long of Halifax, my own town company by Capt. Christopher Dudley, Lt. John Geddie, and Ensign [blank]. And late in November or in December of that year, a detachment of that regiment (say 250) was called into actual service to march to the Great Bridge near Norfolk, in Virginia, to assist some Virginians posted at its upper end in opposition to Captain Fordyce of the British grenadiers posted at its lower end under cover of a fort which Lord Dunmore, the last regal governor of Virginia, had caused to be [e]rected there, when, after the defeat of Fordyce, who was killed on the bridge or causeway, they entered Norfolk, and was there at the time the town was burnt.

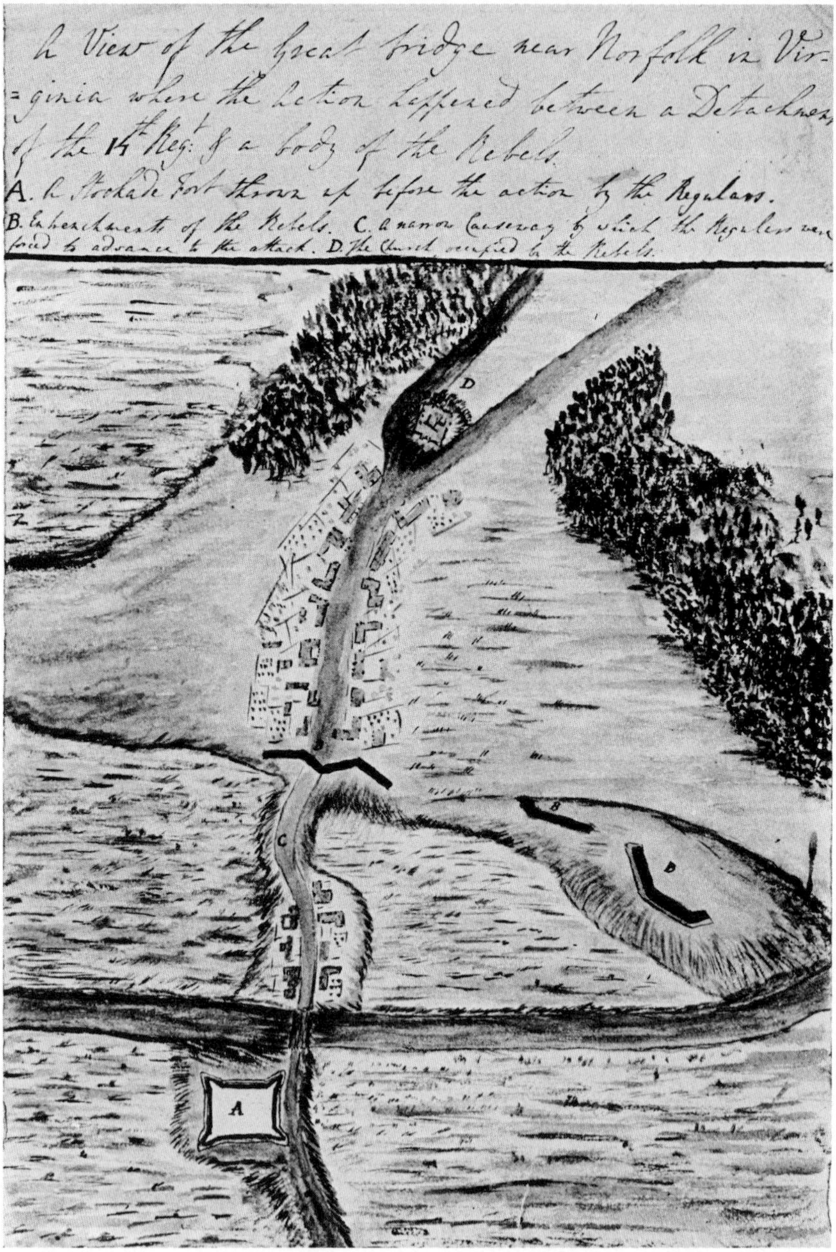

A View of the Great bridge near Norfolk in Vir-
=ginia where the Action happened between a Detachment
of the 14th Regt. & a body of the Rebels.

A. A Stockade Fort thrown up before the action by the Regulars.

B. Entrenchments of the Rebels. C. A narrow Causeway by which the Regulars were
forced to advance to the attack. D. The Church occupied by the Rebels.

A

B

C

D

In the month of February following (1776), the whole of that regiment being called into actual service again to suppress a most formidable insurrection of the loyalists (Tories) in the south and west assembled at Cross Creek on Cape Fear River, I also marched with said regiment, and after the defeat of the said loyalists at Moore's Creek Bridge, near Wilmington (sixteen miles), by Colonels Caswell and Lillington, detachments from this regiment were sent up the country in pursuit of the fugitives, when Brigadier General McDonald, their commanding officer, and many others of distinction were made prisoners and conducted to Halifax, where they were for a while shut up in the common prison with a strong guard around it, and then the minutemen were, for the present, dismissed. This tour, performed in the months of February and March, 1776, continued about forty days as well as I can now recollect.

The details of my other military services during the Revolution will be seen in my answers to the interrogatories propounded by the court aforesaid, which follow here. . . .

I was called into actual service as a minuteman in February 1776 and marched against the insurgents who had assembled at Cross Creek in great force, having belonged to a regiment of this description of troops from July 1775, commanded by Col. Nicholas Long of Halifax as already related in the first page of this declaration. I was neither drafted, nor was I a substitute, but a volunteer of said regiment and performed all the duties of a private soldier from the repeated calls of my captain and the colonel commandant for nine months, until the minute regiments were dissolved about the month of May, 1776, after the provincial Congress which sat at Halifax that spring had completed the quota of North Carolina troops (nine regiments of foot and three companies of light horse). In this service, performed by minutemen, there were no regular officers of the line with us, although North Carolina had raised two regiments the summer before. The next actual service I engaged in was in June 1780, after the fall of Charleston, in a company of volunteers raised in Halifax (mostly by myself), commanded by Lt. Col. Samuel Lockhart, lately an officer of the Continental line of North Carolina, then at home, acting as captain, Lt. John Geddie, and Ens. Dolphin Davis, having with us Capt. James Bradley, another Continental officer serving as a private soldier.

Under the direction of Captain Lockhart, the company marched into South Carolina after taking a most circuitous route for want of proper information, crossing the Yadkin first, above the narrows (a great natural curiosity), and then falling down that river to Colson's on Pee Dee and Rocky River and thence to Anson Old Courthouse, where the British had a small garrison but which was withdrawn before our arrival. Finding himself too far ahead of all other troops about to enter South Carolina and out of reach of support from any quarter, Captain Lockhart's situation became very perilous. He therefore determined to recross Pee Dee at Mask's or Haley's Ferry and fall down that river on its eastern side to Cheraw Hill, where he hoped to overtake Major General Caswell's division of militia just then penetrating into South Carolina in that direction, but who had crossed the river one day before us.

In the meantime, Lord Rawdon had broken up the post at Cheraw, commanded by Major McArthur, an experienced British officer with 350 prime troops, and called them to him, as well as the small garrison at Anson Courthouse, concentrating his whole field force at Big Lynch's Creek, about forty-two miles above Cheraw Hill on the Camden road. Captain Lockhart, with his volunteers in prime order and high spirits, by forced marches in the sultry weather of the last of July over bald sand hills and pine plains overtook Caswell's division of North Carolina militia between Brown's and Big Lynch's creeks, who were immediately sent forward to overtake (without halting) Caswell's light infantry, a few miles in front, then under the direction of Maj. John Armstrong, another Continental officer of the North Carolina line and whom we found posted at the fork of Cheraw and Rocky River roads, and remaining under his command three or four days until General Gates, who, marching by the latter road, formed a junction at that point with Caswell's division of militia, when the command of all the light troops was given to Lieutenant Colonel Porterfield, a regular officer of the Virginia line, having under him Capt. Thomas Drew with a company of regular troops of the same line.

Col. Henry Dixon of Caswell County, whom I well knew and who was also at home without employment, likewise a regular officer of the North Carolina line, had the command of a regiment of Caswell's militia and who by his skill in military discipline and tactics had trained his troops to stand and do their duty in battle with great firmness and order.

Col. John Pugh Williams, Col. Benjamin Williams, and Col. Thos. Blount, also Continental officers but of lower grades, likewise took commands in the militia of North Carolina (the latter acting as adjutant general) and were of the suite of General Caswell. These were all the Continental officers then serving with us that I can now recollect, and it would be an endless business to enumerate all the names of the officers of distinction among the militia with whom I was acquainted, except I should mention the names of Brigadier Generals Rutherford and Gregory of North Carolina, both of whom were wounded in battle and the former taken prisoner. Nor will I attempt to mention the names of the Continental officers of the Maryland and Delaware lines with whom I served, except Col. Otho Holland Williams of the Maryland line, adjutant general of Gates's army and a most valuable officer, whom I happened to meet at General Caswell's quarters at Clermont (Rugeley's Mill) when sent there from the advanced corps upon business the day preceding the fatal disasters of the morning of the sixteenth August, 1780, at which very time the detachment of Maryland troops under Colonel Woolford was turning out to march over the Wateree River to join General Sumter, who was then ready to strike the British convoy coming from Ninety Six to Camden, and who did actually capture the same with the escort the next morning (the eighteenth) near the latter place with the assistance of the Maryland troops just mentioned.

I was in the night action of the fifteenth of August, 1780, on the plains above Camden and fought near the person of Colonel Porterfield, who was mortally wounded, and carried him off to a place of safety for the present, and remaining by his side the rest of the night. And after providing for the proper assistance to carry him off further (for I was unable to do it by myself), just at the dawn of day, left him with Capt. Thomas Drew, Lieutenant Vaughan, three surgeons, and eight or ten privates whom I caused to be searched for that night, and, forming a litter and, placing the colonel upon it, was in the act of moving away with him to a place of greater safety from the enemy when the rattling of our cannon about a mile to the east of where I had lain with him that night announced the commencement of the battle, to which I hastened with all the speed in my power upon my starved, broken-down horse (for I was a light dragoon), leaving Colonel Porterfield and the party steering north to someplace where we hoped he would be safe until the battle should be over, not dreaming of a defeat. Here I encountered the difficulties and dangers of that disastrous morning, and remained on the ground, rendering my unavailing aid, sometimes nearly surrounded by the enemy, and then chased by his cavalry until our army was entirely defeated, and yet I escaped with all my arms and equipage. The result is but too well known. Then falling back with the relics of our army, first to Charlotte (North Carolina), then to Salisbury, and Hillsboro, where I remained ten days, and then finally home.

I have no written discharge to produce from my services heretofore, the proper officers verbally discharging their men when they returned home, and it is well known that everybody, after this disastrous battle was over or during the conflict, discharged himself. I served three months, however, during this unprosperous campaign.

Remaining at home after this expedition in the prosecution of my private business until February 1781, and during the arduous and skillful retreat of General Greene across the state of North Carolina into Virginia, when I entered into the service of my country again and joined a volunteer corps of 250 mounted infantry and cavalry raised also in the town and county of Halifax and placed under the direction of Maj. James Read, a Continental officer, by the legislature then in session in that town, which corps was forthwith marched to join General Greene wherever he might be found, Lord Cornwallis with the British army then lying in Hillsboro.

This corps (after joining General Greene, whom we found posted above Reedy Fork of Haw River and a few miles below Guilford Courthouse, Lord Cornwallis lying upon Little Alamance about twelve miles southeast), serving day and night with the American army, most frequently on detachment until about seven days after the Battle of Guilford, that is on the twenty-second of March, General Greene then having his headquarters at Troublesome (Speedwell's) Ironworks, twelve miles from the courthouse, when the corps was reorganized, and instead of horse, became foot, at which time I was called from the ranks and appointed major of the First Battalion of North Carolina militia (all the field officers having at that place retired from the service with consent, and a new set through the management of General Greene was commissioned by Governor Nash, then in camp, mostly taken from the Halifax volunteers and put in their place in such regiments as could be collected there) and was in the pursuit of Cornwallis down to Ramsay's Mills on

Deep River, a distance perhaps from the ironworks of between ninety and one hundred miles.

General Greene having at Ramsay's Mills discharged all the Virginia and North Carolina militia except one regiment of the latter commanded by Col. James Read, who had before commanded the corps of Halifax volunteers, I was promoted to the rank of (senior) lieutenant colonel of one of the battalions of that regiment about the last of March of 1781. And General Greene, after mature deliberation having determined to carry the war back into South Carolina, I marched also into that state, crossing Deep River at Searcey's Ford, about thirty miles from Ramsay's, thence to Colson's on Big Pee Dee, where the river is about 500 yards wide, which we forded, horse, foot, and artillery and, crossing a very narrow point of land, immediately forded Rocky River (of Pee Dee), also about 150 yards wide, a rapid stream with an appropriate name, and thence on to Camden, crossing Big and Little Lynch's creeks at the points where Colonel Porterfield crossed them the year before when conducting General Gates's advanced troops to the same scene of action. I should not have been so minute in describing our route, but it seems to be required in order to show my knowledge of the marches of our armies where I served and the geography of the countries through which we passed, and I am perfectly willing to be interrogated not only on all such points, but on every other within my knowledge that may tend to give satisfaction at the War Department.

In the morning of the nineteenth of April, 1781, General Greene arrived before Camden and sat down upon the beautiful eminence of Logtown, which overlooked the enemy's works three-quarters of mile north of Camden, with his little army in excellent spirits, the great Waxhaw Road passing over its eastern point, Logtown then in flames, and the houses crumbling down, the enemy having, upon our approach, withdrawn their pickets, etc., and applied the torch to that small appendage to the village of Camden. Here we lay three days in full view of the town, our militia riflemen often venturing down near the enemy's works to skirmish with the Yagers and other marksmen, who, under cover of a few trunks of pine trees left here and there and from behind their abatis, began a desultory game that provoked our men to retaliate.

Camden stands on a peninsula formed by Pine Tree Creek on the east and the Wateree on the west, the forts stretching across an open, lovely plain, divested of its timber on the north side and about three-quarters of a mile in extent every way, the forts bearing no particular names, but numbered from Pine Tree Creek in the east, 1, 2, 3, 4, 5, 6 to the Wateree in the west, under the protection of the last of which stood the British hospital on the banks of the river, the ferry one mile below the town and then covered by a fort also.

In the afternoon of the twentieth, the day after General Greene sat down on the eminence of Logtown, a most unpleasant and disgusting circumstance occurred which seemed for a moment to disturb even the equanimity of the general himself. Lieutenant Colonel Webb's battalion of militia, which with my own constituted the command of Colonel Read, insisted on their discharge, alleging that their term of service had expired. This was at first refused and the allegation denied, when they evinced a spirit of mutiny, encouraged and heightened by Captain R. of that battalion, who was their chief spokesman. Persuasion and even entreaty was used by the field officers of the regiment, pointing to the enemy's works staring us in the face at a short distance and telling them not to desert their general but have patience and wait only a few days longer, when their services might be all important to him in the plain before us. But all this only made them more eager and determined upon being discharged, and finding our entreaties unavailing, one of us went to the general and gave him the unpleasing information, when he, with great condescension, mounted his horse, and, accompanied by Col. O. H. Williams, rode into our camp on the aforesaid eminence at a short distance from the regular troops and used all his persuasion and eloquence to detain them but a few days longer, when, as before observed to them, they might be of important service to him. The general was seconded by Colonel Williams, who in the most persuasive manner reasoned with them and urged their delay, but all to no purpose. Captain R. and the others became more clamorous, and General Greene, mortified and disgusted, directed Colonel Williams to write their discharge, which done, they were instantly off, and Lieutenant Colonel Webb had the mortification to attend them back into North Carolina.

There was General Greene, in a moment, and that one of danger and difficulty too, deprived of 250 of his efficient force—men who, though but militia, he had considerable hopes from their services since the change of field officers which took place at the ironworks and their subsequent training. My battalion, with Colonel Read still at its head, were now the only militia in the southern army, and they were soon to experience the reality of uncommon active service and hard fighting.

The general having determined, for reasons too long to detail here, to shift his position from Logtown on the north to the lower side of Sand Hill Creek on the east, four miles from Camden on the Charleston road, and finding his baggage and artillery would be only an encumbrance to him when crossing the deep and muddy swamps he had to wade through, resolved to send them away to Upton's Mill on Big Lynch's Creek, twenty-seven miles from Camden and near the Cheraw Road, escorted by my battalion, having with us all the quartermasters and commissaries together with our herds of lean cattle and swine, all the provisions the southern army had to subsist upon. This movement took place on the twenty-second of April. Here (at Upton's Mill) we remained until about one or two o'clock P.M., the twenty-fourth, when unexpectedly an express arrived from General Greene ordering the whole, troops, baggage, and artillery, etc., to return with all haste to our former position near Logtown. In half an hour all was in motion again, and marching all that day and until three or four o'clock the next morning without halting, sat down about five or six hundred yards in the rear of General Greene's Continental troops, then returned from Sand Hill Creek and posted in one line upon the lofty summit of Hobkick's or Hobkirk's Hill, in the rear of Logtown, having the great Waxhaw Road running directly over it, a favorable position with a handsome rivulet running by its northern base.

On the morning of the twenty-fifth of April, 1781, after breakfast, my battalion, with the artillery in front, Colonel Harrison of Virginia at its head, slowly moved on to take our post in the line wherever ordered. Lord Rawdon finding himself more and more straitened for provisions, despairing of the safe return of Colonel Watson to the garrison, and for other cogent reasons, had determined upon giving General Greene battle that morning and accordingly made his sally about nine o'clock. We were just ascending the hill with the militia and artillery when the firing commenced by our sentries and pickets, which brought on the fierce and sanguinary Battle of Hobkick's Hill. When about halfway up, we were met by Col. O. H. Williams, adjutant general, from whom we received this very brief order, "March to the right and support Colonel Campbell," for there was no time to say more. This movement was made with great celerity, obliquely up the hill with trailed arms and open files, the deep sand sliding from under our feet at every step. But, before we had reached a third of the way to our destined post, the artillery, which had so opportunely arrived and taken its station in the road between the two wings of our army, commenced a spirited and well-directed fire with cannister shot upon the British column as it advanced, and in a moment, notwithstanding some disorder and confusion that happened at first, there was an universal blaze of musketry from left to right throughout our whole line for an hour, every officer exhorting all the bravery and energy of his soul, the general himself, with his cool intrepidity risking his invaluable person in the thickest of the battle. Yet at last a retreat became necessary, which was effected with very little loss after we fell back to the foot of the hill, although the enemy pursued our right wing for a mile through the woods, keeping up their fire upon us, whilst our flying troops, in their quarter, were repeatedly rallied by the activity of their officers, faced about, and would pour in volley after volley as the enemy rushed upon us, until we finally gave up the contest.

The left wing of our army fell back to Saunder's Creek, three and a half or four miles from Camden, whilst the right, not knowing precisely their fate, but judging merely from the awful silence that had prevailed there for an hour, nor the fate of General Greene personally, whom we knew had greatly exposed himself during the conflict, especially on the left, nor yet what had become of the artillery and baggage, shaped our course through the woods, over bog and morass, at a respectful distance from the road until we first crossed Saunder's Creek, then Sutton's, and lastly Gates's battleground on the plains above Sutton's, when it was agreed to oblique to the right, and we soon entered the great road, nearly seven miles above Camden, where we most fortunately met General Greene, who, as well as the left wing which had halted at Saunder's Creek below, were equally uncertain what had become of us.

With the general at our head, the right wing of our army then fell down and reunited with the left at Saunder's Creek about three or four o'clock in the afternoon whilst Rawdon was burying the dead on both sides on Hobkick's Hill and affording what relief he could to the wounded in the absence of four of his surgeons brought off by Colonel Washington from the enemy's rear during the engagement.

Thus the battle terminated unfavorably to the American army, though without affording the least advantage to Lord Rawdon and the British garrison. Lieutenant Colonel Kosciusko, chief engineer to the southern army, and Major Pierce, aide-de-camp to General Greene, were both separated from the general in the course of this action, probably sent with orders to Hawes and Campbell on the right about the time that wing gave way, and continued with us during the remainder of the time we were disputing the ground with the enemy, in our ultimate retreat, and until we joined the rest of the army at Saunder's Creek.

On the twenty-sixth (the day after the battle), Colonel Read of the militia (who was a Continental major) was sent back into North Carolina to attend to some matters there, when I became commandant of the remaining militia and continued so until expiration of our tour, as may be seen by my discharge from the southern army.

On the twenty-sixth also, General Greene fell back from Saunder's Creek and by a rapid march passed by Rugeley's Mill and took post that night about one and a half miles higher up the Waxhaw Road, thirteen miles above Camden. Here, on the twenty-seventh, General Greene directed a court-martial to convene near headquarters for the trial of twenty or twenty-five deserters whom we had taken in battle on Hobkirk's Hill on the twenty-fifth. They were all equally guilty as to matter of fact, but some of them were more notorious offenders than the rest. The general therefore was pleased to order the execution of five of them only. The rest were pardoned and returned to their duty in their respective companies in the Maryland line.

This and some other transaction which took place in our camp above Rugeley's being finished, and General Sumter not yet joining as was expected when we first sat down before Camden on the nineteenth, General Greene became restless for want of employment and from his too-remote position from the garrison in Camden. He therefore determined to change his position once more, from the eastern to the western side of the Wateree, and accordingly, on the twenty-eighth, broke up from that camp, and passing down by Rugeley's a mile or two, filed off from the Camden Road to the right, and soon reached the Wateree at a very rocky ford about nine miles above that town, four or five hundred yards wide, which we forded, horse, foot, and artillery, as we had done before at Colson's on Big Pee Dee, and, keeping out from the river a mile or two until we entered the main road leading down from Rocky Mount, etc., to the ferry below Camden, pitched our tents opposite to that village, in an open plain covered with pine about two miles from us and with the river interposed. This movement was made for the double purpose of more effectually cutting off the supplies coming down on that side or from Ninety Six, if that should be attempted, as well as to intercept Colonel Watson on his return to the garrison, should he evade Marion and Lee on Santee and then, crossing Congaree at Fort Motte or elsewhere, force his way to Camden on the upper road, on the west side of the Wateree.

Watson, however, at last evaded Marion and Lee and made good his passage to Camden on the eastern side of the Wateree altogether unexpectedly. It was not long, however, before General Greene got intelligence of this circumstance, and therefore was upon the lookout for a visit from Lord Rawdon with his increased force, which we were not exactly in a situation to resist with our mortified troops, whose spirits were yet rather depressed by their late repulse before Camden.

General Greene, knowing his adversary would strike at him as soon as Watson reached Camden, hastily broke up from this camp about an hour by sun in the evening of the sixth or seventh of May and, falling back by a rapid march, gained the heights of Sawney's Creek, the strongest position I ever saw anywhere in South Carolina or perhaps anywhere else, and sat down on its summit, a stupendous hill faced with rock, having a difficult pass of steep ascent to climb up, his artillery posted in the road, on the eminence, where the gap was somewhat lower than the hill on either side.

In the morning of the seventh or eighth, before day, Rawdon put his army in motion and, crossing the ferry below town, was at the dawn of day in General Greene's deserted camp, greatly disappointed by not finding his intended victim there, but still determined upon his destruction, followed him up to the lower side of Sawney's Creek, covered with lofty timber, both of pine and oak, and where his advanced troops met our strong pickets and Colonel Washington's cavalry (always their terror) judiciously posted. Instantly a handsome firing took place. Lord Rawdon paused, examined with caution the ground his adversary occupied, Washington keeping himself raised up in his stirrups, watching the exact moment when to strike with the saber his quondam friend Major Coffin, with the British cavalry in view.

In the meantime, on the upper side of the creek all was in motion, General Greene in person and the adjutant general

forming our troops on the heights in battle array, my battalion ordered down the hill to cross a narrow, lengthy field in the bottom, not in cultivation that spring, and to post myself in and around sundry deserted houses near the ford of Sawney's Creek under the supposition that the enemy would force a passage, and there to maintain my post as long as I could. This order I received from the general himself on the brow of the hill. But scarcely had I reached the houses before I was recalled. At this moment the general had received information of another crossing place about two miles lower down the creek, quite convenient for the enemy's purpose of getting at him and attacking him in the rear of his present position on the lofty summits of the hill. This intelligence instantly changed the mind of the general and produced the determination to retrograde again and once more fall back three or four miles to a large creek of still, deep water (Colonel's, I believe it was called), having over it a framed bridge covered with plank. Lord Rawdon, not liking to risk an attack upon his adversary in his strong position on the heights, thought it best to retire into Camden, at the same moment Greene was retrograding, and prepare for its evacuation. On the upper side of this bridge I posted my battalion, having in charge the baggage of the army, our herds of cattle, swine, etc., whilst the general with his suite halted about a mile below and took up his headquarters in a comfortable dwelling house on the margin of the road. Here (at the bridge), I remained until the evening of the tenth, when the general rode up to visit my quarters and did me the honor to invite me to breakfast the next morning at headquarters, an occurrence, or to dine with him in rotation with other officers, [which] not unfrequently happened. This invitation it may be easily imagined I readily accepted and, accordingly in the morn of the eleventh, at the proper hour, waited on him, when the general, who seemed to have been expecting me, came to the front door of his apartment and saw me close at hand and ready to dismount at the gate in the upper corner of the yard. At the first glance I thought I perceived in the general's countenance an expression of something of a pleasing and interesting nature, and so there was. With his accustomed politeness he stepped out of the door, his fine manly face wearing the smile of complacency and benevolence so natural to him, and met me at the yard gate, where, hardly taking time to present his hand, his invariable practice whenever an officer visited him, with apparent eagerness asked me if "I had heard the news?"

Struck by the manner of his asking the question, I hastily replied, "No, sir, what news?"

"Rawdon evacuated Camden yesterday afternoon," and added in a facetious way, "[and] has left Capt. Jack Smith commandant of the place, in the care of his sick and wounded, as well as ours, and pushed towards Nelson's Ferry on the Santee."* This pleasing intelligence the general had but just received himself, no patrols of our cavalry having been on that side of the river for several days, nor down about the ferry the evening before, nor that morning, where they must have seen the conflagration of houses,

*Capt. Jack Smith had been made a prisoner on the twenty-fifth April, on Hobkick's Hill, and carried into Camden that night, and threatened with death, under the law of retaliation for the alleged murder of Lieutenant Colonel Stewart of the British guards at the Battle of Guilford (utterly false), but Greene interfered by a flag and prevented it.

etc., which Lord Rawdon, in his clemency, thought proper to destroy by fire.

Things being in the situation in our camp at Colonel's Creek before described, and Rawdon returning to Santee with great celerity as if afraid of being overtaken by General Greene, the latter ordered his army to be put in motion and directing me, while at headquarters, to bring down my battalion and the baggage. We broke up from that place and continued our march down the river a couple of miles below the ferry on the west side of Wateree and halted on the upper road leading from Camden to Friday's Ferry on Congaree, where I was, with my battalion, "discharged from the Southern army, by order of Major General Greene," as may be seen by my written discharge signed by O. H. Williams, adjutant general, now in file with other original papers of mine and left in the hands of the chairman of the Committee on Pensions, in the Senate of the United States.

There were many and uncommon incidents that occurred in this Battle of Hobkick's or Hobkirk's Hill such as I never heard of before, and which I witnessed myself and was a sharer in them, wholly dissimilar, however, to anything that happened in Gates's defeat, a few miles farther off on the piney plains above Sutton's Creek, and which I must forbear to detail here because this declaration is already swelled to too great a length perhaps for those whose official business it may become to read it. I therefore forbear at this point, but I must yet go on some further with my declaratory narrative. . . .

Having left the southern army beyond Camden on the road leading from the ferry there to Friday's Ferry on the Congaree, and returning through that town with my battalion, marched them back into North Carolina on the road General Greene marched them out, where I discharged them at the request of my officers, that they might take the nearest routes to their respective homes, determining myself to take the road leading from Pee Dee to Searcey's Ford on Deep River (where we crossed before) and thence to Chatham Courthouse, being my nearest route home. But when I got upon Little River of Pee Dee, I found the country in my front all the way to Haw River and Chatham Courthouse (on my right down along Drowning Creek and the Raft Swamp to Wilmington, on my left to Uharie Creek and the Yadkin River) in a state of insurrection and parties of armed Tories spreading themselves in every direction before me and on either flank. I nevertheless determined to push on with my baggage wagon and its valuable contents to Chatham Courthouse, not only as my best route home, but as my nearest point of safety, with only one companion in arms, a youth of nineteen years old and a cadet in Washington's regiment of cavalry. But before I got to Searcey's Ford I found we were hemmed in on every side; yet I was still determined to go on and cut my way through if possible, for there was no alternative, and retreat in any direction was equally hazardous for want of correct intelligence from some person upon whom I could rely, for they were all Tories and in arms. Crossing the ford, and leaving the wagon to come on with all expedition, I went forward with my young friend, both of us well armed with sabers and holster pistols.

I soon fell in with the infamously celebrated Col. David Fanning, a loyalist (Tory), then and long before in the British service, and his party, lately recruited, well armed, and mounted upon the best horses the country afforded, with whom I had two rencounters in the space of little more than an hour, in the last of which I was forced to give up my baggage wagon with many valuable effects, both public and private, and retreated up the country to Randolph Old Courthouse, in a direction quite contrary to that I wished to go, and chased for about six miles by the party, when they had to decline the pursuit owing to the fleetness of our horses. Finding myself at the courthouse upon the old trading road leading from Hillsboro to Salisbury, I turned down it to the east and reached Bell's Mill on Deep River, three miles below, where I lodged in secret that night, being surrounded at that time by Tories in arms on every side, having traveled sixty miles that day, twenty of which was with my baggage wagon.

Rising at daybreak the next morning, instead of keeping the direct road down to Hillsboro, about fifty-five miles, I had to turn to my left, among three roads that centered at Bell's Mill, and, directing my course in a north direction, entered the New Garden settlement of Quakers in about sixteen or eighteen miles, considerably above Guilford Courthouse, and at last reached this latter place, where I deemed myself safe from further pursuit and molestation and where I halted to see my acquaintance Captain Barrett, who was left there in March so dangerously wounded and whom I found in a convalescent state, and from thence down to Hillsboro, about fifty or fifty-five miles, having been turned out of my proper course by Fanning and other royalists about an hundred miles. Here (at Hillsboro) I was met by Brigadier General Butler of that district and solicited to take the command, as colonel of a regiment of volunteer mounted infantry and cavalry that he was then raising, which office I accepted on the twenty-second of May, 1781, and in a few days thereafter took the field in the prosecution of my duty against the infamously celebrated Col. David Fanning already mentioned, who had free ingress and egress into the British garrison at Wilmington with his plunder and prisoners at all times. Having, after various marches and countermarches, obtained the object for which this regiment was sent into the field, to wit, either to defeat Fanning or compel him to disband his forces and quit the country, the latter alternative was his choice when he could no longer avoid coming to action and retired to Wilmington with such of his followers as chose to adhere to his fortunes, whereby peace and safety for a time at least was restored to that part of the country, and the legislature, which had convened early in June at Wake Courthouse (now the city of Raleigh), protected from certain captivity or dispersion, when I received a letter of thanks and discharge from General Butler and returned home after an absence of five months in the unintermittent and active service of my country. But here I was not permitted to remain at rest, being engaged in reconnoitering the enemy (Tarleton and Simcoe) when making their excursions into the parts of Virginia contiguous to North Carolina, from James River, and whose alarms spread over the country.

When the French fleet and army under the command of Count de Grasse and Marquis St. Simon arrived in Virginia and blocked up the Chesapeake, about the last of August, 1781, the news of which event reached Halifax on the second day of September, where the governor and his suite then were on public business, when the opinion of the executive, as well as the general expectation, was that Lord Cornwallis, of whose headquarters and movements we then knew nothing, would endeavor to save himself and his army by retreating through North Carolina to Wilmington or to Charleston. I was applied to by the governor and requested to take the command of a party of observation, consisting of light dragoons belonging to the new state legion, some recruits of which were assembled there, and proceed immediately into Virginia, search out where his lordship might be, what route he was taking, throw myself in his front, ascertain his force of every description, and lastly to give the executive information by express, from time to time, of these particulars. I accepted the command because the occasion was urgent and important, and in the space of two hours, which I waited to give Governor Burke time to draw up my instructions and write two letters, one to General Muhlenberg and the other to Colonel Parker of Norfolk or Princess Anne County, marched at the head of my party with all the expedition the nature of the service would admit.

On this service I was gone about a fortnight or upwards, my men and horses often suffering for want of food, such being the scarcity in Virginia owing to the previous marching and countermarching of the enemy through that part of the county where my route lay, which, from the circumstances of the times and our ignorance of the movements of the British, was of necessity a devious one. At last I reached Swan's Point on James River opposite to old Jamestown, near to which I had marched before I got my intelligence of Lord Cornwallis's last movement from Portsmouth to Yorktown. Waiting here for several days without a possibility of crossing the river (three miles wide) for want of boats, and happening by mere accident to hear of the arrival of General Washington and Count Rochambeau with their respected suites at Williamsburg, where the Marquis Lafayette with his small army lay, whilst Count St. Simon had debarked his troops at old Jamestown and were in full view of Swan's Point, where I was posted, having fulfilled the governor's wishes as far as practicable by frequently conveying to him such intelligence as I could procure of the condition of Lord Cornwallis and the situation of the combined forces, I withdrew from Swan's Point on James River and returned home with my party, adding two months more service to the tours already enumerated from the time I received my discharge from General Butler in July.

I have indeed been, it may be thought, too prolix in drawing up this my declaration, but the occasion seemed to require it, and the rules and regulations adopted by the War Department in regard to applicants for pensions under the late law of Congress I hope will justify it, being, as I am, desirous of giving every evidence of my Revolutionary services and all other satisfaction in my power, but especially to avoid every imputation of suspicion of imposition.

JOHN CHANEY *(b. 1757) was born in Randolph County, North Carolina, and served two tours in the latter part of the war as a volunteer in the South Carolina infantry. He was wounded with a broadsword in hand-to-hand combat in a skirmish with Rawdon's army on the road to Ninety*

Six and wounded again, while serving in William Washington's cavalry, in the Battle of Eutaw Springs (September 1781). Unlike Washington, he escaped capture. The anecdote about Billy Lunsford's effort to shoot "one damned British son of a bitch" provides a glimpse of the blood-chilling humor that any war can produce.

Chaney moved to Tennessee in 1801 and to Indiana in 1824 and was living in Greene County, Indiana, when he submitted this application in 1833 and was granted a pension.

About the age of seventeen or eighteen he went to South Carolina in the district of Ninety Six to live with his cousin John Chaney. Having been there about a year, he met with Capt. James Lepham [?] and enlisted with him in the presence of John Hargrove, John Toles, W. Tapley, and other not recollected who had previously enlisted under said captain. This applicant then and there volunteered and enlisted under said officer to serve in the service of the United States in the war of the Revolution in the state troops of said state of South Carolina, probably by a call of Congress, he cannot say certainly, for one year. He was promised one hundred pounds sterling and lands, the quantity of which he has forgotten, as bounty, no part of which he has ever received.

The same day of his enlistment, which he thinks was in the year 1780 or 1781, he is not positive, he thinks in the early part of one of said years, the latter part of spring or first of summer (he was living at or near Cook's Mills in said district of Ninety Six when he enlisted), he marched off with said captain and other recruits toward Augusta in Georgia and then to where said Lepham [?] kept a public store, perhaps five or six miles from Augusta. He was some time at said store and was put under charge and command of said John Hargrove, who was their ensign, and by said ensign marched back to Ninety Six or near it, said Captain Lepham [?] remaining at said public store near Ninety Six. With and under said ensign, he joined and was put in the regiment commanded by Colonel Middleton, whose first name he was under the impression was William. The major's name in said regiment was Moore, whose first name he has forgotten. He cannot state the length of time which he stayed at said public store but thinks it was several months. Under the charge of said ensign and in joining said regiment of Colonel Middleton, he was put in the company commanded by Capt. Isaac Ross. The lieutenant's name of said company was Dinkin, first name forgotten, the brigade commanded by General Rutherford. He thinks the oldest colonel in said brigade was Henderson. Another of the colonels in said brigade was Pogue, another Wade Hampton. General Rutherford about this time being absent, the command of said brigade devolved on Colonel Henderson, who marched said brigade, including this applicant, down near Moncks Corner. They were there met by Lord Rawdon (who had been some time lying at said place and had moved from it) with, as was said, several thousand footmen and one thousand dragoons going to relieve Colonel Cruger who was in Ninety Six besieged by General Greene. Upon meeting Lord Rawdon, they retreated and was pursued by the enemy.

From Moncks Corner to Ninety Six he thinks it was about 160 or 150 miles. The British pursued them to Little Saluda or near it, to the Juniper Springs at West's Old Fields, where they had a fight with the enemy's dragoons (all said Rutherford's men with this declarant being mounted men). This declarant mounted near Ninety Six (where was our guard pasture). Knowing they had foot to support them, we were compelled to retreat with the loss of about twenty-eight killed and a number wounded.

In this action the declarant was wounded in three places with the broadsword by a Hessian dragoon whom he met in full charge. His antagonist, being well skilled in the sword exercise and uncommonly strong, was greatly his superior. The first wound was a slight cut across the fingers of the sword hand. The next, a severe cut across the wrist of the same hand, at which, turning his horse round a pine sapling to escape, he received a severe cut and wound a little back of his left temple which brought him to the ground. He jumped to his feet, and whilst running round a pine, one of his companions rode up and with his pistol shot the Hessian dragoon dead in his saddle.

A fever rising in his wounded wrist, and no doctor being to be had, he suffered much. He lost his horse, saddle, holster, pistol, and sword and saved himself by mounting behind his companion.

The Americans continued to retard as much as possible the British army until they arrived at Saluda Old Town, where they camped about one hundred yards from the British picket. Col. William Washington had, with his command, been with said brigade and was there at this time. One of his dragoons, Billy Lunsford, requested of his captain leave to steal upon and shoot a British sentinel. The captain told him it could not do the cause any good, and, as the sentinel was doing his duty, it was a pity to shoot him. Billy swore his time was out, and, as he was going home to Virginia, he would have it to tell that he had killed "one damned British son of a bitch." Accordingly, Billy commenced passing backwards and forwards with a pistol, creeping on his all fours and grunting like a hog. The sentinel was heard to slap his cartouche box and fired, and Billy changed his grunting to groaning, being shot through the body, entering his right and coming out his left side. It was as pretty a shot as could have been made in daylight. The British sentinel, being reinforced, carried Billy a prisoner into their camp, where, by the kind attention of a British surgeon who nursed him and had him nursed all night to prevent his bleeding inwardly and to make him bleed outwardly, he recovered. (This declarant afterwards traveled with him, Billy, down to Congaree.) The next day was kept up and continued from that day for several days in succession skirmishing for the purpose of checking the enemy until General Greene could raise the siege of Ninety Six and escape with his baggage. We always encamping at night, and making fires, with the appearance of intending to remain until morning and fighting, but soon after making our fires, marched on all night (halting to sleep in daytime just after crossing a river or suitable place to gain advantage of ground). Between Ninety Six and Broad River, this declarant and army joined General Greene. The British having turned from the pursuit at the old Saluda Town to go to Ninety Six, having gone there and finding that General Greene had gone, immediately resumed the pursuit, the Americans retreating with great speed and halting to rest on the banks of streams after crossing and planting his cannon against the fords. Whilst fleeing from the neighborhood of Moncks Corner before Lord Rawdon, he, this declarant, crossed Davenport's Creek, Tiger River, Broad River.

The British at length turned back to Ninety Six, and the American army with this declarant marched down to Congaree and there remained a long time. There this declarant got a furlough and traveled up to Saluda Old Town in company with Clark Spraggins. Was gone about twenty days. Billy Lunsford, being there with his wounds and better, returned with him down to the army. Said Spraggins was a brother to Capt. Thomas Spraggins in Rutherford's brigade. In a few days after his return to the army from Saluda Old Town on said furlough, his period of service expired. Having served said twelve months faithfully and to the acceptance of his officers, he received a written discharge from his said captain, which discharge he afterwards kept in a little trunk at his sister's, Margaret Allred's, whose house was destroyed by fire and his discharge with it. He was dismissed on the Congaree at a ferry, the name of which he has forgotten. He never left the camp but enlisted to serve another year. Said company was cavalry, or mounted men.

Within a few days after the expiration of his said year's service voluntarily entered, he enlisted in a corps of troops raised by the state of South Carolina by a call from Congress to serve with Col. William Washington in the company, the name of the captain of which he cannot recollect, to serve for the period of one year at least. At this encampment of the army, which was on the north side of the Congaree and at said ferry, the name of any town, or county, or place near or there he does not know, he was opposite and not far from the British army lying on the south side of the said river. The British moved down to Orangeburg and thence to the Eutaw Springs. The Americans, including Colonel Washington's command and Colonel Henderson's, moved down to the Eutaw Springs, and the battle there ensued, as well as the fight at the potato patch, two or three miles from the springs. This applicant was in the rear of Washington's troops in the heat of said battle. The British, after giving way, rallied at the brick house and planted some fieldpieces. Washington attacked these pieces, supported by some of Lee's footmen. Washington jumped his horse into the midst of the enemy and was suddenly taken prisoner. A British soldier appearing to be in the posture of attempting to stab Colonel Washington, one of his men rushed forward and cut him down at one blow. Washington being a prisoner, and his men mingled in confusion with the enemy, and not knowing what else to do, this applicant with about twenty-five retreated and left the field. Afterwards they were joined by five of Washigton's other soldiers, stating that they only escaped out of a great many who attempted to charge through the enemy's lines, they having succeeded by flight after penetrating through. Said twenty-five having no officers and being joined by said five men, they marched from the High Hills of Santee up to the other state troops and joined them at Brown's Old Fields.

Said Washington's troops were entirely broken up. After the Battle of the Eutaw Springs, he was taken sick and was at Colonel Middleton's house about three weeks. John Toles was sick with him. Speaking of his wish to go to the state troops, Colonel Middleton's overseer advised him on account of the Tories to go a near route and pathway, in which he was, owing to sickness and fatigue, very near perishing before he reached the camp, when Adjutant Weathers took him in his arms and, carrying him to a shade, gave him brandy and cheese, etc., and he was there sick about a month. The state troops crossed the Congaree about this time. John Toles, who was sick with him at Colonel Middleton's house, was about this time (being on his way to Ninety Six) hung by the Tories. After being sick about said month, he seemed better and, when the state troops marched, marched with them but soon relapsed and continued sick probably something near a month, not positive.

Washington's troops were never collected and reorganized within his knowledge after the Battle of Eutaw Springs. There being no officers, and the Negroes or Tories having stolen his horse while he was sick, he considered himself at liberty to return home and done so to North Carolina, having served in said last period of serivce about four months from the time of his enlistment to the time of quitting the service as above stated. He states that he quit the service as above with the advice of his friends who were officers in the state troops, and one reason for his doing so and their advice was his feeble state of health, having suffered greatly from sickness and fatigue and being completely worn out. The time of his quitting the service as above he thinks was in the latter part of summer on in the fall of the year 1781 or 1782.

7

VIRGINIA, TO YORKTOWN

EDWARD ELLEY *(b. 1751) was born in Culpepper County, Virginia, and resided there and in Spotsylvania County throughout his life. He volunteered in the militia for three months, apparently in 1780, was drafted for the same term, and was drafted twice in 1781. He was older and apparently wealthier than the average private soldier, and he hired a substitute. When Lafayette passed his plantation in the period just before Yorktown, Elley entertained the general and his staff, and when drafted shortly afterward, he joined the army at Williamsburg. He gives a good description of building the fortifications that would soon bring about the British surrender. Like a significant percentage of his fellow soldiers, familiar with the word "corn" and with the surname "Wallace," he thought of his opponent as "General Corn Wallace" and refers to him as General Wallace in the narrative.*

Elley obviously had a loving wife, and she vastly overpaid a substitute to replace him for the last month of his service. He just missed the surrender. He was ninety-four years of age when he submitted this deposition in 1846, and he was granted a pension.

I entered the service of the United States under the following-named officers and served as herein stated. Volunteered for the term of three months and went into service under Captain Herndon, Lt. James Cunningham, Francis Thornton, ensign, and Hezekiah Ellis, sergeant, and marched to Fredericksburg and took the prisoners brought from the south to that town and carried them over the mountains to Staunton in Augusta County, Virginia. And on our march with the prisoners we passed through Spotsylvania and Orange counties, Virginia, and crossed the ridge of mountains called the Blue Ridge at a place called Swift Run Gap. And after crossing the ridge, we came to and crossed a river called Shenandoah River and crossed said river at a place called Hast Mackett's [?] Ford. And after delivering the prisoners at Staunton, we returned to Fredericksburg. Our company numbered about sixty men, and the prisoners were about forty in number and were taken in South Carolina, as I understood. We continued through the remainder of this turn about the armory at Fredericksburg. A British fleet was expected about this time upon our waters, and just before this term expired, the enemy's fleet passed along our coast from the south to the north. By reason of old age and the consequent loss of memory, I cannot state particularly the date of this term of service as to the beginning or end but recollect that [it] was about the time of General Gates's defeat. This service was performed in the spring season of the year. We were kept out as sentinels on watch, and there were companies in the neighborhood ready to be called out if necessary. Col. Richard Young was commissary at Fredericksburg during this term of service.

I had been, prior to this term of service, a resident of the above-mentioned county, but after returning from the service I removed to Culpepper County, Virginia, and settled near Elley's Ford in said county, where I resided when called into service the second term.

The second term, I was drafted a soldier and called into service under Gen. Joseph [*sic*] Weedon of Fredericksburg and marched to Hunter's Forge near Falmouth, Virginia, and on our way to said forge, we crossed the Rappahannock River at or near the junction with Rapidan and soon to the forge and joined General Weedon's regiment at said forge. This regiment or army was, I understood, separated into three divisions, and one division was stationed on the Potomac and another stationed on the Rappahannock River below Fredericksburg, and the third division was stationed at the said forge near Falmouth on the said Rappahannock River. The British fleet was about this time lying on the Potomac waters and threatened an attack upon us. There were in Fredericksburg at this time several disaffected citizens who were tarred and feathered and drummed out of the town, and several Scotch merchants closed their business in Fredericksburg and set off for home to Scotland, as they said.

This term lasted within a few days of three months, but the commencement or end I do not now recollect owing to the loss of memory in regard to dates. I recollect the name of John Heall, Joseph Ficklen, John Noe, and Bennet Noe who served with me during this term. The British, after remaining in our water for some time, left and went to the north. At this time we were then discharged, and I returned to my home in Culpepper County, Virginia.

The third term I was drafted for the service, I hired a substitute who filled my place and was in General Lafayette's army when he passed on by Elley's Ford in Culpepper County, Virginia, by circuitous route through Spotsylvania County and into Culpepper in order to strengthen his army, and he joined, I think, General Morgan's army at the Fork Church in Culpepper County and crossed over the Rapidan River at the Raccoon Ford into Orange County and so on down towards Williamsburg on the James River. And whilst passing Elley's Ford, some fifty or sixty of Lafayette's officers and soldiers called at my house near said ford, and I gave them dinner, it being that time of day when the army passed. A short time after this army passed, another requisition of men was called as a relief, which included me, and having just hired a substitute and not feeling myself able to hire if I could have obained another substitute, I determined to fill my own place and took my horse and joined Lafayette's army before it reached Williamsburg. I do not recollect the day or month when this term of myself or substitute commenced or ended. The armies halted a short time at Williamsburg to receive reinforcements from the surrounding country and then marched down to Yorktown in Virginia. And we had several little engagements with the enemy before they were hemmed in at said town. A council of war was held by our officers, and some were in favor of storming the enemy's fort there under General Wallace [Cornwallis], but General Washington was opposed to that course and recommended a siege, as I was told. The enemy frequently fired upon us whilst engaged in making preparations for the siege and killed a few of our men. The militia officers were at this time employed with the soldiers getting brush, etc., to make wattling required in the fortifications. I was put among the able-bodied men to throwing up bomb batteries, Washington's Grand Battery having been previously finished, and whilst engaged in throwing up the bomb batteries night and day, we were ordered to squat in the ditch when the enemy fired upon us, of which we were notified by the sentinel on guard. And Captain Welch ordered the men to hurry with the work, else they would not sink deep enough to shelter them from the enemy's cannon by morning. And we who were on the front works were industrious and advanced with the work, and in the morning those behind wanted to crowd upon us when fired upon, but Captain Welch ordered them to keep their place as it was their own fault that they were exposed. And whilst engaged in this work, a cannonball from the enemy came so near me that the wind of the ball blew my hunting shirt from the bank just by me, and another ball came and struck within three feet of us in our work. After throwing up these works, I was ordered to the park where the ammunition was kept, put to swabbing and cleaning the cannons and bombs, to assist in sending off the battery guns, ammunition, etc.

The works of the battery were thrown up by the militia soldiers, and whilst they were cutting brush a cannonball came bounding along on the ground, and a youngster put his heel against it and was thrown into lockjaw and expired in a short time. And I recollect another circumstance which occurred near me. A ball came from the enemy, struck a man, and cut off his leg at the thigh, and then struck a stack of arms and rendered them unfit for service. After serving at the park as above stated, I was ordered to the works. The works were thrown up by the militia soldiers. The Continentals at this time were encamped about a mile off towards Williamsburg. I frequently saw General Washington riding around and directing the operations, and after the siege began my place was at the guns in the battery called Washington's Grand Battery. There were in this battery four twenty-four-pounders, four eighteen-pounders, four twelve-pounders, and twelve mortar pieces, and these were fired in platoons, four at a time, and the mortars three at a time, making four rounds of mortars, in order to keep up a constant fire. And, whilst firing, the elevator of the guns got in a violent passion because the men in assistance dodged when fired upon by the enemy from their portholes and produced a considerable confusion. And General Clinton, coming up just at that moment, put things to rights, and I remarked to the men in his hearing, "Come, my brave fellows, stick to your posts and the day will soon be ours," and for this remark I was very soon rewarded with a good breakfast from the general, which was very acceptable as I had not had a meal for twenty-four hours. And I never saw men more mystified than were these serving with me at the guns when I received the reward. Shortly after the siege began, thirty-three of the enemy deserted and came around in a boat about midnight and joined us, and General Clinton gave them a pass to General Washington. And whilst engaged in firing the guns, it appeared to me as if the earth would sink beneath us.

I continued in this service until within a few days of Wallace's surrender. My wife having hired a man and sent him down to take my place, and so I put the man in my [place] and took my horse sent for me and set for home immediately. And before I reached Fredericksburg on my way home, I understood that Wallace had surrendered. Before I left the service, I saw a number of dead horses on the beach which the enemy had drowned. I served myself in this turn two months, besides my substitute who served three months and paid him to his satisfaction. The amount paid I do not recollect, and my substitute who relieved me from the said siege continued in the service and guarded the prisoners from the siege over the mountains to Winchester and then returned, and I paid him a suit of good new clothes, a blanket, a knapsack, a cheese, and a thousand dollars in Continental paper, and thirty silver dollars, the price previously agreed upon by my wife.

JOHN SUDDARTH *(b. 1765) was born in Amherst County, Virginia, and moved to Albemarle County in 1778. He served three months as a substitute for his brother at age thirteen, guarding prisoners from Burgoyne's army at the Charlottesville prison camp, and in 1781 he served five and a half months at Yorktown. His narrative is of historical value for his anecdote about Washington. The commander-in-chief narrowly missed being killed several times in the course of the war, most notably at Princeton and at Brandywine. But dauntless courage inspires men, and a sense of invulnerability, shared by most of the military heroes in history, helped make Washington the great leader he was.*

Suddarth moved to Simpson County, Kentucky, in 1839, submitted this narrative that year, and received a pension.

That he volunteered in the army of the United States about the last of June (he recollects it was just before harvest), 1778, as a substitute for his brother James Suddarth under the command and in the company of Capt. John Burley or Burleigh and in the regiment of Colonel Bland of the Virginia troops, but he cannot state whether of the state or Continental line. Under the command of these officers he was engaged as a private in guarding the prisoners in the county of Albemarle, about four miles westwardly of Charlottesville, Virginia, which prisoners had been taken by General Gates in the defeat of General Burgoyne. He continued in this service until the last of September (a period of three months), when he was relieved by the return of his brother for whom he had substituted as aforesaid and who had been compelled to leave the service in consequence of sickness. This declarant, at the time of joining the service, resided in the county of Albemarle, Virginia. He recollects that Capt. Holman Rice and Captain Garland were in this service at the same time with this declarant, and that Captain Garland was shot by a sentry whilst there.

This declarant again joined the army of the Revolution from said county of Albemarle and state of Virginia about the middle of July, 1781, in the company of Capt. Benjamin Harris and joined a portion of the main army at Williamsburg, which to the best of his recollection was under the command of Major Merriweather. He will not say that Merriweather was the highest officer in command there, but from his indistinct recollection, he now seems to him to have been so. From Williamsburg we marched to Travis Point, at the mouth of Queen's Creek into York River, where we remained a few days guarding a number of beeves, etc., belonging to the American army. From thence we were marched down to the main encampment before Yorktown. We were here immediately placed to work in rearing the breastworks around the town. We were put on duty during this time at eight o'clock in the morning and not relieved until the succeeding morning at eight o'clock, only taking time to eat our meals. We then rested the succeeding twenty-four hours and so on till the works were finished. He was present at the taking the two British redoubts, the one stormed by the French and the other by the Americans. He was not a participant in the storm, except so far as that he was drawn out with a large body of other troops to render such aid as might become necessary. Each man of the troops with him had a fascine, and as soon as the redoubts surrendered they were thrown down and the work of circumvallation was recommenced.

Your declarant, during the progress of these works, witnessed a deed of personal daring and coolness in General Washington which he never saw equaled. During a tremendous cannonade from the British in order to demolish our breastworks, a few days prior to the surrender, General Washington visited that part of our fortifications behind which your declarant was posted and, whilst here, discovered that the enemy were destroying their property and drowning their horses, etc. Not, however, entirely assured of what they were doing, he took his glass and mounted the highest, most prominent, and most exposed point of our fortifications, and there stood exposed to the enemy's fire, where shot seemed flying almost as thick as hail and were instantly demolishing portions of the embankment around him, for ten or fifteen minutes, until he had completely satisfied himself of the purposes of the enemy. During this time his aides, etc., were remonstrating with him with all their earnestness against this exposure of his person and once or twice drew him down. He severely reprimanded them and resumed his position. When satisfied, he dispatched a flag to the enemy, and they desisted from their purpose.

Your declarant continued at Yorktown till the surrender of Cornwallis. He then marched as a guard to the prisoners as far as Nolan's Ferry on the Potomac, where we delivered them to the Maryland troops. Thence he returned and was discharged about Christmas of that year, making this period of his service five months and a half, thus making the entire period of his service eight months and a half.

SARAH OSBORN *was born in Blooming Grove, New York. She was a servant in the household of a blacksmith in Albany, New York, when she met and married Aaron Osborn, a blacksmith and veteran. Without his wife's knowledge, Osborn reenlisted for the war as a commissary sergeant with the Third New York Regiment. He insisted that Sarah travel with the army, and, after momentary doubts, she "volunteered" for the duration of the war.*

The deposition that she submitted at age eighty-one to obtain her husband's pension is a narrative of her personal experiences as a cook and washerwoman with the Continental army. It is in all likelihood the only autobiographical narrative of a woman traveling with the army, and it has been previously unknown to scholars.

Sarah Osborn was an acute observer. In 1837, at eighty-one, her memory was remarkable; most of the details that can be verified are accurate. The pathetic Capt. James Gregg had indeed been scalped on 13 October 1777; the two bargemen's story of Arnold's invitation to join him in treason agrees with the most credible narrative; a man named Burke was court-martialed and his execution delayed because of popular support; the British did drive Negroes out of Yorktown when food became scarce, and many were killed between the hostile armies. Her accounts of proudly riding on horseback through Philadelphia, of exchanging quips with Washington in the trenches, and of meeting Governor Thomas Nelson in what is now called "the Nelson House" in Yorktown are priceless. Her narrative of the surrender at Yorktown, where General O'Hara surrendered his sword, is as fine an eyewitness account as we have.

She was a remarkable person in many ways. Although her husband proved to be an irresponsible character and a bigamist, she accepted it with graceful resignation and remarried. In 1854 she was pictured and was the subject of an article in the American Phrenological Journal *(20, no. 5 [November 1854]:101–2). She claimed to be 109 years of age, although her 1837 deposition indicates that she was 98. In the article she also speaks of an earlier husband, preceding Osborn, who was not mentioned in the pension application. However, she was still spry, and her recollections of the Revolution in no way contradict earlier statements.*

Sarah Osborn received a double pension for her veteran husbands Osborn and Benjamin, and she deserved every penny of it.

On this twentieth day of November, A.D. 1837, personally appeared before the Court of Common Pleas of said county of Wayne, Sarah Benjamin, a resident of Pleasant Mount in said county of Wayne and state of Pennsylvania, aged eighty-one years on the seventeenth day of the present month, who being first duly sworn according to law, doth on her oath make the following declaration in order to obtain the benefit of the provision made by the act of Congress passed July 4, 1836, and the act explanatory of said act, passed March 3, 1837.

That she was married to Aaron Osborn, who was a soldier during the Revolutionary War. That her first acquaintance with said Osborn commenced in Albany, in the state of New York, during the hard winter of 1780. That deponent then resided at the house of one John Willis, a blacksmith in said city. That said Osborn came down there from Fort Stanwix and went to work at the business of blacksmithing for said Willis and continued working at intervals for a period of perhaps two months. Said Osborn then informed deponent that he had first enlisted at Goshen in Orange County, New York. That he had been in the service for three years, deponent thinks, about one year of that time at Fort Stanwix, and that his time was out. And, under an assurance that he would go to Goshen with her, she married him at the house of said Willis during the time he was there as above mentioned, to wit, in January 1780. That deponent was informed by said Osborn that while he was at Fort Stanwix he served under Capt. James Gregg and Colonel Van Schaick, the former of whom she was informed by said Osborn was scalped by the Indians near Fort Stanwix while he was on an excursion pigeon hunting, which in the sequel proved to be true, as she will show hereafter.

That after deponent had married said Osborn, he informed her that he was returned during the war, and that he desired deponent to go with him. Deponent declined until she was informed by Captain Gregg that her husband should be put on the commissary guard, and that she should have the means of conveyance either in a wagon or on horseback. That deponent then in the same winter season in sleighs accompanied her husband and the forces under command of Captain Gregg on the east side of the Hudson river to Fishkill, then crossed the river and went down to West Point. There remained till the river opened in the spring, when they returned to Albany. Captain Gregg's company was along, and she thinks Captain Parsons, Lieutenant Forman, and Colonel Van Schaick, but is not positive.

Deponent, accompanied by her said husband and the same forces, returned during the same season to West Point. Deponent recollects no other females in company but the wife of Lieutenant Forman and of Sergeant Lamberson. Deponent was well acquainted with Captain Gregg and repeatedly saw the bare spot on his head where he had been scalped by the Indians. Captain Gregg had turns of being shattered in his mind and at such times would frequently say to deponent, "Sarah, did you ever see where I was scalped?" showing his head at the same time. Captain Gregg informed deponent also of the circumstances of his being scalped: that he and two more went out pigeon hunting and were surprised by the Indians, and that the two men that were with him were killed dead, but that he escaped by reason of the tomahawk glancing on the button of his hat; that when he came to his senses, he crept along and laid his [head near] one of the dead men, and while there, his dog came to his relief, and by means of his dog, [caught the attention of] the two fishermen who were fishing near the fort.

Deponent further says that she and her husband remained at West Point till the departure of the army for the South, a term of perhaps one year and a half, but she cannot be positive as to the length of time. While at West Point, deponent lived at Lieutenant Foot's, who kept a boardinghouse. Deponent was employed in washing and sewing for the soldiers. Her said husband was employed about the camp. She well recollects the uproar occasioned when word came that a British officer had been taken as a spy. She understood at the time that Major André was brought up on the opposite side of the river and kept there till he was executed. On the return of the bargemen who assisted Arnold to escape, deponent recollects seeing two of them, one by the name of Montecu, the other by the name of Clark. That they said Arnold told them to hang up their dinners, for he had to be at Stony Point in so many minutes, and when he got there he hoisted his pocket handkerchief and his sword and said, "Row on boys," and that they soon arrived in Haverstraw Bay and found the British ship. That Arnold jumped on board, and they were all invited, and they went aboard and had their choice to go or stay. And some chose to stay and some to go and did accordingly.

When the army were about to leave West Point and go south, they crossed over the river to Robinson's Farms and remained there for a length of time to induce the belief, as deponent understood, that they were going to take up quarters there, whereas they recrossed the river in the nighttime into the Jerseys and traveled all night in a direct course for Philadelphia. Deponent was part of the time on horseback and part of the time in a wagon. Deponent's said husband was still serving as one of the commissary's guard. A man by the name of Burke was hung about this time for alleged treason, but more especially for insulting Adjutant Wendell, the prosecutor against Burke, as deponent understood and believed at the time. There was so much opposition to the execution of Burke that it was deferred some time, and he was finally executed in a different place from what was originally intended.

In their march for Philadelphia, they were under command of Generals Washington and Clinton, Colonel Van Schaick, Captain Gregg, Captain Parsons, Lieutenant Forman, Sergeant Lamberson, Ensign Clinton, one of the general's sons. They continued their march to Philadelphia, deponent on horseback through the streets, and arrived at a place towards the Schuylkill where the British had burnt some houses, where they encamped for the afternoon and night. Being out of bread, deponent was employed in baking the afternoon and evening. Deponent recollects no females but Sergeant Lamberson's and Lieutenant Forman's wives and a colored woman by the name of Letta. The Quaker ladies who came round urged deponent to stay, but her said husband said, "No, he could not leave her behind." Accordingly, next day they continued their march from day to day till they arrived at Baltimore, where deponent and her said husband and the forces under command of General Clinton, Captain Gregg, and several other officers, all of whom she does not recollect, embarked on board a vessel and sailed down the Chesapeake. There were several vessels along, and deponent was in the foremost. General Washington was not in the vessel with deponent, and she does not know where he was till he arrived at Yorktown, where she again saw him. He might have embarked at another place, but deponent is confident she embarked at Baltimore and that General Clinton was in the same vessel with her. Some of the troops went down by land. They continued sail until they had got up the St. James River as far as the tide would carry them, about twelve miles from the mouth, and then landed, and the tide being spent, they had a fine time catching sea lobsters, which they ate.

They, however, marched immediately for a place called Williamsburg, as she thinks, deponent alternately on horseback and on foot. There arrived, they remained two days till the army all came in by land and then marched for Yorktown, or Little York as it was then called. The York troops were posted at the right, the Connecticut troops next, and the French to the left. In about one day or less than a day, they reached the place of encampment about one mile from Yorktown. Deponent was on foot and the other females above named and her said husband still on the commissary's guard. Deponent's attention was arrested by the appearance of a large plain between them and Yorktown and an entrenchment thrown up. She also saw a number of dead Negroes lying round their encampment, whom she understood the British had driven out of the town and left to starve, or were first starved and then thrown out. Deponent took her stand just back of the American tents, say about a mile from the town, and busied herself washing, mending, and cooking for the soldiers, in which she was assisted by the other females; some men washed their own clothing. She heard the roar of the artillery for a number of days, and the last night the Americans threw up entrenchments, it was a misty, foggy night, rather wet but not rainy. Every soldier threw up for himself, as she understood, and she afterwards saw and went into the entrenchments. Deponent's said husband was there throwing up entrenchments, and deponent cooked and carried in beef, and bread, and coffee (in a gallon pot) to the soldiers in the entrenchment.

On one occasion when deponent was thus employed carrying in provisions, she met General Washington, who asked her if she "was not afraid of the cannonballs?"

She replied, "No, the bullets would not cheat the gallows," that "It would not do for the men to fight and starve too."

They dug entrenchments nearer and nearer to Yorktown every night or two till the last. While digging that, the enemy fired very heavy till about nine o'clock next morning, then stopped, and the drums from the enemy beat excessively. Deponent was a little way off in Colonel Van Schaick's or the officers' marquee and a number of officers were present, among whom was Captain Gregg, who, on account of infirmities, did not go out much to do duty.

The drums continued beating, and all at once the officers hurrahed and swung their hats, and deponent asked them, "What is the matter now?"

One of them replied, "Are not you soldier enough to know what it means?"

Deponent replied, "No."

They then replied, "The British have surrendered."

Deponent, having provisions ready, carried the same down to the entrenchments that morning, and four of the soldiers whom she was in the habit of cooking for ate their breakfasts.

Deponent stood on one side of the road and the American officers upon the other side when the British officers came out of the town and rode up to the American officers and delivered up [their swords, which the deponent] thinks were returned again, and the British officers rode right on before the army, who marched out beating and playing a melancholy tune, their drums covered with black handkerchiefs and their fifes with black ribbands tied around them, into an old field and there grounded their arms and then returned into town again to await their destiny. Deponent recollects seeing a great many American officers, some on horseback and some on foot, but cannot call them all by name. Washington, Lafayette, and Clinton were among the number. The British general at the head of the army was a large, portly man, full face, and the tears rolled down his cheeks as he passed along. She does not recollect his name, but it was not Cornwallis. She saw the latter afterwards and noticed his being a man of diminutive appearance and having cross eyes.

On going into town, she noticed two dead Negroes lying by the market house. She had the curiosity to go into a large building that stood nearby, and there she noticed the cupboards smashed to pieces and china dishes and other ware strewed around upon

SURRENDER OF CORNWALLIS
at Yorktown Va. Oct 19th 1781. Seven thousand men were made prisoners by the Americans & French under Washington, *this event decided the Rev.y war.*

the floor, and among the rest a pewter cover to a hot basin that had a handle on it. She picked it up, supposing it to belong to the British, but the governor came in and claimed it as his, but said he would have the name of giving it away as it was the last one out of twelve that he could see, and accordingly presented it to deponent, and she afterwards brought it home with her to Orange County and sold it for old pewter, which she has a hundred times regretted.

After two or three days, deponent and her husband, Captain Gregg, and others who were sick or complaining embarked on board a vessel from Yorktown, not the same they came down in, and set sail up the Chesapeake Bay and continued to the Head of Elk, where they landed. The main body of the army remained behind but came on soon afterwards. Deponent and her husband proceeded with the commissary's teams from the Head of Elk, leaving Philadelphia to the right, and continued day after day till they arrived at Pompton Plains in New Jersey. Deponent does not recollect the county. They were joined by the main body of the army under General Clinton's command, and they set down for winter quarters. Deponent and her husband lived a part of the time in a tent made of logs but covered with cloth, and a part of the time at a Mr. Manuel's near Pompton Meetinghouse. She busied herself during the winter in cooking and sewing as usual. Her said husband was on duty among the rest of the army and held the station of corporal from the time he left West Point.

In the opening of spring, they marched to West Point and remained there during the summer, her husband still with her. In the fall they came up a little back of Newburgh to a place called New Windsor and put up huts on Ellis's lands and again sat down for winter quarters, her said husband still along and on duty. The York troops and Connecticut troops were there. In the following spring or autumn they were all discharged. Deponent and her husband remained in New Windsor in a log house built by the army until the spring following. Some of the soldiers boarded at their house and worked round among the farmers, as did her said husband also.

Deponent and her husband spent certainly more than three years in the service, for she recollects a part of one winter at West Point and the whole of another winter there, another winter at

Pompton Plains, and another at New Windsor. And her husband was the whole time under the command of Captain Gregg as an enlisted soldier holding the station of corporal to the best of her knowledge.

In the winter before the army were disbanded at New Windsor, on the twentieth of February, deponent had a child by the name of Phebe Osborn, of whom the said Aaron Osborn was the father. A year and five months afterwards, on the ninth day of August at the same place, she had another child by the name of Aaron Osborn, Jr., of whom the said husband was the father. The said Phebe Osborn afterwards married a man by the name of William Rockwell and moved into the town of Dryden, Tompkins County, New York, where he died, say ten or twelve years ago, but her said daughter yet lives near the same place on the west side of Ithaca, in the town of Enfield. Her son Aaron Osborn, Jr., lived in Blooming Grove, Orange County, New York, had fits and was crazy, and became a town charge, and finally died there at the age of about thirty years.

About three months after the birth of her last child, Aaron Osborn, Jr., she last saw her said husband, who then left her at New Windsor and never returned. He had been absent at intervals before this from deponent, and at one time deponent understood he was married again to a girl by the name of Polly Sloat above Newburgh about fifteen or sixteen miles. Deponent got a horse and rode up to inquire into the truth of the story. She arrived at the girl's father's and there found her said husband, and Polly Sloat, and her parents. Deponent was kindly treated by the inmates of the house but ascertained for a truth that her husband was married to said girl. After remaining overnight, deponent determined to return home and abandon her said husband forever, as she found he had conducted in such a way as to leave no hope of reclaiming him. About two weeks afterwards, her said husband came to see deponent in New Windsor and offered to take deponent and her children to the northward, but deponent declined going, under a firm belief that he would conduct no better, and her said husband the same night absconded with two others, crossed the river at Newburgh, and she never saw him afterwards. This was about a year and a half after his discharge. Deponent heard of him afterwards up the Mohawk River and that he had married again. Deponent, after hearing of this second unlawful marriage of her said husband, married herself to John Benjamin of Blooming Grove, Orange County, New York, whose name she now bears.

SARAH BENJAMIN. (109 YEARS OF AGE.)

About twenty years ago, deponent heard that her said husband Osborn died up the Mohawk, and she has no reason to believe to the contrary to this day. Deponent often saw the discharge of her said husband Osborn and understood that he drew a bounty in lands in the lake country beyond Ithaca, but her husband informed her that he sold his discharge and land together in Newburgh to a merchant residing there whose name she cannot recollect. Her son-in-law, said Rockwell, on hearing of the death of

Osborn, went out to see the land and returned saying that it was a very handsome lot. But said Rockwell being now dead, she can give no further information concerning it. Deponent was informed more than forty years ago and believes that said Polly Sloat, Osborn's second wife above mentioned, died dead drunk, the liquor running out of her mouth after she was dead. Osborn's third wife she knows nothing about.

After deponent was thus left by Osborn, she removed from New Windsor to Blooming Grove, Orange County, New York, about fifty years ago, where she had been born and brought up, and, having married Mr. Benjamin as above stated, she continued to reside there perhaps thirty-five years, when she and her husband Benjamin removed to Pleasant Mount, Wayne County, Pennsylvania, and there she has resided to this day. Her said husband, John Benjamin, died there ten years ago last April, from which time she has continued to be and is now a widow.

8
THE INDIAN FRONTIER

John Struthers *(1759–1845) was born in Cecil County, Maryland, and moved to the frontier settlement on the north branch of Chartiers Creek, Washington County, Pennsylvania, in 1775.*

In traveling west with his father, he had met Dunmore's party. The governor was a loyal Scotsman, and he undoubtedly greeted Struthers's father enthusiastically and urged him to join their party. Backwoodsmen, annoyed that Dunmore would not pursue the Indians more vigorously, convinced Struthers that the expedition had been a cover for forming a western British-Indian alliance against the colonies, but modern historical evidence proves they were wrong. Struthers's memory of the conversation with the governor was faulty, obviously influenced by post-Revolutionary frontier opinion and perhaps by some of the early frontier histories such as Alexander S. Withers's Chronicles of Border Warfare *(Clarksburg, Va., 1831), which reflected these views.*

In company with most able-bodied males on the frontier, Struthers served as a "spy and wood ranger" year after year during Indian season, spring to fall, interrupting the routine only to participate in McIntosh's campaign to Fort Laurens in 1779. His narrative gives an excellent picture of this type of service. Considerable rivalry existed between the frontiersmen and regular soldiers, and Struthers presents convincing arguments at the end of his deposition for the greater importance of the former in dealing with the Indians. Unfortunately, the pension officials did not see it that way, and frontier service, except in the rare cases where formal records were kept, was not credited for eligibility. Struthers was not granted a pension.

He remained in Washington County, Pennsylvania, until 1798, then moved to Ohio and was living in Coitsville, Trumbull County, when he submitted this deposition in 1841.

I was born in Cecil County, in the state of Maryland, on the eleventh day of February, 1759, according to the best of my knowledge, information, and belief, having no record of that event, the record thereof being destroyed with other papers and effects of my father in 1774 by the destruction of his house by fire. In 1773 migrated with my father and his family from Cecil County to the headwaters of the north branch of Chartiers Creek, then the utmost boundary of the few settlers towards the Ohio River in that region, now in Washington County, Pennsylvania. In 1774 the few settlers fled into the interior and erected forts for their protection at Bowland's and White's, near the main branch of Chartiers, in the latter of which I performed an equal share of duty with the men from the latter end of April till about the first of November.

If it be true, as was then believed by many persons, that Lord Dunmore's main object in his campaign of this year was to engage the savages as British allies against the frontiers, and his subsequent conduct proved it, then in the Battle of Point Pleasant was shed the first blood in the War of Independence. I distinctly remember that, when, with my father, crossing the Allegheny from the east, we met Lord Dunmore at Faucet's tavern on or near the Laurel Hill, and, it being announced to him that a Scotchman had arrived (my father was a Scotchman), he approached my father, and, having asked his name, he took him aside, and, casting a look of disapprobation on me, my father told him I was his son, and I was permitted to hear the conversation. After extolling the Scotch for the most loyal subjects in His Majesty's dominions, he said a crisis was approaching and near at hand, when it was probable there would be a rupture between the mother country and her American colonies and exhorted my father to continue his allegiance to his liege sovereign and firmly to withstand all attempts to seduce him. Notwithstanding all this and much more on the same subject, my father, as soon as civil government was established by the states, took me with him to a justice of the peace, and we both swore fidelity to the United States. This may be considered a digression perhaps and irrelevant.

Having no written discharge or evidence of my services, I must depend mostly upon my memory for the facts which I have to state. During the Revolution, or the most of it, I kept a record of the principal events in which I was concerned, but long since, with other papers considered of no value, they were destroyed. Nearly sixty years have elapsed since the termination of our struggle for

Independence, and I have been absent from the scenes of action more than forty years. Almost everyone who was with me as a spy or an army scout, from its commencement till its termination in 1794, in which I performed my last tour of one month, has ceased to live, and of those who know anything of my services, there are but two persons to my knowledge now living, viz., John White, Esq., and my brother, Thomas Struthers, who is younger than I am. I cannot specifically state dates.

The year 1775 was a time of peace and quiet to us, and the settlement progressed rapidly, a militia company was formed, and, as Virginia had assumed jurisdiction over that part of the country, I (being then sixteen) was enrolled and in May 1776 was drafted for two months and served that period under Capt. Robert Miller in the blockhouse on Grant's Hill near Fort Pitt (now Pittsburgh) as first sergeant and clerk of the company. The captain, though a brave Irishman, could but barely write his name. The only military prowess performed during this tour was the capture, or rather finding, of five new bark canoes while on a scout up the Allegheny River headed by Captain Miller. We saw no Indians. We did not serve quite two months, being relieved by our neighbors. General Hand commanded at this time in Fort Pitt. There was no militia officer, to my recollection, higher than captain. Names of lieutenants I do not recollect.

The summer of 1777 was a season of great alarm, and the whole settlement from Fort Pitt to Kentucky was broken up. A number of families assembled at the house of my father in order to erect a fort, but, hearing that families had collected at Hoagland's and Beelor's, eight or ten miles nearer to the Ohio, for the same purpose, they only repaired the cabins as well as they could to resist an attack and remained in them during the summer. The others went on and built forts.

It was early resolved to raise a small company of volunteers to act as spies and wood rangers. Capt. James Scott, a brave and experienced officer, offered his services and appointed a place of rendezvous, and in a few days had upwards of twenty, of whom I was one, enrolled and ready to march with as much provision as we could conveniently carry. We started about the first of May, as nearly as I can now state, and I state it accordingly to be on that day. The country traversed was from a few miles below Fort Pitt, down the Ohio, crossing Raccoon Creek, Traver's and Tomlinson's Runs, Cross Creek, King's and Heoman's creeks, near their junction with the Ohio, passing on our way down Reardon's and

Holliday's stations, where we occasionally drew provisions. From Holliday's Cove, we traversed the country backward and forward, carefully watching the Indian warpaths until we arrived at some one of the forts or stations on the headwaters of some of the streams above mentioned, in the vicinity of which most of our company resided, where we remained a day or two to get washing and mending done and a recruit of provisions, and at every station would spend an hour or two in the exercise of the tomahawk and rifle, not only for our own improvement in the use of these weapons of warfare but also to alarm the savages if they should be lurking in the neighborhood.

In the latter part of the season, the alarm was still kept up and increased by the attack (as was reported at the time) of two or three hundred Indians on Wheeling Fort, and in this stage of alarm many others volunteered to protect the frontier, and so effectually was the country scoured from Holliday's Cove to Fort Pitt, that, though we had no triumphs in battle to record nor defeats to lament, yet not an individual was massacred by the savages in that region during this year. I ask credit for six months only during this season, that is from the first of May till in November, when the cold weather forced the Indians to return to their towns. And I am quite confident that I served at least six months this year.

In the spring of 1778 the Indians broke out earlier than usual and committed several murders on Ten Mile Creek, which was then considered an interior settlement and, although not within the range of my excursions the preceding year, was within ten or twelve miles of my father's dwelling. I believe it was in March, and the whole settlement, from Wheeling upwards, was broken up and retired into forts, of which there was now perhaps too many, as from the paucity of males in each they could spare none to act as spies or wood rangers and scarce enough to defend the forts if they should be attacked. On my return from an ineffectual scout in pursuit of the savages who had committed these barbarities, though we passed two men whom they had murdered and scalped and who were not yet cold, yet they escaped punishment. On my return from this scout, which lasted but three or four days, a request was sent me from Hoagland's Fort to turn out with as many volunteers as I could collect. I did so and, referring to my previous acquaintance with the woods and Indian warpaths, was (though among the youngest) elected to head about fifteen or sixteen active and brave men and continued during the greater part of the season, that is, from March to November with short intervals to obtain ammunition, clothing, etc., on the same route as in the preceding year but not quite so extensive. The result, however, was that no Indian depredations were committed in that settlement during the whole season. . . .

In March 1779 I entered a volunteer in Capt. David Vance's company of mounted men, in General McIntosh's campaign to Fort Laurens on Tuscarawas, found my own horse, provisions, forage, and accoutrements, and, instead of being mounted, going out carried a load of flour or bacon on each horse. This was saved, whilst the balance of the flour and meat was very much scattered through the woods and lost by reason of a salute fired from the garrison on our arrival. The next day, after commencing our returns, it was ascertained that it would be more tedious than was anticipated, and the general sent an officer to request Captain Vance to proceed with all possible speed to Fort McIntosh and return with provision sufficient to subsist the army at least two days; and, being piloted by friendly Indians along a path nearer than the main road, we met the army a considerable way back. I returned home in April and spent the remainder of the Indian season on the same route and in the same manner as during the two preceding summers. And during this season, according to the best of my knowledge and belief, I served at least six months.

Early in the spring of 1780 intelligence was received, I do not remember how, that a large body of Indians were on their march to devastate the whole country from Wheeling to Fort Pitt. This news was either not believed or at least not heeded until a party of them, crossing below Wheeling, had penetrated nearly halfway from the Ohio to Catfish Camp, now the seat of justice for Washington County, Pennsylvania. They had taken a number of prisoners but, becoming alarmed, speedily retraced their steps to the Ohio and murdered all their male prisoners on the way. The main body of those who were expected to have ravaged Raccoon Settlement, it was supposed, never crossed the Ohio, but sent two of their warriors to reconnoiter, who, approaching Dillow's Fort late in the evening, spied two boys at play and tomahawked and scalped them within two hundred yards of the fort and escaped. And it was supposed that their report was rather unfavorable, and that they immediately commenced their retrograde march, as no other mischief was done by them this season. Colonel Broadhead commanded at Fort Pitt, and this was the summer of his campaigns to the Muncee towns up the Allegheny River and to

Coshocton at the forks of Muskingum, at which two places he was supposed to have destroyed five hundred acres of corn. My services this year were of the same character with those of preceding years and amounted, according to the best of my knowledge and belief, to at least five months, commencing early in the spring and terminating late in the fall, and deducting such time as was not occupied in active service.

Early in the year 1781 the Indians made an incursion into the upper settlements of Buffalo Creek and, notwithstanding the vigilance and bravery of Col. David Williamson and his party, cruelly murdered several persons in his immediate neighborhood and took others prisoners. This caused a general alarm through all the settlements, and the people crowded into the forts, but still their great dependence for safety was on the volunteer spies and wood rangers; so I spent from April till November, at least five months, in scouting the frontier and watching the Indian crossing places and warpaths.

In the fall of this year too was the first expedition of Colonel Williamson to the Moravian Towns on the Tuscarawas, in which I (at the risk of my popularity as a soldier) declined taking a part. In the latter part of February 1782, the Indians invaded the settlement of Raccoon and murdered the family of a Mr. Wallace and took John Carpenter prisoner and took his two horses. He, however, soon made his escape and brought his horses with him.

In March, another expedition under Colonel Williamson started to the Moravian Towns and destroyed them with the inhabitants, amounting to nearly a hundred of all ages and sexes. In this, also, I refused to be concerned. These occurrences were considered by the settlers as harbingers of great distress and suffering during the summer. Yet such was the vigilance of the settlers and spies that no other mischief was done, save in one instance, and they paid dearly for their temerity. Six Indians had crawled up ten or twelve miles into the settlement and captured an old lone man of the name of William Jackson and plundered his cabin and retreated; but, so instant was the pursuit, they were overtaken at the river before they had time to embark, and a skirmish ensued wherein five Indians were killed and the other wounded in the abdomen. He dropped into a deep hole in the run, on the bank of which he was standing, and eluded search. He was often at Pittsburgh after the peace [and] would show his wound and exult in his dexterity in hiding himself. He said the white man's gun was double load, they made his head ache. Of the whites, John Cherry

Moravian martyrs

was killed and Andrew Poe and the prisoner badly wounded with the tomahawk. The latter received a deep gash in the shoulder as he turned to run towards the whites on their approach. This was the only skirmish that I recollect took place in that region during the Revolutionary War.

In the spring of this year I was elected to the command of a militia company, and my attention to the duties of that office caused necessarily a relaxation of my excursions on the frontiers; yet I spent at least two months in that service during the season, which, added to the services heretofore listed, will amount to two years and seven months. Although from the lapse of so many years and the absence of other data than memory it is impossible to specify correctly the weeks and months spent as a volunteer on the frontier during the Revolutionary War, yet I believe the statement several months less than the services really performed. I am the more confirmed in this opinion by this, that in frequent conversations with several young men, my neighbors, who had listed for three years and returned at the close of the war, it was admitted by all that I and my companions had actually served longer and endured more fatigue and hardship than they had. These conversations it is probable would not now be thought of, but that they were sometimes carried on with a considerable degree of acrimony, the regulars affecting to consider the volunteers as an inferior class, and these retorting on those as a worthless set, not daring to set heads outside the gates but under the protection of volunteers and so on.

The regular soldier performs only during the summer and then retires to winter quarters, receiving pay and clothing and rations for the whole year. The volunteers, to whom I belonged, performed at least an equal amount of service and retired home during the winter, not receiving either pay or rations and not even clothing for any part of the time, with the trifling exception of a little flour obtained now and then at the posts, or stations, and furnishing their own ammunition. Justice therefore requires that these volunteers, on applying for pensions, should have their time calculated in the same rule as the regulars. The few regulars stationed along the Ohio, from Pitt to Wheeling, and I here speak of them only, the only reliance placed on them was to defend the forts should they be attacked. Indeed, it was admitted by everyone at the time that the only security of the people along the river and adjacent settlements was the vigilance of the volunteers in watching their crossing places and warpaths and ferreting them out of their lurking places near the stations, and that by their means, principally, was the settlement saved from savage vengeances.

GEORGE ROUSH *(b. 1760) was born near Hagerstown, Maryland, and resided in Hampshire County, Virginia, when he volunteered at Fort Pitt in June 1777, as an Indian scout.*

Samuel Brady, his captain, is one of the legendary figures of frontier warfare. His company disguised themselves as Indians and ranged far into the wilderness of western Pennsylvania and Ohio, fully matching the natives in stealth and viciousness.

Brady's brother and father were both murdered in the course of the war, and he acted on the principle that "the only good Indian is a dead Indian." The 1777 massacre of an Indian hunting party that Roush minutely describes—remarkably similar in detail to Brady's killing of the great Bald

Eagle in June 1779—exhibits the deadly method of warfare for which Brady was famous.

George Roush returned to Hampshire County, Virginia, after three years' Indian service and went out for several tours with the militia, including a march to Yorktown, where he witnessed the surrender.

He resided in Mason County, Virginia, where he successfully applied for a pension. When he applied for a bounty land warrant in 1855, at age ninety-five, he was living in Meigs County, Ohio.

In the year 1777, in the month of June, declarant thinks about the seventh day, in Fort Pitt in the state of Pennsylvania, at the place where Pittsburgh now stands, declarant enlisted into the service of the United States for three years as an Indian spy. Declarant states that his services were accepted by a man by the name of Capt. Samuel Brady and continued under his command until the expiration of his said term, three years. The subaltern officers' names who belonged to Captain Brady's company were Lt. Timothy Murphy, Ens. James Ervin.

Declarant states that he was then stationed at Fort Pitt, the place aforesaid. Declarant states that in obedience to the order of his said Captain Brady, he proceeded to tan his thighs and legs with wild cherry and white oak bark and to equip himself after the following manner, to wit, a breechcloth, leather leggins, moccasins, and a cap made out of a raccoon skin, with the feathers of a hawk, painted red, fastened to the top of the cap. Declarant was then painted after the manner of an Indian warrior. His face was painted red, with three black stripes across his cheeks, which was a signification of war. Declarant states that Captain Brady's company was about sixty-four in number, all painted after the manner aforesaid.

Declarant states he was engaged in spying the country by regular tours from Fort Pitt on to the waters of Big Beaver, from thence to Little Beaver, from thence to Yellow Creek, from thence to Stillwater, from thence to Tuscarawas River, from thence to White Woman Creek, from thence to Black Fork of Mohican, from thence to the Clear Fork of Mohican, from thence to Owl Creek, from thence to the waters of Licking River, a branch of the Muskingum River, from thence to Black Lick Creek, from thence to Walnut Creek, from thence to Big Elm Creek, from thence to the Scioto River, near where the town of Columbus now stands, the seat of government of Ohio State. Declarant states that he then retraced his steps to the fort aforesaid. Declarant further states that he did not always return the direction that he went, that he sometimes returned striking the Ohio River at Wheeling Fort and following the meandering of the river up to Fort Pitt aforesaid.

The occurrences which took place during three years' laborious servitude were so numerous that declarant cannot at this time enumerate them all. The following are a few of the many that took place in the month of October, 1777, whilst declarant was on a spying tour on Stillwater, a stream which empties into the Tuscarawas River.

A party of Indians was espied by declarant and those who were with him, to wit, Captain Brady and fifteen of his soldiers. It was late in the evening. The Indians encamped in an old hunting camp which had been built by the Indians. Declarant is of opinion that the Indians had come for the purpose of hunting. There were six in number, five men and [an] old squaw. When it was ascertained that the Indians intended to remain in the camp all night, Captain Brady ordered his men to encamp not far distant from the Indians, and at the hour of twelve in the night Captain Brady marched his men within about thirty paces of the Indian camp, and we lay behind a log until it began to get light, at which time we were discovered by the dogs which the Indians had brought with them for the purpose, as we suppose, of hunting. The barking of the dogs alarmed the Indians, and one of them awoke and knocked the priming out of his gun and primed it fresh and walked the way we were laying and encouraged the dogs, which continued fiercely barking, during which time the other four Indians were yet asleep in the camp. Declarant thinks that the Indian discovered Captain Brady, who lay behind the log. Captain Brady had on a French capa coat made of fine sky blue cloth, which declarant thinks the Indian discovered above the [log]. We lay behind the log.

The Indian wheeled and walked carelessly back towards the camp, keeping his eye on the spot where we lay. We did not let him take but few paces toward the camp before Captain Brady gave the signal agreed on, which was an alternate hunch of the elbow. Declarant and a man by the name of Applegate fired, and the Indian fell dead to the ground. The report of our guns awaked those in the camp, and they got up and stood by the fire. We fired and killed three, one of which was a squaw, and then approached the camp, and an Indian sprung out of the camp and run up the hill. Captain Brady gave orders for us not to shoot running, as of the fifty Indians that we had seen on the evening before.

Whilst we were examining their guns, an Indian boy, which we supposed to be of the age of fifteen or sixteen years, came near and halloed to us and said, "Unhee, what did you shoot at?"

And a man by the name of Fulks answered in the Indian language and said, "A raccoon." The Indian came across the creek, and when he come in shooting distance one of our company shot him. On our return to the fort on Yellow Creek, we were retarded by a party of Indians. From intelligence afterwards, about forty-four in number in all were engaged. [A skirmish] took place. Six or seven rounds were fired. The result was that one of our men was killed by the name of Rickantaua [?], two wounded. We were soon overpowered by number, that we were compelled to retreat. The number of the Indians killed we at that time could [not] ascertain, but from intelligence after received by James Whiticar, who was a prisoner amongst the Indians at that time, the Indians lost twenty-four killed on the first of action, and six wounded which reached the Sandusky towns, and four of the six wounded died.

And again in March 1778, as declarant and fourteen of his fellow soldiers were on a spying tour on the Allegheny River, about eighteen miles above Fort Pitt near the mouth [of] Puckity Creek, declarant together with his fellow soldiers espied five Indians crossing the Allegheny River on some logs which they had lashed together. They had in company a woman by the name of Kiser, wife of Benjamin Kiser, who they had taken. Declarant states that he, together with those who were with him, fired on the Indians whilst in the act of crossing, aforesaid, and the Indians were all killed the first fire we made. Declarant states that he fired the first gun and aimed at an Indian who had a pole in his hand, steering the raft. The result was that the Indian fell dead. Declarant states he was engaged in seven other skirmishes during his term of service but cannot entail them with precision. Declarant states that he continued engaged in the service as aforesaid until the time for which he was volunteered had expired, at which time he was discharged by his said Captain Brady. . . .

JAMES HUSTON *(1758–1841) was born near Marcus Hook, Delaware County, Pennsylvania, and moved to Westmoreland County in 1777, where he served two tours of fort and ranger duty. When Indian hostility made normal life impossible in 1781, Huston's mother with other settlers retreated to Conococheague Settlement, Franklin County. He served three months, August to October 1781, in the malitia, scouting in central Pennsylvania.*

Forts, in most cases simply a single house and an outbuilding or two strengthened by a wooden stockade, were a common feature of the western frontier. When the threat of Indian attack made life on separate farms dangerous, especially true when able-bodied men were absent on military service, women, children, and the elderly united at the most defensible dwelling. A few militiamen guarded the inhabitants while in the fields, and the remainder performed regular, wide-ranging scouting tours, looking for any signs of Indians. Except in rare instances, the danger existed only from spring to fall, and settlers moved back to their cabins in the winter. Huston's narrative gives a sense of this service and its dangers.

After the war he moved to Indiana County, Pennsylvania, where he resided in 1834 when granted a pension.

That in the beginning of the year 1777 he resided in that part of Westmoreland County, Pennsylvania, which is now Indiana County, and that about the fifth day of April in the year 1777, he volunteered in a company of rangers commanded by Capt. John Pumeroy; the first lieutenant was John Hopkins; second lieutenant, William Lemon; ensign, Joseph Hopkins. The company rendezvoused at [the house of] James Ramsey, who resided at that time about two miles northeast of where the borough of Indiana is now located. That early in the month of June, 1777, Capt. John Pumeroy was elected colonel, and the command of the company was transferred to John Hopkins. William Lemon was first lieutenant, John Lemon was second lieutenant, and Joseph Hopkins continued ensign. That on the fifth or sixth of August, 1777, deponent was discharged, having served four months in this tour. That during the whole four months, the company was stationed at James Ramsey's, whose house was converted into a blockhouse, and deponent was almost constantly engaged in searching parties against the Indians for the protection of the frontiers, being seldom more than a day at one time in the station, and during the time the major part of the company were twice as far as Kittanning, once under Captain Pumeroy and once during the command of Captain Hopkins, but deponent was not engaged during these four months in any skirmish with the Indians, although they frequently saw what they supposed to be their trails. James Ramsey was the commissary and furnished the company with rations during the whole time. Deponent did not ask for, nor receive, any written discharge.

That about a week after deponent was discharged from Hopkins's command, on or about the thirteenth day of August, 1777, deponent volunteered in a company of militia commanded by Capt. Samuel Dickson. Robert Rayburn was first lieutenant, John Miller, second lieutenant, and Robert Mitchell, ensign. The company was formed from the militia residing within the bounds of Captain Dickson's company, volunteering as rangers and put under pay and rations under a requisition from Archibald Lochry, county lieutenant.

The company was stationed at Samuel Dickson's, about a mile from Campbell's Mill on Black Lick Creek, then Westmoreland County, now Indiana County. Colonel Campbell was commissary, and, being scarce of salt, Lieutenant Rayburn and deponent were sent for some salt in kegs which deponent had left at his place covered over with flax in an old house. While deponent was gone for the salt, Colonel (afterward General) Campbell, David Dickson (a brother of Capt. Samuel Dickson's), John Gibson, and Randall Laughlin went to the plantation of Randall Laughlin to examine whether that would be a suitable place for a station, being six or seven miles further out than Dickson's. As deponent was on his return to the station with the salt, he killed a deer and took the meat past the station (where he left the salt) to his mother and sister at Wallace's Fort and stayed that night at the fort. He returned to the station next morning and continued there that day, and, Colonel Campbell and those with him not returning according to their promise, the next morning Captain Dickson, Levi Gibson, and this deponent started over to Laughlin's plantation to learn what had become of them. When Gibson got near the house and opposite the door, he turned round, started, and run back and said that was enough. Captain Dickson called on him several times to stop, but he continued on, and Captain Dickson and the deponent pursued him, and when they came up with him, he said he had seen Campbell's dog dead at the door of the house. Captain Dickson proposed to go back to the house, but Levi Gibson refused and continued on his way to the station, and Dickson and deponent went with him.

And the company evacuated the station and went to Wallace's Fort in Westmoreland County, and expresses were sent out for men from other forts, and there was upwards of one hundred men collected, and they started to discover what had become of Colonel Campbell and his companions. Captain Dickson commanded the advance guard, which consisted of deponent and eleven others. When they got near to Dickson's Station, they heard a dog bark, and the captain sent Lieutenant Rayburn and deponent round through the field to come up behind the house and send word to the main body to come up, intending to surround the house. The main body came on so fast that the Indians got the alarm, and before Rayburn and deponent had got to the place assigned them by Captain Dickson (having a considerable circuit to make), Joseph Campbell and John Scott, two of the main body, came between them and the Indians and got before them and fired at the Indians, who were in a piece of ground Dickson had cleared for a meadow. Joseph Campbell was about reloading his gun where he was when he was shot by an Indian and ran about fifty yards and fell dead. The Indians then started to run, and Colonel Pumeroy shot at one through the fence, which brought him to his hands and knees, but rose again and ran off. The troops pursued them about three-quarters of a mile, but the Indians escaped, and the troops returned to Dickson Station and buried Joseph Campbell and continued there all night, and next morning went to Randall Laughlin's house, which the troops surrounded, but it was empty, and a letter was found sticking in the door which had been written by some of the British to the inhabitants urging them to give up and return to their allegiance. Colonel Campbell had written on the letter that they were all taken prisoners but were well used. The greater part of the men then went home, but Major Wilkins, Captain Dickson, and the deponent with a scouting party went across the county to Two Lick Creek to endeavor to make of them discoveries. But, not making any, they returned to Wallace's Fort, Dickson's Station being then abandoned.

And deponent continued from that time to be engaged on scouting parties through the county until Wallace's Fort was attacked by the Indians, which was in the month of October, 1777, about the middle or towards the latter end of the month. In the morning of that day, Major Wilkins and William Campbell (a brother of the colonel's) had left the barn where they had been feeding their horses. The Indians came on and shot a calf and a black sheep. Deponent, not knowing that Wilkins and Campbell had returned to the fort, ran out of the fort towards the barn, when Captain Dickson called to know where he was going. Deponent replied that he was going to the barn, that he expected the Indians had shot Campbell and Wilkins. Captain Dickson told him to go back, that he had seen them go into the fort. Deponent and Dickson then both went into the fort, where he found Campbell and Wilkins, whom he had not observed before, they being in Chapman's cabin. Major Wilkins then stationed every man at his porthole round three sides of the fort. Only a few men were stationed on the fourth side, that being covered by the Wallace's Mill in which there were ten men stationed, and Captain Dickson went out and took the command of them. The mill was grinding corn at that time for the troops, there being no wheat.

About an hour after this, nine Indians came out of a thicket which was between the fort and the barn, and coming near the fort, raised their guns and fired toward it and raised the whoop and run off beyond the barn. In about half an hour, fifteen Indians came out of the same thicket and repeated the same evolution. The most of the men in the fort wanted to go out and fight them, but Major Wilkins refused permission, as he said the Indians only wanted to draw them out by that maneuver. Shortly after, a white man came up the tail race of the mill with a red flag hoisted on a pole. He got beside a buttonwood tree, and John Donehy fired from the fort and struck him in the right side, and the ball went through him. He shifted round the tree, when he was struck in the breast by a shot from the mill and fell dead. Deponent afterward understood from Captain Dickson that it was he that shot from the mill. There was another man with this white man who made his escape when the man was shot, but they could not discover whether he was a white man or an Indian. Immediately after this man made his escape, the Indians commenced a general fire upon the fort, which was returned. In the fort they could hear the bullets of the Indians strike against the stockade, but they were so far off that very few of the bullets penetrated into the wood. After the firing was over, the Indians took five horses out of the barn, three of which belonged to Major Wilkins, one to William Campbell, and a stud horse belonging to Richard Wallace.

After the Indians had gone, Major Wilkins halloed down to the mill to know whether they wanted any men from the fort to assist in taking in the white man who had been shot. They replied from the mill that they did, and deponent and four others ran down from the fort to the mill, and those in the mill refused to go out until deponent and Edward Cahill ran beyond where the man lay to the top of a hill to see if the Indians were gone, when those from the mill hauled in the body. By a subsequent account which was received, it was stated that the Indians were three hundred strong when they attacked the fort.

Deponent from this time continued to be engaged in scouting parties continually so long as Captain Dickson continued in command while the Indians were burning the houses and laying waste the plantations, but he never came up with them but once, when a scout was out commanded by Major Wilkins, and they were accompanied by a scout commanded by Capt. John Hinkston from Fort Palmer, Ligonier Valley, Westmoreland County, Pennsylvania. While on scout, they followed an Indian trail across Cowanshannock Creek in what is now Armstrong County, Pennsylvania. Captain Hinkston, Daniel McClinlock, and deponent were sent in advance, and when they had got about three miles beyond Cowanshannock, they espied the Indians kindling a fire, and they fell back and informed the main body of it, and they came to the top of the hill and then retired to a deep hollow where they kindled their fires and stayed there till they allowed the Indians would be in their first sleep. The company was then divided into two detachments so as to surround the Indians and tomahawk them without giving any alarm, but one of Hinkston's men named Wilson, when they got near the Indians, shot one of them dead as he lay, when the rest started up and endeavored to make their escape. Three more of them were killed, and a fifth one made his escape.

About the middle of February, 1778, Captain Dickson left the company and Capt. Andrew Lowers assumed the command, and some additional men joined it. Lt. John Miller died about this time, and the other officers remained as under Dickson. While under command of Captain Lowers, the company was engaged in guarding there people who had grain to thresh and continued engaged in this service two months. About the middle of April, deponent was discharged as well as most of the company, deponent having been engaged eight months in this tour under Captains Dickson and Lowers, during the whole of which time he held the appointment of first sergeant, but he never asked for nor received a written discharge, nor does he believe it was customary to give any.

The settlements in Westmoreland County being broken up, deponent took his mother down to Conococheague in what is now Franklin County, Pennsylvania, where he was drafted in the latter end of August, 1781, in a company of militia commanded by Capt. John McConnell. David Shields was lieutenant, but the ensign's name deponent cannot recollect. Col. Thomas Johnston and Maj. William McFarland of the Big Spring were with the company and had the command, when they marched to the Standing Stone on Juniata River, now Huntingdon, Huntingdon County, Pennsylvania, and the company lay there about two weeks, going out occasionally to assist the country people in putting in their grain and hay, after which the company marched to Frankstown settlement in what is now Huntingdon County and lay at Peter Titus's and there met two other companies of militia, one of which was commanded by Capt. Samuel Holliday. Does not recollect who commanded the other company. The militia lay there three or four weeks, watching the gap of the Allegheny Mountains where the Bedford scout were killed by the Indians. The provisions ran out, and Captain McConnell's and Captain Holliday's company were marched back to the Standing Stone. The other company was sent to Rickett's Fort. While the militia lay at the Standing Stone, Captain McConnell was directed to detail a number of men from both companies and set out after a scout. Deponent was one of the men selected, and they left the Standing Stone, went up through Frankstown settlement, up what is now called Blair's Gap, and across the Allegheny Mountain to the headwaters of Two Lick Creek and returned back through the gap where the Bedford scout had been killed to the Standing Stone. And shortly afterwards the company was discharged, which was in the latter end of October, deponent having been engaged on this tour two months. Deponent did not ask for nor receive any written discharge.

To ANNA OOSTERHOUT MYERS *(b. ca. 1747), as to many women of the frontier, Indian attacks were a normal part of life. When she was a child, her parents, four sisters, and a brother were murdered by Indians. She and another brother were captured, and she lived with the Indians long enough to forget most of her native Dutch.*

The Revolution brought the Indians back to the Mohawk Valley in full force, and Anna Myers's deposition, forwarded in 1840 to support a claim for her husband's pension, is very much a personal narrative of her own experiences.

The Revolution on the frontiers of the upper Susquehanna, Delaware, and Mohawk rivers inspired a considerable body of romantic historical literature. Works such as William Leete Stone's Life of Joseph Brant *(New York: A. V. Blake, 1838) and Jeptha R. Simms's* History of Schoharie County, and Border Wars of New York *(Albany: Munsell and Tanner, 1845) are classic narratives of Indian-white conflict that remain primary sources of information. Yet for no theater of the war is it harder to get concrete information on names, dates, and places.*

The standard sources do not confirm an attack at Canajoharie on 17 April 1778, when Anna Myers's account seems to suggest her settlement was overrun, but they are vague on many aspects of their subject. If she were ninety-three in 1840, her capture by Indians as a child of three would have occurred in 1750, several years before the outbreak of the French and Indian War. On the other hand, by the same reckoning of her age, her last child would have been born when she was fifty-five, improbable from a medical standpoint. It seems likely that she was eighty-six or eighty-seven at the time of her application. Even if her memory was faulty on dates, the narrative has an unquestioned air of credibility as to the reality of the events themselves.

Anna's husband and son eventually made it back home, and she went on to bear a total of twelve children. She lived at Minden, Sullivan, Hastings, and Mexico, New York. She was granted a pension for her husband's one year of military service. One could make a good case that she had earned it in her own right.

Says she is now, as near as she can recollect, about ninety-three years old; that she has no record of her age and therefore cannot state the precise time when she was born. Her maiden name was Anna Oosterhout. She was born at Canajoharie, in the present county of Montgomery, in the state of New York. During the French War, and when she was about three years old as near as she now recollects, she was taken prisoner by the French and Indians and carried to Canada. She well recollects the transaction. The house in which her father and his family resided was attacked and surrounded by the Indians, and her father and mother, four sisters, and one brother were killed by them, and she and a brother by the name of John, then about fifteen years of age, was taken prisoner. She understood and believes that the reason why she and her brother were not killed was that one of the Indians belonging to the party had lost children of about the same age, and wanted them to adopt. One other brother escaped, whose name was Frederick. At the time, he was sick with the whooping cough, and when the Indians saw him cough, they were frightened of it and let him alone. The Indians took her and her brother to their camp, but where or which way or how far they traveled she cannot state, but supposes and believes they went to Canada, as she recollects they called the place "Canda." She was with the Indians about three years, when she learned to speak the Indian language, and when she returned to the Mohawk, she had almost entirely forgotten her native language, the Dutch. Afterwards she was sent to Albany, where she was met by an uncle of hers who had come there to see if any of his brother's children were alive. She was taken by her uncle to his residence at Canajoharie.

She then went to live with her grandmother, Mrs. Katharine Hess, with whom she resided until she was about fifteen years old. She was married to Henry Moyer or Myer [Myers] about the fifteenth day of May, 1770. She was married at the house of her father-in-law in Canajoharie, where she had been residing for several weeks previous. She was married by the Reverend Mr. Ehle, a clergyman of the Low Dutch church. David Hess was present at the time of said marriage, as she well recollects he being a fiddler and played for the company to dance the evening of the marriage. She believes the said David is now living, and she knows of no other person who was present at said marriage. She knows of no record of said marriage. A record was made of said marriage in the family Bible, but the same was destroyed afterwards as will appear from what appears afterwards. She has had by said Henry Moyer twelve children, the oldest of whom is about sixty-eight years and the youngest about thirty-eight years. There are eight only of her said children now living. The said Henry Moyer was several years older than this deponent and died on the nineteenth January, 1830.

Soon after the Revolutionary War commenced, the valley of the Mohawk became the scene of many important operations and bloody transactions. He was frequently called out for the purpose of defending the frontier from the incursions of the Tories and Indians and was on guard at the fort nearly the whole time. For about a year before the Battle of Oriskany, the said Henry held the office of ensign or lieutenant in the militia in a company commanded by Captain Diefendorf. As soon as it was announced, in the spring and summer of 1777, that Colonel St. Leger was raising an army of Tories and Indians at Oswego for the purpose of invading the valley of the Mohawk, the whole country was in a state of excitement. General Herkimer issued a proclamation for every able-bodied man to turn out, leaving the old men and those who were not able to bear arms to guard the forts and other places where the women and children were assembled. The company commanded by the said Diefendorf turned out under General Herkimer and proceeded with him towards Oriskany. The said Henry was at that time an ensign or lieutenant in the company of said Diefendorf and went with the said Diefendorf as far as German Town, then called, about eight miles below Utica. The said Henry was there taken lame in consequence of having cut his foot, which had previously healed up, but in consequence of traveling it had broken out, and his foot had swelled to such a degree that it had cracked open when he returned. Said Diefendorf was killed in the Battle of Oriskany and was the brother-in-law of said Henry, having married his sister. It was said at the time that said Diefendorf was killed by an Indian who was in a tree. During the summer of 1777 the said Henry was absent most of the time in the service. After the Tories and Indians had left Fort Schuyler, in August or September, the said Henry returned to his home.

After the return of said Henry, as aforesaid, he was engaged for the greater part of that time and until the seventeenth day of April following in assisting about the erection of a fort in the present town of Minden, in the county of Montgomery and state of New York, about six miles east of Little Falls, which was called Fort Willett. Said fort was nearly completed on said seventeenth of April. It was intended for the people living near said fort to remove therein on the next Monday.

General Herkimer

On Sunday, which was on the seventeenth day of April aforesaid, about sunrise in the morning, and while some of the children of this deponent were sent a few rods from the house to feed some calves, this deponent discovered the horses then owned by the said Henry run past the door of the house greatly frightened, and at the same time she heard her children scream. She went to the door to see what was the matter and there saw several Indians who had taken the two children who had been sent out as aforesaid. One of the Indians was near the door when she went out, and he yelled and whooped and seized her by the arm. The Indians took her and her four children about fifty rods from the house and stopped. Soon after they stopped, they were met by another party of Indians who had been up to a neighbor's by the name of Christian Durt, who had taken the said Durt, his wife, and one child, and the said Henry Moyer. A few minutes before she had been taken by the Indians, as aforesaid, her husband, Henry Moyer, had left the house and gone to the said Durt's to see about moving into the fort they had been building, as aforesaid, and while there, was taken prisoner with the said Durt and his family.

She was discharged by the Indians soon after the parties met, as aforesaid, with a sucking child then about two years old. Her husband, the said Henry, and three of her children were then taken away by the Indians, and where they went she does not know except from information. After she was discharged, as aforesaid, she returned to her house, which she found rifled of such articles as the Indians could carry and set on fire. The Indians had put brands of fire between one or two beds, which were on fire when she returned. She succeeded in getting the beds out of the house and extinguished the fire and prevented the building from being entirely consumed. About two hours after the Indians left, two of her children returned, who were daughters, leaving the said Henry, her husband, and one of her children, a boy named Henry, then about three years old, prisoners with the Indians. When her daughters returned, they informed this deponent that the Indians discharged them, and that their father also wanted the Indians to discharge the boy Henry, but they refused to do so and told the said Henry, her husband, that if he attempted to run away, they would kill his boy. The wife of said Durt was also discharged by the said Indians, and her husband and child, a boy about seven years old, were carried off by the Indians. Alarm was soon made, and she on the same day went to a house called Fort House where the people had assembled and where she remained about a week, when she went into Fort Willett, where she remained for two or three years, until it was understood that it would be safe for the people to go onto their farms.

The said Henry, her husband, returned in the fall of 1779, having been absent more than a year and a half. When he returned, the said Henry informed this deponent, which she believes true, that the Indians took him to Niagara, where he was forced to run the gauntlet. While there, he was struck by an Indian with a tomahawk over the left eye, which produced a wen of considerable size and which remained there until his death. He also, at the same place, received a cut on the right side of the head which left

a scar about three inches long. From Niagara, they went to Oswego. While there, he was set to chopping wood in company with a man by the name of Stimet near the lakeshore. While a party of the British were endeavoring to get a boat ashore for the purpose of receiving the wood, the same was capsized, when he and the said Stimet escaped and went up the Oswego River, which was then a wilderness. They went to Three River Point, about twenty-five miles south of Oswego, where they discovered that they were pursued. The party pursuing encamped overnight, and then he and the said Stimet crossed the river from the west to the east side and escaped. They were five weeks in the woods and finally were found by a party of friendly Indians about six miles from Schoharie in the present county of the same name. He remained there several days until he got recruited and had recovered his strength and then returned to Fort Willett, where this deponent was. This deponent's son remained a prisoner with the Indians until peace was declared, when he returned home.

During harvest the year before the said Henry was taken prisoner, the people in the neighborhood where she resided lived in a house called Fort Walradt. The fort was burned by the Tories and Indians after the people had escaped. This fort was situated about two miles from the Mohawk River, and an alarm had been made that the enemy were in the neighborhood, when the people left Fort Walradt and went to the river for greater safety. All the furniture, clothing, and all the household stuff of the said Henry was then destroyed, and also the Bible in which her marriage with the said Henry was recorded. And this deponent further says that she is now the widow of the said Henry Moyer, never having been married to any other person.

DAVID S. WELCH *(b. ca. 1761) enlisted in February 1777 for three years in Col. Seth Warner's regiment. He served until October 1779 at Rutland Fort, Vermont, doing garrison duty and making frequent scouting expeditions in the surrounding wilderness.*

He was, to use his own words, engaged in only one fight, but it was a spectacular hand-to-hand conflict with an Indian, and after fifty-four years he could still remember it, blow by blow, and describe it so that the reader feels like an eyewitness.

Welch, living in Middlebury, Ohio, at the time, submitted this narrative in 1832.

He enlisted in the army of the United States at Rutland Fort in Vermont in the year 1777, in the month of February, in a regiment, the number of which he has forgotten, of the Vermont line under the following-named officers: his colonel was Seth Warner, one Thomas Lee was his captain, John Mott his lieutenant, and he is not confident as to the name of the ensign but thinks it was March. He enlisted for the term of three years and continued in the service until sometime in October immediately preceding the end of his term of service, when he was taken sick and received a furlough, under which he returned home, and in consequence of his continuing sick, the furlough was continued to the end of his enlistment, which was in February 1780.

The place of his enlistment was at Rutland Fort, which was in the territory now called the state of Vermont, being situated near the town of Rutland in the last-named state. The company in which he enlisted were termed a company of rangers, and the nature of his whole service was such as placed him in detachments separate from his regiment and frequently separate from the main body of his company. He was engaged during his whole service in various scouting parties and guarding the country between Union River upon the east side of Lake Champlain, now in the state of Vermont, and extending south as far as Wallingsford in Vermont, and he was during his service as far west as Fort Ann in the state of New York.

The only fight in which he was engaged occurred in the summer of 1778. He was detached on a scout with five other men, including a corporal from Fort Rutland, to range the woods north of Rutland about twenty-five miles to see if we could discover any approach of the enemy, either Tories, British, or Indians. We took our course near the west side of the mountains, desiring to return nearer to the lakeshore. As we were traveling on the second day, we came to the determination to separate and travel as near as practicable about forty rods apart, this for the double purpose of making as small a trail or track as possible and the better to explore that part of the country in which we had reason to apprehend we might meet the enemy.

It fell to my lot to be placed the most westwardly man of our party as we marched northward. In this way of marching, about the middle of the day, I had, as I afterwards found, become separated upward of half a mile from my companions, when I discovered through a thicket of hemlock brush the appearance of a smoke evidently indicating the fact of there being a fire. We were then in a wilderness some fifteen miles beyond our then most frontier garrisons. Immediately on making this discovery, I crept with the utmost caution toward the spot from whence the smoke rose. Presently I saw through the brush two Indians sitting by a smoke that appeared to have been kindled to keep off the mosquitoes. I instantly laid myself flat down, keeping my eye upon the spot to see if there were more than the two. In a few moments I became impressed with the belief that there were but the two. I was not more than eight rods distant from them.

After much hesitation as to what might be most proper, I finally came to the conclusion that my companions were proceeding on and might perhaps soon be surprised, as there might be more Indians within a short distance. I drew my gun, and whilst lying thus flat on the ground, I took deliberate aim at one of the Indians and shot him dead. The other Indian instantly sprung upon his feet, seizing his gun, and started to run. Without reflecting upon the consequence, I immediately run after him, having my gun unloaded. The Indian made but a few leaps after I started before he turned and fired upon me, but his fire missed as I supposed by several feet. He then dropped his gun and came at me with his tomahawk. I encountered him with my empty gun. The first blow which he aimed with his tomahawk I warded off with my gun, and in doing it I was so fortunate as to hook the deadly weapon from him. It fell upon the ground rather behind me. I was then encouraged and sprung to get the tomahawk, in which effort I succeeded. Whilst I was yet bent in picking up the tomahawk, the Indian, who had drawn his knife, gave me a cut, giving me a deep but short wound upon my right leg a little above my knee. He than aimed a second stroke at me with the same weapon. This blow I warded off with my left hand, in doing which I received a wound between the thumb and forefinger. About the same instant, with the tomahawk I hit him a blow on the head which brought him to the ground, and with another blow after he had fallen I made sure he was beyond doing me any further harm.

I immediately secured the guns of the two dead Indians and had the three, including my own, ready charged before my companions, who had heard the fire, came up. The corporal, after seeing what was done, ordered our immediate retreat, which we did toward Rutland Fort, where we arrived the next day sometime in the afternoon, bringing with us the guns of the two dead Indians and their tomahawks and knives. The nature of our expedition was reported to the officer, but as usual we were charged not [to] tell what had happened to the soldiers. And this applicant also by direction of the officers disguised from the soldiers the nature of his wounds and their cause. The person who in that scout acted as corporal I think was of the name of James Woodward. I do not know that him or either of the six beside myself are now living or what has become of them.

I was also present during my service in an [encounter] near a place called in those days Bull's Creek, now called Lewis Creek. Our scout at this time consisted of about fifteen. We met the enemy and fired, but they fled, and no lives were lost on either side. I was never present at any other fighting during my aforesaid enlistment. It now occurs to me that in the scout last mentioned, our march was farther north than Vergennes. I think the place called Bull's Creek was some six miles north of Vergennes. I also remember that one Peleg Eda (who I understand has been many years dead) was the sergeant who had command of the last-mentioned scout.

During my aforesaid enlistment, I was sometimes at Fort Rutland (which was my principal headquarters), sometimes Castleton Fort, sometimes at Fort Edwards, sometimes at Fort Ann. And I was, except during my aforementioned furlough, during each campaign of the three years almost constantly engaged on scout or in spying out the situation and movements of the enemy. I never received any discharge, the reason of which was my being at home on furlough at the end of my service.

JOHN COCK *(b. 1756) was born in Bedford County, Virginia. He served four tours of duty as a private in the militia between 1778 and 1782 guarding the lead mines, accompanying the commissioners treating with the Cherokees, and protecting the frontier. While stationed at Osbourne's Station on Clinch River, he went to the cabin of one John English, a mile from the fort. He was caught outside the cabin without his gun by two Indians and scalped; a hatchet was buried in his skull, and he was left for dead.*

Although Cock's brain injury destroyed the use of one arm, he lived a full, natural life, moving to Kentucky after the war and to Warren County, Tennessee, where he made this deposition in 1834 and was granted a pension.

In the month of May (he does not recollect the day), in the year of 1777, he entered in the service of the United States during the then-existing war. He was enlisted by a recruiting officer called Maj. Thomas Quirk in Montgomery, now Grayson, County, state of Virginia, by whom he was carried to the lead mines in Montgomery County in the state of Virginia. He was there attached to a company commanded by Captain Miles [Miller?], whose given name he does not now remember and of which company Robert Nuckels [?] was lieutenant.

This company, as well as one other commanded by Capt. James Newell, was stationed at the lead mines for the purpose of guarding the same. He does not know whether Newell's company was regular or not. He supposes that the company to which the applicant was attached constituted a part of what was then called Virginia state troops. At this place he remained for eighteen months, during which time he was together with his company marched up New River to Chestnut Creek after a company of Tories. They came upon them at the Round Meadow, fired upon them, and took one prisoner; the balance escaped. Then returned to the lead mines, and in a short time afterwards was marched together with [a] company of militia under the command of Harry Francis over to the Yadkin River, North Carolina, to take or surprise a gang of Tories under the command of a Tory called Capt. Ben Burke. They found them in the neighborhood of the Shallow Ford of the Yadkin, attacked them, and had a skirmish in which Burke was killed and also Captain Francis. The latter was shot through the head. Applicant and his company then returned to the lead mines, and by the consent of Col. John Montgomery, who occasionally visited that place, hired one Edward Hardin to take his place as a substitute, which he did for the sum of $150. Applicant was there at the lead mines, in Montgomery County in the state of Virginia, discharged in writing from the service by Col. John Montgomery. In this tour he served one year and six months. He thinks it was in the month of November, 1778, that he was discharged and thinks that Col. John Montgomery was the only field officer that exercised any authority at the mines. During the time he stayed there, there was not a full regiment, and Montgomery was only occasionally there.

In the month of March, 1781, he was drafted into the service for three months in Montgomery County in the state of Virginia and attached to a company commanded by Capt. John Cocks or Cox. This company was intended for the use and protection of the commissioners appointed by the state of Virginia to treat with the Cherokee Indians and was not called into actual service until the latter part of May, 1781, at which time they were ordered to rendezvous at Jacob Catron's [Cahoon's] mill on the road to the Big Island of Holston River near that place. He does not recollect what county it was in, but it was on Reed Creek, a branch of New River. In the latter part of May, 1781, he found his company and marched immediately to the Big Island of Holston, where they in a few days arrived. There was already there a great many militia, and in a few days many others arrived, making in all about sixteen hundred. He thinks the commissioners was there at the time he reached the island, at all events some of them were. He knows that Col. Evan Shelby was there. He was a relation of applicant's. Col. Joseph Martin, William Preston, and he thinks others were there when, or in a few days after, he reached the island. He remained under the command of Captain Cox for he thinks a little better than two months, when Cox, for some cause or other, with the most of his company were sent home. Applicant immediately took the place of William Holder, who belonged to Capt. John Dollison's [?] company, as a substitute. He remained in this company until his term of service expired, during which time the commissioners consummated the treaty with the Indians. He was then, at the Big Island upon the Holston River, as he now thinks in the latter part of August in the year of 1781, discharged in writing by Col. Evan Shelby, who appeared to be the superior officer over the militia there. He does not think that the companies were formed into regiments. He served in this tour three months. He then returned to his residence in Montgomery County (now Grayson, as he is informed), Virginia.

Shortly after this, sometime in the month of September in the year of 1781, he, being a single man and without a family, went to Osburn's or Osbourne's Station on Clinch River and there volunteered into the service for six months. He does not recollect what county it was in. He found a company stationed there to give protection to the frontier and to keep the Indians in subjection commanded by Robert Trimble, of which one Osbourn, whose given name is not recollected, was lieutenant. There was also another company stationed there at the same time commanded by Capt. Samuel Newell [?].

Here he remained for several months, during which time, in the month of December, John English, who lived in the neighborhood and had come to the station for protection, wished to go to his plantation a mile off and got permission of applicant's captain to go with him, as well as one Oxshir [Oxter?] and English's wife. Applicant accordingly went to English's house with him and stayed all night. Their guns were laid away. In the morning, about sunup, the dogs barked exceedingly fierce. Applicant stepped out into the yard to see what they were baying and got some distance from the door and discovered four Cherokee fellows, all armed. He ran to the door, but the inmates of the house had by this time discovered the Indians and closed it. They were afraid to open the door to let him in for fear the Indians would also enter. Being thus situated and without his gun, applicant had no hope of safety but by flight. He accordingly ran through a field, the only way he could go, the outlet towards the woods being the direction at which the Indians had gone and where they then were. After he had gone some distance, perhaps two hundred yards, he, as he run, turned his head to see if he was pursued, when to his misfortune he beheld two Indians close to him, each running with their guns presented at him. An effort to escape being hopeless, applicant stopped and signed to them that he would surrender.

Each of the merciless savages instantly drew from their belts their tomahawks and stepped up to him. One of them immediately struck him upon his bare head, for he had left his hat in the house, with the point [?] of his tomahawk and sunk it in applicant's skull and gave him a second lick with the edge of the ax which sunk into his head and touched the brain. Applicant fell lifeless, and the Indians no doubt believed him to be so. They immediately scalped him and pulled his hunting shirt off of him and cut one-half of his waistcoat off and took these with them. In a short time, applicant came to his senses. His neck was entirely limber. He had no use of his left arm or shoulder, nor has he ever regained the use of his shoulder or arm. The arm has wasted away. The places where the tomahawk entered his head healed up, but the holes never filled up. They remain yet, and one of them is perhaps two inches long and one wide and about one deep.

Shortly after this occurrence, the information was carried to the station, and a company immediately came to the place and carried him to the station, where he remained for one month longer than his six months, at which place and about the last of March or perhaps the first of April in the year of 1782, he was by his captain, Robert Trimble, discharged in writing. In this tour he served six months. He was detained the other month in consequence of his wounds. He then returned to his residence in Montgomery, now as he understands, Grayson County in the state of Virginia. This ended his military service.

ANSEL GOODMAN *(b. ca. 1752) resided in Bedford County, Virginia, and volunteered in 1777 for service in the Virginia militia. In company with fifty men under Capt. Charles Watkins, he marched to Kentucky. He was stationed at Boonesboro, and with Daniel Boone he was captured by the Indians at Blue Licks on 8 February 1778. Held captive for eight months, he managed to escape to the falls of the Ohio.*

He was living in Russell County, Kentucky, when he submitted this narrative in 1832 and was granted a pension.

That in the state of Virginia, in the county of Bedford, in the year, as well as he can now remember, 1777, he enlisted in the service of the United States under Capt. Charles Watkins and was ordered to Kentucky with the balance of the company for the purpose of assisting the inhabitants in their battles against the British and Indians. That the company was composed of fifty-odd men. That they were promised forty shillings per month, and the period of their enlistment was for six months. That very soon after their enlistment, they were marched to Kentucky by their captain and arrived at Boonesboro on the Kentucky River, in the now state of Kentucky, which was a fort, sometimes called station, at which place we found Col. Daniel Boone and some men and families under his command. We were placed under the command also of Colonel Boone and acted in the capacity of defenders of the fort against the enemy and also as Indian spies.

Some considerable time after being so employed upon constant duty and very short allowance, himself and as well as he can now recollect about thirty others under the command of Colonel Boone were ordered out upon an expedition to make salt for the use of those in the fort. They marched to a place about seventy or eighty miles from the fort, then and now known and called the Blue Licks. After being there about three weeks engaged making salt, Colonel Boone was absent from the company hunting and trapping, when a party of the Shawnees of about one hundred Indians, commanded by their chief, Black Fish, fired several guns at him, as he, Boone, told this applicant, and run him some distance, and he, Boone, discovering he would be taken, stopped, put his gun behind a tree, stepped out, and gave up. The Indians then marched with Colonel Boone to where the balance of us were, and we were ordered by Colonel Boone to stack our guns and surrender. We did so.

We were all taken first to the Indian towns over the Ohio River on the Little Miami. Some of the company were taken to the

British. This applicant and a few others were retained by the Indians, and from the day he was taken up to the time he run off, a period of eight months, he suffered misery and wretchedness, hunger, cruelty, and oppression of almost every sort. The night after he was taken, his arms were tied behind him, a rope of buffalo's leg tied fast around his middle and then made fast to an Indian on each side of him, and the one around his arms was made to go around his neck and tied fast to a tree, and in that position he had to sleep upon the snow. A little while before he reached the Indian town, he was compelled to strip himself, cold as it was, entirely naked, his arms again made fast, and a load of bare meat packed upon him. It was a heavy load. Indeed, he was packed heavily from the time he was taken until he arrived at the town, and just as he got there he was met by many Indians from the town and run the gauntlet with the load of meat and was very severely beaten and bruised in the race. Before they got in sight of the town, he was made to sing as loud as he could holler. The object of that, he afterwards learnt, was to give notice of their approach. After running the gauntlet, he and the other prisoners were ordered to dance like the whites. A Negro, who was prisoner with them, acted as interpreter. Colonel Boone was taken awhile to the British, and they give him a little horse and a saddle, and he returned with the Indians and was taken off with a party, mostly of squaws, to make salt. There he made out to run off and got to Boonesboro safely.

This applicant, having stayed as he before mentioned eight months, he, in company with two others, George Hendricks and Aaron Ferman, run away, and, having learnt from some of the Indians before they started that there was some white men at the falls of Ohio, they made their course that way. Before they arrived there, being pressed with hunger, they were getting some red haws, when a party of Indians came upon them and, after a chase, retook George Hendricks, but his other companion and himself arrived at the falls. He remained there upwards of two months, having engaged as a soldier, and performed duty under Capt. William Harrod. He has no discharge, no written evidence of his services whatever. From the time of his enlistment until he got back to Virginia was one year and nine months.

JAMES THOMPSON *(b. 1744) was born in Chester County, Pennsylvania, and had settled in the rich Buffalo Valley, near present-day Lewisburg, in*

1776. He volunteered in the Pennsylvania militia and served as a private, then captain, for two tours with the main army, 1776 and 1777. He then served two years on the frontier, scouting the area between the upper Delaware and the western branch of the Susquehanna.

Indian attacks having rendered the Buffalo Valley uninhabitable in the latter part of the war, Thompson moved his family down the river to Penn's Creek, below and across from Sunbury. In April 1781, while briefly visiting his abandoned home, he was taken prisoner by the Indians. He and a female captive were taken north, up the western Susquehanna to the site of Williamsport, north along Lycoming Creek, and northeast to Towanda Creek, where he escaped and managed, without food, to make his way back to Fort Swartz, near where Milton now stands.

Thompson spent the rest of his life in Buffalo Township, submitted this deposition in 1832, and received a pension.

. . . In the spring of 1778 we were called out to guard the frontiers against the incursions of the Indians. I marched as captain under Col. John Kelly, who had been promoted, from Buffalo Valley in Northumberland County up the north branch of the Susquehanna as far as Fishing Creek and across the country as far as Loyalsock, Jersey shore, and Williamsport on the west branch. And, as parties of Indians were almost daily making attacks upon the inhabitants, killing some and taking others prisoners, we were almost constantly engaged in skirmishes with the Indians.

Many of the inhabitants had fled to the lower counties of Dauphin and Lancaster, and some families had collected on Penn's Creek. to which place I had removed my family. And I continued in this service at different times, making all together my service as captain two years and two months, occasionally visiting my family until I was taken prisoner by the Indians on the first Monday in April, 1781. The manner in which I was taken is as follows. I resided in Buffalo Valley in Northumberland County. The inhabitants principally had fled, and I had removed my family to Penn's Creek and was returning to my house for the purpose of procuring more necessary articles for the family, when I was taken by four Indians who were secreted in a wood near a path along which I was passing.

They had not taken me far until they also took a young woman of the name of Mary Young a prisoner. They took us up the west branch of the river Susquehanna, and when night came on they struck up a fire, and they tied me by each arm to a grub, and two of the Indians, one at each side of me, lay on the rope. The girl lay between the other two Indians, on the other side of the fire, untied. The next day we traveled up the river a considerable distance, crossed the river in a canoe, and spent the night in the same manner. The next morning we set off and went up Lycoming Creek some distance and spent the night in the same manner. The next day, waded the creek, and when night came on and they were about to tie me as before, I lay on my side so as to get a little more rope to enable me to turn, which I could not do before. During the night, when I found the Indians were all asleep, I got the ropes loose and got up and could have effected my escape but could not bear the idea of leaving the girl with them. I looked round for a tomahawk but found the Indians had taken care to lie on them. I then observed two stones which the Indians had procured in the evening to pound their corn. I took one in each hand and resolved on making an attempt to rescue the girl by dispatching the Indians. I placed myself between the two Indians in the manner I was before, struck one, intending to hit him on the temple, but struck him too high up on the head. He immediately gave the alarm, and the other Indians sprang up, and one drew his tomahawk and made an attempt to strike me, but stopped and spoke to the Indian who was wounded, and then drew it again to strike me, but again stopped, and at length concluded to take me on.

The next day, we crossed Lycoming Creek and continued our march, day after day, until Sunday night, when we encamped on the banks of Towanda Creek, now in Bradford County, Pennsylvania. The Indians sent me out for some wood to make fire. It was getting dark, and I made my escape. I traveled on all night, directing my course by the North Star. Towards morning it commenced raining and continued to rain all day, and, it being cloudy, I could not tell the course I was steering. The succeeding night was also cloudy. The next day, when it cleared up, I found from looking at the sun that I had been traveling entirely out of the course I intended. I changed my course, and after traveling several days without any food except a few grains of corn which I had when I left the Indians and the marrow of a bone which I found in the woods, I arrived at the same place on Lycoming Creek where we had crossed when in company of the Indians.

I then crossed the creek, and, avoiding the Indian paths, I traveled on till I came to the west branch of the river at the same place where we had crossed, where I found two canoes, one drawn out on shore and the other sunk in the river. I tried to push the canoe into the river but was too weak. I then got some round sticks shoved under the canoe so as to raise it off the gravel and with a handspike succeeded in getting it into the river. I found a couple of paddles, and I concluded it would be safest for me to bail out the other canoe and take them both, lest I might be seen by some Indians as I was passing down the river and they might get the canoe and follow me. I got some bark and lashed the two canoes together and got out into the middle of the river and came down some distance, when I came to a tree that had falled into the river which my canoes struck, and one of them sunk. I had then become so weak as not to be able to raise it. I remained in the other canoe but had lost my paddles. They drifted down the river before me. At last my canoe struck the shore, and on looking round, I discovered both my paddles lying near me on the edge of the river. I got them and again set sail down the river.

When I came near to Fort Swartz, which was on the river just above where Milton (in Northumberland County) is now situate[d], I was seen by some persons who were in the fort and came out and brought me to shore and took me into the fort, being nearly exhausted with fatigue and hunger. Captain Daugherty and Captain Ferguson, who were in the fort with their wives, were very kind and attentive to me. This was on Thursday after I left the Indians at Towanda. This terminated my services, having lost the use of my right arm in consequence of being tied so tight as to prevent the circulation of the blood.

JACOB ZIMMERMAN *(c. 1757–1835), a lifelong resident of Oppenheim, Montgomery County, New York, volunteered in the militia and served seventeen tours of duty on the New York frontier between 1776 and 1781. His narrative of service is long and repetitious, and only the last tour is published here.*

While on a five-man scouting party traveling between Fort Zimmerman and Fort Walradt, 9 August 1781, he was wounded and captured. Although carrying a ball in his neck, he was taken by rapid forced marches to Swagotchie, now Ogdenburg, New York, and on to Montreal, where he was sold to a British officer. In spite of the excruciating pain and the privations of captivity, he provides an objective account of his Indian and British captors, free of the bitterness usually present in such narratives.

Zimmerman was returned by way of Boston in 1782. He applied successfully for a pension in 1833.

On the ninth day of August, 1781, he still belonged as a private in the company whereof Christian House was captain, in the regiment whereof Jacob Klock was the colonel. On said day he still resided in the said town of Oppenheim and was in Fort Zimmerman guarding same. He and about five others of said company, to wit, his lieutenant, John Zimmerman, his cousin Jacob Zimmerman, Adam Zimmerman, Peter Hellegas, and himself went from Fort Zimmerman on their way to Fort Walradt. He understood it was done by the order of Col. Marinus Willett, then stationed at Fort Plain in the town of Minden. The orders were that six men more from Fort Walradt were to go on a scouting party to see whether the traces of any Indians could be discovered in the neighborhood. On said ninth day of August, 1781, according to his recollection, they so started to go to Fort Walradt.

After going about a quarter of a mile or so from Fort Zimmerman on their way to Fort Walradt, they were fired upon by a large party of Indians and Tories who were concealed in the brushes, by which fire John Zimmerman, the lieutenant of said House's company, and said Jacob Zimmerman were wounded and killed and scalped by the Indians. Adam and Henry Zimmerman made their escape. He was badly wounded in his neck and throat. The Indians did not discover his wound at first. They took him a prisoner together with Peter Hellegas, and he saw the Indians tomahawk and scalp his said lieutenant and said Jacob Zimmerman.

The ball struck in his neck or throat. After going but a short way with the Indians, they discovered his clothes bloody and then saw his wound. They halted and ordered him to spit, to see, he supposed, whether he spit any blood and was dangerously wounded, and if so, to kill him also. As directed he did spit but not any blood, when they started off again on a hard trot, and he was obliged to keep up with them. In consequence, his wound gave him a great deal of pain. He several times began to feel faint and thought he should fall and be unable to proceed. His clothes were bloody. The Indians halted several times and made him spit, but as he did not spit any blood he was told he must go along. He suffered a great deal on the way. Peter Hellegas, who was taken a prisoner also, would dip up water with his hands on their way to give him to drink, as he could not stoop to drink at the brooks by reason of his neck being swelled and stiff. They traveled about a week through the woods until they got to a place commonly called Swagotchie, where was a British fort. On the way, he lived chiefly on roasted cornmeal with which the Indians mixed water, almost the only food he could swallow. When they came to a stream of water, he was not suffered by the Indians to wet his feet, but they would take him on their backs across the streams. The ball still remained in his neck. His right hand he could hardly raise to his mouth by reason of the swelling of his wound, and he suffered more than he can express. The Indians treated him well enough, as much so as he could expect. Some leaves the Indians found and applied to his wound, which eased his pain some.

When he arrived at the fort at Swagotchie, he saw some Tories he had been acquainted with before the war. They examined him as to the state of affairs at home and whether the people had anything left to eat. He told them that Colonel Willett commanded at Fort Plain and was an active and good officer, that the Indians had destroyed much of their grain, etc., but that those whose property was spared would give to those that wanted, and thus they got along well enough. Major Ross it was said then commanded the fort at Swagotchie. He told some of the Tories he knew he wished the ball to be cut out of his neck. They told him that unless the Indians consented it could not be done. The Indians, however, consented. He was taken to the room occupied by a surgeon. He was placed on a chair with his head held back over the chair by an Indian. The surgeon cut or extracted the ball, and who told him that a few days more he would have died of his wound if the ball had remained.

From Swagotchie he was taken to Montreal, where he saw many of his fellow soldiers or countrymen prisoners of war. Colonel Campbell at Montreal purchased him of the Indians. He saw said Campbell pay the Indians some money on said purchase. A Captain Jones at Montreal he became acquainted with, who was a captain in the British service and who, he thinks, had to see to the prisoners; to said Jones he had told the manner of his being taken a prisoner and his sufferings, etc. The Tories at Montreal wished him to enlist. He refused, telling them in substance he would rather perish on the spot than enlist among them. Captain Jones had previously informed him that the Tories dare not hurt him and he could freely express his mind to them. Captain Jones and his lady were kind to him. He would go often and see Captain Jones and ask him for a little tobacco, and he always got some, but once was refused when his lady told him, "Oh! Do give him some coppers," which the captain did, adding that he did not want to be troubled so much for tobacco and told him to go and buy some with the coppers.

From Montreal he was taken to Quebec, thence to Boston, and from Boston he traveled home on foot, to wit, to the now town of Oppenheim where he resided when he was taken a prisoner and has ever since his return from imprisonment. He returned home from his imprisonment about ten days before Christmas in the year 1782, that is, on the fifteenth or sixteenth day of December, 1782, according to the best of his recollection. He believes he has given correctly the time he was taken a prisoner and when he returned home but has stated same only from the best of his recollections, having no memorandum thereof. He was a prisoner as aforesaid from the time he was taken, as he considers, to the time he returned home, to wit, for one year, four months, and six days. A special law was passed by Congress allowing him a pension on account of his said wound as under which law he has received his pension up to the fourth day of March, 1833. He believes from information that Ogdensburg is now situated on or near the place called in that war Swagotchie or Oswegatchie. On reflection, he thinks that Captain Robenson commanded instead of Ross the fort.

DAVID FREEMOYER *(b. 1761) was born in Albany County, New York, on 28 February. At age seventeen, residing on Cobleskill Creek, he enlisted in the militia for thirteen months and participated in the engagement at Cobleskill, 30 May 1778, retreating with the rest of Captain Patrick's company to Fort Clinton. In the fall of that year he went out as a ranger on Butler's Indian expedition.*

Freemoyer's description of his third term of service is the most important, but the narrative raises certain historical problems that are unlikely ever to be solved. On the evening of 12 September 1779, Sullivan's army encamped at the present site of Conesus, New York, near the southern end of Lake Conesus. At 11 P.M. *on 12 September the commander dispatched Lieutenant Boyd and his party to reconnoiter an Indian town some miles ahead near Canaseraga Creek. Boyd's party crossed the marshy outlet at the bottom of Lake Conesus, as Freemoyer seems to indicate.*

There are dozens of contemporary journals of the Sullivan expedition by men with the main army, but none of the authors accompanied Boyd's party. Their narratives, therefore, describe the "Groveland massacre" of 13 September after the fact, and their accounts both support and challenge Freemoyer's description. On one point all contemporary sources except Freemoyer's agree: that Boyd's party was ordered to reconnoiter the Indian village some four miles west on Canaseraga Creek, and that Boyd and a scout made contact with several Indians there. Tim Murphy, the scout, supposedly killed one Indian. Freemoyer, in his narrative, says that no contact with Indians was made at all. Freemoyer himself apparently did not see any Indians, and it is true that, until ambushed, Boyd's party had found no trace of the large army of Brandt and Butler that lay concealed on the banks west of the Lake Conesus inlet. Leaving camp at night, Boyd and his party came very close to the enemy but failed to spot them. When the scouting party was returning to the main army (on the next day, not the following one, as Freemoyer suggests) they were attacked, and most of the men were killed. Boyd himself and one other man were captured and taken to an Indian town five miles farther on, where they were tortured and killed. It makes perfectly good sense, since the Indians lay between them and Sullivan's army, that Freemoyer, Murphy, and "Captain Yoke" (an Indian, Captain Jehoiakim, is listed as a survivor elsewhere) headed north, around Lake Conesus, to reach safety.

Freemoyer is wrong about Sullivan's route home. The main army did not go as far south as Harrisburg (although he and some companions may have accompanied supply boats down the Susquehanna). They returned east by way of Tioga and present-day Wilkes-Barre, Pennsylvania. He served three tours of duty after this at Middle Fort on the Schoharie River and was involved in several exciting adventures related here.

David Freemoyer remained in Albany County until 1810, when he removed to Washington County, Ohio. He submitted this deposition in 1834.

He entered the service of the United States under the following-named officers and served as herein stated, to wit, that in May 1778 affiant was residing in Albany County, then a frontier county of the state of New York on a creek called Cobleskill, a branch of the Schoharie River, when a party of Indians consisting of Mohawks, Senecas, and Anaquaquas, besides some Tories, principally from the Unandilla and Anaquaqua settlements of Indians on the north branch of the Susquehanna River, having penetrated into the settlement where affiant lived, Capt. Christopher Brown of the militia with his whole company was ordered out, of which applicant was one (he, affiant, having been enrolled on this occasion for the first time). A company of Continental troops was also detailed and sent from Fort Clinton, which was situated on Schoharie River about nine miles from the settlement in which affiant lived, to go against the Indians, which company was commanded by a Captain Patrick. Captain Patrick's company joined affiant's company at the house of George Warner, who resided on Cobleskill, aforesaid, thirty-first [*sic*] day of May of said year 1778.

Just before the junction of the two companies, Indians had been seen running across the fields backwards and forwards, which was done no doubt for the purpose of decoying affiant's company into the woods where the Indians would be lying in ambush for them, as it afterwards proved to be the case, for as soon as Captain Patrick's company arrived, the officers sent out three men as scouts, and when but a very little way in the woods, they were fired on and one of them shot through the body. Nevertheless, being so near to the house, he got in and afterwards recovered. Affiant states that as soon as they heard the guns fired, they all ran in great haste out in pursuit of the enemy, being entirely ignorant of their number, and met the scouts in the edge of the woods returning and a parcel of the enemy in close pursuit. Affiant states that they immediately encountered the fire of the enemy, who kept firing and retreating for at least a mile until they fell back upon their main body, who was commanded by Colonel Brandt. Affiant states that they were in such hot pursuit of the Indians that they were precipitated upon the main body of them before they were aware of it, who were lying in ambush behind a small knoll of some two or three hundred yards in length and about four feet in height. A singular break of nature this, if natural, but being on a level gravelly spot of ground and of such equal height and width, and withal so straight from one end to the other, that affiant thinks it was the work of some ancient race of people long since extinct and at present unknown to the world (if ever), thrown up for defense in some of their wars with hostile foes. This knoll or ridge was covered with timber, but not so large as the timber on the ground surrounding, owing probably to the fact that the knoll was not so rich. There was no ditch on either side, but on the side the Indians lay, the surface of the earth near the knoll seemed to the affiant, when viewing the ground since the battle, to be somewhat lower than on the opposite side. Behind the knoll the Indians had driven stakes into the ground, fastened a stick across the top, on which they had put pieces of blankets and stuck a hat or cap thereon in order to deceive affiant's party. An excellent device, too, as affiant states that many in their zeal to destroy the enemy, and not being able to distinguish well for the smoke occasioned by the firing, were deceived and fired at the supposed bodies of the Indians, while the real Indians were lying or stooped below their imaginary men and firing upon affiant's party.

As soon as Captain Patrick (who was in advance of his men and a brave officer) discovered the situation of the enemy, he directed his men who had fixed bayonets on their muskets to charge upon the enemy, but before his order could be executed, he was shot dead, and one of his lieutenants was killed at the same instant. The death of Captain Patrick and his lieutenant so damped the ardor of the Americans, and the enemy was found to be so much superior in numbers, being about 300 or 350 while that of the Americans was only about 200, Captain Brown ordered a retreat, and they retreated with great precipitation to Fort Clinton before spoken of. The enemy only made prisoner the ensign belonging to Captain Patrick's company, who they kept about two years before he was exchanged, when he returned home and reported that the enemy in this engagement was 350 strong and had lost thirty-six killed. Affiant states that affiant's party lost twenty-one men killed including officers and had nine wounded. That the enemy laid waste the whole settlement on Cobleskill by burning houses, barns, stables, etc., and shooting such horses as they could not conveniently catch to take away with them.

That he remained voluntarily in the service of the United States until in September or October (he thinks) of said year, when he was sent from Fort Clinton in a company of rangers, about thirty-two in number, and placed under command of a Capt. John Ditz and, attached to a regiment commanded by Colonel Butler, sent on an expedition against the towns of the Unandilla and Anaquaqua Indians. That the Indians had left their towns when Colonel Butler arrived, leaving only two very old squaws who affiant's party left in a hut together with some provision to sustain them until they might be taken away or be provided for by the tribe to which they belonged. Colonel Butler burnt all their buildings, save the one just spoken of, and destroyed their orchard and a large quantity of corn, after which they returned to Fort Clinton again, where affiant remained in the service stationed in Fort Clinton until the latter end of June, 1779, under Captain Brown, aforesaid, Lieutenant Boist, and Ens. Nicholas Warner. That the fort was commanded by Col. Peter Vrooman. Affiant was employed in guarding the fort, aforesaid, which contained . . . women and children who had taken refuge there from the savage ferocity of the enemy [as well] as soldiers for the protection of the fort and the inhabitants generally. Affiant, being at that time amazingly fleet and a good marksman as well as woodsman for one of his years, was frequently while in service sent out as a spy or scout to range the country round about, which he performed faithfully, sometimes skirmishing with small parties of Indians, the relation of which would swell this narrative to too great a length to admit insertion. That affiant was discharged about the last of June, 1779, after having served one year and about one month, but whether he received a discharge or not he does not now recollect. Affiant, in this thirteen-month service, knew, in addition to the officers already named, Colonel Ziele, Captain Hager, and Lts. John Lawyer, John Baker, and Ditts or Ditz. The five last named were militia officers, as affiant believes. The names or number of any Continental or militia regiment with which he served he does not now recollect, but believes the regiment commanded by Colonel Butler was called the Fourth Pennsylvania Regiment.

That an expedition being meditated against the Six Nations of Indians, affiant volunteered for that campaign immediately after his discharge in the latter part of June, 1779, aforesaid, and was sent under a Captain or Major Parr of the Continental troops, who commanded a company of rangers, and was marched from Fort Clinton, aforesaid, and joined Colonel Butler's regiment at what was then called the Middle Fort on Schoharie River and marched by way of Cobleskill Creek, thence through Cherry Valley to Otsego Lake, at which place they were joined by General Clinton with a large body of the American army. Finding the water too low to float their boats down to Tioga Point, General Clinton ordered a dam erected across the mouth of the lake, which caused the water soon to raise to the height of the dam, and, having everything in readiness, they opened a passage through the dam for the water to flow, which raised the river so as to enable them to embark and float down to Tioga Point, at which place in a few days they were joined by General Sullivan, the commander-in-chief of the expedition. The two divisions then united and marched up what was called the Cayuga or western branch of the Susquehanna River, which led them immediately into the Indian country. That, after having routed a few small bodies of the enemy while on their march, they found the main body of the enemy collected near Newtown, well fortified, composed of Indians and Tories, who they defeated and routed after a somewhat obstinate resistance on the part of the enemy, who escaped across the Cayuga River and made for the lake of that name.

That General Sullivan with his army pursued the enemy to the Cayuga [Conesus] Lake, where General Sullivan detached a

Lieutenant Boyd with this affiant and some eighteen or twenty men, including two friendly Indians who went as pilots, and sent them in the night across the river at its outlet from the lake to ascertain if the enemy were not lying in ambush in a large cedar swamp on the opposite side for the purpose of attacking General Sullivan's army as they crossed the river. Their orders were to cross over (which they did on rafts made of cedar poles tied together with leatherwood bark) and examine the banks along. If the enemy were not discovered, they were then to penetrate the swamp and go through, which was not more than from one-quarter to a half mile wide, and to go to a certain high knob which was a quarter of a mile or more beyond the swamp, upon which knob the detachment was to lie concealed on the next day and watch the movements of the enemy in case any were there, and the succeeding night they were to return to General Sullivan's camp.

Affiant states that they crossed as aforesaid in the night, examined the banks, made no discoveries of the enemy, passed through the swamp also without making any, and passed on to the high knob before spoken of, where they remained until the next morning, all the next day, and the next night (as Lieutenant Boyd refused to return the second night as he was ordered to do) until the second morning after they had crossed the river, when the unfortunate Boyd determined to return to Sullivan, declaring that there were no Indians there, as they had had scouts out all the day before, who had not been able to make any discoveries of them. True, scouts had been out, but the enemy had not left the swamp, into which the scouts did not penetrate, and of course they had made no discoveries. Against this rash proposition of the lieutenant, affiant declares every man he believes remonstrated, urging upon him the danger of returning by day in case any of the enemy should be lying in wait, because if they had left a force sufficient to annoy General Sullivan in crossing the river, it must be a large party and of course much superior to the lieutenant's detachment, and in that event, being between them and our crossing, we must certainly be destroyed. But all in vain.

The ill-fated lieutenant declared that there were no Indians there, and having determined to return that morning, no entreaty availed to shake him from his purpose. So about eight o'clock the lieutenant started with the detachment to the swamp, where they commenced marching by a single file, this affiant and one Timothy Murphy in front, Lieutenant Boyd in the rear. When they had passed [the] greater part of the swamp along a path leading through, the enemy, lying in ambush for affiant's party (having discovered their trail no doubt the day before and expecting their return), commenced firing upon their rear and instantaneously thereafter fired all along the two lines they had formed on each side of the path extending beyond affiant and Murphy, at the same time closing the extremes of the two lines, whereby the whole detachment were entirely surrounded and hemmed in by the enemy.

Affiant and Murphy, upon the first fire of the enemy in front, dropped and lay flat on the ground to avoid the effects of their fire and so continued to lay until the firing had nearly ceased, when they sprang to their feet, and fortunately for affiant and Murphy the morning was foggy, and amidst the fog and smoke occasioned by the firing of the enemy in front, affiant and Murphy were enabled to escape through the line of the enemy unhurt, running against and knocking over several Indians as they broke through their lines. Affiant and Murphy kept together and, holding a consultation as they can, agreed to run around the lake, although a distance of about ninety-two miles, to reach General Sullivan again, as Murphy declared (which affiant knew well to be true) that it was out of the question to attempt an escape by recrossing the river again, as the enemy would certainly be upon them before they could leave the shore.

Affiant and Murphy ran about four or five miles, when they were overtaken by five large dogs the Indians had set after them. Three of these dogs were very severe and would take hold in an instant. The other two would not bite but would follow after and bay them. Two of these dogs ran up to Murphy and seized and lacerated him much before he could kill them, which he succeeded in doing with his tomahawk. While Murphy was engaged with the two dogs, affiant was engaged with the third dog, who had seized affiant just at the time the others had seized Murphy. But affiant was not so well prepared by far for the fight as his companion was, although affiant had but one to contend with while his companion had two, for affiant had lost his tomahawk at the time he fell down to avoid the fire of the Indians in the swamp, and he and Murphy thought it most prudent and had agreed, when they discovered the dogs coming after them, not to shoot the dogs for fear some of the Indians, who they were certain were near them, might come upon them while their guns were empty. And, excepting his rifle, affiant had no weapon to defend himself with other than a very thin case knife ground sharp at the point, affiant having sometime before lost his butcher knife.

The dog first seized affiant by the fleshy part of the thigh, in front and near his crotch. Affiant struck at him with his knife and occasionally with his fist but did not hurt the dog materially. He eventually succeeded in disengaging the dog's hold of his thigh, however not until he had torn it considerably. The dog next seized affiant by the side of the leg and sunk one of his tusks deep into his leg just by the side of the bone. After loosing the dog's hold of the leg, he seized affiant by the throat and held on until from loss of wind occasioned by affiant's choking him severely, he was compelled to let go, when he dropped to the ground on his forefeet and stood close by affiant an instant, gaping for breath. In this situation, affiant made an underhanded thrust at the dog's flank, which struck low and penetrated into the intestines, when affiant making a considerable effort (considering his exhausted state) and ripped the dog open across to the backbone and let out his entrails. Notwithstanding this, the dog made another spring at affiant's neck, but from exhaustion and the wound just given him, only sprang high enough to reach affiant's breast, upon which he inflicted a wound of some three or four inches in length, when he fell down and died.

Just at this instant, Murphy, having finished the two that had attacked him, came to affiant's assistance. Glad would affiant have been, after he was in contact with the dog, to have been able to shoot him. The consequence of the enemy coming upon him and he with an empty gun he would willingly have risked; but then it was too late. He could not disengage himself from the dog, and his knife was so weak in the blade that he was afraid to make a heavy plunge for fear it would break, and sorely indeed did he repent not shooting the dog while it had been in his power.

Immediately after the conclusion of the fight, Murphy discovered standing at a small distance and pointed out to affiant Captain Yoke, a friendly Indian of the Stockbridge tribe who had went out as one of the pilots on this excursion. Simultaneously with discovering Captain Yoke, affiant and Murphy discovered about forty naked Indians within fifty yards of them, all with tomahawks in their hands, affiant thinks not a rifle amongst them, having left them to make the better speed, no doubt expecting to find affiant and those they pursued with no guns, or empty, if any, when they would be able, with the assistance of their dogs, to deprive us of, or take our scalps. Here, had affiant and Murphy not been wounded, and fresh as when the race commenced, the Indians would have paid dearly for their temerity in leaving their guns behind, but, situated as affiant and Murphy were, wounded much by the dogs they had killed, already much fatigued by running and their fight with the dogs, and having a great way to travel before they could reach camp, and withal two dogs and about forty Indians close at their heels, prudence forbid any other course for them to pursue but to seek safety in flight and reach the army they had left with all possible speed. Affiant and Murphy, therefore, instantly on discovering the Indians so close, put off at the top of their speed and ran on, followed by the dogs and Indians, about fifteen miles as affiant supposes from where they had had the encounter with the dogs, when affiant and Murphy, believing the Indians to be some distance behind, had leisure and shot the remaining two dogs. To this place affiant thinks the enemy pursued him and his companion and gave up further pursuit.

Affiant and Murphy went on until in the night sometime, when, being much fatigued, they stepped out of the path to one side to rest and to observe if any of the enemy passed. After sitting and resting some time, they discovered Captain Yoke passing along, who they had not seen before, since the time they started when the Indians were so close upon them. They, knowing it to be Yoke, hailed him, and from that time went on in company, all three together, to where they had left General Sullivan encamped, which they reached the next morning about eight o'clock. When they arrived, General Sullivan had with his whole army crossed the river, whereupon affiant, Murphy, and their Indian ally constructed a log raft, immediately crossed the river, and overtook the army just as they were engaged in collecting for burial the bodies of the scouts killed the previous morning and putting together the body of Lieutenant Boyd, which the enemy had severed in five pieces—the head cut off, the body then split in twain, and then each half cut into again. Here affiant and Murphy had their wounds dressed for the first time after their infliction, except the wound on the side of affiant's leg, which gave affiant so much pain in traveling the day before that he was compelled to do something if possible to relieve it, which he done by killing a striped squirrel and putting the brains of the squirrel on the wound and fastening them on with the skin thereof. Affiant's wounds were so bad and disabled him so much, that he was placed on a packhorse and rode for six days.

In due time, General Sullivan reached the Indian settlements on the Genesee River, but, finding no enemy to contend with, he destroyed all their buildings, orchards, gardens, and their immense crops of corn, after which General Sullivan returned by the same route again to the Susquehanna River, thence down the same to Harrisburg, Pennsylvania, thence to Easton, Pennsylvania, where affiant and such of the rangers as were yet living were discharged and ordered to return to Fort Clinton again, where they arrived about the last of October, 1779, making in all which he served this tour four months. Affiant did not receive any written discharge for this tour that he remembers of. A letter was sent by them to Colonel Vrooman, who was in command at Fort Clinton, stating the particulars of the expedition and that the rangers (of which affiant was one) had acquitted themselves well, etc. In this campaign, affiant knew Generals Sullivan, Clinton, and Maxwell, Colonel Butler, Major Parr, Lieutenant Boyd, and many other officers whose names he has now forgotten.

That about the first of May, 1780, affiant still residing in Albany County, New York, enlisted under Captain Cannon or Kennon for the term of one year and was attached to a regiment commanded by the said Col. Peter Vrooman and stationed at the Middle Fort on the Schoharie River. That affiant was appointed and served as orderly sergeant of the company to which he was attached during the whole term of his enlistment. That he served during the season of 1780, until the expiration of his tour in May 1781, mostly as a ranger, generally having command of scouting parties sent out to scour the country for the protection of the fort and safety of the settlement.

That, sometime in the fall of the year 1780, a large body of British, Indians, and Tories from Niagara, under command of Sir John Johnson, penetrated the country, meditating an attack on the Middle Fort, it being the strongest and of most consequence to the enemy to possess. The enemy marched by the Upper Fort without molesting it, which they could easily have taken, as that fort was weak, being only a picket fort with two small pieces of artillery. As soon as the enemy passed the fort, the garrison perceiving it to be the object of the enemy to take either the Middle or Lower Fort by surprise, they fired off one of their pieces of artillery to alarm the Middle Fort, which was only about four miles off. This gun they heard very plainly at the Middle Fort, and immediately Colonel Vrooman sent out a detachment of about one hundred riflemen, of whom affiant was one, under command of

Captain Woolsey of the Continental or state troops, but who just happened there by accident (as affiant believes), he not belonging to the fort. This detachment were to go with all possible speed to the Upper Fort to ascertain the cause of the alarm and then act as circumstances might require.

As they were proceeding along in haste by a route not usually traveled, affiant voluntarily took the place of one Jacob Franks who was placed as a flank guard on the left of the company. Franks was a messmate and particular friend of affiant's, and affiant, knowing him to be unwell, took his place on the left as aforesaid. While they were passing through a large pasture in which the cattle and horses belonging to the fort were usually pastured (this pasture was very large and considerably grown up with willows and other bushes growing about in bunches), affiant, proceeding expeditiously and cautiously along, discovered in front of him five or six Indians running very closely together in the same direction affiant was moving. Affiant took deliberate aim and fired at the bunch, for they were running as before stated in very close order, and affiant noticed immediately after that his shot produced considerable confusion among the squad. Affiant does not therefore doubt that he killed one of them, as it was the only gun fired at the enemy there, and an Indian was found a few days afterward lying dead with a rifle and knapsack at a spring near where affiant fired. As soon as affiant fired (as was his duty), he ran in and joined his company. By this time the enemy made their appearance in sight, and so numerous were they that Captain Woolsey ordered a retreat to the fort, which was effected without any loss, although the enemy closely pursued, firing many shots at them, but fortunately none took effect. The enemy then invested the fort and threw three bombs at it, one of them only falling into it, which, however, done no particular injury. Sir John Johnson then sent two men with a flag of truce, it was supposed to summon the fort to surrender, and, contrary to the order of Colonel Vrooman (whose valor the men in the fort placed but little reliance upon), the man bearing the flag was shot when about 140 yards of the fort by Timothy Murphy, the same person with whom affiant had suffered so much in the unfortunate expedition under Lieutenant Boyd. The other person ran back without attempting to proceed further with the flag.

The enemy succeeded only in killing one man in the fort. This was a Samuel Runnels, or Reynolds, who went on top of one of the buildings in the fort and there foolishly and indecently exposed his hind parts to the enemy in contempt of them and there remained, contrary to the admonition of those in the fort, until one of the enemy under cover of some sprouts put up from bushes and saplings that had been previously cut off crept near enough to shoot and fired at him, the ball just breaking the skin across above one of his eyebrows. This stunned Reynolds, and he fell off the house on the pavement or some stone below on his head and broke his neck.

It was afterwards said that Sir John Johnson, having discovered Reynolds's contempt of them with a spyglass, gave a guinea, half johannes, or some gold coin to an expert marksman to shoot Reynolds, which was accomplished in the manner before related. But for the truth of this story affiant cannot vouch. Colonel Vrooman then commenced firing at the enemy, who were some four or five hundred yards off, with some small brass cannon, when the enemy marched off, not, however, without getting a good warming before they left the neighborhood. Seeing the route they took and knowing that the enemy had to head a long and deep ravine after leaving the fort, the road passing very near the same place back again after heading the ravine, Captain Woolsey, aforesaid, with about one hundred riflemen, including affiant, was dispatched to a certain place from which the enemy could be much annoyed without endangering Captain Woolsey's men. This was an elevated spot of ground on which had been erected a blockhouse (but at this time not in use) which commanded the road on the opposite side of the deep ravine, by which road the enemy must of necessity pass and where it would be impossible for them to cross the ravine to drive Captain Woolsey from his position and impracticable to return by the road, being one and a one-fourth miles. This place Captain Woolsey and his men reached in time, from which they fired three rounds at the enemy, when they retreated to the fort again, as the enemy instantly started a large detachment back by the way of the road to dislodge them, which detachment Captain Woolsey did not think it prudent to wait for. They followed Captain Woolsey to the fort, but, on firing a cannon shot at them, they again retired. In this engagement across the ravine, affiant believes they killed many of the enemy, as on viewing the ground soon afterwards, he seen much blood in and about the road and a very large fresh-dug grave nearby, where they had buried their dead. But what number they killed, affiant did not know, as they did not open the grave.

Previous to the enemy's attack on the Middle Fort, they set fire to and burned a mill on the Schoharie River which ran six pair of stone, owned by John Baker. This mill the enemy had made frequent attempts to burn before but did not succeed until the present time. After this the enemy passed down the Schoharie and then up the Mohawk River, laying waste and destroying everything before them, and returned to Niagara again. When affiant completed his one year's service as orderly sergeant, he was regularly discharged, but who signed it, affiant does not recollect, but remembers that about 1790 he had some pieces of it, the same having worn out where folded, but what became of them, he does not now recollect. In the course of this last year's service, affiant knew in addition to the officers already named, Colonel Ziele, Captains Hager, John Ziele, and David Baker, and Lieutenant Ditts or Ditz, besides others at present not recollected.

That in the year 1781, affiant, still residing in Albany County in the state of New York, in the month of May volunteered under Colonel Vrooman for a term of eight months and served as orderly sergeant in a company commanded by Capt. Christopher Brown and was stationed at the Middle Fort on the Schoharie River. That he served principally as a ranger, having generally when out (as in the last year) command of a parcel of scouts.

That sometime in the year 1781 (affiant thinks it was), the time affiant cannot now recollect, affiant was in an engagement under Colonel Willett with the enemy under command of Colonel Brandt, who had taken a number of whites prisoner on Tripes Hill, a place not far from the Mohawk River, and Colonel Willett with about four hundred men had been sent in pursuit of Brandt, who he surprised and defeated at the place called Turloch, or Turlach, on a water emptying into the Mohawk River, killing many of the enemy, number not now known. But before Colonel Willett succeeded in recapturing the prisoners, the enemy had put them to death. In this engagement affiant received a slight wound on the left side, just above the hip, by a rifle ball.

That sometime in October of said year 1781, the country was penetrated by a large body of British, Indians, and Tories commanded (affiant thinks) by a Major Ross; that they commenced hostilities on the Mohawk River, whence an express was immediately sent from Colonel Willett, the commander of Fort Plain on the Mohawk River, to Colonel Vrooman, who had in command the three forts on the Schoharie River, for assistance. That detachments were detailed and sent from each of the forts on the Schoharie and rendezvoused at the Middle Fort and were

Brandt

marched (affiant being one of the number) under Capt. John Titts, Ditts, or Ditz to Fort Plain, where they joined Colonel Willett, who marched on in quest of the enemy and came in contact with them at a place known by the name of Johnstown. Affiant states that, when they discovered the enemy, they were engaged in killing and destroying cattle. That a sharp skirmish ensued, which continued a considerable time. Colonel Willett gained a partial victory over the enemy, and, night coming on, they retreated and marched up to the top of a very high ridge and encamped.

That Colonel Willett encamped at Johnstown and early on the following morning marched in pursuit of the enemy, when, after pursuing them affiant thinks about twelve miles, they overtook them, with whom they had a considerable skirmish in which several of the enemy were killed and wounded. Some of Colonel Willett's men were also wounded, but none killed. The enemy retreated, and Colonel Willett ordered Captain Titts, or Ditts, with his company of riflemen, to which affiant was attached on this excursion, together with fifty or sixty friendly Indians of the Oneida tribe commanded by Colonel Looey, an Indian officer of the same tribe, to pursue the enemy at least to Canada Creek, with the expectation of being able to annoy them in crossing said creek, which they did and overtook part of the enemy while they were making their way over the creek, the crossing of which was attended with some difficulty, as the water was at that time rather deep to ford.

That affiant's party fired on the enemy several times and killed a number of them, the amount affiant cannot now recollect, if he never knew, but amongst the slain affiant thinks there was a Major Butler, who had taken an active part in the British service against the frontiers of New York and who had signalized himself for his savage barbarity. That affiant was then marched back to Fort Plain and thence to the Middle Fort again. That, after having been at the Middle Fort affiant thinks but a few days, a party of the enemy near two hundred strong were discovered near the Upper Fort who had killed several families. That affiant with about thirty rangers and ten or twelve militia were sent from the Middle Fort to the Upper Fort, at which place affiant with the rangers, aforesaid, were attached to Captain Woolsey's company of riflemen, and with a company of militia commanded by Capt. Jacob Hager marched under command of Major Woolsey in pursuit of the enemy and overtook them at a place known at that time by the name of Harpersfield, at the head of the Delaware River, where they had an engagement with the enemy, of whom they killed and wounded several, the number not now recollected. That, of affiant's party, only two were killed and seven wounded as well as affiant recollects. That affiant was marched to the Middle Fort again, where he was discharged sometime in January 1782, after having served his term of eight months as orderly sergeant, the time for which he volunteered. Whether affiant received any written discharge from the service for this last tour, he does not now recollect. That affiant knew in this last campaign Majors Woolsey, Van Alstine, and Tygart, and Captains Woolsey, Cox, and Lieutenant Loop, Colonel Willett, Colonel Peterey (or Peteree), Major Fader, Captain Peteree, and a lieutenant of the same name, besides others whose names affiant has now forgotten.

That sometime in May 1782 affiant, still continuing to reside in Albany County, New York, enlisted under Captain Stenbrough or a captain of some such name for a term of nine months. That affiant, with twenty-seven others constituting a part of a rifle company, was attached to a part of a company of state or Continental troops commanded by Captain Harrison and was again stationed at the Middle Fort on the Schoharie River under command of Colonel Peter Vrooman, at which fort were also stationed two companies of militia commanded by Capts. David Baker and John Ceiley.

That affiant was appointed and served as orderly sergeant of the company to which he was attached during the nine-months tour. That affiant served principally as a ranger, having frequently command (as theretofore) of scouting parties. That sometime (affiant thinks) in July of the same year, Indians were frequently discovered by the scouting parties, which induced affiant and others to believe that a body of Indians were encamped in some place not far distant. That some of the scouts from Fort Clinton ascertained that this party of Indians were in camp on the top of a ridge near Cobleskill Creek and immediately informed Colonel Vrooman of the fact, whereupon Colonel Vrooman ordered affiant to select a few of the best men in the fort and go by night and ascertain if possible the strength of the enemy. That in obedience to this command affiant chose Abraham Baker, Henry Hager, William Mackindice, and Adam Folk, men in whose bravery and skill in Indian warfare affiant thought he could confide.

That affiant with his party set out on this expedition directly after dark, having about ten miles to travel in order to reach the camp of the enemy, being directed by Colonel Vrooman to return the same night if possible. After having traveled some two or three miles, affiant and his party missed their way by reason of the darkness of the night and were obliged to lay by till the next morning, when they resumed their march and reached the place at which the enemy were encamped about nine o'clock. Affiant and his party came within a few steps of the camp of the Indians before they discovered any sign, in consequence of a rise of ground. That before their campfires there was a great parcel of meat stuck round about on spears or sticks roasting and not an Indian there. They had gone down the hill some distance to an old waste field to gather (as affiant supposes) rasp and black berries. On discovering the enemy's camp, affiant's "chosen few" immediately deserted him and fled to a man.

Affiant, feeling himself bound to comply with the orders received from his colonel, or at all events not to return until he had made some further effort to discover the strength of the enemy, went off some small distance from the encampment and lay concealed in some brush near a place where he supposed the Indians would pass in returning to their camp by the way of an old trail. After being there a little while, affiant heard some noise in the leaves and looked behind, or rather to one side, and discovered an Indian alone approaching very near affiant and making towards the camp but coming from a different quarter from which affiant expected and entirely to one side of the trail. He came very near before affiant discovered him. Affiant being but poorly concealed, and knowing from the direction of the camp for which the Indian was evidently making that he would certainly pass within a few feet of affiant and that it would be impossible for him to remain undiscovered to the Indian, affiant therefore instantly determined to shoot him, as the best and perhaps only means of escape, although danger and great hazard to his life attended him either way, as the main body of the Indians must in all probability be very near, as (before stated) they had left their meat roasting before their fires, to which they would of course soon return. Affiant rose from his squatting position to his feet unperceived by the Indian. As the Indian was coming up a little rise within eighteen or twenty feet of affiant, about half the length of his body being exposed to affiant, affiant shot him through the breast. The Indian fell and was dead in an instant.

Affiant, seeing that the Indian had a beautiful English fusee such as (from information affiant received) the English were in the habit of presenting to the chief warriors and captains of their savage allies to stimulate them to greater action in their murderous and predatory incursions upon the whites, determined to make himself master of that. From the circumstance of his having this gun and of his having so many silver ornaments about him, affiant is confident he was an Indian chief and probably the commander of the party. One of the principal silver ornaments affiant also took a fancy to, being a large one that bound his hair growing immediately on the crown of his head. Being cylindrical and so fastened that it was not easily disengaged from the hair, affiant with his knife severed it from the Indian's head, hair and all, together with a little of the skin, which was accidental, affiant being in great haste.

Affiant put off at full speed in the direction to the fort, and when he had run about three hundred yards or more, he heard the Indians setting their dogs on his trail. That he ran on until the first crossing of a small stream on his route that empties into Cobleskill, after crossing which he heard the dogs at some distance back coming on his trail. When he came to the second crossing of said stream, he ran up some distance in the stream to prevent them following him further. After he left the stream, he ran up a bottom about two miles, when he took to a ridge. At this time he heard the dogs again and, supposing them to be on his trail (it somewhat alarmed him, recollecting well his former scrape with the dogs), but which affiant afterwards learned was the trail of his deserting companions, the dogs at the second crossing, aforesaid, taking theirs, and at this place, affiant passing near thereto and hearing the dogs, was deceived. And the better to enable affiant to escape the Indians and dogs, affiant pulled off his clothes, except pantaloons and moccasins, and threw them behind a log and then ran on until he reached the fort, where he arrived safely and some time before his comrades arrived, who reported affiant dead, as they were within hearing of affiant's fire at the Indian, aforesaid, and supposed that it was affiant that was shot at. It was purposely kept secret from them that affiant had reached the fort for the purpose of seeing what tale they would tell, and, on being asked what had become of their leader, [they] replied that "the damned fool was dead," that they had discovered the enemy's camp, etc., and that Freemoyer would not leave there with them, and before they were out of hearing, they heard the report of a rifle, and they were certain he was dead. After they had finished their tale and at the expense of affiant, as they supposed, affiant left his concealment, much to their astonishment and chagrin.

The place where affiant killed the Indian was afterwards always called and known while affiant lived in that country by the name of Freemoyer's Battleground. Affiant served nine months as orderly sergeant, the time for which he enlisted, and received a discharge from Col. Peter Vrooman, which he has long since lost; he neglecting to take care of it as well as all other discharges he received in the service, as he considered them of no value to him whatever. That this last tour completed affiant's service in the Revolutionary struggle. . . .

SAMUEL RIGGS *(b. 1760) was born in Morris County, New Jersey, moved to Surry County, North Carolina, in 1765, to Powell's Valley, Tennessee, in 1777, and, because of Indian attacks, back to North Carolina, where he volunteered in 1778 for frontier service.*

It is Riggs's narrative of the Sevier expedition in the winter of 1780–81, one of the few existing accounts of a southern campaign, that makes his story historically important. Expeditions of this sort rarely resulted, and were only partially intended to result, in heavy Indian casualties. They were, in fact, precursors of Sherman's scorched-earth policy. They were aimed at supplies and towns, intended to destroy both the means and the will to fight. The expeditions' effectiveness in preventing frontier attacks could be debated, but their success in destructiveness was unquestionable.

Samuel Riggs returned to Tennessee after the war and successfully applied for a pension in 1833.

Shortly after his removing to the north fork of Holston, declarant volunteered under Capt. Isaac Shelby in the summer of 1778, in the month of July, day not recollected, for the purpose of protecting the frontiers against the Indian incursions and of garrisoning a fort on Beaver Creek. There were about thirty men under Capt. Isaac Shelby, lieutenant and ensign not recollected. The company were for the greater part of the time engaged in keeping the fort. This fort was capable of containing five hundred people. Repeated attacks were made by the Indians upon the settlements and the people compelled to take shelter in the fort until the company had driven off the Indians, and the people thus cultivated their land under the protection of Captain Shelby's company. Captain Shelby's company were constantly in service in doing the duty of sentries or in scouting parties and in all such service as was necessary for the protection of the families of that frontier settlement. While declarant was in service under Captain Shelby at this fort, General Chrystie, in the fall of 1778, in October, day not recollected, came by the fort with his troops on his expedition against the Cherokee Indians, and, it being thought that the people would not need the protection of Capt. Isaac Shelby's company during this invasion of the Cherokee country, Captain Shelby went on with General Chrystie. The declarant was anxious to go on this expedition, but his health being then bad, he was not permitted to do so. The declarant's father received a written discharge from Capt. Isaac Shelby for declarant's service, setting forth that the declarant had served a tour of three months under him in garrisoning the fort on Beaver Creek. Whether his father ever received anything for declarant's services or not, declarant does not know. Declarant did not receive anything, nor does he know what has become of the discharge obtained by his father.

In the month of December, 1778, day not recollected, declarant volunteered under Capt. Isaac Bletcher, Maj. Anthony Bletcher commandant. Lt. George Hart was the lieutenant of the company, other officers not recollected. Captain Bletcher's was one of three companies raised for the purpose of garrisoning a large fort on the north side of the Holston River, opposite to the Long Island. This fort was on the remotest part of those frontiers. These three companies under Major Bletcher were constantly engaged on duty in keeping the fort or in scouting parties protecting the settlers and ascertaining the approaches of the Indians. This garrison was regularly detailed for guard duty and for the duty of scouts and was regularly paraded night and morning and were every Sabbath day taught the manual exercise. In the month of April, 1779, day not recollected, this declarant was discharged after a service of four months by Captain Bletcher on the application of declarant's father, who was then about to move back to North Carolina. Whether declarant's father received anything for his services or not, declarant does not know. Declarant himself received nothing. Declarant moved back to Surry County, North Carolina, with his father and there remained until the fall of 1780, when he again moved with his father to Greene County, North Carolina, now East Tennessee.

Early in the month of December, 1780, declarant volunteered under Capt. William Pruett (John Howard lieutenant, no ensign) to go under Col. John Sevier against the Cherokee Indians. We were mounted riflemen. Colonel Sevier commanded the men from Washington and Greene counties. Major Tipton, Captain Hawkins, and Capt. Landon Carter were officers under Colonel

Sevier. There were four companies under Colonel Sevier, about two hundred men. The company of Captain Pruett started after Colonel Sevier had started. The first night we encamped on Lick Creek; the second night we overtook Colonel Sevier on Long Creek in what is now Jefferson County; the third day we started two hours before day and crossed French Broad River at Buckingham's Island and encamped on the other side of the river. The fourth day we marched for Chota Town. We started early in the morning, and after marching two miles we came to where the Indians had encamped the night before on their way to attack the whites.

The Indians had fallen back to waylay us. Our spies, having gone on and met the advanced spies of the Indians, made us acquainted with their situation. They had fallen back about two hundred yards from where they had encamped. Colonel Sevier was leading one division and Major Tipton the other. Suddenly a gun was fired about fifty yards off from the midst of a field of tall grass before us at Colonel Sevier. Maj. Jesse Walton, a volunteer, being next to Colonel Sevier, jumped from his horse and fired at the Indian who had discharged his gun at Colonel Sevier and broke the Indian's leg. The Indians immediately jumped up and fired. Our men jumped from their horses at the fire of the first gun (except Colonel Sevier) and commenced firing and immediately drove the Indians, completely routing them. We killed sixteen of them. None of our men were killed; one of our men was slightly wounded in the hand, and one of our horses was killed, and one of our men was injured by being thrown from his horse. We pursued them to a canebreak in which they took refuge, and we were ordered to halt. We got a good many guns and knapsacks which were thrown down by the Indians. The same day we returned to Buckingham's Island and there remained encamped for eight days, waiting for reinforcements from Virginia. A considerable body of men, about five hundred, came on, commanded by Col. Archibald Campbell. Other Virginia officers are not recollected. Colonel Campbell took the command of the united forces, and the whole body, the day after the junction, marched towards the Cherokee Towns. After leaving Buckingham's Island, we crossed Little River and arrived the second night at an Indian town on the Tennessee River. Here we found provisions, deer skins, horses, cattle, and a swivel. After burning this town, we marched up the river on to Chota, several miles above the mouth of Tellico River. We remained some time in Chota, finding here corn that had been concealed. An Indian was killed at this town. After burning Chota, we marched back down the Tennessee River to the mouth of Tellico River to Tellico Towns. Here we remained for some time, when the army divided. The larger part, of which declarant was one, marched under Colonels Campbell and Sevier to the Hiwassee Old Town, the remainder being left at the Tellico Towns. We arrived at the Hiwassee Old Town the second day, burnt it, and immediately returned to Tellico, where we again remained for several days.

At our entrance into Tellico Towns, Captain Elliott of Virginia was killed by an Indian. There were some Indians getting corn in Tellico on our arrival. Captain Elliott was in front. One of his men had wounded an Indian. The Indian having fallen, Captain Elliott rode up to him, and as he approached the Indian rose and shot him dead through the head. Elliott fell so near to the Indian that the Indian got Elliott's gun and fired it at one of the men before he was killed, which was immediately done. We found several Negroes in the town.

After burning Tellico, we marched back together until we came to Long Creek in what is now Jefferson County, where we separated, Colonel Sevier returning with his men through Greene County, and Colonel Campbell to Virginia through Hawkins County. The men who were engaged in this tour were informed that they would receive certificates for a three-months tour at Jonesboro from a committee of the North Carolina legislature, and those who applied did receive certificates for a three-months tour, though this declarant never did and never received any other than the verbal discharge of his captain on his return into Greene County. The declarant was engaged in this expedition from November 1780, day not recollected, until February 1781, day not recollected, a period of three months.

ANGUS MCCOY *(b. 1760) emigrated from Scotland to Philadelphia in 1772 and to Chartiers Township, Washington County, Pennsylvania, in 1781. He participated in local defense efforts and went on a brief expedition with Captain Van Swearington in 1781. He was drafted and defended Burgett's Fort the following spring, and, in place of a brother, he joined William Crawford's expedition against Sandusky. His narrative of the expedition, the 4 June defeat, and the retreat was unknown to C. W.*

Butterfield, author of An Historical Account of the Expedition against Sandusky *(Cincinnati, 1873), and it provides certain details unrecorded elsewhere.*

McCoy served one further tour of duty in late 1782 and was residing in Washington County, Pennsylvania, in 1833 when he submitted this deposition and received a pension.

I, Angus McCoy, according to my mother's statement, was born March 1760 in Scotland. We landed at Philadelphia in the fall of 1772, I being upwards of twelve years old (my father dying in Scotland). After I arrived to twenty-one, I moved to the western part of Pennsylvania, in Washington County and Chartiers Township, and there in the summer of 1781, the Indians being very troublesome on the then frontier or new settlements, I, having no family at that time, volunteered to guard the then frontiers on Chartiers Creek and now Chartiers and Strabane townships during the time of cutting and gathering in their harvest in their collective capacity from field to field and house to house, forting together at night and laying with our firearms in our arms occasionally.

In the same summer after the before-mentioned service, it was rumored that three hundred Indians were in hostile array at the Moravian Towns by a squaw that came to Fort Pitt (now Pittsburgh), at which report Captain Van Swearington raised a company of volunteers of which I was one. We marched to Robenson's Run in this county, where we had to detain until we procured ammunition from Pittsburgh. We then took up our line of march and proceeded by streams and ridges, having no road until we struck the Ohio River at or near the place where Georgetown now stands. There was three of our men went into the river to swim or bathe themselves. They discovered the Indians about a mile below us, making over to the other side. We ran down with all the might or speed we could. They discovered us. They sprang off the horses which they had stolen from our side. They principally swam back, but the Indians made their escape. We proceeded about ten miles down the river bottom to opposite Yellow Creek and returned up Harmon's Creek, a circuitous route, making no other discovery of Indians. The time I lost as a volunteer this summer in first guarding during harvesttime and the above expedition my memory will not serve me. The last expedition, we traveled sometimes the meanderings of streams and ridges. I find that the direct road at present exceeds a hundred miles circuitous. The committee on this petition will please allow me what time they think proper on the above and following services.

In the following year, 1782, early in the spring, I was drafted a tour of military duty according to the then Pennsylvania law and served it faithfully under Capt. Andrew [Van] Swearington at Burgett's Station, at or near where Burgettstown now stands, guarding the then frontiers by traveling from point to point and house to house and field to field while the people were working in their collective capacity. Immediately at the close of the above draft, I volunteered and served a tour of military duty in the room or place of my brother, William McCoy, who had a charge of a family and was legally drafted next in rotation to the one I had just served. I have no documentary evidence in my possession by discharge if any was given for these two drafts, and I do not know of any of my comrades living and shall therefore give you a detailed account of the last above volunteer service in the room of my brother who was drafted in succession of my former draft according to the then Pennsylvania law (this tour was of such a nature as to leave a lasting impression).

I was placed under Capt. Charles Bilderback, a noble officer who was under the command of Colonel Crawford. We each found our own horses, firearms, and equipments. We crossed the Ohio River at the Mingo Bottom. We there detained until ammunition was procured from Pittsburgh. Our number being 489, our distance was computed by our pilots, who were Messrs. Nicholson, Slover, and Zane, to be two hundred miles without any road. We proceeded through the woods and across the Tuscarawas waters. At length we reached the Sandusky Plains. It was about midday when we entered. We found a path which our guides knew led to their towns. We traveled until night and camped as usual.

On the morning of the fourth of June (for on this day we had our battle), we took up our line of march, and, having come to the place where their town formerly stood, it was removed except their back walls of their fireplaces, we being by computation then thirty miles in the plains. Here we sent our spies ahead, who had not gone far before they discovered the Indians. The Indians gave chase to our spies and ran them hard. William Midkirk, one of the spies, having a swift horse, soon appeared, giving us the signal. We each mounted and went to meet them as fast as we could. There was one Indian who did outrun his comrades to meet us, but he was the first killed. We dismounted and endeavored to screen ourselves behind the few remaining trees and let them advance on us. The play of human destruction began. I think it was a little after the middle of the day when this powder music began. We continued watching and firing at our adversaries and them at us until dark occasionally. Soon after the commencement of the battle, a number of our men got wounded, some badly, and some fell to rise no more. I got my own clothes riddled with balls, but a merciful Providence preserved my flesh.

Finding that the Indians were concealed in the long grass, Daniel Leet mounted his horse and, as he passed me, looked me in the face, said "Follow me." I immediately gave the same invitation to those around me who were on foot. I took after Leet, who rode between a canter and a gallop and I suppose between fifteen and twenty after me. We routed them in groups out of the grass in this daring maneuver. In their consternation, not a gun was fired at us until Leet wheeled to the left, at which time two Indians discharged at Leet. I saw his horse bounce as if mortally wounded (but neither injured). Our pass was so quick we had no time to fire on them, and a kind Providence prevented them. We supposed that we passed at least one-half of the Indian line. The reason why Leet I suppose selected me was we were well acquainted, having served on a former draft together (but he is a few years past numbered with the dead, or I have not the least doubt would corroborate this statement).

Shortly after this, a brother soldier close by me got wounded. I asked him for the loan of his gun, it being a superior one to that of mine. He gave it me and his ammunition (mine I left on the battleground). I confess I felt myself stouter, being prepared with my additional stock of ammunition. We had some of as brave a men as ever shouldered a gun. We had some, it is true, were no credit to themselves, but they were the fewest number. I think we were at this work of destruction for at least five hours; dark at length prevented us, the night being short at this season of the year (being the fourth of June). We were all anxiety and expected that the same course would be pursued in the morning. But the Indians did not advance on us, and our officers gave us no orders to advance on them.

During all the night past and all the fifth of June, they were reinforcing themselves and forming a circle around us, keeping at a distance. A while before sundown, there was a company of Indians coming up to their place in the circle who discharged their pieces at the sun. Near or about this time they had completed their circle and began to show themselves except where there was a deep swamp. Here they had placed a sentry and nearly central in this swamp. We supposed their intention was, when all their forces were collected, to close on us at or after dark. We, however, got everything in readiness, our wounded on horseback. Through the day, we buried our dead and burning what stuff we could gather over where they were buried in order to deceive and prevent them from raising them. We left none on the ground but one man who was shot through the breast, who could not live long, by the name of Thomas Ogle.

In this critical situation, after sundown, about the closing of the day, we made an attempt to retreat, at which time the sentry in the center of the swamp discharged his piece, and immediately all in the circle discharged their pieces, we suppose at us, but without effect, which proved very favorable to us, for before they could load, we passed them, principally through their lines and some through the swamp, some of which stuck fast and fell a prey to the enemy. We marched all night as fast as the wounded could bear and circumstances permit. The Indians did not annoy us any more that night, we suppose from our taking a wrong road or path from that intended.

The next day we made across through the plain and continued our course as fast as our wounded could bear, keeping together as well as we could in the evening, some of our small army being a small distance ahead. The Indians, laying in ambush, rushed on them and caught John Hayes, and before we could rescue him they had his scalp half raised off his head and inflicted a mortal wound with the tomahawk on the same. And shortly after, and before we were out of the plains, a body of Indians both on horseback and foot attacked our rear. Our small army gave them powder and ball in exchange, while our front gained the woods with the wounded. Some of our men were here killed and others wounded. John McDonald got his thighbone broken with an Indian ball or slug. Captain Bilderback requested me to take charge of McDonald. We got to the woods about dark, and there we camped for the night. It commenced and poured down rain and that very heavy for the forepart of the night. Hayes, who was still living, and McDonald was laid on one blanket. My business was to guard them. I walked around them all night, with the lock of my gun under my arm in order to keep it dry. At the break of day, things in readiness, we started. I got McDonald on a horse. Hayes was still living but could not live long. We left him there. The Indians did not attack us any more. I brought McDonald home with much difficulty, having to lead his horse all the way, as we had no road. He died in a few days after his arrival at home. I believe all the rest of the wounded were able to guide their own horses.

While I am on this sickening campaign, not wishing to wound or hurt the feelings of any connected or concerned, I understood that Colonel Crawford, the first night of our retreat, left our little army, taking with him Slover the pilot, Harrison his son-in-law, and Dr. Knight. One thing I know and am certain of is I never saw Colonel Crawford after the forepart of the first night of our retreat. I understood they were taken by another party of Indians who were coming to assist those engaged against us. Colonel Crawford, I understood, was burnt to death. Slover I saw some years afterward. He, I understood, was tied to a stake or tree to be burnt, but, there coming on a great rain, the Indians supposing that their hellish pleasure would not be gratified, loosed him for that time as he supposed for a better evening, during which time he made his escape. Dr. Knight as miraculously made his escape but had nearly perished with hunger. I never learnt what became of Harrison.

In the same fall after Crawford's defeat, I was again drafted. Our frontiers being few in population, we had to be nearly one half of our time on public duty from spring to fall. Shortly after my time had expired wherein I had volunteered to serve in place of my brother before stated and when on our way to Fort McIntosh, our orders were countermanded. Here I cannot recollect the time lost. I know it was late in the fall, and I was glad when our orders were countermanded, for I dreaded the winter's campaign in our unprepared state. One thing I know, that from early in the spring to late in the fall of 1782, my principal business is above stated. Our difficulties of fatigue, hunger, and uneasy sensation of mind is bright to my recollection, but the exact time I served I cannot recollect. Yet I feel fully persuaded that whatever time the Pennsylvania drafts were for, I served for myself and for my brother as before stated. I shall here state that I never received anything for my military services other than certificates, which I traded for little or no value, to the best of my recollection. I have never received any pension. I never was an applicant until at present for a pension, and now I only claim your lowest grade of pension, which from the former and after services rendered by your petitioner, will I hope appear sufficiently satisfactory to your committee to place me thereon.

COMBAT MEMORABLE ENTRE LE PEARSON ET PAUL IONES
Combat memorable entre le Pearson et Paul Jones donné le 22 7bre 1779 le Capitaine Pearson commandant le SERAPIS et Paul Jones commandant le Bon homme Richard et son Escadre
Das merckwürdige See Gefecht zwischen Capitain Pearson und Paul Jones welches 1779 den 22 September sich ereignet wo der Cap: das Schiff den Serapis und der Paul Jones, den guten Homme Richard genañt commandirte

9
MARITIME COMBAT

ABEL WOODWORTH *(b. 1758) was born in Lebanon, Connecticut. He volunteered for service on the twenty-gun Connecticut naval vessel* Oliver Cromwell *in August 1776 and remained a member of its crew from the time it was fitted out until captured. The ship left New London in May 1777, and under the command of Seth Harding and Timothy Parker it compiled an enviable record of captures. The ship the* Cromwell *cruised with in 1778 was the* Defense. *The vessel was captured in the middle of 1779, and Woodworth was imprisoned on the* Jersey *and exchanged. He served on privateers for the rest of the war.*

He resided in Columbia County, New York, after the war and successfully applied for a pension in 1833.

On or about the last of August, 1776, he enlisted as a marine and private to serve on board of the *Oliver Cromwell,* a twenty-gun ship built, as he understood, by the colony of Connecticut.... He enlisted under recruiting officer Bela Elderkin of Windham County. This applicant, as he well recollects, at the time of his enlistment was in the employment of one David Young in tending a grain mill in the aforesaid town of Windham, although his home or native place was in Lebanon County.

This declarant, from the time of his enlistment and soon after organization, was one of the *Cromwell*'s constant hands to the time of her capture by the enemy in 1779. This capture of the *Cromwell* by the enemy's armed ship *Daphne* of twenty-two guns, copper-bottom, the *Delaware,* thirty-two gun frigate, and the *Union,* an eighteen-gun brig, was according to the best recollection of this declarant about the middle of May, 1779. The time of his exchange as a prisoner of war he well recollects was the day on which the attack was made on Paulus Hook by the Continental troops. This declarant was aboard of the *Cromwell* every time she made a cruise or sailed excepting one. Captain Coit sailed to the island of Nantucket to recruit and did enlist, as he understood, one James Hill, Harris, and others who had been whalemen. This declarant, during the winter of 1776 and 1777, was some part of the time on board the *Cromwell* and a part of the time home on a furlough.

In the spring of 1777, Capt. Seth Harding took the command of the *Cromwell.* Timothy Parker was first lieutenant, and John Chapman was second lieutenant, and Bela Elderkin was lieutenant of marines. The *Cromwell* cruised, and the first prize this declarant recollects of taking was sometime the last of August or first of September, 1777, this declarant doing duty as a mariner on board through choice of his own and that of his officers, though he enlisted as a marine. And this declarant had the command of the maintop in cruises performed after he received his sergeant's warrant subsequent to this cruise.

Whilst cruising, a sail was espied in the afternoon. The *Cromwell* gave chase, and in the forepart of the night of the same day, she came alongside. The lamps of the *Cromwell* were lighted up, her portholes were knocked open; the enemy had there a view of her strength. She struck to the *Cromwell* with but little firing. She proved to be a British packet from one of the West India islands to Britain, on board of which was a sum of specie, some gentlemen, officers, and a few women. She was sent to Boston. The packet had [a] number of guns; he does not recollect the number.

The latter part of the year 1777, he believes in the month of December, Capt. Timothy Parker took the command of the *Cromwell;* John Chapman was first lieutenant and James Day of Norwich had the command of the marines, either as captain or lieutenant, he does not know which. Beriah Hillyard was first sergeant, and Abel Woodworth, this declarant, was second sergeant. This declarant's warrant was under the hand and seal of James Day, who at one time came up to Lebanon, Connecticut, the residence and home of this declarant, and he with Capt. James Day, as he was called, went out and recruited in that vicinity a number of hands. The names of some he well recollects, viz., Chandler Wattles, Samuel Wattles, Walter Hunt, Joseph Allen, and one White, son of Captain White of Lebanon. This Mr. White, as he well recollects, was seasick during the whole cruise made subsequently and was sent in the first prize taken into port. The hands thus recruited, this declarant traveled on foot with

[them] by land to Boston, as he well recollects, the *Cromwell* lying in that port. The sergeant's warrant under which this declarant then acted and stood had been in the possession of the declarant for many years after the war and during his residence in the state of New York. He recollects to have seen it amongst his papers not many years since, but upon due search lately he has not been able to find it and verily believes it to have been lost.

In the year 1778, the *Cromwell* cruised in company with a ship of eighteen guns, the name of which he does not recollect, but well remembers that she was commanded by a man by the name of Smedley. They had not been to sea long when they espied two or three sail and during the day gave chase, but towards night gave over the pursuit, for what reason he, this declarant, knew not, but it was said by some that it was owing to cowardice in the commandant.

But in a few days after they saw another sail, gave chase, and before twelve o'clock at night came up with her. She was a French ship, the officers of which informed them that at four o'clock P.M., she, the French ship, was in sight of the *Cromwell* and Captain Smedley's ship and also in sight of two British letters of marque, the latter of which had for some time been examining the papers of the French ship in order to make a prize of her but had released her. They further said they were cruising for Yankee privateers, and that at the time aforesaid the *Cromwell* was sailing so and so, and the letters of marque were sailing in such and such a direction (the points he does not recollect).

Then the *Cromwell* and Smedley's ship altered their course to get into the course of the British letters of marque, and at daylight they were in sight and not far off. They did not try or make sail to avoid us, and when the *Cromwell* was in about a mile of the large ship, she fired a bow gun. The enemy then wore round and fired a broadside and had fired a number more guns, when someone inquired of Captain Parker if it was not time for the *Cromwell* to fire. The captain walked round on the gangway and observed to the crew, "The other day when I gave over chase, you called me a coward. Now I mean to bring you so close that you can see the whites of their eyes before you fire a gun. No firing till orders."

The *Cromwell* neared the large ship, and a close action commenced, Captain Smedley's ship and the small ship not joining in action. The action continued some time and without heaving in stays till the letter of marque struck to the *Cromwell*. The other ship was nearing the *Cromwell* and getting under her stern to give her a broadside as was supposed, but too late. The latter also struck. The action was said to have been severe, but does not recollect the number killed. It, however, appeared by the obstinacy of the fight that they, who were cruising for Yankee privateers, were unwilling to knuckle to Yankee valor. They proved to be a couple of very valuable prizes loaded with dry goods, etc. The larger ship carried eighteen guns; the number the other carried he does not recollect. They were sent into Boston. During the aforesaid action or some subsequent one, he does not distinctly recollect which, a nine-pound shot was fired into one of the portholes of the *Cromwell* and killed two men, one a prize master by the name of Knowles, and a quartermaster whose name he does not recollect.

In the year 1779, the particular month or day of the month he does not distinctly recollect but thinks it was in the forepart of that year, the *Cromwell* sailed out of New London to Charleston, South Carolina. When at Charleston, well recollects that it was a time of watermelons at that place. The *Cromwell* took in a quantity of indigo and sailed with an intention of going to France, if we were not fortunate enough to come in sight of the Jamaica fleet which was expected. That we might pick up some of their straggling vessels, at Charleston Captain Parker was advised by one Captain Gillings or Gillian to sail in company with him through what was called the "hole in the rock" to shorten the distance, as he understood. Went through and spoke [to] a Spanish palacca, and she informed that the Jamaica fleet had been past eight days.

The *Cromwell* then experienced a severe gale (nearly a hurricane) which blew the compass round and was blowing onshore. We cut away our foremast. The wind shifted so quick instead of carrying the mast to the leeward, it carried it to the windward, and some of the rigging on the bowsprit hung, and the mast lay surging against the ship. Before the storm was over, the *Cromwell* had lost all her masts and rigging and was under the necessity of putting up jury masts and then sailed toward New London in the Gulf Stream. We spied a sail and gave chase during that day, and the next morning, assisted by the stream, the *Cromwell* had neared her and before night made a prize of her. She proved to be a victualing ship belonging to the enemy. We carried her into New London. The *Cromwell* was there rigged out with all haste and went out back of Long Island and New York, and in eight days she took four prizes, brought them into New London again, went out back of Long Island, saw three sail, gave chase till their strength was discovered and that they were armed vessels. The *Cromwell* then hove in stays and steered before the wind. As soon as that was observed by the enemy, they hove in stays and made after. The ship, afterwards proved to be the *Daphne,* a copper-bottomed ship of twenty-two guns, gained on the *Cromwell* pretty fast.

As soon as the *Daphne* got near, she began to fire to cut away our rigging, and one Capt. Joshua Palmer (brother to the well-known Bob Palmer), who commanded the two stern chases of the *Cromwell,* with a six-pound shot cut away the main topmast of the *Daphne,* which dropped down on the deck. The *Cromwell* then wore round, gave the *Daphne* a broadside, and passed on. The *Daphne* got up her mast with all speed and finally overtook the *Cromwell.* The *Cromwell* fought under a running fire till the *Delaware,* a thirty-two-gun frigate, was nearly under the stern of the *Cromwell,* and the *Union,* an eighteen-gun brig, not far off. Then it was that, to save lives, the *Cromwell* struck the Yankee colors.

Then one of the crew of the *Cromwell* by the name of Charles White, an Englishman who had before been taken by the British after desertion and branded on the face, came forward before the enemy came aboard, and to save the brave fellow we took a razor and cut out the brand. He then passed for a wounded man, and the deception, as he believes, was not discovered. White was a brave fellow, artful and cunning.

The *Cromwell* and crew were sent into New York, and as many of the enemy as they would take on board of the prison ship *Good Hope* were put on board, and the remainder were put on board of a man-of-war condemned, by name as he thinks the *Gold and Jersey.* In three or four weeks, those which were put on board on the prison ship were exchanged and went to New London. During their stay on board of the prison ship, fifteen had died, and two more before they got to New London. It was this declarant's lot to be put on board of the condemned ship *Jersey.* The lieutenant of the said ship frequently took the declarant and others to row him where he wished to go, and for a time fared tolerable, till four of our crew made trial for escaping. They were pursued and brought back. The names of two he recollects, viz., Bunce and Watson of Hartford. We were then put into the prison ship *Good Hope,* which had been cleansed since the first imprisonment and rendered tolerable healthful. We there remained prisoners of war for about five weeks longer, until we were exchanged on the 19 August 1779. He recollects it was the night on which the attack by the Americans on Paulus Hook took place. This declarant was then on board of a sloop then ready to carry them to New London. The firing commenced, as near as he can recollect, about two or three o'clock at night. Recollect distinctly at daylight of seeing the British crossing over.

And further, this declarant, after being exchanged as aforesaid, did go out twice in private vessels to cruise for British prizes and had some hard fighting, but he is informed that the law makes no provision for the crews of private vessels. This declarant verily believes that he was on board of the *Cromwell* or one of her crew and under monthly wages as second sergeant not less than one year, seven months, and fifteen days, and as a private also he served not less than one year and five months. This declarant sometimes went home on a furlough and returned again by the time stipulated in such furlough, but was one of her constant hands from the time he first went aboard to the time of her capture before stated.

ELNATHAN JENNINGS *(1754–1841) was born in Southampton Township, Long Island. He had served in the militia in 1775, and his family, with other pro-Americans, were forced to abandon their houses when the British occupied New York and Long Island in 1776. Like many of the refugees, they settled in Connecticut. Jennings knew the sound and the island itself. He briefly served as commander of three whaleboats employed in stopping Tory commerce in provisions with New York. He vol-*

unteered in the Connecticut line in summer 1776, was in the Battle of White Plains, and volunteered as a sergeant in the Continental army in April 1777.

In mid-May 1777, clearly a few days earlier than 24 May, as he remembered it, Jennings went to Col. Return J. Meigs and suggested a bold attack on Sag Harbor. Meigs had an interview with Washington, and the plan was accepted, with Meigs in command. Jennings provides a detailed account of what was one of the most daring and successful initiatives of the war. The 23 May 1777 raid netted six killed, twelve ships burned, and ninety taken prisoner, without the loss of a man on the American side.

Fearing reprisal for his known involvement in the exploit, Jennings changed his name to Nathan B. Jennings. He served two more turns in the Connecticut line, guarded cattle at Valley Forge, and received a medical discharge in December 1778.

He resided in Middletown, Connecticut, until the conclusion of the war. He then moved to Philadelphia, where he lived in 1820 and from which he submitted this narrative and was granted a pension.

I, Nathan B. Jennings, was born in the township of Southampton, near Sag Harbor, on the east end of Long Island, in June, the sixteenth day in the year of our Lord 1754, and in the year 1775, in the month of April, I was drafted in the militia in Captain Holabord's company, in Colonel Dayton's regiment for the term of six months; then was ordered to march to Montauk Point on the very end of Long Island to prevent the British from taking off cattle and sheep, as part of their fleet then lay in Gardiner's Bay, within three-quarters of a mile of Long Island shore. Within about five weeks after we encamped there, we received orders to embark from Sag Harbor to New York and from New York to Albany. Then we was ordered to join General McDougall's brigade to prepare for a march to St. Johns. The very day that we received orders to march, the express came to our commander that the fort was taken. Then our troops was ordered back to New York and there continued until my six months was up; received my discharge, then returned back to my parents on Long Island; there continued till sometime in March 1776. My father and family all fled before the British and left a large stock of horses, cattle, and sheep behind us for want of vessels to carry them off. We left them in the power of the enemy. We went over to Connecticut River and went up the river near Middletown. A very short time after, I was recommended to His

Excellency Governor Trumbull, Esq., for a warrant to take command of three whaleboats with ten men each to pilot them to Sag Harbor, and in Southold Sound to take vessels and boats that was found guilty of supplying the British with wood and any kind of stores. We soon captured three vessels loaded with flour and wood and took them up Connecticut River for trial, and they was condemned and sold according to law. Soon after, the British cutters prevented our cruising there.

Then I enlisted for six months in Captain Ely's company, Colonel Sage's regiment, commanded by General Putnam. We marched to New York and was stationed on Governor's Island. The British fleet lay in view of us at Staten Island about five miles of us. The twenty-fourth [*sic*] of August, 1776, was the Battle of Long Island fair in our view when General McDougall was defeated the twenty-eighth day. Our regiment retreated off Governor's Island to the city of New York in flat-bottom boats in the night, and, within a few days after, the whole British fleet came up to the city and parted. Some went up the East River and some up the North River; some of their troops landed at Harlem, above our army, which obliged us to fight our way through; then fought on our retreat to Kingsbridge, fourteen miles from city. There we stood our ground for some time. Then we was ordered to march to White Plains, and the twenty-eighth of October, 1776, we had a sharp battle with the British at White Plains, and I received two slight wounds, one musket ball in my right foot, and one in my right groin, cut four inches in length, but never applied for a pension until the fourteenth day of April, 1818, after the law of Congress was passed (a law of the eighteenth of March, 1818). The thirty-first of October, 1776, His Excellency General Washington give orders to march to Northcastle for winter quarters. There I continued until my time was out, then received my discharge and returned back to Connecticut to my parents. There remained until the spring following, sometime about the first of April [when I] enlisted for three years a sergeant in Captain Cole's company in the First Connecticut Regiment. Was ordered to march to New Haven. There we was stationed.

The twenty-fourth [*sic*] of May, 1777, I, said N. B. Jennings, volunteered myself to Colonel Meigs, stating the situation of Sag Harbor and the strength of the British guard and how easy they might be taken, and that I would pilot him and a detachment of troops across the sound to Long Island and carry our boats across Oysterpond Branch, about 150 yards, into Southold Bay. Then we could land and come on the back of the guard. The colonel was highly pleased with my plan. Then Colonel Meigs showed it to His Excellency General Washington. Then the general sent for me to come to headquarters with Colonel Meigs. Then, after asking me many questions, he was highly pleased with my conversation and plan.

The next day, the troops was ordered on the green at New Haven. The orders was read that about 110 men of good oarsmen to volunteer themselves to go on a private expedition, and when the word march was given there was upwards of 300 men stepped four paces in front in less than three minutes, and, after Colonel Meigs had picked out 110 men, the rest fell back in the ranks. At the same time, there was a number of whaleboat[s] lying at the Long Wharf at New Haven. Then we crossed over the sound to Long Island, carried our boats across the beach into Southold Bay, crossed bay, landed just before daylight on Joseph's Island, and carried our boats into a thicket of red cedars. There lay all day. The next night, I conducted the boats within about two miles and a half of Sag Harbor, on the back of the guardhouse. The guard was kept in a schoolhouse where I had gone to school. After landed, we left a few men to keep our boats afloat. Then I conducted our detachment a back way across fields and through thick brush until we came in sight of the guardhouse. We kept under the side of a thick swamp within about fifty yards of the two sentries. We immediately surrounded the guard and sentries and took all except one sentry that made his escape through a piece of marsh. Then we left a guard with our prisoners and marched down about two hundred yards to my uncle. There we took a man by the name of Chew. The said Chew was appointed a commissary in Connecticut and went to the British with a large sum of the public money. Then we marched about one [hundred?] yards to their barracks. We made prisoners of all that was there. Then we went on the Long Wharf. There we took more prisoners and burnt twelve brigs and schooners, a quantity of hay and corn. Then the British was playing on us with grapeshot. Then we returned back to our boats with ninety prisoners the same way to the Oyster Point beach, carried our boats across the beach, then put our prisoners on board of two small vessels and guarded them across the sound to Black Rock, and from there we marched our prisoners to New Haven without the loss of a man.

There was not a man in the attachment that ever had been on Long Island except myself and one man who said that about twenty years ago he was ashore about two hours. And, in a few days after, we guarded our prisoners from New Haven to Hartford prison up Connecticut River, then returned back to New Haven. There I fell in with two young men that was looking for me. We had been schoolboys together. They had made their escape from Sag Harbor in a boat. They told me not to venture over there no more, for the Tories and the British swore that if they could take me, as I had been cruising about that shores and piloting Colonel Meigs with a detachment of troops a few days before, that if they could get hold of me, they swore they would put me to death without judge or jury. Then I asked the two young men to go with me to Colonel Meigs's lodging. We went together. They told the colonel the same that they had told me. The colonel asked me what my mother's maiden name was before she was married. I told him it was Bishop. Then he advised me to go to His Excellency Governor Trumbull, the governor of the state of Connecticut, with a recommendation which he would give me. Accordingly I procured a furlough and went to His Excellency the Governor Trumbull with my recommendation stating my danger in case I should fall in the hands of the enemy. He said in such a case it should be lawful for me, as my name was Elnathan, to leave out the two letters "El" and write it Nathan, and as my mother's maiden name was Bishop, to write my name Nathan B. Jennings, although it was wrote in the enlistment Elnathan Jennings, but ever since the governor decreeded it lawful, I have wrote my name Nathan B. Jennings, which is well known in this city for near thirty-eight years by the first gentlemen in Philadelphia.

And when we received orders to march from New Haven into the state of New York, we had several marches to different places in that state before we came into New Jersey, from Jersey to Whitemarsh in Pennsylvania and to Swedes Ford. From Swedes Ford, sometime in December 1777 we marched to Valley Forge, and soon after I was ordered to take charge of a stationed guard called the bullock guard under the directions of Commissary Conrad Huff. I had seven hundred head of cattle to guard besides other stores for the use of the United States army. There I continued on that guard till June 28, 1778, then followed the British to Monmouth in New Jersey sometime after the Battle of Monmouth, which was on the twenty-eighth of June, 1778. Some short time after, I joined the First Connecticut Regiment, which I enlisted in and continued there until our troops was ordered to march to Middlebrook in New York State for winter quarters. Soon after, I was struck with a fit of apperplacks [apoplexy] and lay three days in the fit. Then Dr. Holmes of the same regiment recommended me for a discharge from the service of the United States, which I received the latter end of December 1778. The above statement is true to the best of my knowledge.

THOMAS MARBLE *(b. 1763) was born in Lebanon, Connecticut. He volunteered in Connecticut regiments three times between 1779 and 1781 and did uneventful service at New Haven, in New Jersey, and at West Point. While stationed at Peekskill in 1781, he was one of thirty privates selected for a whaleboat raid on East Chester. Setting out in six whaleboats and a gunboat commanded by Captain Lockwood, they captured, on 13 November 1781, a schooner and three sloops, one of them a manned ten-gun vessel. They returned safely to Stamford with vessels and prisoners.*

Marble moved from Lebanon to Cazenovia, New York, in 1795 and to Camillus in 1812. Although he returned to Lebanon in 1832 to make this deposition, either from lack of proof or perhaps death, he did not receive a pension.

In the year 1779, about the first of July, I enlisted in the town of Coventry, county of Tolland (then county of Hartford), and state of Connecticut as a soldier in a regiment of Connecticut state troops for eight months in Capt. Daniel Tilden's company. Alexander Mack was our lieutenant; the ensign I do not recollect. In Colonel Wells's regiment, Mr. Root of Coventry was our adjutant. The lieutenant's and major's names I cannot recollect.

After the regiment was formed, we entered into quarters at New London and remained stationed there until December. We then started on a march for Staten Island, as we were informed by some of the noncommissioned officers. We reached New Haven the last of December, and on account of the severity of the weather, we were obliged to make a halt for ten or twelve days as nigh as I can recollect. We then marched to Fairfield, Connecticut, the weather still continuing so severe, and the snow had been so deep that we could not march any farther. We then remained stationed there until the last of February, 1780. We were then discharged by our colonel.

I then went to Hebron, Connecticut, and resided there until about the first of July, 1780. I then enlisted in Hebron (Connecticut) as a soldier in the United States army for six months. I was then, with about twenty other soldiers, put under the command of a subaltern officer, whose name I cannot recollect, and started in a march for New Jersey, where the main army was then stationed. We arrived at headquarters about the middle of July as nigh as I can recollect. I then joined Captain Hart's company in Col. Samuel B. Webb's regiment. Ebenezer Huntington was lieutenant and [commander?] of the regiment (Colonel Webb being then a prisoner). Our adjutant's name I think was Loomis, but I am not positive. The major's name I cannot recollect. We then remained in New Jersey, occasionally marching from one place to another, until the time General Arnold attempted to give up West Point to the British. The brigade then marched to West Point, where we remained stationed until the first of January, 1781. My time of enlistment being then expired, I was discharged by Lieutenant Colonel Huntington. I then returned to Hebron, Connecticut, where I resided until the first of July, 1781.

I then went to Lebanon in Connecticut and enlisted as a soldier in the United States army for six months (to Ensign Berman, he then officiating as a recruiting officer). I then went to Peekskill, New York, where the main army was then stationed. I then joined Capt. John H. Buell's company in the regiment of Leather Caps formerly commanded by Colonel Meigs, but I think it was then commanded by Colonel Durkee, but I am not positive, in General Parsons's brigade. We then remained stationed there and near there until sometime in September. While we were there stationed, General Lafayette with his army of French marched up on the opposite side the river at Kings Ferry, and I and about sixty or eighty other soldiers assisted in ferrying the army across the river. General Washington then selected about half of the army (as nigh as I can recollect) and started on a march together with General Lafayette and his army for the southward. I was left with the remaining part of the army at or near Peekskill.

Soon after this, I and twenty-nine other privates were detached from the main army and placed under the command of Lieutenant Deforest and marched from there to Stamford in Connecticut. On our arrival at Stamford, we there found General Parsons and his aide-de-camp Oliver Lawrence. We remained stationed there as near as I can recollect about six weeks. During that time we were frequently called out to go to Horseneck to protect the inhabitants from being plundered by the British light horse and refugees who were frequently scouting about for that purpose.

Likewise, we joined Captain Lockwood, who had the command of six whaleboats and one gunboat. We manned the boats about eight o'clock in the evening and directed our course to East Chester. Thither we arrived a little before day the next morning. We then being within British lines, we immediately repaired to a house cellar, where we lay concealed during the day, and while we were there concealed, the British light horse passed the house.

About eleven o'clock the following night, we returned to our boats, took one of our whaleboats out of the small cove where we landed the night before, and carried it on poles across a neck of land about a half mile above the mouth of East Chester Creek. We then espied a small sloop lying at anchor about twelve [rods?] opposite of our boat. We then manned our boat, made up to her, and there being but one man aboard of her, we took her without opposition. We then lashed our boat to the sloop, weighed anchor and hoisted the foresail, and with a fair breeze, moved down to the mouth of the creek where we found a ten-gun sloop belonging to the British. When we come in about ten rods of the sloop, the British, supposing us to be their own men, hailed us to know whether we were coming alongside of them. We made them no reply but kept our course until we ran afoul of her. Our men then lying flat on deck, we all rose up and fired a shot. Engagement ensued in which several wounded on both sides, and among the wounded among the British was the captain of the sloop, who died the next day about four o'clock in the afternoon. We took the sloop and made twenty-six prisoners. The sloop being a good deal out of repair, we set about repairing her, which employed all hands about two hours. We then weighed anchor and steered our course for Stamford.

About sunrise we discovered a sloop and a schooner, loaded with wood, steering their course for New York. We immediately manned our whaleboat, our gunboat (we got on our return), and gave chase. On coming up with them, we found only two men aboard of each one. We took them, sloop and schooner, and made them prisoners without much opposition. We then continued our course for Stamford. Thither we arrived about sunset. We then remained at Stamford until we received news that Lord Cornwallis and his army had surrendered. General Parsons then ordered Lieutenant Deforest to march us onto a rise of ground which was about a half mile from Stamford Town, when we had a day of rejoicing by firing, etc. At the close of the day, we returned to Stamford Town. Soon after this, under the command of Lieutenant Deforest, we marched and joined the main army which was stationed near Peekskill. The exact place I cannot recollect. I then remained with the main army until my time of service expired, and I was discharged by the colonel.

JOHN INGERSOLL *(b. 1750) was a resident of Tuckahoe, Gloucester County, New Jersey. He was drafted in 1776, and between his own monthly tours and alternately substituting for his father, he spent nine consecutive months in the militia, stationed at various locations in southern New Jersey and participating in several skirmishes.*

Ingersoll had no recollection of dates, but it appears that in about 1778 he entered the New Jersey sea service to avoid the draft. He shipped on the schooner Enterprize *at Somers Point and participated in the capture of several prize vessels. He then volunteered as a crew member of the lookout boats harbored at Cape May. He was captured by Tories while on patrol at Cranberry Beach, Barnegat Inlet, and was incarcerated on the prison ship* Scorpion, *then on the* Huntress, *where he was instrumental in staging a spectacular escape. He returned to lookout boat service until peace was declared and helped capture several Tory vessels.*

Ingersoll submitted this application in 1832 and was granted a pension.

. . .The law at that time being for one half the militia to perform duty one month, the other half the next, by this time I began to [be] wearied with the marchings and countermarchings which I was continually subject to, and being informed that, if I entered on board a privateer and served continually, it would answer the same purpose, that is, clear my father and myself from any other military duty, accordingly I entered on board the schooner *Enterprize* then laying at Somers Point, New Jersey, with twenty-four guns and seventy-five men; Captain Gardner; Humphrey Hughes, first mate; George Wanton, second mate.

The second day after I went on board, we set sail on a cruise. We put to sea, and after being at sea about two weeks we fell in with an English brig off the Capes of Delaware. His cargo was sugar, molasses, limes, salt, boots, shoes, and English blankets, etc., which we succeeded in taking. We put a prize crew on board the brig and sent her on to Philadelphia. Her former crew we made prisoners of war and landed them in Philadelphia, where they were kept in prison until duly exchanged.

We again put to sea, and after clearing the Capes of Delaware we espied a brig. She bore down upon us. We beat to windward until sometime in the night, when we came alongside of her. We hailed her. She proved to be a brig belonging to the enemy from New York, bound to Halifax. We captured her and had her in tow until the next day about eleven o'clock A.M., when one of the enemy's ships of the line came down upon us. We cast our prize loose and effected our own escape. We made Barnegat Inlet, where we ran in. We lay in Barnegat Bay that night. The next morning we espied a schooner close under the beach. We got under way, ran out, and gave chase. We soon came up with her. We fired upon her, and she struck her colors. She proved to be a schooner belonging to the enemy from the island of Jamaica, bound to New York. She had forty hogsheads of rum on board. We took out one hogshead of the rum, put a prize crew on board of said schooner, and sent her to Philadelphia. We then ran into Barnegat, aforesaid, where remained for two days.

On the third day, if my recollection serves, we espied another schooner close in with beach. We again put to sea and gave chase. She kept out of the reach of our guns for near five hours. We at length, however, came alongside of her and captured her. She proved to be an American schooner and had been recently captured by the enemy. Her loading was boards and scantling and was bound to New York. We dispatched her on to Philadelphia to the care of Colonel Gurney, our prize master.

We then ran into Little Egg Harbor, where was laying a cutter recently taken from the enemy. She was at this time commanded by Captain Welsh of Philadelphia. A part of our crew being desirous to return home, and a part of Captain Welsh's crew being anxious to continue on a cruise, Captain Welsh and Gardner exchanged five of their crews. I was one of the five who then went on board of Captain Welsh in the said cutter, and in about two days we landed safe in Philadelphia. I then took my discharge from Captain Welsh and returned home. And at that time I thought I never would go again. But I remained at home about a month, and I was solicited to go again. At that time there were boats fitting out from Cape May called lookout boats.

The seashore was at that time much infested by refugees, who collected in bodies and plundered and annoyed the inhabitants whenever they could. They frequently burned the private dwellings, deprived the families of their stock of provisions, drove off large stocks of cattle from the beaches; in fact ruin and desolation marked their footsteps wherever they went. It was to protect the coast from their depredations that these lookout boats were fitted out. There were two of said boats started out together. One was commanded by Captain McGee, with a crew of sixteen men. The other was commanded by Captain Willets of Cape May, with an equal number of men. To the latter boat I belonged.

We followed along the coast until we came to Barnegat Inlet. We there ran in and landed on Cranberry Beach. We there fell in with a larger body of refugees. They were far superior in number to us, and they succeeded in taking us prisoners. They handcuffed us and conveyed us into the prison ship then laying in the North River opposite the city of New York, whose name was the *Scorpion.* I remained on board the *Scorpion* about three weeks. It being then in the month of July, I was taken sick with a camp fever, when I was removed out of the *Scorpion* and put on board the *Huntress,* also a prison ship but then converted into an hospital. I was on board the *Huntress* but a short time, when I was attacked with dysentery. Here I thought would be an end to my sufferings, but, although death relieved some of my messmates from the horrors of that prison (Captain Willets was among the number who fell a victim to the disease), I was one among those who recovered. The water was bad and the provisions worse. Our allowance was a half pound of mutton per day, but, to our surprise, when the mutton came on board it was only the heads of sheep with the horns and wool thereon. Our bread was oatmeal, neither sifted nor bolted. Our manner of preparing it was as follows: pound up a sheep's head until the bones were all broken, then sink the oatmeal in a bowl of water and float out the hulls; with this we would thicken the broth and thus we kept soul and body together.

I had been on board about two months, sometimes almost famished for the want of provisions, when the officers of the hospital ship made a proposal to me. In case I would keep the cabin clean, boil their teakettle, black their boots, etc., I should have a hammock to sleep in, should be better fed, and should be exchanged when the rest of my company was. I accordingly accepted of the offer. The hospital ship was anchored in what is called Buttermilk Channel with their cables and anchors. The center one was a tremendous chain cable. There were but one gun kept on board said ship, and that was an English musket which the officers kept in the cabin. There were about two hundred prisoners on board said ship, with seven officers and one physician.

I had been doing my duty in the cabin about two weeks, when we laid a plan for our escape. It was as follows. One day while the officers were absent on Long Island, I took down the said musket, poured out the priming, poured water into the barrel of the gun until the load became thoroughly wet. I then wiped the pan thoroughly dry, reprimed her, and put her back in her place. One or two days had elapsed, but we could get no boat wherein to make our escape, for they universally at night chained and locked her fast.

An opportunity at length presented itself, to wit, the officers had a mind to go on shore, and, it being tremendous stormy weather, they unlocked their boat from the chain, brought her up alongside, and ordered a boy to get in the boat and bail the water out of her. I had communicated the secret of the gun being out of order to some of my fellow prisoners, and there being at time a heavy storm, with the wind blowing directly upon the Jersey shore together with a thick, dense fog in the air, we considered this a favorable time to make our escape. We accordingly embraced the opportunity which then offered.

Seven prisoners (beside the boy which was in the boat) sprang into the boat. We shoved off, but before we had fairly cut the boat loose, one of the officers came on deck and discovered us. He screamed out for the gun, which he readily obtained, took aim at us, but as he pulled trigger, she only flashed. He reprimed her, but as oft as he pulled trigger, she would only flash. They then abandoned their musket, all ran upon the quarterdeck, halloed as loud as they could to give the alarm to the fleet then laying at anchor around us, but the wind was blowing so heavy it was impossible for them to be heard at even so short a distance. They then hoisted a flag on the flagstaff on the stern of the ship as a signal of distress, but, the fog being so dense, none of the fleet discovered it. By this time we were pretty nearly over to the Jersey shore, which we reached at length.

We landed on an island in the meadow called Communipaw, between Staten Island and Paulus Hook, but here we were in great danger of being taken up as runaways, for the enemy had possession of the whole country through which we had to travel for some miles at least. We were emaciated with hunger and sickness, and vermin covered our bodies. We were, however, fortunate enough to reach the camp of General Lafayette in safety, who received us joyfully and sent a sergeant of his guard to pilot us on to General Washington's army. We stayed with General Lafayette's army about one day, when we left it and reached General Washington's camp, which was about two miles distant.

General Washington's army was then under arms and about to remove from that place of encampment. We marched with his army about two miles further, when he again encamped and furnished us with passes to return to our homes, which I reached in safety. My pass which I received from General Washington at that time I kept for many years, and I was under strong impressions that I had it to this day, but I have had my papers searched, and it cannot be found. What has become [of it], it is impossible for me to say.

I remained at home for about two weeks, when I again entered on board of another boat commanded by Captain Enoch Willets (brother to my former captain, who died on board the prison ship). We sailed from Great Egg Harbor and ran into Shark River, between Barnegat and Sandy Hook light. We sailed from Shark River and ran into Little Egg Harbor, where lay a heavy ship nearly loaded with goods. Said ship was an English ship. The crew a few days previous had mutinied, succeeded in taking the ship, and ran her into Little Egg Harbor, aforesaid, but, in running her in, she struck on the bottom. They were unloading her, conveying their goods in scows up to Chestnut Neck. In going up with a scowload one evening, the refugees in that section of country waylaid the crew, captured the scow, and took charge of her load. The crew informed us of this. We went in pursuit of said refugees. We came up with them at a place called Osborn's Island, distant about six miles from where the ship lay. Said refugees had two wagons loaded of four horses each and one wagon load of two horses. They fired upon us and then fled, leaving their booty behind. We took charge of the ten horses, with the wagons and goods, and returned to our boats. Said goods were condemned agreeably to law and sold at public sale.

I again entered on board a boat commanded by Capt. Hope Willets of Cape May. We set sail from Cape May and again landed at Shark River. We stayed at Shark River two or three days, when we espied a refugee boat alone close in with the beach, steering apparently for the Delaware. As they came opposite the inlet wherein we lay, they gave three cheers. We put to sea and gave chase. We kept up a steady and well-directed fire for about four miles, when they endeavored to run their boat into Squan Inlet, but in their attempting to do so they ran her ashore and fled. And before we could get on shore they had concealed themselves in the woods which were nearby. We took their boat, in which we found a six-pounder on her stern together with a quantity of dry goods, with hardware, and one barrel of rum, which we took. We then made sail for Cape May, and before we arrived we were informed of peace being proclaimed between this and the mother country.

JOSEPH SAUNDERS *(b. 1757) was born in Lancaster County, Virginia, and served slightly over three years in the Virginia navy. Like most of the state navies, that of the Old Dominion was no match for regular British vessels, but it provided valuable support to land militia forces. He served with the* Dragon *from before its launching until the summer of 1781. When Cornwallis's army invaded the James River, Saunders was assigned by Lafayette to destroy stores and scuttle his vessel. At the time of the surrender, he patrolled the York River and searched a British vessel for contraband slaves.*

Joseph Saunders moved to Brunswick County in 1789 and Lawrence County, Alabama, in 1823. He successfully applied for a pension in 1832.

I do hereby certify that I was born in Lancaster County, Virginia, in June 1757, and I enlisted to serve three years in navy of Virginia on seventh March, 1777. The recruiting officer was named Thomas Downing, who never, I believe, came into active service. I was placed on board ship *Dragon,* then on the stock building at Fredericksburg, Virginia, commanded by Captain Eleazer Callender, John Lurty, first lieutenant. I helped to rig her, was launched in her, and as soon as she drifted from the wharf into the channel and ship's crew came on board, I was entrusted with charge of the provisions and issuing rations. And when the guns came on board I was entrusted with the charge of magazine and making cartridges, etc. I continued to act in both of these stations until a gunner was engaged, and he took charge of that department. I continued to fill the other place for some time. Mr. David Henderson from Fredericksburg was clerk of the ship.

A board of officers were organized, styled the Navy Board, by whose authority the navy of Virginia was regulated, commissioned, etc. They held their office at Williamsburg prior to the transferring [of the] seat of government to Richmond. To this board clerks of ships reported the rolls and stations of ships' crews, etc., etc., and from them drew money for payment of ships' crews. If those records could be referred to, ample evidences could be obtained for those claiming pensions of the Navy Department for some two or three years from first establishment, but my age and infirmity prevent my benefiting therefrom.

Three ships, a brig, and tender were commissioned and ordered on a cruise, destination not published. On the second or third day, fell in with a large ship. Proved to be a British seventy-four, which gave chase to our fleet; came up fast with us. Night came on, our fleet separated, changed course, and evaded pursuit. Returned to our station near the Capes of Virginia in order to protect the commerce of the Chesapeake Bay, which was much harassed by the British privateers, etc. After this, nothing worthy of note transpired for some time. (But find I omitted the names of ships and commanders thereof, that was ordered on a cruise. I now state them: ship *Tartar* commanded [by] John Taylor, ship *Tempest* commanded by Early Saunders, ship *Dragon* commanded by Eleazer Callender, brigs, name forgot, commanded by John Lurty, former first lieutenant of ship *Dragon,* and a tender.)

On this station a sail came in sight; gave chase to our ship. We housed our guns, concealed our men, and let our sails hang loosely; let some of sails hang half-mast. She proved to be a privateer, came down upon us, and fired ahead of us; began to take in sail. Found her mistake. We gave a broadside or two. She hauled up her sails, ran by us giving us a broadside, and made her escape. The firing was heard by Captain Taylor, who came alongside to know what it meant, and took out of our ship men and officers and gave chase to [the] privateer. Came up with her and engaged her. The action was warmly contested, and the Captain Taylor, who was commodore of the squadron, was dangerously wounded and several of the men, and Lieutenant Hamilton, I think, next in command. Bore away and left her to take care of his wounded.

Commodore Taylor never came into actual service again. Capt. William Saunders then commanded ship *Tartar,* Capt. James Barron the elder was then commodore, and Captain Callender resigned, and Capt. James Markham, an old seaman, commanded ship *Dragon.* He was an old, inferior man and soon resigned. Then Capt. Edward Travis commanded *Dragon.* About or before the time for which I enlisted expired, I was promoted to master's mate, and, being pleased with my station, I continued in the service, while many of my comrades took discharges and went home.

And when the British came into Hampton Roads, ship *Tempest* I think, however one of the ships commanded by Capt. Richard Barron, and the *Dragon* that lay there were obliged to give way to superior force and go up James River. Some British ships came up

James River, up as high as Chickahominy, and Lieutenant Chandler and myself obtained permission of Capt. James Maxwell, the commissioner of the navy, to take a galley and man her and go and attack a British ship then off the mouth of the river. We accordingly went down and made the attack. The ship was a letter of marque of twelve or fourteen guns, and the action continued until our ammunition failed, and we had to bear away. No lives lost on our side, but shot, langrage, and round shot flew thick around and through our sails and rigging until we got out of reach.

I was promoted to a lieutenant in the navy and instructed to man and fit out a galley as quick as possible (my commission was signed by Capt. James Maxwell, then commissioner of navy) and go down near the British fleet to watch their motion, if any motion there took place worth notice. I was to give notice to General Lafayette or the commander nearest thereto and attend to any orders from General Lafayette. I did so and joined Lieutenant Chandler, then on the said station of lookout, who in a few days was taken by a decoy fitted out by the British for that purpose and died a prisoner in their possession.

About the time the British army came from Charleston to Petersburg, Virginia, their vessels began to come higher up James River. They sent a number of gunboats up to our shipyard to destroy what was there. I had filled my galley with naval stores to take up the river to conceal them, but wind and tide being against me, could not go on, came to, put a spring on my cable, and awaited their arrival. It was not long before they came in sight, and, as soon as near enough, I discharged my cannon at them, sunk my vessel, and made my escape to shore with the men I had with me. This was the last active service I had in the navy, but rendered service to the army in conveying forage and provisions to them in a set of small craft I had procured by command of Captain Travis of the navy, considering me as a naval officer. And on this service, when off mouth [of] York River, I received a signal from French admiral that General Cornwallis had surrendered to the American arms. I went right up to York through British fleet and delivered the loads. While there, I was ordered by Capt. Edward Travis to take a sergeant and guard and go on board a British ship who was about to sail unrestricted as to load. But information said she had many slaves on board, contrary to stipulations. I was entrusted to search her, and all I found, bring on shore. I did search her, found only one, brought her on shore, and delivered her to the proper authority. There was no more call for the officers or mariners of the navy that I ever heard of.

10
BEHIND ENEMY LINES

ENOCH CROSBY *(b. 1750) is the best known spy of the Revolution. Born in Harwich on Cape Cod, he grew up in New York State and was living in Danbury, Connecticut, when the war broke out. He served one tour in Waterbury's Connecticut regiment, marching to St. Johns and back. On his way to join his regiment for a second tour of service in August 1776, he fell in with and gained the confidence of a Westchester Tory named Bunker. Crosby had the temperamental fascination with danger that is a primary qualification for a spy, and he was encouraged by John Jay and the New York Committee on Conspiracies. He infiltrated the Tory recruiting system, and the intelligence he provided aided the capture of numerous loyalists about to join the British army.*

James Fenimore Cooper's The Spy *(1821) was apparently based partly on Crosby's career. H. S. Barnum's* The Spy Unmasked *(1828), a biographical account intended to prove the connection between Cooper's novel and Crosby's career, raised him to preeminence in the annals of Revolutionary intelligence. His importance was confirmed in the 1950s and 1960s when John Bakeless and James H. Pickering found and publicized this pension narrative.*

In 1779, after previous spy work made further involvement of the sort too dangerous, Crosby joined a New York regiment and served two tours of duty along the Hudson. He submitted this deposition and was granted a pension in 1832.

In the month of April or in the forepart of May, 1775, he enlisted in the town of Danbury in the state of Connecticut into Capt. Noble Benedict's company in Colonel Waterbury's regiment of troops to defend the country for eight months' service. The regiment met at Greenwich in Connecticut. Stayed there two or three weeks, then went to New York under General Wooster. Stayed in New York a few weeks. The regiment was there carried to Albany in sloops and went directly to Half Moon; was there a few days. Went then to Ticonderoga; stayed there a few days to have the batteaux finished which were to convey them further. General Schuyler had the command to the Isle aux Noix, when, General Schuyler being unwell, General Montgomery had the command. The declarant went to St. Johns, which, being by us at time besieged by the Americans, in about five weeks surrendered, and the fort was taken. The declarant then went to Montreal; that he came from there with Colonel Waterbury's regiment to Albany and, having served the eight months, was at [that] place (Albany) permitted to leave the regiment and return home. That he had no written discharge.

And this declarant further says that in the latter part of the month of August in the year 1776, he enlisted into the regiment commanded by Colonel Swartwout in Fredericksburgh, now Carmel, in the county of Putnam, and started to join the army at Kingsbridge. The company had left Fredericksburgh before declarant started, and he started alone after his said enlistment, and on his way, at a place in Westchester County about two miles from Pines Bridge, he fell in company with a stranger who accosted the deponent and asked him if he was going "down." Declarant replied he was. The stranger then asked if declarant was not afraid to venture alone and said there were many rebels "below" and he would meet with difficulty in "getting down." The declarant perceived from the observations of the stranger that he supposed the declarant intended to go to the British, and, willing to encourage that misapprehension and turn it to the best advantage, he asked if there was any mode which he, the stranger, could point out by which the declarant could "get through" safely. The stranger, after being satisfied that declarant was wishing to join the British army, told him that there was a company raising in that vicinity to join the British army, that it was nearly complete and in a few days would be ready to "go down," and that declarant had better join that company and "go down" with them. The stranger finally gave to the declarant his name, it was Bunker, and told the declarant where, and showed the house in which he lived, and also told him that Fowler was to be the captain of the company then raising and Kipp, lieutenant.

After having learned this much from Bunker, the declarant told him that he was unwilling to wait until the company could be ready to march and would try to get through alone and parted from him on his way down and continued until night, when he stopped at the house of a man who was called Esquire Young and put up there for the night. In the course of conversation with Esquire Young, in the evening, declarant learned that he was a member of the committee of safety for the county of Westchester and then communicated to him the information he had obtained from Mr. Bunker. Esquire Young requested the declarant accompany him the next morning to the White Plains in Westchester County, as the committee of safety for the county were on that day to meet at the courthouse in that place.

The next morning the declarant, in company with Esquire Young, went to the White Plains and found the committee there sitting. After Esquire Young had had an interview with the committee, the declarant was sent for and went before the committee then sitting in the courtroom and there communicated the information he had obtained from Bunker. The committee, after learning the situation of declarant, that he was a soldier enlisted in Colonel Swartwout's regiment and on his way to join it, engaged to write to the colonel and explain the reason why he did not join it, if he would consent to aid in the apprehension of the company then raising. It was by all thought best that he should not join the regiment but should act in a different character, as he could thus be more useful to his country.

He was accordingly announced to Captain Townsend, who then was at the White Plains commanding a company of rangers, as a prisoner, and the captain was directed to keep him until further orders. In the evening after he was placed as a prisoner under Captain Townsend, he made an excuse to go out and was accompanied by a soldier. His excuse led him over a fence into a piece of corn then nearly or quite full grown. As soon as he was out of sight of the soldiers, he made the best of his way from the soldier, and when the soldier hailed him to return, he was almost beyond hearing. An alarm gun was fired, but declarant was far from danger.

In the course of the night, the declarant reached the house of said Bunker, who got up and let him in. Declarant then related to Bunker the circumstances of his having been taken prisoner, of his going before the committee at the courthouse, of being put under the charge of Captain Townsend, and of his escape; that he had concluded to avail himself of the protection of the company raising in his neighborhood to get down. The next morning

Bunker went with declarant and introduced him as a good loyalist to several of the company. Declarant remained some days with different individuals of the company and until it was about to go down, when declarant went one night to the house of Esquire Young to give information of the state and progress of the company. The distance was four or five miles from Bunker's. At the house of Esquire Young, declarant found Captain Townsend with a great part of his company, and after giving the information he returned to the neighborhood of Bunker's, and that night declarant, with a great part of the company which was preparing to go down, were made prisoners. The next day all of them, about thirty in number, were marched to the White Plains and remained there several days, a part of the time locked up in jail with the other prisoners. The residue of the time, he was with the committee. The prisoners were finally ordered to Fishkill, in the county of Dutchess, where the state convention was then sitting. The declarant went as a prisoner to Fishkill. Captain Townsend with his company of rangers took charge of the company at Fishkill.

A committee for detecting conspiracies was sitting, composed of John Jay, afterwards governor of New York, Zephaniah Platt, afterwards first judge of Dutchess County, Colonel Duer of the county of Albany, and a Mr. Sackett. The declarant was called before that committee, who understood the character of declarant and the nature of his services. This the committee must have learned either from Captain Townsend or from the committee at White Plains. The declarant was examined under oath and his examination reduced to writing. The prisoners with the declarant were kept whilst declarant remained at Fishkill in a building which had been occupied as a hatter's shop, and they were guarded by a company of rangers commanded by Captain Clark. The declarant remained about a week at Fishkill, when he was bailed by Jonathan Hopkins. This was done to cover the character in which declarant acted.

Before the declarant was bailed, the Fishkill committee had requested him to continue in this service, and on declarant mentioning the fact of his having enlisted in Colonel Swartwout's company and the necessity there was of his joining it, he was informed that he should be indemnified from that enlistment, that they would write to the colonel and inform him that declarant was in their service. The committee then wished declarant to undertake a secret service over the river. He was furnished with a

Enoch Crosby

secret pass, which was a writing signed by the committee, which is now lost, and directed to go to the house of Nicholas Brawer, near the mouth of Wappinger's Creek, who would take him across the river, and then to proceed to the house of John Russell, about ten miles from the river, and make such inquiries and discoveries as he could.

He proceeded according to his directions to said Brawer's and from thence to John Russell's and there hired himself to said Russell to work for him but for no definite time. This was a neighborhood of loyalists, and it was expected that a company was there raising for the British army. The declarant remained about ten days in Russell's employment and during that time ascertained that a company was then raising but was not completed. Before declarant left Fishkill on this service, a time was fixed for him to recross the river and give information to someone of the committee who was to meet him. This time having arrived and the company not being completed, the declarant recrossed the river and met Zephaniah Platt, one of the committee, and gave him all the information he had then obtained. Declarant was directed to cross the river to the neighborhood of Russell's and, on a time then fixed, again to meet the committee on the east side of the river.

Declarant returned to Russell's neighborhood, soon became intimate with the loyalists, was introduced to Captain Robinson, said to be an English officer and who was to command the company then raising. Captain Robinson occupied a cave in the mountains, and deponent, having agreed to go with the company, was invited and accepted of the invitation to lodge with Robinson in the cave. They slept together nearly a week at the cave, and the time for the company to start having been fixed and the route designated, to pass Severns to Bush Carricks, where they were to stop the first night. This time for starting having arrived before the appointed time to meet the committee on the east side of the river, the declarant, in order to get an opportunity to convey information to Fishkill, recommended that each man should the night before they started sleep where he chose, and that each should be by himself, for if they should be discovered that night together, all would be taken, which would be avoided if they were separated. This proposition was acceded to, and when they separated, declarant not having time to go to Fishkill, and as the only, and as it appeared to him the best means of giving the information was to go to a Mr. Purdy, who was a stranger to declarant and all he knew of him was that the Tories called him a wicked rebel and said that he ought to die, declarant went and found Purdy, informed him of the situation of affairs, of the time the company was to start, and the place at which they were to stop the first night, and requested him to go to Fishkill and give the information to the committee. Purdy assured the declarant that the information should be given.

Declarant returned to Russell's and lodged in his barn. The following evening the company assembled, consisting of about thirty men, and started from Russell's house, which was in the town of Marlborough and county of Ulster, for New York, and in the course of the night arrived at Bush Carricks and went into the barn to lodge after taking refreshments. Before morning the barn was surrounded by American troops, and the whole company, including Captain Robinson, were made prisoners. The troops who took the company prisoner were commanded by Capt. Melancton Smith, who commanded a company of rangers at Fishkill. His company crossed the river to perform this service. Colonel Duer was with Captain Smith's company on this expedition. The prisoners, including the declarant, were marched to Fishkill and confined in the stone church, in which there was near two hundred prisoners. After remaining one night in the church, the committee sent for declarant and told him that it was unsafe for him to remain with the prisoners, as the least suspicion of the course he had pursued would prove fatal to him, and advised him to leave the village of Fishkill and to remain where they could call upon him if his services should be wanted.

Declarant went to the house of a Dutchman, a farmer whose name is forgotten, about five miles from the village of Fishkill and there went to work at making shoes. After declarant had made arrangements for working at shoes, he informed Mr. Sackett, one of the committee, where he could be found if he should be wanted.

In about a week, declarant received a letter from the committee requesting him to meet some one of the committee at the house of Dr. Orsborn, about one mile from Fishkill. Declarant, according to the request, went to the house of Dr. Orsborn, and soon after John Jay came there, inquired for the doctor, who was absent, inquired for medicine, but found none that he wanted. He came out of the house and went to his horse, near which declarant stood, and as he hopped he said in a low voice, "It won't do. There are too many around. Return to your work."

Declarant went back and went to work at shoes, but within a day or two was again notified and a horse sent to him requiring him to go to Bennington in Vermont and from thence westerly to a place called Maloonscack and there call on one Hazard Wilcox, a Tory of much notoriety, and ascertain if anything was going on there injurious to the American cause. Declarant followed his instructions, found Wilcox, but could not learn that any secret measure was then projected against the interest of the country at that place, but learned from Wilcox a list of persons friendly to the British cause who could be safely trusted. From that place quite down to the south part of Dutchess County declarant followed the directions of said Wilcox and called on the different individuals by him mentioned but could discover nothing of importance until he reached the town of Pawling in Dutchess County, where he called upon a doctor whose name he thinks was Prosser and informed him that he wished to go below but was fearful of some trouble. The doctor informed him that there was a company raising in that vicinity to go to New York to join the British army; that the captain's name was Sheldon; that he had been down and got a commission; that he, Prosser, was doctoring the lieutenant, whose name was Chase; that if declarant would wait a few days he could safely go down with that company; that he could stay about the neighborhood and should be informed when the company was ready. That declarant remained in that vicinity, became acquainted with several of the persons who were going with that company, was acquainted with the Lieutenant Chase but never saw the captain to form any acquaintance with him.

The season had got so far advanced that the company were about to start to join the enemy to be ready for an early commencement of the campaign in 1777. It was about the last of February of that year when a place was fixed and also a time for meeting. It was at a house situated half a mile from the road and about three miles from a house then occupied by Colonel Morehouse, a militia colonel. After the time was fixed for the marching of Captain Sheldon's company, the deponent went in the night to Colonel Morehouse and informed him of the situation of the company, of the time appointed for meeting, of the place, etc., and Morehouse informed declarant that they should be attended to. The declarant remained about one month in the neighborhood and once in the time met Mr. Sackett, one of the committee, at Colonel Ludington's and apprised him of what was then going on and was to have given the committee intelligence when the company was to march, but the shortness of the time between the final arrangement and the time of starting was that declarant was obliged to give the information to Colonel Morehouse.

The company consisting of about thirty met at the time and place appointed, and, after they had been there an hour or two, two young men of the company came in and said there was a gathering under arms at old Morehouse's. The inquiry became general. What could it mean? Was there any traitors in the company? The captain soon called one or two of the company out the door for the purpose of private conversation about the situation, and very soon declarant heard the cry of "Stand! Stand!" Those out the door ran but were soon met by a company coming from a different direction. They were taken, the house surrounded, and the company all made prisoners. The colonel then ordered them to be tied together, two and two. They came to declarant, and he urged to be excused from going, as he was lame and could not travel. The colonel replied, "You shall go dead or alive, and if in no other way, you shall be carried on this horse with me." The rest were marched off and declarant put onto the horse with Colonel Morehouse. All went to the house of Colonel Morehouse, and when the prisoners were marched into the house, the declarant with the permission of Morehouse left them and made the best of his way to Colonel Ludington's and there informed him of the operations of the night. He reached Colonel Ludington's about daylight in the morning. From thence he went to Fishkill to the house of Dr. Van Wyck where John Jay boarded and there informed him of all the occurrences on that northern expedition. Said Jay requested the declarant to come before the committee the next night, when they would be ready to receive him. He accordingly went before the committee, where he detailed under his oath all that had occurred since he had seen them. There was no more business at that time in which they wished to employ declarant, and, he, being somewhat apprehensive that a longer continuance in that employment would be dangerous and the time for which he enlisted in Colonel Swartwout's regiment having expired, he came home with the approbation of the committee. This was about the last of May, 1777, and in the course of the fall after, the declarant saw Colonel Swartwout at his house in Fishkill and there talked over the subject of this employment of the declarant by the committee, and the colonel told declarant that he had drawn his pay the same as if he had been with the regiment. That the paymaster of the regiment lived in the town of Hurley in Ulster County; declarant went to the paymaster and received his pay for nine months' service or for the term for which the regiment was raised. The declarant was employed in the secret service for a period of full nine months. . . .

JOHN L. MERSEREAU *(1756–1841) was a native of Staten Island and the son of Washington's deputy commissioner of prisoners. He was recruited by Washington himself to remain in New Brunswick after the American evacuation and gather intelligence from behind the British lines. He had several hair-raising escapes, as he relates here, but he successfully relayed information on British activity in New York for eighteen months in 1777–78, until withdrawn from enemy territory because of British suspicion. He then became an assistant commissary of prisoners and served eighteen to twenty months as commissary at the Rutland, Vermont, prison camp.*

He submitted this deposition in 1840 and was granted a pension.

The memorial of the undersigned, a citizen of Tioga County, state of Pennsylvania, respectfully sheweth that your memorialist was in the service of the United States in the war of the Revolution for a period of something more than three years; that during about eighteen months he acted as a spy for the Americans while the British held possession of New York and Staten Island and for the remainder of said period was at Rutland in Massachusetts, acting in the capacity of assistant deputy commissary of prisoners quartered at that station.

When the British took possession of New York and Staten Island, my father with his family (including myself, my brother Joshua, and others) resided on the north side of Staten Island. A large amount of property was taken or destroyed by the British. About this time we moved to New York, and your petitioner was for some time afterward engaged in transporting provisions for the American army to Bergen Neck and Paulus Hook, the then outposts. I also superintended the building of twelve large flatboats which were used by the American troops under General Sullivan to cross to Staten Island for the purpose of attacking the British forces there. These boats were built, as I understood, by the orders of General Washington. After this, we went to New Brunswick, landing about the time that Washington retreated through New Jersey.

Before General Washington left New Brunswick, it was arranged between him and my father, Joshua Mersereau (as I was informed at that time by my father), that I should remain at New Brunswick until it should be included within the British lines and afterwards go to New York and Staten Island and continue at one or the other of those places (or other places within the enemy's lines) for the purpose of obtaining intelligence that might be useful to the Americans and conveying the same to the headquarters of the American army. Explicit instructions came for this purpose to me through my father. I did so and spent in this service as before stated, according [to] the best of my recollection, about eighteen months. It was arranged that intelligence should be conveyed beyond the British lines by a young man of the name of John Parker, an apprentice of my father to the business of shipbuilding. After this young man had made three or more journeys from Staten Island to New Jersey or Pennsylvania on this business, he became suspected by the British, was captured by them at Amboy, and imprisoned in New York until his death. Your memorialist visited him in the prison about twelve hours before his death and offered to supply him with clothing and food. His answer was that it was of no use, for he should not live long; they kept the prisoners several days without food and then supplied them with poisoned bread; that numbers had been killed in that way, and that he, without being aware of it, had eaten of the bread and felt sick then. I went to the door of his room the next morning. He was not there, and the gaoler informed me he had died and was taken out the night previous.

After the arrest of Parker, I went in the night to the Jersey shore and saw my father at the house of my uncle John La Grange in Elizabethtown, where we concerted another mode of communicating intelligences, which was practiced as long as I remained in this service. The information was committed to paper and enclosed in a bottle secured by a thread passing out by the side of the cork. This was conveyed in the dead of night and generally by means of a small temporary raft to Shooters Island, between Staten Island and the Jersey shore, where it was deposited under the side of a large rock, where it was found by the proper person from the Jersey side and an answer if necessary deposited in the same bottle. When intelligence was left at the place aforesaid, the person depositing it there notified his correspondent by a light, a plan previously fixed upon (at a certain hour of the night), visible from the opposite shore. The reception of communications was acknowledged by a similar signal.

Your memorialist sometimes carried intelligence to the Jersey shore in person. At one time, learning that my father was at Elizabethtown and having important intelligence to communicate and further instructions to receive, I repaired in the night an old skiff which lay among the grass on a part of the island not then guarded by the British and passed over and had an interview with my father. But when my business was concluded it was too late to return that night, and I remained on the Jersey side the next day, concealed in a barn. During my absence, the British had noticed the absence of the old skiff and placed a sentry near the place where I had embarked and expected to land on my return. I landed there without knowing the place was guarded. The sentry hailed, and I fled on my hands and feet to a ditch, along which I could run without being much exposed to his fire. He fired his musket just as I got into the ditch, and his ball struck a post just over my head. I then jumped out of the ditch and ran directly to my lodgings. The sentinel, with others, pursued me and reached the out door just as I entered my room. Had they persevered, I must have been discovered and taken. It happened, however, that a British "Major Tenpenny" (so-called) quartered at the same house and, being drunk at the time, countermanded further search, swearing "there were no rebels in the house where he lodged," or words to that effect.

Your memorialist has no writing by which he can fix the time when he left the service aforesaid, but believes it was near the end of 1778 or the beginning of 1779. The reason of my leaving the spy service was that my friends had learned that I was suspected by the British. From this, I went immediately to the Rutland barracks and took charge of the commissary department there and remained there in that service about eighteen or twenty months, except that during a part of this time I went to New York with a flag of truce to procure clothing and money for the prisoners of Burgoyne's army stationed at Rutland barracks, and at another time I went to Philadelphia to deliver up one Chapman to the governor of Pennsylvania (Governor Mifflin, I think). Chapman was supposed to be guilty of burning an American soldier in a stack of hay somewhere in Pennsylvania.

In consequence of a weakness in his right arm, your memorialist never was gratified to carry or use a musket or other arms, which was the reason that he was employed in the service aforesaid, while his father and brother entered into a more active and regular service, in which the former continued till the end of the war, and the latter until he was taken a prisoner by the British.

My father was one of the confidential friends of General Washington and was frequently employed by him in important business. He was the same Mersereau who removed the boats on the Delaware and thus prevented the British from crossing to Pennsylvania.

The services rendered by your memorialist were, as he verily believes, important and useful to the American cause. Much of it and the most important and dangerous was from its nature known to very few persons, and I know of no living witness except my brother Joshua Mersereau, my father having deceased in the year 1804 or about that time.

JOHN WYATT *(b. 1748) was born in London, immigrated to Virginia sometime before the Revolution, and early in 1778 volunteered for one year with the Eighth Virginia Regiment. He participated in the Battle of Monmouth and, after a leave, joined, in Petersburg, the Virginia troops that were sent to defend Charleston. He surrendered with Lincoln's army on 12 May 1780, and after being imprisoned for six months he purchased a pass from a British sympathizer and made his way in the guise of a Tory through the British lines and back to his home in Botetourt County, Virginia.*

The American officers were quick to appreciate the potential value of Wyatt, a man with a British "protection." He was sent to the New River settlement and succeeded in identifying Tories and preventing them from actively taking up arms for the British.

Wyatt moved to Kentucky in 1792 and was residing in Rush County in 1833 when he successfully applied for a pension.

That in the winter or early in the spring (the month he does not recollect) of the year 1778, in Botetourt County, Virginia, where he then resided, he volunteered for one year in a company commanded by Capt. Joseph Crockett in the Eighth Regiment of Virginia troops commanded by Col. Abraham Bowman; Clark, major. The names of the other officers he does not remember except a Captain Wales who belonged to the same regiment.

That from Botetourt County he marched to Petersburg in the state of Virginia, where he lay for a short time until the levies were collected, when he with the troops took up the line of march for Valley Forge, where he joined the main army under General Washington, at which place he remained for a short time, when he marched into New Jersey and was present in the Battle of Monmouth, after which battle he marched to Robinson's Farm on North River, where he lay until late in the fall, and from thence marched to Bound Brook, New Jersey, where he remained until in the winter. Being sometime in the month of December, 1778 (as he believes), he enlisted into the Virginia troops in a company commanded by a captain named Steed or Steeth or some such name in the Eighth Regiment commanded by Colonel Heath (Colonel Bowman having returned home as well as he recollects). The brigade to which he belonged was commanded by Gen. Charles Scott. After enlisting, he returned home upon furlough, where he remained three months.

At the expiration of his furlough, he repaired to Petersburg under Lt. Andrew Scott, where he remained until the next fall, when he marched under Colonel Heath and Wallace (the latter being lieutenant colonel) through Hillsboro and Camden to Charleston in South Carolina, where he lay during the siege of that place and was, while there, made a prisoner by the British and remained a prisoner for about six months, when he purchased the protection of one Joseph Seal who had been made a prisoner at Waxhaw and had taken protection under the British and enlisted with them. He gave him about a quart of rum for the protection, and with it, and by passing under the name of Joseph Seal, the applicant effected his passage through the British lines, made his escape, and returned home to Botetourt.

After his return to his home, and it being understood by the officers there how he had escaped, they had an interview with him, when General Lewis, Colonel Preston, Colonel Chrystie, and Colonel Crockett prevailed upon him not to rejoin the army, as they would have him excused. They then prevailed upon applicant to act as a spy among the Tories on New River, which he was enabled to do by having the protection aforesaid. Col. Hugh Crockett had an old captain's commission under Governor Dunmore which he altered by erasing out his name and inserting that of Joseph Seal. With this commission and his protection and some newspapers he had got at Charleston, etc., he, under the direction of the aforesaid officers, started for the Tory settlement on New River, where he arrived and made himself known to them as a British captain and was kindly received and entertained by them. After remaining awhile with them, the Tories communicated to him the objects they had in view. He learned from them that it was their intention to attack, break up, and destroy Chiswell's lead mines on New River and to attack the homes, destroy the property, and take the lives of our leading men in that section of the country. He obtained from them a written list of their force, which amounted to a considerable number.

Finding that their attack was to be made at a period so early that he could not return in time to apprise Colonel Preston and other officers so that they could be prepared, he told the Tories to desist for the present, that in a short time there would be British troops in the neighborhood who would assist them in their enterprise. With this arrangement the Tories agreed, when he, applicant, left them and started on his return to communicate to Preston and the other officers what he had learned. He immediately went to Colonel Preston and communicated to him, Crockett, Chrystie, and other officers what he had discovered and learned, who immediately raised the militia and took a large number of the Tories prisoners. Applicant was along with the militia at the time.

After this, sometime in the summer of 1781, the precise time he does not recollect, he, in Botetourt County, entered into a company of militia for a two-months tour as a man furnished by two of the persons who were taken as Tories, as some of them were compelled to pay men to perform duty as a punishment for their disaffection. He marched under Colonel Campbell (his captain he does not recollect) to the neighborhood of Yorktown, where he with his regiment were employed in reconnoitering the country until his term of duty expired, when he returned home about a week before the surrender of Cornwallis, which was the last duty he performed.

WEDNESDAY, FEBRUARY 10, 1779.] THE [No. 247.]

ROYAL GAZETTE.

NEW-YORK: *Published by* JAMES RIVINGTON, *Printer to the King's Most Excellent Majesty.*

New-York, 15thNov. 1778.

Mr. RIVINGTON,

CAPTAIN Duncan, late of the Rose Letter of Marque, with his crew, who so bravely distinguished themselves in a severe action with a French frigate, arriving here late last night in a Flag of Truce from Elisabeth-Town, several of those gallant seamen were by mistake detained at their landing, in order to be put on board the ships of war; but Admiral Gambier being informed thereof, he was pleased to direct, that they should immediately be set at liberty, and to give express orders, that no prisoners returning from captivity in future, shall be obliged to serve on board the King's ships. I therefore think it my duty to request, that his Majesty's faithful subjects may be made acquainted therewith, through the channel of the Public News-Papers.

I am, Sir,
Your most obedient Servant,
JAMES DICK, Commissary for Naval Prisoners.

All Seamen and others that shall come in from the rebels after the 20th instant, and produce a certificate from any officer of the out-posts, or from any commander of the King's ships of their having come in after that date, will be at liberty to enter on board any of the privateers or letters of marque fitting out at this port, and not be liable to be impressed on board the men of war, whilst in that service.

JAMES DICK.

New-York, 15th Dec. 1778.

By MAJOR GENERAL JONES, Commandant of New-York,

PROCLAMATION,

BY a Proclamation of His Excellency Sir Henry Clinton, dated New-York, December 20, 1777, the farmers of Long-Island and Staten-Island, were ordered to thrash and bring to market, by stated periods such proportions of Wheat, Rye, and Indian Corn, in their possession, as they did not stand in need of for the support of their families, and the sowing their lands: They were required also, to give an account to the Colonels of militia of their respective districts, what quantities of grain they possessed, and what it might be necessary to reserve for the above uses. The Commander in Chief has been pleased to order that Proclamation to remain in force, and be strictly observed, the rates excepted, which, as an

Forage-Office, New-York, Sept. 10, 1778.

THE Farmers on New-York-Island, Long- and Staten-Island, are hereby required immediately to thrash out their grain, as the STRAW is wanted for the use of his Majesty's troops, for which they will be paid at the usual rate, on producing certificates of the delivery from the Deputy Commissaries at the different posts of Brooklyn and Flushing, on Long-Island; at Coles-Ferry on Staten-Island; and at Kingsbridge, Marston's Wharf, and Bear-Market, on New-York Island; with the same allowance for transportation as they received last year.

GEORGE BRINLEY,
Commissary of Forage

PUBLIC NOTICE is hereby given to the distressed Refugees, that the Gentlemen appointed to distribute the money collected by subscription for their relief, attend at the Police Office in Smith-Street, every Thursday from the hours of Eleven till One.

Notice is hereby given to the Citizens,

THAT JOHN NORRIS, at the corner house, near the Main Guard, and DAVID HENRY MALLOWS, near the Tea-Water Pump, have the care of the Chimney-Sweeps, and that on a note in writing being left at either of their houses; a Sweep will be sent to the place required; the fine of Five Pounds, heretofore established, will be punctually exacted from every inhabitant whose chimney shall take fire through neglect. Each chimney to be swept once in every four weeks.

Office of Police.
Nov. 12, 1778.
ANDREW ELLIOT, Superindent General.
D. MATHEWS, Mayor.

To all OWNERS and MANAGERS of PRIVATEERS.

NOTICE IS HEREBY GIVEN,

THAT Privateers and their Prizes, arriving in this harbour, are to put their Prisoners on board the GOOD HOPE or PRINCE of WALES PRISON-SHIPS, and bring Receipts for them from the master of the latter, to the Commissary for Naval Prisoners, before

Forage-Office, New-York, Dec. 9, 1778.

The Commander in Chief having taken into consideration the price of Forage, does not think it adequate to other articles, and is pleased to order, that from and after the above date, the following prices should be paid untill further orders.

	Currency.
For good Upland Hay,	8s. per cwt.
Salt Hay,	4s. per ditto.
Straw,	3s. per ditto.
Indian Corn,	10s. per bushel.
Oats,	7s. per ditto.

And Two Shillings and Six Pence a Ton for every mile carting or water-carriage; he has allowed these ample prices, that no further delay may be made by the Farmers in bringing in all the Hay, both Fresh and Salt to the most contiguous Magazines, where they will receive certificates for the quantity delivered, which will be paid at the Forage-Office, New-York, and has directed me to acquaint them, that any person that is found delinquent after this notice, will have their Forage taken, and no receipts given.

GEORGE BRINLEY,
Commissary Forage.

TO BE SOLD,
By GEORGE WEBSTER,
At the Sign of the TEA CANNISTER,
No. 1077, WATER-STREET.

ONE hundred and seventy dozen of Ramsay and Marshall's best red PORT WINE in casks, containing 6 dozen and a half each; likewise a quantity of London bottled PORTER, and excellent Liverpool BEER in the like packages; the lowest price for the port wine will be One Guinea per dozen; a purchaser for the whole, or part, will be extremely agreeable.

A few quarter Casks of LISBON WINE to be had at the same place.

MOORE and KEKR,

AT their Store in Wall-Street, No. 16, have for Sale, choice Irish mess Pork in barrels, an assortment of yard wide Irish linens, mens & womens shoes, French lint for the use of surgeons, a few quarter chests of Green Tea, an assortment of French locks, Indigo, bottled

A Quantity of
ROCK-SALT,
For Sale.
Enquire of the Printer.

SELLING OFF FOR CASH,
By JAMES GAUTIER,
No. 324, DOCK-STREET.
The Remainder of his Stock in Trade;—Going to Europe by the first Conveyance.

A Compleat set of Turner's Tools.	Officers Canteens, large and small
Bar Iron and German Steel.	Medicines and Bark
Stays and Whalebone.	Common Shoes
Sieve bottoms.	Leather Portmantuas
Ironmongery of various kinds	Best mahogany houshold Furniture.
Needles and Fish-hooks	Four post and tent Bedsteads, &c.
Shirts	Superfine scarlet Cloth
Bridles and Saddle cloths	White Cassimirs
Black Stocks	Womens finished heels.

LAMP Oil, and white Pine Boards, and a few Carpets to be sold, at No. 49, Wall-Street.

THE Vestry hereby give public notice to all persons who have or may hereafter hire any of the Houses, the rents of which are appropriated for the maintenance of the Poor of this city, that they are not under any pretence whatever to assign or transfer to any other person their term in such house or houses, without obtaining the previous consent and approbation of the Vestry; and that no premiums will be permitted to be given to, or taken by any such tenants, for, or in consideration of such transfer. The intention of this inhibition is if possible to prevent the great abuse that has been practised by tenants, some of whom availing themselves of the right of preference, they were intituled to by virtue of their pre-occupancy, have renewed their engagements for houses for another year, without any intention to reside in them, but solely with a view of extorting extravagant sums over and above the stipulated rents from the necessitous and distressed.

Vestry-Chamber, Feb. 4, 1779.

A Tory newspaper

WILLIAM JOHNSON *(b. 1760) was born in Freehold and resided at Newark, New Jersey, when the war broke out. He was a volunteer in the state militia throughout most of the war and served almost continuously, substituting for others in the alternate months for which he was not personally subject to the draft. He was called out frequently and participated in skirmishes on Staten Island and in the Battle of Connecticut Farms.*

Sometime after the Battle of Monmouth, William Johnson and a friend, Abraham Ward, were recruited by Washington through Johnson's uncle to serve as spies in British-held New York City. Setting themselves up between New Jersey and New York as black-market merchants, of which there were many operating with full British support throughout the war, they periodically went into the city and reported on any observable activity. Their contact in New York was a Barney Savage.

In late summer 1781 Johnson noticed unusual military activity. He learned that reinforcements were being amassed for Cornwallis's beleaguered force in Virginia, reported the intelligence to Washington, and was sent back to the city to spread a false report that Washington was about to attack the British simultaneously at Staten Island, Paulus Hook, and Manhattan. He successfully carried out the mission.

Johnson resided at Newark, in Bergen County, New Jersey, and in New York City after the war. He submitted this deposition in 1834, but his application was rejected for lack of documentary evidence.

In the month of October or November, 1776, deponent became a volunteer in the company of militia commanded by Capt. Caleb Wheeler. The other company officers were David Sears, first lieutenant, Isaac Davis, second lieutenant, Stephen Hays, orderly sergeant. The company was attached to Col. Philip Van Cortlandt's regiment, Samuel Hays, major, James Hedden, adjutant. The regiment was under General Dickinson, who commanded all the militia of New Jersey. That he continued attached to this company during the whole of the Revolutionary War; that same individuals, who are above named, continued as officers of the company during the same period, none of whom he believes are now living. The company was composed principally of residents of Newark, New Jersey, and was stationed at that place throughout the war.

The first marching service which this and the other militia companies stationed at Newark rendered was to cross over from Elizabethtown Point to Staten Island to attack the British troops who were stationed at different places on that island. On our approach, the enemy retreated to their principal fortifications at the Narrows, and our troops then returned to Newark. General Wines commanded the American troops on duty on this occasion, who in all numbered about fifteen hundred men. This must have occurred more than a year after deponent was first attached to the militia.

In this skirmish some British were killed. One in particular he remembers was lying on the ground mortally wounded. He had a green coat on, which one of our company (an Irishman) espied and said, "Your coat is better than mine; I'll have it." He immediately took the coat off the wounded soldier and put it on his own back, and immediately run his bayonet in the body of the wounded soldier, who on his march back lay quite dead.

In the spring, about a year after this, about daybreak, we were suddenly surprised by a body of British troops and refugees from Paulus Hook, about a thousand or twelve hundred in number, who marched into Newark and threw us at first into great disorder. The alarm was given, and our troops were soon in readiness and enabled to drive them back. He remembers that the refugees were part of Van Buskirk's corps. Deponent's brother was at this time shot above the knee and fell beside him, who in consequence of the wound he then received was confined for nine months after. Captain Knox of General Wayne's brigade, who volunteered on this occasion, was shot through the jaws a few minutes after. The captain had been married the evening before, and deponent and his brother were at the wedding, and while there, deponent jokingly said to Captain Knox that if they were attacked by the British that night he would call upon him to assist in the defense. The captain requested him to do so. We were attacked about daylight, and deponent did call upon Captain Knox and loaned him a gun.

A few months after this, we were alarmed in the morning by the firing of cannon and musketry on the road leading to Springfield. Our companies were soon in readiness and marched towards Springfield, where we were joined by the other companies. We found that General Knyphausen had landed with about three thousand Hessians. Our troops attacked them, and they, towards evening, retreated to Elizabethtown, where on the following morning our troops again attacked them. They defended themselves by a breastwork which had been erected by our troops sometime previous. We had several skirmishes during the day, and we remained at Elizabethtown until the next morning, when we returned to Newark.

Deponent was on duty in his company, which was under arms at Freehold, Monmouth County, at the time of the Battle of Monmouth, but the company was not in the engagement. After the battle, we marched to Englishtown and quartered there during the night. It was the practice of the members of this company during their service to perform duty alternately one month at a time. Deponent, in addition to his regular month's duty, was in the habit of serving as a substitute for others during their month's duty, for which they remunerated him, and consequently he was scarcely ever off duty. Gilbert Smith is the only individual whose name he can now remember as one for whom he thus served.

In the winter before the Battle of Monmouth, about eleven o'clock at night, deponent was called out of his bed at his residence near Newark by Col. Marinus Willett, who with his regiment were on their way to Paulus Hook and was by the colonel desired to act as a guide to conduct them in the most unfrequented way to that place. Though quite ill, the ground covered with snow, and the weather exceedingly cold, deponent, having been particularly recommended for that duty to the colonel by Captain Wheeler, did not hesitate but immediately proceeded with them, where they remained for about an hour and then returned to Newark. Colonel Willett's object was to obtain a survey of the place.

The uncle of deponent, Isaac Johnson, then residing near Morristown, was well acquainted with General Washington while his headquarters were established at Morristown. About a year before the termination of the war, the general wished deponent's uncle to recommend some persons of discretion on whom he might rely to procure information of the enemy's movements at New York and elsewhere. Mr. Johnson recommended for the duty Abraham Ward (who was attached to Captain Wheeler's company) and deponent. We were associated together in business, purchasing goods in New York for country merchants, which business was necessarily conducted by us with great secrecy and without the knowledge of the officers or members of our company. Sometime after, Ward received a letter from General Washington with instructions, enclosing a pass containing our names to protect us in case we were suspected or taken by our own people for being seen in the enemy's lines. We were often engaged in this business and frequently communicated information that we obtained to General Washington. Those with whom we conferred in New York supposed us to be friendly to the British cause.

About two or three weeks before the surrender of Cornwallis, deponent was in New York for the above purpose (his partner on this occasion was not with him in consequence of sickness in his family) when he perceived an unusual bustle. Press gangs were passing through the streets to impress men to man the vessels. The streets were lined with troops from the Battery to the old

Federal Hall where the barracks were erected. Deponent, instead of making any purchases, immediately called upon Barney Savage, the individual who had been designated to us by General Washington with whom we could safely communicate and get information. Mr. Savage told deponent that an express had just arrived from Cornwallis to send a reinforcement to the South of five thousand troops and all the disposable shipping, and he advised deponent to hasten with this information to General Washington. As soon as deponent procured a permit from the mayor, Mr. Matthews, with whom deponent was well acquainted, he supposing deponent was friendly to the British cause, Mr. Savage landed deponent over to Bergen shore in his boat, and deponent immediately walked over to Newark Bay, where his boat lay, and rowed hard to get to his home, where he arrived about three o'clock in the afternoon. Deponent requested Mr. Ward, who resided in the same house, to write to General Washington immediately, which he did, and the general received the letter about nine or ten o'clock that night. The next evening we received a letter from General Washington directing us to go to New York immediately and circulate as well as we could the information that he intended to attack New York, Staten Island, and Paulus Hook.

In company with a young man hired for the purpose, deponent proceeded that night to Bergen Point, where Colonel Ward's regiment of refugees, composed of blacks and whites, were garrisoned. Deponent called upon the colonel and communicated to him the intended attack of General Washington. The colonel, upon this, ordered two fieldpieces to be fired and conveyed deponent in his barge to a British galley which was lying in the kills opposite Colonel Ward's garrison. Deponent communicated the same information to the officer commanding the galley, who immediately conveyed deponent in his barge to New York and introduced him to General Birch, who was in command of the British troops there. Deponent informed the general that a friend of their cause had sent him from Morristown to let them know of General Washington's intended attack. He thanked deponent for the information and said deponent ought to be well rewarded for it. Deponent then went to Mr. Savage and from thence to the mayor's to get a permit and returned home. The British troops did not leave New York as was contemplated, and General Washington, instead of making those attacks, immediately proceeded to the South, where the surrender of the British army ended the Revolutionary struggle.

JOSEPH KERR (b. 1760), of Scotch-Irish parentage, was born in Chester County, Pennsylvania, and moved to York County, South Carolina, before the war. Young in appearance and a cripple, he was not subject to the draft, but he volunteered to serve as a spy. His innocuous appearance and his reckless daring made him exceptionally effective, and the information he gathered was used to good advantage at the Battle of Blackstocks Ford and the complete American victory at Kings Mountain, 7 October 1780.

His narrative of the last engagement presents problems. On 12 July 1780, almost three months before *Kings Mountain, Col. William Bratton and more than two hundred North Carolina militiamen, according to the* State Records of North Carolina, *ambushed a Capt. Christian Hook or Huck, killing thirty-six men and capturing twenty-nine. Kerr's memory, at age seventy-two, was presumably faulty as to either officers' names or time sequence.*

After the war Joseph Kerr lived in York District, South Carolina; Wilson County, Tennessee; and White County, Tennessee. He submitted this deposition and was granted a pension in 1832.

In the year of 1778 or 1779, he cannot remember which, he lived in Mecklenburg County, North Carolina. The British and Tories were very troublesome in that part of the country and at that time. This declarant has been a cripple from his infancy, properly termed an invalid, and not subject to military duty.

At the pressing solicitation of his suffering neighbors, who were exposed to the ravages of the enemy, this declarant went to General McDowell in Rowan County (as he now thinks) and offered his services to him as a "spy." The offer was thankfully received, and this declarant entered the service in that character. He was sent by General McDowell from Rowan, North Carolina, to Tiger River in South Carolina, near Blackstocks Ford, to watch the operations of the British and Tories. He found some British and Tories, to the number of about fifteen hundred as well as he now recollects, quartered on Tiger River, on the south side, about half a mile below the above-mentioned ford. He then returned to Rowan County, North Carolina, and apprised General McDowell and Colonel Stein of the discoveries he had made. From Tiger River to General McDowell's station in Rowan County he believes was about ninety miles. He was well mounted and traveled night and day until he reached General McDowell. On receiving this information, General McDowell, Colonel Stein, and the troops with them marched to Smith's Ford of Broad River, South Carolina. Here General McDowell remained with a part of the troops and detached Colonel Stein, with about six hundred men as well as declarant now recollects, to go against the British and Tories at Blackstocks Ford on Tiger River, where their situation had been particularly spied out by this declarant. Colonel Stein with his troops came upon them rather by surprise, routed, and defeated them. Colonel Stein in this engagement lost four men killed and had seven wounded. He took no prisoners but killed, as declarant thinks, from fifty to a hundred of the British and Tories.

Declarant then returned to North Carolina and joined Colonel Williams as a spy. He thinks it was Rowan County. By this time the above-named Colonel Stein, who commanded the South Carolina "Refugees," had joined Colonel Williams. From there they marched near to the Cowpens in order to join what were called the "overmountain troops" under the command of Colonels Sevier, Cleveland, and Shelby.

Colonel Stein informed the other officers that this declarant was known to him as a faithful and efficient spy, as a true friend to his country, and one in whom the utmost confidence could safely be reposed. Colonels Sevier, Cleveland, Shelby, and Stein then held a council in presence of this declarant. They knew that Ferguson with his British and Tories was then stationed about twenty miles from them at Peter Quin's old place, about six or seven miles from Kings Mountain and between said mountain and where our troops then were. The result of this council held by the officers was that this declarant should go and reconnoiter Ferguson's position, which he did. He found the British and Tories encamped about one hundred yards apart and their arms stacked up and no sentinels. This declarant gained easy access to them by passing himself for a Tory, as Tories were then numerous in that part of the country. He believes, but in this he may be mistaken, that Ferguson's strength, including British and Tories, was not exceeding fifteen hundred. He ascertained from the Tories that they intended on the evening of that day to go from Quin's old place to the top of Kings Mountain and remain there a few days in order to give protection to all the "rebels" who would join Ferguson's standard. After obtaining this information and making these discoveries, this declarant returned the next day to Colonels Sevier, Shelby, Cleveland, and Stein, having stayed all night at the house of a Tory who lived about ten miles from Quin's old field. He reached our encampment about sunset.

The officers immediately collected round this declarant in order to ascertain what his discoveries had been. He gave a brief but circumstantial account of them to the said Sevier, Shelby, Cleveland, Stein, and Williams, whose name has been unintentionally omitted in his last references to the officers. Williams was present at each council that was held. The conclusion was that they would march that very night in the direction of Kings Mountain, a distance he believes of about twenty-seven miles or perhaps only twenty-six.

Sevier, Cleveland, Shelby, Stein, and Williams, with their troops, reached Kings Mountain the next day (having marched all night) about ten o'clock and completely surprised Ferguson and his troops by surrounding them, Sevier occupying one position, Cleveland another, Williams another, Shelby another, and Stein another. The engagement he thinks lasted about an hour, but in this he may be mistaken. The defeat of Ferguson was complete. About 250 were killed on the ground, about 750 taken prisoners. The balance escaped. They were principally Tories. We lost about twenty-five men killed on the ground, many wounded, of which number was Colonel Williams, who was wounded in several places. A mortal wound in the groin, as this declarant believes, terminated his life on the next day after the battle before twelve o'clock. This declarant well remembers conversing with him after the battle. He knew he must die and did so, cheerfully resigned to his fate. From the time this declarant first entered the service as a spy until the Battle of Kings Mountain was something like one year and some few months, but how many he does not know.

This declarant then left the service by permission and returned to Mecklenburg County, where he remained some little time, how long he does not remember. He had before the war lived in South Carolina in the country or district of York, had been well known there, and his fame as a spy had reached the settlement where he had lived. His acquaintances, to the number of eight or ten, in York County, South Carolina, wrote a letter to him describing their distressed and exposed condition and imploring aid. He showed this letter to the officers commanding the refugees in North Carolina near the Yadkin River. Colonel Stein was now dead, having been killed by the Tories, and who commanded these refugees he cannot now tell for the reason that he does not remember. Thirty-one of the refugees came with this declarant back to Mecklenburg, where he made his home at the house of his uncle Joseph Kerr. It was about fifty miles from here to York, South Carolina, as he now thinks, from whence this cry of distress above spoken of proceeded.

At the instance of Captain Barnett, who commanded the few refugees who returned with him to Mecklenburg, this declarant proceeded to York for the purpose of making discoveries. Barnett's object was to get accurate information and then procure force sufficient from other sources to make a successful attack upon them. This declarant went, and in the character of a Tory gained access to the camp of General Floyd and Captain Hook, British and Tory officers. Hook commanded the dragoons. But here this declarant was recognized by some of the Tories. They were there in great numbers under General Floyd, and on this occasion he came very near losing his life. He was personally known to some of the Tories, who told Captain Hook that he was "a damned rebel spy." Hook drew his sword over the head of this declarant and repeatedly menaced and threatened his life. After continuing to menace and threaten for some time, Hook told him, as there was no positive proof against him, he would spare his life on condition that he would remain there until next Thursday (and take the oath of allegiance, and come under his protection, he having, as said, appointed the next Thursday as a day on which he would administer the oath to rebels in general), stating at the same time, in these words, "Young man, I am damned suspicious of you. You can do us more damage than two hundred men in the field," stating that if ever this declarant returned to North Carolina and was brought before him again, he should not live two minutes. This declarant was not retained in custody but pledged himself to remain until the following Thursday and take the oath and come under protection of Captain Hook. He, however, effected his escape, as there were no sentinels and as Captain Hook believed and so expressed himself that there was not "a rebel army" in five hundred miles. This declarant made his way to his horse where he was tied in the bushes some distance from the camp. He traveled all night. Leaving the British and Tories in the afternoon, he reached Captain Barnett and his thirty-one refugees a little before day.

The next morning he described the condition of the enemy to Captain Barnett, which was this: the British and Tories were encamped in an old field near a house without sentinels, as above stated; adjoining them was another old field. measurably grown up with pines and was tolerably thick set with pine saplings. Captain Barnett, with his thirty-one men, determined to set out for the British and Tory encampment. They did so, and traveled daylight till they came in about fifteen miles of the encampment.

The balance of the way they traveled in the night and reached the above-mentioned old field, viz., the one which was grown up with pines, between midnight and day. This was on the second night after declarant left the British and Tory encampment.

Barnett and his men, having tied their horses behind the field, cautiously and silently advanced upon the British and Tories and found them asleep. Captain Barnett's orders were that, as the night was very dark, his little band should advance to where the men were asleep and ascertain from their breath, or breathing, which way their heads lay. At a concerted signal, every man was to fire and fire all at once, which signal was this: old Mr. Gipson at the head of the line was first to fire and the balance to fire immediately. They did as they were ordered and literally obeyed the directions given. The fire was fatal. Captain Barnett's men commenced reloading and halloing and giving the word of command and calling upon generals and colonels to surround the enemy. This was done for the purpose of impressing the enemy with the belief that they were attacked by a large force. The artifice succeeded. There was killed of the enemy about ninety-seven, principally British, amongst whom was Captain Hook. The enemy retreated in the utmost confusion, leaving their arms, ammunition, horses, and saddles, and some of them leaving their hats. In short, the defeat and rout of the enemy was decisive. This was the last of this declarant's services to his country.

11
LOGISTICS

JOHN CLASPY *(b. 1760) was born in Maryland and moved to Berkeley County, Virginia (now West Virginia), in 1772. He volunteered in the Virginia militia for three months in 1776, was stationed at Wheeling as a drummer, and in December 1776 he volunteered for six months and helped construct Fort Laurens on the Scioto River. Later in 1777 he joined the Tenth Virginia Regiment as an hostler, but, desiring less confining work, he was placed in the recruiting service. He served in this capacity for close to three years.*

In the Revolutionary War, where volunteer units of all sorts, local militia, state troops, and Continental regiments were actively competing for the same men, the recruiting sergeant was a vital component of any regiment. Moving from area to area, to use his own words, "his destination was always where there were the largest gathering of the people in their civil capacity and where whiskey was most likely to induce them to assume a military one."

Claspy served a short militia tour late in 1781 at the time of the siege of Yorktown and guarded prisoners to Shepherdstown. He submitted two depositions, in 1832 and 1833, in Warren County, Kentucky, where he then resided, and was granted a pension.

On this twenty-sixth day of November, 1832, personally appeared in open court before the judge of the circuit court for the county of Warren, now sitting, John Claspy (called during the Revolutionary War Gillaspee), a resident of said county and state, aged seventy-three years on the seventeenth of April next . . . .

He volunteered into the service as a private in the militia of the State of Virginia from the county of Berkeley and said state on or about the twenty-fourth of April, 1776. His captain was named

John VanMeter, his lieutenant, McIntire, the sergeant, Nathaniel Lender. There was no major or colonel at that time out with him. A Colonel Pendleton, who he thinks was stationed about Pittsburgh, occasionally visited the post at which your applicant was stationed.

He rendezvoused at Martinsburg in said county of Berkeley and marched thence to Wheeling with a view of defending the fort then at that place and the settlements about it from the ravages of the Shawnee Indians. He was engaged here three months, during which time he was wounded in the arm by a ball from the Indians, and at the same time a comrade, Thomas McClary, was killed. He was mainly engaged on this tour as a drummer. At the expiration of the three months, he returned home to Berkeley County. He received no written discharge, but the whole company was verbally dismissed or discharged by the captain.

In the winter of the same year, he thinks about the first of December, 1776, he again volunteered from the same county and state, having rendezvoused at the same place in the company of Captain Lucas and Lt. Nathaniel Lender (the same who was sergeant on his first tour), and Sergeant Duke. Major Scott was, he thinks, the only officer of a grade higher than captain who was out on this tour. We marched from Martinsburg to a point on the Scioto River, near, he thinks, if not the very place where Chillicothe stands, for the purpose of finishing a fort called Fort Laurens which had been begun by companies that had been out before him. He aided in completing the fort and occupied it for the purpose of defending this country from the Shawnee Indians. This was a six-months tour, and he served the whole time. He does not remember to have received a written discharge.

Sometime after this, but he cannot recollect the year, he joined the army of General Darke, who he thinks was the commander of the Tenth Regiment of the regular army. It was at the time that Darke's army was lying near the mouth of Bull Run Creek on the Potomac River, a little below Alexandria, while the army of General Morgan was just above that town. He was employed for a while, say four months, by General Darke in the capacity of hostler, but for that service was promised soldier's pay. Becoming weary of the confinement incident to that station and desiring a more active service, he joined the recruiting service and continued in that employment for about three years. He acted as a recruiting sergeant but had no other commission than orders from General Darke to act in that capacity. Your applicant had always expressed a disinclination to enlist, although he had received many solicitations to do so. He messed, however, with Captain Merriwether's company whenever he was with the main army, but his business was such that he was but rarely with it. Of the regulars, he knew General Darke, Colonel Stephens, and a Major McIntire of Darke's army, but being so frequently away and not being in regular service, his recollection of this is imperfect. He was finally discharged from this service by General Darke in consequence of ill health occasioned by his exposure. This discharge he has lost.

He again volunteered just previous to the surrender of Cornwallis from said county and state under Captain Vestill, whose lieutenant was named Blair. Marched to Yorktown; was present at the surrender of Cornwallis. After the surrender, he attended as an escort or guard of that part of the prisoners which were sent to Winchester under the command of Colonel Holmes and was detained in this service little more than three months. He also guarded them as far as Shepherdstown, where they were received by some other escort.

Supplemental Application

Upon examination of his original declaration, he observes an error in the statement of the length of time he was engaged as a recruiting sergeant under General Darke. He was (and had supposed he had so stated) three years under General Darke. But he was not, as he then stated either by the mistake of himself or of the draftsman of his declaration, all that time engaged as a recruiting sergeant. In that capacity he was engaged to the best of his recollection only two years and eight months. Four months of the time that he was under Darke he was engaged as he stated in his declaration as hostler, which makes the three years as stated.

As to the "tours, etc.," of his recruiting service, concerning which he is required by the War Office to speak more particularly, he can only say that he had no particular "tours" in such service, but one long "tour" which lasted as he has just stated two years and eight months. Recruiting was his regular duty then, from day to day and from year to year, as plowing his farm is now, and he states that he was constantly and actively engaged in it for the whole period of two years and eight months. He recruited for no particular company. The men he obtained were delivered by him to General Darke and placed by him where and in what companies he pleased. During the time of his service, Darke marched with his army from Bull Run to West Point, from there to Richmond, and to Washington, etc., guarding the ports in the Chesapeake and the coasts generally. At one time he believes he marched as far as Trenton, New Jersey, but during these several movements your applicant did not always attend him, but visited him wherever he might be when his recruit was full. *His* destination always was where there were the largest gathering of the people in their civil capacity and where whiskey was most likely to induce them to assume a military one. He was always attended by his fifer named John Roe and his drummer named John Hart.

During his recruiting service, your applicant was taken prisoner but was confined but a short time, and that latter circumstance prevented him from stating it in his original declaration. The circumstances were these. He and his comrades had stopped at the house of a Mrs. Boyd, who was then churning and who promised to give them the buttermilk as soon as she was done. While she was still engaged, your applicant walked alone down to the spring and, having slept none for two or three nights, threw himself on the ground and fell asleep. He was too soon awakened by the tramp of horses. He arose and attempted to retreat by leaping a fence near him. He was instantly followed by two British dragoons, who caught him and carried him to the house of a Tory in the neighborhood. At night he was placed in the upper story of a two-storied stone house, and a Negro man was designated to guard him. He succeeded in bribing the Negro to assist him, by means of the bedcord, to make his escape through the window. He directed the Negro, for his own inculpation, to arouse the family after your applicant should have escaped, and when he had got one or two hundred yards from the house, he had the tremendous pleasure of hearing the noise and bustle which his escape occasioned.

EPAPHRODITUS CHAMPION *(1756–1834) was born in Colchester, Connecticut, son of Col. Henry Champion, chief purchasing agent for the Continental army. The son joined the service in a similar capacity: as deputy commissary of fresh provisions from April 1776 to October 1777 with the main army; purchasing commissary from October 1777 to February 1778, also with the main army; deputy to his father, supplying fresh beef from the Connecticut Valley to Valley Forge from February to May 1778; and again as a regularly appointed purchasing commissary from May 1778 until January 1780, stationed in the Connecticut Valley, buying and sending on cattle to the army.*

Champion had the mind of a merchant, a head for figures, and a decidedly mercenary outlook. His narrative gives an excellent glimpse of a side of the American war effort that does not get into the standard histories.

He moved to East Haddam, Connecticut, after the war and served in Congress as a Federalist from 1807 to 1817. He submitted this narrative in 1833 and was granted a generous pension of $480 a year.

In July 1775 Congress appointed Col. Joseph Trumbull commissary general to supply the American army with provisions. He resided with the army and was commissary general of issues and purchases. On the ninth of April, 1776, I left home, Colchester, for New York, and by the twelfth of April joined the main army then in New York and assembling there. On my arrival at New York, I was employed by the Commissary General Trumbull as a deputy commissary and acted under his orders.

The appropriate duties of my office were to receive, provide for, and safely keep all the beef cattle, sheep, and livestock which were purchased for the army, cause the same to be butchered as the daily necessities of the army required, deliver the meat into the issuing stores, sell the hides and tallow, and keep and render all accounts of the weight of the meats and of all issues of meat and fresh provisions which I made to the issuing commissaries or stores. In short, I had the sole charge of the magazine of fresh provisions for the use of the main army.

The army was furnished with salt meat on Sundays and with fresh meat the other six days of the week. I was also required by the orders of the commissary general to keep him constantly informed of the state of supplies of fresh provisions and the number and condition of the beef cattle on hand, and to keep Col. Henry Champion, the principal purchasing commissary of beef cattle, constantly informed of the consumption of beef by the army, the number of cattle on hand, and the number required.

I continued with the army in its retreat to the White Plains. After we were driven from our issuing stores in New York, I sometimes delivered the meat and sometimes the beef cattle alive to the issuing commissaries. I attended the movements of the main army in the years 1776 and 1777 through New Jersey and Pennsylvania, until I left it as hereinafter stated. I continued with the army and discharged the duties of my office from the time of my arrival during the remaining period that Colonel Trumbull continued or acted as commissary general. But in August 1776 I was taken down with a fever while with the army in New York, the only sickness which I have ever had in my life, and which I believe was occasioned by the excessive duties and labors of my offices, and rendered incapable of attending to the duties of my office for about four weeks, in which time my place was supplied by Capt. John Isham in Colonel Chester's regiment in the Connecticut line upon the request of Colonel Trumbull and with the permission of Colonel Chester and Adjutant General Reed.

A few days before the Battle of the White Plains, the commissary general being absent from the army and in Connecticut, I went to headquarters by order of General Washington and received orders directly from him relative to the beef cattle and their disposition. About this time, Captain Delevan of the New York troops, with a party of men, returned from a tour of duty below our lines and brought off nine beef cattle and brought them to me to receive and receipt. I declined to receive them, knowing them not to have been bought for the army, upon which he obtained an order from Adjutant General Reed ordering me to receive and receipt for the same, which I did. The order I cannot find among my papers. Some years afterwards Captain Delevan made an unsucessful claim on me for the pay for these cattle.

In consequence of the regulations of Congress of June 1777, Colonel Trumbull resigned the office of commissary general but continued to act in that capacity some time longer, until the department could be reorganized under the new regulations. I continued with the army, acting under him. The last delivery of beef cattle which I made to the issuing commissaries was at what was called the Crossroads, some fifteen or twenty miles northward of Philadelphia, on the twenty-first of August, 1777. I then left the army and by order of Colonel Trumbull went to Ulster County in the state of New York to collect and deliver over to the order of Col. Ephraim Blaine, the deputy commissary general of purchases, five hundred head of beef cattle which had been placed there for fattening and as some security for supply in case the enemy should get command of the North River and cut off supply from the eastward. This delivery to the order of Colonel Blaine was completed in September 1777. I then returned to Colchester, Connecticut, and closed my services under Commissary General Trumbull on the second of October, 1777, making a service at this time of 542 days.

Colonel Trumbull died not long after his resignation, and his brother, the late Governor Jonathan Trumbull, was appointed, as I understood by Congress, sole commissioner to settle the accounts of the Commissary General Trumbull. My accounts were settled with Governor Trumbull as such commissioner in the year 1780. My receipts and vouchers were all delivered to him. In the settlement of my account, I was allowed for my aforesaid services four dollars per day for the 542 days. I had no written appointment from Commissary General Trumbull nor any written discharge, and I believe it was not his practice to give written appointments to his deputy commissaries or those acting under him. . . .

In August 1777 Peter Colt was appointed by Congress deputy commissary general of purchases. On the third of September, 1777, he wrote to me while I was at Peekskill to accept from him the office of a purchasing commissary. . . . I concluded to accept. I received the appointment from him, and on the third day of October, 1777, immediately after closing my services under Colonel Trumbull, I commenced my services under Mr. Colt as a purchasing commissary. Afterwards, on the twenty-third day of November, 1777, our first Governor Trumbull gave his certificate of my appointment, upon a letter of Mr. Colt. . . . Whether that certificate was required by some law, or why it was made, I do not now recollect. I find no other written evidence of my appointment except the letters of Mr. Colt and the certificate of Governor Trumbull.

I commenced my services under said Colt as purchasing commissary on the third of October, 1777, and continued to serve in that capacity until the thirty-first of January, 1778, making 121 days on daily pay allowed by Congress at four dollars per day. In addition to the daily allowance, the deputy commissary general was authorized to make an allowance for horse and expenses not exceeding one dollar and one-third per day, by virtue of which I was allowed twenty-four pounds, sixteen shillings, lawful money . . . .

In February 1778 my father, Col. Henry Champion, received from General Washington a letter dated February 17, 1778. . . . Under the pressure and necessity of the case, he considered this letter was an authority for him to act as a deputy commissary general for supplying the army with beef cattle. He immediately commenced the most active exertions, using his own credit and the credit of his purchasing commissaries for the relief of the army. He immediately visited those parts of the country most capable of fattening cattle in the winter season, particularly the towns bordering on Connecticut River in Massachusetts, a district of country at that time far more capable of fattening cattle than any other in the United States. His object was to induce the people to fill their stalls and fatten their cattle, assuring them that they should not be losers by it. To promote that object, he read that letter probably a hundred times over, which is the reason why it appears so much worn and defaced.

In the month of February, 1778, while I was serving under Mr. Colt, Colonel Champion appointed me a commissary under him, and I continued to serve in that capacity until the fifteenth of May, 1778. So active were our exertions that on the fifth of March, 1778, I forwarded a drove of seventy-three beef cattle to the army at Valley Forge. Colonel Champion directed the purchasing commissaries to conform as far as practicable to the regulations of June 10, 1777, which required them to make monthly returns of their purchases. In consequence of that direction, I charged the whole of the month of February to Colonel Champion, instead of dividing it and charging a part to Mr. Colt and a part to him. Including the time I served under Mr. Colt in the month of February, 1778, my service under Colonel Champion amounted to 104 days, for which I was allowed by Congress four dollars per day with an allowance for horse and expenses. At the time my father received General Washington's letter, I resided in his family and was well acquainted with the measures he adopted to carry into effect the requirements of General Washington. . . .

On the fifteenth of May, 1778, I commenced my services as purchasing commissary under Henry Champion, deputy commissary general of purchases, who was appointed by Jeremiah Wadsworth commissary general of purchases. From this time, my compensation as commissary was not a per diem compensation, as formerly, but a commission of 2 percent under the resolutions of Congress of April 14, 1778. In pursuance of these resolutions, I gave, if I mistake not, the bond required of ten thousand dollars, with two good and sufficient sureties, which was, as I have understood, lodged in the Treasury Office. I also, as I think, took the oath prescribed in the resolutions of Congress before the Honorable William Williams of Lebanon, Connecticut, then a magistrate and an assistant or member of the Upper House of Connecticut.

I continued a purchasing commissary in constant service from the fifteenth of May, 1778, to the twenty-second of January, 1780. In January 1780 I purchased a drove of 142 head of fat cattle in the county of Hampshire, Massachusetts. The last of this drove were purchased on the twenty-second of January, 1780. When I made this purchase, I was in Massachusetts, where I had to remain, collect, and deliver the cattle to the drovers and then return home to Colchester and settle my accounts. How long after the twenty-second of January, 1780, I was employed, I do not recollect. Exclusive of that, my service in this last term, viz., from May 15, 1778, to January 22, 1780, was one year, eight months, and eight days.

It is my belief that I received a written appointment from Colonel Champion on or about the fifteenth of May, 1778, at the time of giving my bond, but I cannot find any such document. Prior to the twenty-seventh of July, 1778, my purchasing district was much larger than afterwards, but at that time, it seems, . . . I was limited to a particular district. Yet, notwithstanding that, I afterwards, by direction of Colonel Champion, went into Massachusetts and there made large purchases. . . . From the year 1776 to the year 1780, both inclusive, Col. Henry Champion was the great purchasing commissary of fresh provisions and furnished the army with the greater part of the beef during these years.

During the 542 days I was with the army under Colonel Trumbull, I received alive and delivered slaughtered or dressed for the use of the army 3,019,554 pounds of beef, 40,275 pounds of mutton, 18,639 pounds of pork, 19,913 pounds of fat. Also, I received and delivered alive 3,257 beef cattle, 657 fat sheep, and 35 fat hogs. During the aforesaid time that I acted as purchasing commissary, I purchased and delivered for the use of the army 3,710 fat cattle and 758 fat sheep. . . .

During the whole of that period, my time was wholly devoted to the public service, and I did no other business whatever. My credit and at all times my wages, except what was necessary for my personal expenses, were made use of for purchases for the army, and no part of my pay was realized by me until July 1778, when, owing to the depreciation of the currency, the price of common beef cattle for the army was twenty-five dollars per hundredweight, computing the weight of the beef, hide, and tallow.

WILLIAM BURNETT *(b. 1764) was born "between the cut banks of the Apermatock [Appomattox] River and Walker's Church," Prince Edward County, Virginia. He volunteered as a wagoner in summer 1780 and served five or six days in the infantry in October 1781.*

Wagoners were crucial to the mobility of fighting units, and they were the most numerous support troops in the army. Burnett was an uneducated runaway servant of very marginal intelligence, but his narrative gives a rare portrait of a person of very low status, the sort who normally leaves no records.

Burnett moved after the war to Henry County, then Wythe County, Virginia, then Kentucky, and finally Tennessee, from which he unsuccessfully applied for a pension in 1841.

That he entered the services of the United States under the following-named officers and served as hereinafter stated. That he run away from his master, as he was a bound boy, and volunteered under Capt. Henry Walker, Lt. Thomas Arnold; other commissioned officers' names not recollected, Orderly Sgt. John Black. The next day, rendezvoused at Prince Edward Courthouse, state of Virginia, and stayed there several days, and from there marched into the state of North Carolina to headquarters, and the same day after his arrival there, he saw his master's wagon and team, which had been pressed. He told Captain Walker that he was acquainted with that team, as it was his old master's team which he used to drive. He was immediately taken from the ranks and put under James Cahoon, a wagon master, and, as the team of his old master to whom he was bound was there, he was ordered by the said Cahoon to drive said team, which he did during the balance of his services, or nearly so.

His loading was provision for the army or principally so. He does not now recollect whether he ever was out of the state of Virginia and North Carolina or not, but thinks his services was confined to them two states or nearly so. He recollects of hauling a load of provision to the mouth of Queens Creek, where there was a number of soldiers stationed. Recollects passing by with the wagon a mountain called Kings Mountain, as they told him. Thinks it was after the battle had been fought there. Also recollects of seeing General Washington twice on the road with his life guard with him and will never forget while he retains his memory the polite bow that the general made to the poor wagoners as he passed them. Also recollects having, at one time when he came to camps with a load of provision, heard of a circumstance that shocked him mightily. That was, as they informed him, his old captain, which was Walker, and several other officers was walking together down the ditch that surrounded their encampment, and Captain Walker happened to raise his head above the ditch, and the Tories fired on him and killed him.

And remembers that one day while resting he heard a noise like the clashing of arms in an old field, and he left his wagon and run to see, and saw the British and Americans fight. They were all horsemen, and that he was so scared that he caught hold of a pine and trembled so that he shook the bush mightily. He instantly remembered his wagon and the wagon master and run to the wagon, for fear the wagon master would come and whip him. And that one night he went to steal some sweet potatoes, and while engaged in graveling them, he latched on the fence and saw three men with a piece of white paper on their hats in front. He instantly knew them to be Tories and run and dropped his potatoes at the fence, that he might be able to go the faster. The Tories followed him and run him into the American lines, and they were taken prisoners by the Americans and the next day was hung for being traitors to the American cause.

He cannot recollect the names of many of the places that he was at during his term of service, as he was kept very close to his team and knew but little else, only what related to them. He hardly ever knew when he started where he was going till he arrived at the place of loading, and when he received his loading, he knew not where he had to take it, as the wagon master did not allow the wagoners to question him, and it seldom happened that the wagon guards knew more than the wagoners.

If he started before the twenty-fourth of July into the service, he was not quite fifteen years old, as that is his birthday, and when he found the service of the United States not to be going to be a frolic, he often wished his term of service out and took but little notice of anything else but the time, as it seemed slowly to pass. And, when his term of time was nearly out, he and some other wagoners were ordered back to Prince Edward Courthouse and was there discharged after remaining in the service eighteen months. He was no scholar and had a bad chance to know much about places even through which he traveled.

After he arrived at home and had stayed there, he thinks three or four days, there was a call for men to guard some prisoners. He again volunteered under James Arnold, captain, other officers not recollected, and went into the neighborhood of Prince Edward Courthouse, and while guarding the prisoners, an officer rode up on a panting horse with a cocked hat on and ordered the guards to form a square with the prisoners in the inside, and then the news of the surrender of Lord Cornwallis was read, and remembers that the officer threw his cocked hat up in the air, and almost every American present done the same, and the words

"America is ours" seemed to almost rend the air, such was the joy at that time. The prisoners were ordered to Prince Edward Courthouse, and there he was discharged, but received no written discharge, after remaining about one week in the service.

EDWARD F. PATRICK *(1760–1834) resided in Salisbury, North Carolina, and performed his military service, two three-month tours in 1780 and 1781, as a prison guard in his hometown. As the war began in earnest and continued year after year, the care of prisoners became a growing problem. Although the majority of regular soldiers on both sides were exchanged, months often went by before arrangements could be made. Tories and members of Burgoyne's Convention army, unless induced to enlist, were prisoners for the duration of the war. Sites for prison camps were selected for remoteness from the active zones of conflict, and, in addition to Salisbury, similar prisons were established at Winchester and Charlottesville, Virginia, Frederick, Maryland, York, Pennsylvania, Rutland, Vermont, and several other inland towns.*

Patrick was an uneducated man, but he conveys a sense of the tense and dangerous life at a prison camp. His account of the stay of execution for the notorious Samuel Bryan because of British pressure is accurate.

Patrick moved to Tennessee after the war and was residing in McLean County, Illinois, in 1833 when he submitted this deposition and was granted a pension.

I did enter the service of the United States under the following-named officers and served as herein stated. First, I was drafted out for a three-months tour and was mustered into service in Salisbury, Rowan County, North Carolina, under Colonel Locke and Capt. Abel Armstrong. From rendezvous, we were marched down toward the south side of the state of North Carolina to guard and fetch on a parole of Tory prisoners that had been taken in South Carolina. We brought those Tories. Colonel Richardson, and one Armstrong, and a man named Fisher, and several more was tried by a court-martial, and Richardson, Fisher, and Armstrong was condemned to be hanged and was accordingly executed on Gallows Hill, one-half mile above Salisbury, and I was one of the guard. Richardson made a confession, neither of the others did, and when Richardson had done, he took a bullet out of his pocket and handed it to the captain that had took him. It had been shot through his cheek and lodged against his teeth, and he said he forgave the captain, and I stayed there about [*blank*] in service until my time was out for the before-named tour of duty, making three months, and received my discharge for the same. This tour of duty was in the winter of 1780, and in the fall of 1781 I was again drafted for three-month tour and was mustered into service in Salisbury and was under the command of Maj. William Lewis. George Gordon was my captain in this tour.

The first I shall give in detail is as respects one Col. Samuel Bryan, who the year before had raised something like twelve hundred Tories and had conducted them safe to the British, but at this time, when I was called into service, he was a prisoner and was in Salisbury gaol with a number of his men and a number of other Tories. We had a number of the northern troops who took up winter quarters in Salisbury with us, and amongst them there was two distinguished French officers, viz., Mountflorence and Major Langham. Our Captain Gordon and Langham here fell out and fought a duel, and Gordon received a slight wound on his wrist, etc., but the before-named Colonel Bryan, the Tory colonel, and several others of the Tory party tried by a court-martial were sentenced to be hanged, but the British declared that, if Bryan was executed, that they would hang twenty of our officers whom they had prisoners, and in consequence of this the execution of Bryan was deferred and afterward changed to banishment. About this time, Major Langham began to enlist many of those Tories (who it appears had seen their folly) and placed them under the United States colors (in during the war), which greatly relieved us both in point of danger from them and from the necessity of keeping a continual guard.

There was amongst those prisoners a man by the name of Elrod, who prevailed with Major Langham to bail him, who on the first night run away but was fetched back. The next day he was bailed again and run away again and was soon brought back again, and it rained and froze that night, insomuch that the next morning, the ground was covered with ice, so that a man could scarcely walk without falling, when we seen Langham and three or four hundred men coming from the barracks, and several of the men were loaded with hickreys [hickories]. They halted within one hundred yards of us. Langham placed two hundred men in two direct lines consisting of one hundred each, leaving a space of six feet between, and the men passing each other all with hickreys in their hands and then calling for the before-named Elrod, who was soon brought, and I was placed at one end of the lines thus drawn up, right opposite to the space between the two lines, with orders to turn Elrod, who was placed in the space between the two lines. He came through, and I turned him twist. Those hickreys were nimbly used on Elrod, as the orders were if anyone favored him, that they should undergo the like discipline. Elrod was in one general gore of blood, and, after having undergone this severe discipline, he was remanded to prison. After this circumstance, one night when I was standing guard, the before-named Colonel Bryan, having by some means penetrated the gaol so far as to get his hands on the ground outside, having got out as far as his waist, at which time I discovered him, cocked my gun, and told him to return back or I would blow him through, but he instantly obeyed, or I would have shot him.

About this time, two men, McClouds by name, were handcuffed together, and one night, when one Corven and Whaley were standing on sentry and thought they had stood too long, and Whaley told Corven if he would stand, he would go to the guard, and he done so, and while he was gone, McClouds having broke their handcuffs, desired Corven to let them out for a special purpose, and, as liberty of this kind had been common, Corven done so, and as soon as they got out, the largest one of them, being a very stout man, seized Corven's gun and tossed him, gun and all, from him, and run off. Corven arose to his feet and heared the sound of McCloud and others running, drew away at a venture in the dark, and in a few minutes the whole army was in parade and at that place, and Whaley was put in prison for leaving his post, and next morning he received forty stripes, save one. But after new sentinels were placed in Corven's and Whaley's place, on the same night of the escape, the sentinel discovered something and thought it had the appearance of a man from the size and appearance of the bulk, and this sentinel halloed out that he believed Corven had killed one of the Tories that had made their escape, and on examination it was found that the slug let loose from Corven's gun had entered McCloud's head near the hole of his right ear and came out above his left eye, and this was an end to him who was the very one that had tossed Corven so. Sometime after this my time expired, and my services as a private footman in the United States amounted in all to six months in actual service.

HENRY SEYMOUR *(b. 1764), apparently a native of Connecticut, moved to Philadelphia in 1780 and was employed by the mercantile firm of Comfort Sands, Richardson Sands, and Joshua Sands, which was con-*

tracted by Robert Morris to supply provisions for West Point in 1782. He carried provisions as well as personal goods for Washington and other officers and brought large sums of money back to Philadelphia.

Why he thought in 1838 that he qualified for a pension is a mystery. His claim was rejected, but his narrative provides some detail on the historically obscure aspects of practical military finance.

That late in the year 1780 he went to reside in Philadelphia with Mr. Richardson Sands, then a merchant there. That in December 1781 Messrs. Comfort Sands, Richardson Sands, and Joshua Sands were, as the declarant supposes, commissaries in the employ of the United States. He entered into their service under them. That the Messrs. Sands, under the direction of Robert Morris, Esq., then financier of the government, supplied the American army at West Point and its dependencies with rations for the year 1782, and their office was kept at Fishkill.

I served under the Messrs. Sands one year, and my services consisted in carrying money to Fishkill to purchase supplies and bringing back to Philadelphia monthly vouchers for the same, upon the delivery of which Mr. Morris usually paid one-half the amount and the residue as soon as the vouchers were examined. I also forwarded at sundry times a considerable amount in dollars and French crowns belonging to the United States by wagons from Philadelphia; also purchased and forwarded quantities of whiskey and other supplies by the wagons. I purchased and forwarded sundry supplies for General Washington's family and table, one wagon with which was robbed in the woods of New Jersey by the cowboys. A part was carried off by them with one wagon horse, part were destroyed, and a part were recovered with three of the horses and the wagon. Also, I purchased and forwarded blue and scarlet cloths and other articles for the officers and sold for them in Philadelphia a considerable amount of "Pierce's notes" and returned the avails at a saving to them of 10 percent.

On one of my trips to camp, in crossing the North River from New Windsor, the boat was nearly upset by a squall and half filled with water and soon after sunk near the shore. I escaped and my horse by swimming. I had then in charge about six thousand dollars for camp of the government money.

Another trip from camp, I crossed the North River towards evening near Newburgh and lodged at the quarters of Colonel Stephens of the artillery. My business being pressing, started early in the morning and called at the quarters of General Knox, a short distance below. He urged me to tarry a few minutes until his aide (Major Shaw, I think) should come and write a pass for me, the general's right hand being lame. I excused myself, stating the necessary haste I was under. He then directed me to take the right-hand road about three miles onward, observing it would be a few miles further but safer, and I should avoid the Clove Road. I, pretty intoxicated, following his directions, but in my haste did not discover my mistake until challenged by a British sergeant with eight men, about two miles within the Clove Road, or Smith's Clove so-called. The men was halted about ten rods from me, facing the road. The sergeant advanced to me and demanded the countersign or a pass. I had neither. After many inquiries, and stating that his orders were "to take up all suspicious persons," and hearing my Yankee story, which was true as far as it went, he observed, "If you are permitted to pass, after I return to the guard, they will face outward. But young man, should you be permitted to go on, you must give me your word of honor that you will not mention this meeting to anyone on this side of the Delaware River." I gave the pledge, and the sergeant, after conversing a short time with the guard, gave the signal for my release. I considered it fortunate that I was then without General Knox's pass. No search was made, and I had at the time about twenty thousand dollars of army vouchers in my portmanteau.

He further declares that he continued to serve as above stated until the close of the year 1782, making one year from the time of his commencement, and for further particulars respecting said service, refers the commissioner of pensions to the papers of Mr. Morris and the Messrs. Sands if they are in existence at Washington.

12
OTHER REVOLUTIONARIES

JUSTUS BELLAMY *(b. 1757) was born in Cheshire, Connecticut. He answered the alarm after Lexington and Concord, and after one week's service he enlisted on the condition that he and five friends might mess together in Wooster's Connecticut state regiment.*

Bellamy was a rough, daring soldier, and General Wooster, while stationed in New York, began to use him for particularly dangerous missions. According to this narrative, he and his friends apprehended the Tory general Philip Skene at Dobbs Ferry in the summer of 1775. Skene, commissioned by the Crown as governor at Crown Point, had made himself obnoxious by uttering pro-British remarks while traveling on a ship from London. He arrived in Philadelphia on 7 June 1775, was made a prisoner by the Continental Congress on 10 June, and was paroled. He was permitted to go no farther than eight miles from the city.

On 27 June Congress ordered Skene sent, under guard, to Connecticut, and on 5 July they urged that Pennsylvania quickly send the prisoner northward. On 12 October a Francis Wade and his party of eighteen men were ordered to be paid for transporting Skene and another prisoner to New York, presumably in July. Although the editor can find no documentation on the prisoner's progress up the coast, Skene apparently attempted to jump parole while in New York and was captured and escorted the rest of the way to Connecticut by Bellamy and his friends.

After a short tour of duty on the eastern end of Long Island, Bellamy enlisted under Wooster for the Canadian campaign. His record of the conversation between Wooster and Montgomery before St. Johns is priceless, and his description of the siege is particularly fine.

He served three more terms of service, participating in the battles of Long Island, Harlem Heights, and Danbury, Connecticut. He resided in Vergennes, Vermont, and Whitehall, New York, after the war, and was living with a son in Augusta, Upper Canada, when he applied for a pension in 1833. His application was successful.

Shortly after the Battle of Lexington, at the commencement of the Revolutionary War, in the spring of the year 1775, this deponent volunteered at Cheshire, in the state of Connecticut, with the militia to go to Boston and was mustered under Capt. Robert Martin and Lt. Reuben Rice at Cheshire, aforesaid, about the last of March or first of April and marched for Boston, aforesaid. There was about one hundred men out at this time. He does not recollect of there being any field officers with them.

Deponent and the other officers and soldiers marched for Boston and went to within some ten or twenty miles of Boston, where they were ordered to halt, and deponent and his comrades stayed there about one week and then marched back to Cheshire, aforesaid, and were discharged. When he returned to Cheshire, no written discharge was given to this deponent. Deponent believes that at this period he served one month. That within a day or two after this deponent returned, he and five other young men of the same age enlisted at Cheshire, aforesaid, in a company commanded by Capt. James Arnold, deponent believes for six months. It was a condition of his and their enlistment that the six should mess together. One Nathaniel Bunnell was our lieutenant and one Tyler was ensign. We mustered, deponent believes, at Durham, Connecticut. This enlistment dated back, as deponent understood it, to the time the order issued for raising the troops. The regiment was under the command of General Wooster, who was then called general, though he seemed to act as a colonel. One Waterbury was our lieutenant colonel. We joined the regiment at Horseneck. Deponent understood the troops then raised and to which deponent was attached were Connecticut state troops. We laid at Horseneck about one month, and we then marched to the city of New York.

While we were in the city of New York, General Wooster sent one day early in the morning for this deponent to come to his quarters. Deponent went. General Wooster asked this deponent if he would go on a tour and endeavor to take General Skene, who was then in New York and was supposed to be on his way to Canada. Deponent answered that he would do his best to accomplish the business. Deponent was informed that he, General Skene, went in disguise, but that he wore a blanket coat and rode in a French caleche and drove a French horse. General Wooster told this deponent that he might pick any six out of his company to go with him and directed deponent to pursue General Skene as far as Dobbs Ferry, fourteen [miles] above the city of New York. Deponent went and selected his five messmates and one David Hitchcock and went in pursuit of General Skene. We overtook him at the ferry just as he was putting off from the shore in the ferryboat. When we went aboard, he told us that we should all be massacred in one hour if we attempted to take him back. He used a great many threats to deter us from arresting him and taking him back. We, however, took him back to New York and delivered him up to General Wooster. General Washington was at his quarters at the time. We went from New York to Dobbs Ferry in one hour and fifty minutes on foot, and we returned to New York in less than five hours from the time we started. We took him back in his carriage, and, to guard him, two went before the carriage, two behind, and one on each side. Deponent went along without reference to any particular place to travel, but kept so as to superintend the whole movement. General Wooster and General Washington complimented us highly for our exploit in taking so important a prisoner. Deponent cannot state what time this was.

Deponent further says that about a week from this time, General Wooster again sent for the deponent and handed him a pair of pistols and a sword and a letter to Governor Trumbull of Connecticut and requested him to take his six associates in taking General Skene and to take charge of him again and convey him to Governor Trumbull at Hartford, Connecticut. General Wooster informed us, when we got our prisoner to Hartford we might go home and stay one week and then return to New York. We did take General Skene to Hartford and delivered him to Governor Trumbull and took a receipt from him for the prisoner and a letter to General Wooster, and, after visiting at home five days, we returned to New York and again joined the army at Harlem, to which place it had been removed during our absence. Shortly after we returned, we were sent to Long Island to a place called the "Fire Place," and then marched to Montauk Point, and thence we went on an excursion to Plum Island to keep the British from driving away the stock there. We exchanged a few shots with their men who came for cattle, and they retreated, and we took the cattle away and returned to Harlem, where we lay a short time, when we were ordered to Canada. We immediately marched up the North River and halted at Greenbush, opposite Albany, and stayed there a few days.

One day, when [we] were paraded, General Wooster informed us that our term of enlistment was about out and that he should not go any further without we engaged to go ahead and stand by him until the end of the Canada campaign. He said he wished all who were sick or lame or had the rheumatism to step out, and they might go home. Deponent thinks that six or seven stepped out forward of the line as being unable or unwilling to go. General Wooster then commenced limping like a lame man and asked if there were no more lame or had the rheumatism in his whole army, and, after doing so a minute or two, all returned to the ranks save two, who were discharged by the general on the spot. General Wooster then praised his men and remarked that with such troops he could go to hell and back with them safe, and from thence we marched to St. Johns in Canada. We went by way of Lake George. This was in the fall of the year. We arrived at St. Johns in November. We went from Ticonderoga down Lake Champlain to St. Johns in boats. General Schuyler and some troops were at this time at Ticonderoga. We landed above St. Johns. Deponent steered the boat which carried Capt. James Arnold and his company. General Wooster directed Captain Arnold to bring up the rear and see that no man was left behind. We struck a brush heap just as we landed, which turned [the boat] over. Captain Arnold and deponent stayed in the boat and handed out the guns to one Jones, who handed them to the men. We made the boat fast and went ashore, and we joined General Montgomery at the north encampment. When General Montgomery and General Wooster met, General Montgomery said, "I welcome you to this place. I am heartily glad to see you. My commission is older than yours, and I must command, and I think it a goddamned shame. I am but a young man, and you are an old man, experienced in war. I shall always take your advice as a son would that of his father."

The night after, we were on fatigue in erecting a battery against Fort St. Johns, which was occupied by the British. Deponent and one other person, a stranger to this deponent, were selected by General Wooster and Colonel Waterbury to go and reconnoiter about the fort to see how things were situated and what was going on. We went out accordingly. The British threw up skyrockets and discovered us, and when we were a little separated they captured the person with deponent. Deponent was informed at the time that he told the British that General Wooster had come on with fifteen hundred troops, and he feared the fort would be all blown

MAJOR GEN.L RICH.D MONTGOMERY
Slain in Storming Quebec Decbr 31st 1775

to pieces within three days and requested them to put him in a secure place. When the place was taken, we found him. He had been in the bombproof. This exaggerated account of General Wooster's strength was intended to alarm the British, for in truth he had only about three hundred men with him. The next day after we built our breastwork, the British demolished it, and then we proceeded to erect one of more strength, on which we placed three cannon. They fired shot and hove shells at us but did not destroy our works. Deponent was at work repairing the works when General Montgomery came up and put his hand on deponent's shoulder and sprung upon the top of the breastwork to see if it was as it should be, and the instant he struck his feet on top, a cannon shot passed him and cut off the skirt of his coat and turned him round, and he pitched into the breastwork but struck upon his feet, but this did not seem to hurt or frighten him.

As soon as our cannon were fixed, we brought balls on our shoulders to the works to be used. Deponent on this occasion brought six twelve-pound cannon shot about half a mile on his shoulders in the leg of his old trousers. He carried them across his shoulders, then on one side, then on the other. Before he arrived at the breastwork, a soldier got tired of his load who had but three and threw one down, and deponent picked it up and carried it in his hand and arrived at the breastwork with seven balls. We commenced firing and kept it up for three days, and we, on the third day, got a thirteen-inch mortar going and threw one shell into the top of a chimney, which went down and exploded within three feet of the powder magazine.

On the fourth night we were all mustered to storm the fort and got within about a hundred yards. A parley was beat by the British, and we returned to our camp and laid upon our arms all night and with orders to turn out at the beat of the tattoo and not at the beat to arms. A flag of truce came from the fort, and a parley was held at General Wooster and General Montgomery's marquee. The British officers offered to come out and march off to Montreal and Quebec and go home to England and not take up arms again during the war. These terms were not accepted, and the British officers returned to the fort. And our officers ordered the tattoo beat, and we all marched toward the fort again. And then another parley was sounded by the British, and we then returned to camp again and received the same orders as before, and then a flag of truce came again from the British, and they agreed to capitulate and march out in the morning and march out and surrender themselves as prisoners of war and to be treated as such and no guns to be fired on either side. This was to be done at nine o'clock the next morning.

We were all kept up that night and doubled our guards and kept in situation to act to the best possible advantage. General Wooster himself took deponent and stationed him in a little bypath which was a crooked route past our lines to the British fort. Deponent was stationed in a thick, bushy place where it was dark, and General Wooster told him not to fire if he could avoid it at all, but if any person come, to bring him to his quarters. The dark spot selected was a spot where the ground was low, and, it being a very wet time, deponent stood in water about six inches deep. And the weather being very cold, snow having begun to fall occasionally, deponent suffered very much with the cold.

About midnight a man run against deponent's bayonet. Deponent told him to stand or he would be a dead man and to move out of the bush at the point of his bayonet, and if he attempted to escape, he would be blown through. Deponent saw him put something to his mouth, but he could not tell what it was because it was so dark. Deponent took him to General Wooster and informed the general of all the particulars. The general searched him but could find nothing, and he affirmed that he had nothing about him. He would not talk much. The general compelled him to take physic and kept a guard over him. Deponent stayed by him all night, though he had not slept at all in three nights. In about two hours after taking the physic, the prisoner discharged a ball, which on being examined was found to be of silver and went together with a screw, and on taking it apart it contained a small bit of paper on which was written these words: "Hold out and you shall be relieved."

In the morning, the British marched out with their arms six deep and laid them down and surrendered themselves prisoners of war. Our lines, which were only one file deep, was about the same length of theirs, which was six files deep. Major Prescott, who commanded them, came up in front of where deponent stood and said that, "In obedience to what has been done, I lay down my arms, but of choice I had rather die by them," and the tears run down his cheeks, and he cried like a child. The British were then taken on board our lake craft and sailed for Ticonderoga under Commodore Douglass, as he was called. Captain Cook and his company marched into the fort and took and kept possession. I was on that morning transferred to Captain Cook's company and promoted to the office of orderly sergeant. This was late in November. Under the enlistment under Captain Arnold, deponent served, as he believes, seven months and a half.

On joining Captain Cook's company, this deponent found their requisition for provision had not been answered, and Captain Cook sent deponent to attend to it. When deponent went to Commissary Waters, he saw the requisition was not right and pointed deponent to his desk to see a form that was right. Deponent then wrote one out and signed the captain's name by deponent as orderly sergeant. Then deponent got the provisions. In about one hour, General Wooster sent for deponent, and deponent asked Captain Cook to go up with deponent, as he feared trouble for having used the captain's name as he did. Captain Cook went. When we arrived, General Wooster said, "I am going to present you with a quartermaster sergeant's warrant, and I wish you to take charge of the provisions that are here and those that are coming on and send them on to my orders, as I am going to leave for Montreal." Deponent told him that it would be hard for deponent to leave Captain Cook, as neither he nor either of his sergeants could write, but deponent would accept the new appointment and perform both duties, and deponent did do so until the twenty-fifth of December, when deponent was compelled to leave on account of ill health. At this time, deponent served as quartermaster sergeant and also as orderly sergeant one month and a half as he believes. Generals Montgomery and Wooster went with all the forces except Captain Cook's company to Montreal. On the twenty-fifth of December, aforesaid, Captain Arnold returned, and deponent, on account of his continued ill health occasioned very much by standing in the water as above mentioned, was permitted to join Captain Arnold's company, and we went down the lake in boats, and when we got to Bennington, Vermont, we had eat up all our provision, and Captain Arnold said he had no more for us, and we must take care of ourselves. And we then went home to Cheshire, where deponent arrived about the middle of February. At this time after, deponent discontinued to perform the duties of quartermaster sergeant at St. Johns. One month and two-thirds expired before deponent reached home.

Deponent's illness increased, and on the second day after he arrived home, he had to take himself to his bed and was not able to get out of it for two months, and the doctors all concluded that deponent must die and that his disease was occasioned by extreme exposure in the army. Dr. Potter and many other physicians called, and, on asking deponent what he wanted, deponent told him he wished to drink cider out of his mother's silver tankard. The doctor said deponent might drink as much as deponent pleased. On its being brought, deponent drank of it, and deponent began to mend slowly and soon got so as to sit up. One day, when the family were at dinner, deponent was sitting in an easy chair near the fire. He felt an extraordinary feeling about his feet and ankles and which seemed to feel precisely as he felt when standing in the water at St. Johns above referred to, and, while this sensation was powerfully felt, the wood on the fire fell down, and, on deponent's attempting to reach the tongs to put it up, he pitched forward onto the fire. Deponent's father on that instant stepped into the room and caught deponent by the left arm and pulled him back, and in doing pulled his shoulder out of joint. On this being set, deponent gained slowly and was able to walk out at the May training of the militia, and on that occasion this deponent was chosen orderly sergeant in Capt. Ephraim Cook's company, a distant relation of the Captain Cook deponent left at St. Johns.

Sometime during the same month of May, Captain Cook's company was called out to march to New York. We were mustered at Cheshire and went to New York, and one Thaddeus Cook was our colonel. At Norwalk, Connecticut, we went aboard of sloops and sailed to New York, and there we remained until after the battle on Long Island. The night after the battle, this deponent assisted in bringing our men from Long Island, and he recollects that he crossed to the island eleven times in a boat that night. That night or in the afternoon of the day previous, General Sullivan was taken prisoner by the British and was afterwards exchanged for General Skene (who was taken by this deponent), as deponent then understood. Deponent then remained in New York until our army was driven out by the British. On the retreat from the city, deponent was drafted into the rear to guard the baggage and cannon. On the retreat to Harlem or Kingsbridge, we were all the way fired at by the British and cut off amazingly, and deponent expected to be killed but resolved to sell his life as dearly as possible. We made a sort of fortification of rails at Harlem Heights, a little west of the road. We soon found ourselves surrounded, and, on finding no word of command given and on looking about, there was no person in command or that ranked higher than deponent. Deponent then counted and saw that of all, there were but seventy left. He immediately took charge and said to the men that it was best to mount on top of the rails and let them fire at us and then fall back and then pounce upon them in their smoke. We did so, and when they were reloading we rushed upon them with our bayonets and cut all who went in front of us down. When we felt that we touched them with our bayonets, we pulled trigger and fired and in this way cut them all down when we met them. Our different platoons each met them in this way as they approached, but at the same time our party kept retreating as fast as the enemy formed and came up.

When we had retreated as far as the woods, when we filed off and went to the road, and when we had passed a small fortification, we saw General Washington coming on a gray horse and the British cavalry after him. We opened to the right and left and let him pass. When the British horse come up, the front rank kneeled down and set their bayonets so as to strike their horses in their breast, and the rear ranks stood up and fired at the horsemen. They were cut down, and the riders were thrown from their horses, and we stopped their progress, and they returned and gave up the chase. We crossed over Kingsbridge and remained there then from four to six weeks on what was called Valentine's Hill. Deponent believes, but he is not certain, that he remained there until General Washington went to White Plains, and then General Wooster, with the army to which deponent belonged, went to Horseneck, where we went into winter quarters. More than one-half, and probably two-thirds of deponent's company were dead and gone home sick. We remained there through the winter. We kept a guard called a captain's guard at a house called Logger's house, about three miles toward New York from Horseneck. At this time deponent's father was in the same company when deponent served and acted as a lieutenant. His name was Aaron Bellamy. Captain Cook went home sick before or about this time, and one Amos Hotchkiss had been promoted to the office of captain in his place.

Captain Hotchkiss, when the British cavalry were approaching from New York (deponent thinks they were then called De Lancey's horse and were the same that we drove back who were chasing General Washington as above mentioned), thought best to retire from Logger's house. Deponent opposed this and proposed to go into the house, close the lower story, and knock out the upper windows and fire from thence. To this the captain assented, and in a short time the British cavalry retired to their quarters near Kingsbridge, and we returned back to the main army, leaving only a small guard at this place. A short time, say two weeks after, the same cavalry attacked a guard at this place, and on the guard attempting to retreat, they were nearly all cut off. Nothing else of note occurred until the spring opened. We stayed at Horseneck until spring, and he thinks until the last of May, and we were discharged and arrived home the last of May. And deponent further says that at this time he served, he thinks, one year as an orderly sergeant. Deponent thinks this return must have been in May 1777. Before leaving the army, General Wooster offered this deponent a lieutenant's commission and the duty of an adjutant in the Continental army, but, deponent having contracted and arranged to be married at Cheshire, he declined accepting the office. Deponent and his father then hired one man to serve for them during the war, which was to clear deponent and his father from service during the war. Deponent then continued at home with his family for some time.

Afterwards, and deponent thinks in 1778, when the British were marching for Danbury to destroy it, deponent volunteered with the body of the militia and served under Capt. Ephraim Cook in Col. Thaddeus Cook's regiment. We went to Norwalk in Connecticut—stayed there until the British sailed down the sound. We had a brush with them before they embarked at Compo, where they embarked. At this time one of our adjutants, named Goodrich, got hemmed in by the British on a marsh and was in great danger of being taken, and deponent and thirty men went to his relief. Captain Simon, a British officer, was close in pursuit, but we got Goodrich off clear. In getting off, Captain Simon made a set-to at this deponent and ordered his men to take deponent. Deponent was left pretty much all alone, and deponent drew up his musket and shot Captain Simon down, but afterwards he recovered. Deponent then run and jumped over a fence, and on getting over he found he had fallen in with a large number of British soldiers. He then run to go past a house, when he was fired at in another quarter from a fieldpiece. The ball passed into the house about eight feet above his head, but the hay with which it was wadded hit this deponent on the back of the neck and knocked him over. The first thing deponent knew after this, he was across the road and over the fence and endeavoring to escape through the orchard. Deponent run three-fourths of a mile under a fence until he come to an inlet from the sound, and when he got there he fell down entirely exhausted. Still he was shot at but not hurt, and on being rested a little he finished loading his gun and gave his pursuers a shot. Immediately, several guns were fired at deponent, and then deponent escaped and joined his friends. Deponent and friends gave several shots at the British, and then the British all retreated to their ships. Deponent well recollects of hearing that when he was knocked over with the hay wad, that the father of the present United States senator William [*sic*] Foote of Connecticut remarked to deponent's father that he would never see Justus (this deponent) again. The troops stayed some days watching General Arnold's (the traitor) movements and then returned home. At this time deponent was absent and served as an orderly sergeant, as near as he can recollect one month.

Deponent then remained at home until the regiment was called out again by Colonel Cook. Deponent carried the orders from the colonel to each of his captains. When this was, deponent cannot recollect, but he thinks it was after Danbury was burned. At this time deponent mustered as orderly sergeant in Capt. Ephraim Cook's company. We were at New Haven some ten days. Deponent believes that from the time he first started from home on this occasion until he returned, he was gone about two weeks and served all the time as an orderly sergeant. Deponent did not on any time of being discharged receive a written discharge, and he has no evidence of his services within his reach other than what he has annexed hereunto.

JACOB FRANCIS *(1754–1836) was born to a black slave mother in Hunterdon County, New Jersey. He served five masters, and he earned his freedom at age twenty-one on 1 January 1775. It is unclear from the narrative what racial background his father had, and Francis learned his true last name only after his first enlistment.*

In October 1775 he enlisted at Salem, Massachusetts, and served with the Continental army through December 1776. While helping to construct fortifications on Lechmere Point during the siege of Boston, he encountered Israel Putnam, and he records a humorous anecdote that is characteristic of the remarkable general. He participated in the engagements of 1776 in New York and returned to Amwell Township, New Jersey, after the Battle of Trenton. He served numerous monthly tours in the New Jersey militia, was captured in 1777 near Newark but escaped the same day, and was in arms at the time of the Battle of Monmouth.

His account of the Battle of Trenton is inaccurate with regard to his crossing the Delaware, because troops were unable to navigate the ice-filled waters anywhere but at McKonkey's Ferry. Probably he crossed there, did not personally see Washington, and later confused the name of the crossing. The detail of the rest of his account is strongly indicative of his presence during the engagement.

After the war he married and purchased the freedom of his wife, Mary, in Amwell Township. He was living in Flemington when he submitted this application in 1836 and received a pension.

I was born in the township of Amwell, in the county of Hunterdon, on the fifteenth January, 1754. I never had or saw any record of my age. I learned it from my mother and the persons with whom I lived my time till I was of age, as I always understood I was bound by my mother, a colored woman, when I was young to one Henry Wambough (or Wambock) in Amwell. He parted with me to one Michael Hatt. He sold my time to one Minner Gulick (called Hulick), a farmer in Amwell. He sold my time when I was a little over thirteen years of age to one Joseph Saxton. He went in the spring of the year 1768 and took me with him as his servant to New York, from thence to Long Island, where we took shipping in May 1768 and went to the island of St. John's. We visited different parts of that island and spent the summer there. Towards fall we came to the town of St. Peter's, where we took shipping and returned to Salem, Massachusetts, where we arrived about the month of November 1769. In Salem, Mr. Saxton sold my time to one Benjamin Deacon, with whom I was to serve six years and until I was twenty-one years of age. With him I lived and served in Salem until my time was out, which was in January 1775.

I lived in Salem and worked for different persons till the fall of 1775. In the spring of that year the war had commenced, and the battles of Bunker Hill and Lexington had taken place. About the last of October, I enlisted as a soldier in the United States service for one year. I was told they were enlisting men to serve one year from the first of January, 1776, but I should receive pay from the time I enlisted, and I enlisted and entered the service about the last of October and received two months' pay for my service up to 1 January 1776. I enlisted at Cambridge, about four miles from Boston, under Capt. John Wooley, or Worley, or Whorley, in Col. Paul Dudley Sergeant's regiment (Colonel Sergeant, I understood, had lived in Cape Ann). When I left New Jersey and went with Mr. Saxton to St. John's, I did not know my family name, but called myself Jacob Gulick (or Hulic) after the Mr. Gulick I had lived with, and was enlisted by that name; but, after I returned to New Jersey, was informed by my mother that my family name was Francis, and after that time I went by the name of Jacob Francis. Captain Wooley, or Worley, as his name was called, was captain; his brother was lieutenant. His Christian name I forget, and he had two sons, one a sergeant and the other a drummer in the same company in which I enlisted. The major's name was Ashton or Aston; his Christian name I don't recollect. The lieutenant colonel's name was Jackson. I remember there was in the regiment Captains Pope, Scott, Barnes, Ferrington, and I forget the names of the others. General Putnam was the general that I first recollect being under. At the time I was enlisted, the British army lay in Boston. After that, I remained with the regiment at Cambridge and in the neighborhood of Boston until the British were driven out of Boston.

I recollect General Putnam more particularly from a circumstance that occurred when the troops were engaged in throwing up a breastwork at Lechmere Point across the river, opposite Boston, between that and Cambridge. The men were at work digging, about five hundred men on the fatigue at once. I was at work among them. They were divided into small squads of eight or ten together and a noncommissioned officer to oversee them. General Putnam came riding along in uniform as an officer to look at the work. They had dug up a pretty large stone which lay on the side of the ditch. The general spoke to the corporal who was standing looking at the men at work and said to him, "My lad, throw that stone up on the middle of the breastwork."

The corporal, touching his hat with his hand, said to the general, "Sir, I am a corporal."

"Oh," said the general, "I ask your pardon, sir," and immediately got off his horse and took up the stone and threw it up on the breastwork himself and then mounted his horse and rode on, giving directions, etc. It was in the winter season, and the ground was froze.

In 1776, after the British left Boston, the army, with our regiment and myself along with them, marched by way of Roxbury (that way we could go by land) over a causeway into Boston and lay over two or three days, then were ordered out to Bunker Hill. We marched out and encamped there and lay there some time. Then our regiment was ordered to an island at that time called Castle William. The island contained about ten acres. It was about three leagues, or nine miles from Boston. The channel for vessels passed close under it. The island had had a fortification in the shape of a half moon, but it was pretty much destroyed by the British before they left. The British fleet then lay about nine miles farther out. We lay on that island till about harvesttime. Then we left the island and was ordered to New York from the island. We crossed the river, left Boston on our right hand, and marched to New London. There we took shipping and come to New York. Came down the East River; left Long Island on our left. The British was then on Long Island. At that time the people were culling oats. We stayed a day or two in New York. There were no other troops but our regiment with us. After a day or two, we marched out to a place called Hell Gate, on the north side of the East River. There we threw up breastworks, and the British threw up breastworks on Long Island on the opposite side of the East River and used to fire across. We lay there some time.

While we lay there, the Battle of Long Island took place. There was a number of men detailed from our regiment, so many from each company, to go over and join the American army, perhaps two hundred men. I was one. We crossed the river at Hell Gate and marched on to the island in the direction we was ordered, but did not get to join the army till the battle had commenced and our army was on the retreat. We had to cross a creek to get to our army, who had engaged the enemy on the other side, but before we got to that creek our army was repulsed and retreating, and many of them were driven into the creek and some drowned. The British came in sight, and the balls flew round us, and our officers, finding we could do no good, ordered us to retreat, which we did under the fire of the enemy. We retreated back to Hell Gate and recrossed to our fortifications. Soon after that, we had orders to leave that place and marched to Westchester by way of Kingsbridge. We lay there some time, and every night we had a guard stationed out two or three miles from where the regiment lay at a place called Morrisania. I mounted guard there every time it came to my turn. There was an island near there. The tide made up round it. The British had a station on the island, and a British ship lay there. In an attack on the island one night, Colonel Jackson was wounded. After some time, we were ordered to march to the White Plains. We marched there and there joined General Washington's army.

We lay some time at the White Plains. While we lay there, the British landed and attacked some of our troops and had a brush there. Our regiment and I with them marched by General Washington's orders toward a hill where the engagement was, but the British got possession of the hill, and we retreated back to the camp. The British established a garrison on that hill. I stood sentinel that night in a thicket between the American camp and the hill, so near the British lines that I could hear the Hessians in the garrison, which was between one-quarter and one-half mile from me. The British lay there awhile and then left that place, and our regiments marched after them about three or four miles farther east. Then we received orders and marched to Peekskill on the North River. We halted a day and night a little distance from the river and there crossed at Peekskill to the west side of the river. From thence we marched on, and I do not recollect the names of places we passed through till we got to Morristown, New Jersey. We lay there one night, then marched down near to Baskingridge and lay there the next night. That night General Lee was taken in or about Baskingridge. I heard the guns firing. The next morning we continued our march across Jersey to the Delaware and crossed over to Easton. From thence we marched down the Pennsylvania side into Bucks County.

It was then cold weather, and we were billeted about in houses. Our company lay off from the river a few miles below Coryell's Ferry and above Howell's Ferry. We lay there a week or two; then we received orders to march and, Christmas night, crossed the river and marched down to Trenton early in the morning. Our regiment crossed at Howell's Ferry, four miles above Trenton, and marched down the River Road and entered the west end of the town. General Washington with the rest of the army crossed at McKonkey's Ferry, four miles above Howell's, and marched down the Scotch Road and came into the north end of the town. We marched down the street from the River Road into the town to the corner where it crosses the street running up towards the Scotch Road and turned up that street. General Washington was at the head of that street coming down towards us and some of the Hessians between us and them. We had the fight. . . . After about half an hour the firing ceased, and some officers, among whom I recollect was General Lord Stirling, rode up to Colonel Sergeant and conversed with him. Then we were ordered to follow them, and with these officers and Colonel Sergeant at our head, we marched down through the town toward Assanpink and up the Assanpink on the north side of it and to the east of the town, where we were formed in line and in view of the Hessians, who were paraded on the south side of the Assanpink and grounded their arms and left them there and marched down to the old ferry below the Assanpink, between Trenton and Lamberton.

Soon after that, a number of men from our regiment were detailed to go down and ferry the Hessians across to Pennsylvania. I went as one, and about noon it began to rain and rained very hard. We were engaged all the afternoon ferrying them across till it was quite dark, when we quit. I slept that night in an old mill-house above the ferry on Pennsylvania side. The next morning I joined my regiment where I had left them the day before up the Assanpink, east of Trenton. We lay there a day or two, and then the time of the year's men was out, and our regiment received part of their pay and were permitted to return home. I did not get a discharge. At that time I had seven and a half months' pay due to me, and I believe others had the same. I received three months' pay, and all the rest of the regiment received the same, and we were ordered after a certain time to come to Peekskill on the North River, and then we should receive our pay and get our discharges. I was with the regiment and in service from the time of enlistment till that time about fourteen months and never left it until I had received the three months' pay and had permission to return to the place of my nativity in Amwell, about fifteen miles from Trenton. I immediately returned to Amwell and found my mother living, but in ill health. I remained with her, and when the time came to go to Peekskill for my pay and discharge, I gave up going and never received either my pay or a discharge in writing. That pay, four and one-half months at forty shillings a month (nine pounds proclamation money equal to twenty-four dollars), is yet due to me from the United States.

After I came home, I was enrolled in the militia in Capt. Philip Snook's company. One Fisher was lieutenant under Captain Snook. The next spring I was called out in the militia in the month's service. The militia took turns, one part went one month, and then the other part went out a month and relieved them, and then those that were out the first month went again, so that one-half the militia in this part of Jersey was out at a time, and this continued several years. I always went out when it came to my turn to the end of the war as one of the militia and went out once as a substitute for a person who was to go but could not and gave me seventy-five dollars Continental money to take his place, and I did and served the month. The name of this person I am unable to recollect, as I was not particularly acquainted with him. In the spring of 1777, the first month I went out, was under Captain Phillips or Capt. Charles Reading, I cannot recollect which, as I was out under them both at different times.

We marched first to Elizabethtown and stayed a month. We laid part of the time at a place near there called Halstead's Point. Col. David Chambers was colonel of the regiment, William Chamberlain, lieutenant colonel. After that, I went out again another month at Elizabethtown under Capt. Philip Snook.

I was out another month under Capt. Philip Snook. We marched that time to Newark and stayed a month. We lay in a building in Newark called an academy or schoolhouse. At that time, the British and Hessians lay on Staten Island. An alarm came that there was an attack on the militia at Elizabethtown, and our company marched out toward Elizabeth two miles or more along the road till we came to a piece of rising ground, where the British came in sight. When we saw their numbers, we fired on them and then retreated. A piece of low ground covered with bushes lay on the west of the road. We turned into that. The Hessians I think came foremost. There was three columns, blue coats, green coats, and red coats and, when they got on the rising ground, fired on us.

After we got off some distance, some of us concluded to cross back toward the road and get a shot at them. One Joseph Johnson belonging to the company and myself went. We separated, and I crept along among the bushes till I got almost within gunshot, when I heard a noise behind me and looked round, and there was three Hessians near me that belonged to a flanking party and had got between me and the company. They took me prisoner. Johnson was some distance from me and was taken prisoner by another party. I was taken by the Hessians that took me out to the road to the British army and marched with them under guard through Newark and was carried some distance up the river called Second River. Night came on, and sometime in the night we came to a creek that ran down into the river. Some of our militia, but I don't know who, expecting the British, had placed themselves in some bushes on the left of the road near the creek and fired on the British as we came up. This created some confusion and broke the ranks, and the most of them left the road and turned off to the right toward the river. There was four men had me under guard. They turned in the alarm and left me. I stood near a steep bank that ran down into some bushes toward the creek. Finding the men a little way from me, I stepped down the bank into the bushes and laid down. The militia that had fired retreated, and I saw nothing of them. The British stayed a few minutes. One of the captains was wounded. Then they then formed in the road again and marched on. That same party marched on up to Esopus and burnt Esopus at that time. I lay in the bushes some time till they were all gone, then came out and pushed back to Newark and joined Captain Snook's company there about two o'clock in the morning. I stayed my month out.

After that, I went out again under Captain Snook, and we marched to Newark and lay there a month. I think I was at Newark and Elizabethtown several times after that and did tours of duty a month at a time at Newark and Elizabethtown, but I cannot state the number of times or particular circumstances that occurred each time.

I was out afterwards and did a tour of duty of a month, in which we marched up to Pompton; stayed there some time. There was other militia there, and two subaltern officers and about sixty of the militia, and myself among others, turned out to go on a scouting party down toward the British lines. We marched from Pompton to Paramus; from that we marched down to Hackensack and stayed all night there. The next morning, marched down the river toward the British lines and Bergen a few miles to where there was an old guardhouse on the west side of the river that was unoccupied, and on the opposite side another which we supposed to be occupied by the British. We went to the guardhouse on the west of the river and stayed an hour or two. On the other side, a piece from the river, was rising ground. After waiting some time, we saw some troops come over the rising ground at a distance and march down toward the river below us, where they were obscured from our sight by an intervening wood. There appeared to be a much larger number of men than we had, and the subalterns who were with us, apprehending they might cross the river below and come in on our rear, ordered us to retreat and not to fire. We had not proceeded up the river far when a considerable party of the British troops we had seen below came in sight on the opposite side of the river and fired on us. The subalterns took the lead in the retreat and ordered us to hurry on without firing. We marched a little way. The British kept firing. I was behind the rest of our party, and a bullet struck very near me, upon which I suddenly turned round and fired. Then our whole party turned and fired on the British, upon which they retreated again. Our subaltern officers had pushed on ahead, and we saw no more of them. We marched on without them and joined the army at headquarters, and I joined my company.

I was out afterwards under Capt. Philip Snook, I think several times. I recollect particularly being out under him at the time of the Battle of Monmouth. We were in a regiment of the Jersey militia at that time commanded by Col. Joseph Phillips belonging to General Dickinson's brigade. Our regiment and myself with it was on the battleground and under arms all that day but stationed on a piece of ground a little to the northwest of where the heat of the battle was and were not actively engaged with the enemy. But our Captain Snook was permitted to go or went in the course of the day for some purpose, but what I am unable to recollect or state, to another part of the field and received a wound from a musket shot through his thigh. After the battle was over, we were discharged and returned home.

I recollect other occasions when I was out, although I cannot state them exactly in their order of time. I was out in the militia at the time of the Battle of Brandywine. I was at Newark at the time Lord Cornwallis was taken. I am not able to state the times and places of my services more particularly, but I am satisfied that the time I served in the militia added to the time I served in the Continental army considerably exceeds the span of two years. I have no discharge or documentary evidence to know my services or assist my memory.

JAMES JOHNSTON *(b. 1758) was a native of Chester County, Pennsylvania. He served three regular tours of duty in the Pennsylvania militia. He was stationed on Staten Island in the summer of 1776 and at Trenton that winter. Johnston was appointed adjutant to Colonel Hannum's regiment in May 1777, stationed at Chester and Billingsport. His description of taking the loyalty oath at the tavern in Chester is of particular interest.*

Gen. William Howe's landing at the head of Elk River in late August 1777 brought the war close to Johnston's home, and he took an active role in removing American stores from the path of the British army. His father's residence became a military storehouse, and during the British occupation of Philadelphia he served as agent to Deputy Quartermaster Hollingsworth, issuing supplies to wagoners who transported them to the main army.

When Lafayette passed through Delaware on the way to Virginia in the spring of 1781, Johnston visited the general, volunteered, and served a last tour of service as a cavalryman, although he left the army well before Yorktown. His anecdote about Lafayette's refusal to allow American sharpshooters to pick off Generals Phillips and Arnold, which has a parallel in British officer Patrick Ferguson's unwillingness to shoot Washington at Brandywine, is a fascinating commentary on the gentlemanly art of eighteenth-century European warfare.

Johnston moved to Ohio after the war, then to Pittsburgh, where he made this deposition in 1832 and was granted a pension.

He was born in Chester County, state of Pennsylvania, on the twenty-second June, 1758. He is possessed of no record of this fact, nor does he believe that any such record exists. Declarant was living in said county on the farm of his father at the breaking out of the war of the American Revolution. Two of his elder brothers obtained commissions in the army, one, Francis Johnston, as a colonel, and the other, Alexander Johnston, as a captain in the Pennsylvania line. Declarant was at no time in the regular service, having declined a lieutenancy (obtained for him by his brother

Francis, as said Francis informed declarant) from unwillingness to leave permanently his aged father, of whom he was the youngest son and the only one remaining at home.

On the eighth June, 1776, declarant marched from Chester County to New York with a company of militia to which he had attached himself, commanded by his brother-in-law Dr. John McDowell and forming part of Col. William Montgomery's regiment. He is not aware that there was any formal draft but believes that they proceeded on the emergency of the case, there being in the ranks some of the most respectable citizens of the county, amongst whom he remembers Stephen Cochran and Montgomery Kennedy, brother to the surgeon general of the army. The enemy then occupied Staten Island. Declarant was stationed on the opposite Jersey shore at a place called the Blazing Star, where was collected a force of about one thousand men composed of Colonel Montgomery's regiment and of another regiment, also militia, from Lancaster County, commanded, as declarant thinks, by a Col. John Boya.

Declarant recollects one incident which occurred whilst in this position watching the enemy. An alarm having been given during the night of a movement on the water, an officer was directed to proceed in pursuit and examination. He selected for this purpose the members of the mess to which declarant belonged and, manning a boat with them, proceeded (being seven in all, including the officer) to execute the order. After a long and ineffectual pursuit, it was found as morning dawned that the boat had approached close to Staten Island, and she was hailed by a guard of the enemy, consisting of six men under command of a sergeant, and a fire of musketry opened on her. Declarant and a young gentleman named Thomas Evans were then at the oars. The officer and the four others immediately crouched down to the bottom of the boat, whilst declarant was remonstrating against this conduct as leading inevitably to capture. The boat touched a projecting sandbank, and the officer made a spring for the shore but fell into very deep water. He rose, succeeded in getting ashore, and immediately, in the most dastard manner, took to flight. Declarant seized a musket, and taking deliberate aim at the sergeant, wounded him severely, as was inferred from his immediately dropping his gun and disappearing in the tall grass and weeds. Evans also took aim at, and wounded, one of the enemy. Taking advantage of the pause thus occasioned, the boat was got out and returned to the American camp. Declarant on this occasion received a slight contusion from a musket ball. He continued with Captain McDowell's company until September or October, 1776, when it returned to Chester County and was discharged from service.

In November 1776 declarant again marched from Chester County as a member of Captain McDowell's company, the regiment being now commanded by Col. Evan Evans. They remained in Philadelphia until December 1776, when they were taken up the Delaware in the row galleys and landed in the night on the Jersey shore about three miles above the town of Burlington, having in company a body of troops, believed to have been regulars, from New England. Soon after reaching the point mentioned, Generals Putnam, Cadwalader, and Mifflin arrived. Declarant was familiar with that part of the country, having formerly gone to school in the neighborhood, and on hearing inquiries made by these officers as to the route to Bordentown, he stated his intimate knowledge of it and his willingness to take the responsibility of guiding the column. No movement, however, was made, and the declarant well remembers the chagrin expressed by General Mifflin on ascertaining afterwards that, had the troops marched at once in the direction indicated, they would have fallen in with a body of Hessians proceeding from Mount Holly to Princeton.

On the next morning the whole force proceeded to Bordentown and marched thence the same day to Crosswicks. There they lay until New Year's Day, first January, 1777, when an express arrived from General Washington commanding a junction with him at Trenton that night. On beat to arms, the New England troops, whose turn had expired a few weeks before and who were almost destitute of clothing, declared that they would perform no further service. General Mifflin addressed them in a very animated strain and finally desired that all who were willing to march should step forward and give three cheers. Every man of them did so. Declarant particularly remembers the delight of General Putnam at this result. After marching all night, Trenton was reached about daylight, and the force to which declarant belonged was ordered to occupy the greenhouse of General Dickinson, about one mile above that place, but, whilst preparing breakfast, the alarm was given of the approach of the enemy. Hastening back to Trenton across the bridge over the millrace, they joined the army, which was formed into three lines, front, center, and rear. About one o'clock the enemy appeared in sight. General Washington, who was well supplied with artillery, ordered twelve pieces to be placed behind the mill. About three o'clock in the afternoon, the enemy came down the street in solid column, when the artillery opened upon them a most destructive fire, which caused them to recoil.

At night, preparations were made by General Washington for a retreat. Declarant was detailed for the main guard and shortly after relief he found the army about to move. Many of the soldiers, thinking they were about to be led against the enemy, threw away their knapsacks. General Washington inquired at the rear of the column, Who commanded here? Major Bell of Colonel Evans's regiment announced himself as in command and received orders to remain behind for two hours, carefully observing the enemy. Declarant was with Major Bell and was sent forward by him with a party to reconnoiter the enemy. Moving carefully forward, they had a full view of the Hessians sitting round their fires smoking their pipes. A sentinel challenged. Declarant and the others dropped to the ground and lay quiet until the sentinel was heard to resume his walk. They then cautiously retrograded and made report. At the expiration of the two hours, Major Bell proceeded to join the main army. The advance had an engagement with the enemy at Princeton, but the force under Major Bell was not in time to take part in it. In March 1777 declarant was discharged and reached home in April.

In May 1777 a corps consisting of drafts from various parts of Chester County and amounting in the whole to about six hundred men marched under the command of Col. John Hannum. Declarant was specially appointed by Colonel Hannum adjutant of this corps. He believes that he had a written appointment from Colonel Hannum, but it is no longer in existence. The corps proceeded to the town of Chester and subsequently to Billingsport, where it remained in service until sometime in August 1777. During the whole of this period, declarant was in the active and assiduous discharge of the duties of his appointment in every matter connected with the drill and other military duties and may remark that the corps was known and distinguished at the time for its state of discipline and efficiency. Major Hartman, a German who had been in foreign service, took particular pains and a very friendly interest in instructing declarant in the minutest points of duty.

Whilst the corps lay at Chester, General Potter, who commanded a body of militia from western Pennsylvania, urged declarant to act as his aide and, on his assent, imposed on him at once the duty of arresting an officer who commanded a corps composed principally of Germans from Northampton County and who had committed some gross military offense. Declarant proceeded immediately to demand a surrender of the offender's sword. He assented, but a large body of his men insisted tumultuously on its restoration. Declarant drew his sword and was about to meet the exigency in a fitting manner, when a party of his own corps rushed to the spot, and he could with difficulty restrain them from using their arms on the offenders.

Whilst the corps lay at Chester, the declarant was ordered to convene all the officers at twelve o'clock noon at Curling's Tavern. On the arrival of the hour, it was found that the object was to meet three commissioners sent from Philadelphia for the purpose of administering an oath of allegiance to the new government. Colonel Hannum remarked to the commissioners that the subject was of great importance and delicacy and that it would require much time for deliberation. The same was said by others and was becoming the sentiment of the room. The declarant came forward and earnestly insisted on the importance of enabling the government at once to know their true and staunch friends. The deponent declared his readiness to take the oath, which was administered to him accordingly, and before the commissioners left the house, it was taken by every officer.

I Josiah Harmar Lt. Col. of 6th Pennsa. Regt.
do acknowledge the UNITED STATES of AMERICA to be Free, Independent and Sovereign States, and declare that the people thereof owe no allegiance or obedience to George the Third, King of Great-Britain; and I renounce, refuſe and abjure any allegiance or obedience to him; and I do swear that I will, to the utmoſt of my power, ſupport, maintain and defend the United States againſt the ſaid King George the Third, his heirs and ſucceſſors, and his or their abettors, aſſiſtants and adherents, and will ſerve the ſaid United States in the office of Lieut. Colonel which I now hold, with fidelity, according to the beſt of my ſkill and underſtanding.

Sworn at the Valley forge Camp this 11th day of May 1778. before me Josiah Harmar

A Pennsylvania loyalty oath

Shortly after declarant's return from this tour of duty, the enemy in great force ascended the Chesapeake. They landed at Turkey Point on a Saturday. On Sunday morning at eleven o'clock, a hasty letter dated Elkton reached declarant from Col. Henry Hollingsworth, deputy quartermaster general, stating his fear that the public stores would fall into the hands of the enemy, and entreated declarant to use every possible exertion to aid in effecting their immediate removal. Before three o'clock in the afternoon, between thirty and forty wagons engaged by declarant were on their way for that purpose, and before nightfall declarant was himself at Elkton in conference with Colonel Hollingsworth. The colonel spoke of the house and outhouses of declarant's father as fit places of deposit. Declarant feared that they would be in the route of the enemy, and, moreover, that his father's well-known and enthusiastic feelings as a Whig, and the freedom with which he declared his sentiments on all occasions, would be the very means of attracting notice and resentment. It was finally decided, however, to send the stores thither. Five hundred barrels of flour, one hundred barrels of rum, a great quantity of pork, salt, molasses, and other articles were accordingly dispatched. By Tuesday at ten o'clock, everything was carried off, and not until then did declarant close his eyes subsequently to the receipt of Colonel Hollingsworth's letter.

On Thursday the British army marched through Elkton. Declarant repaired to the headquarters of General Washington, where were his two brothers, Francis and Alexander. Being well mounted, he with some other young men reconnoitered closely the enemy's position at Grey's Hill. The enemy were not provided with cavalry, but a party of mounted men closely pursued declarant whilst thus engaged. Declarant had occasion to return to his father's house, but the day before the Battle of Brandywine he rejoined the army. He was mounted and took a position with the force under General Potter. Owing to the unexpected turn which the battle took, General Potter, who was stationed below the lower ford, had no active part in the conflict of the day.

The public stores already referred to remained in safety at the house of declarant's father, and at the express instance and request of Colonel Hollingsworth, declarant issued them during the fall and winter of 1777 and spring of 1778 to the American army at Valley Forge. Great caution was necessary on account of the occupation of Philadelphia by the enemy. The course pursued was a circuitous one by Cochran's Tavern to the Lancaster road.

Declarant had great difficulty and vexation with the wagoners. He also supplied the troops of General Gist from Maryland, who came on a few days before the surprise of General Wayne at the Paoli and the greater part of whom dispersed immediately afterwards. The whole was done under the orders of Colonel Hollingsworth. Declarant thinks he had a warrant in writing from that officer. He kept a regular account of the issues and made return thereof to Colonel Hollingsworth.

In the month of March, 1781, troops were passing to the southward to act under the Marquis de Lafayette in repelling the incursions of the British under Arnold and Phillips. Declarant joined them near Wilmington in the state of Delaware and, whilst crossing the Susquehanna, was introduced to the marquis, to whom he expressed a wish, being well mounted, to be attached to any cavalry corps that might be employed. The marquis yielded a ready and cheerful assent.

At Fredericksburg, declarant obtained permission from the marquis to turn aside for one day to visit a brother residing about twenty-five miles below. Whilst returning next morning, declarant met a party of Americans who had fled from Richmond and who were engaged in sawing asunder some beautiful pieces of cannon presented to the United States by the French government and bearing the arms of France. This was with a view to render them useless in the event of their falling into the enemy's hands. Declarant remonstrated and advised that they should be buried, but was answered that the orders were peremptory. On reaching Richmond, he reported the scene he had witnessed to the Marquis Lafayette and General Nelson. The former showed considerable emotion, and the latter was exceedingly indignant. Adverting to the subject of declarant's wish for employment, the marquis said, "Here are a hundred young gentlemen, Virginians, desirous of serving as officers, but no one is willing to go into the ranks." Declarant expressed the cheerfulness with which he would occupy any position, even under an officer of the regulars.

One incident of that day is strongly impressed on declarant's memory. He was invited by the marquis to dinner at a small log house opposite the ferry below the falls. Declarant happened to be so placed at the table as to be able to see what was passing out-of-doors, and he called attention to the fact that Generals Phillips and Arnold had advanced along the beach and were making an examination with the spyglass whilst their servants held their horses. Immediately after, there was a bustle at the door occasioned by five riflemen in hunting shirts and moccasins who eagerly solicited permission to steal down to a point from which they felt sure they could pick off these officers. The marquis refused his sanction, declaring that he would meet the enemy openly in the field but would authorize nothing like assassination. This refusal excited great dissatisfaction, which was expressed among the rest by his aide Major McPherson.

Declarant was attached by the marquis to the troops of Captain Reed of Virginia. The enemy retired down the river to Petersburg. Declarant served with Captain Reed until a call of business and the absence of any immediate prospect of active duty induced his return to Pennsylvania, which he reached after an absence of two months.

Declarant has no formal discharge from the service on any occasion, and it is out of his power to state the circumstances under which have disappeared the warrants under which, as he believes, he acted from Colonel Hannum and Colonel Hollingsworth.

ISRAEL TRASK *(b. 1765) was born in Massachusetts and volunteered at age ten in Colonel Mansfield's regiment, for which his father was recruiting in Essex County in 1775. He served as cook and messenger.*

Trask served two tours in the Massachusetts line, from spring or summer 1775 through December, and from January until the next summer. His regiment was stationed with the Continental army, first at Winter Hill, then at Cambridge, and finally on Dorchester Heights. He was a normal ten-year-old boy, excited by army life, and he noticed and records the sorts of things that would impress anyone of his age–not only the military events of the siege itself, but a great snowball fight between frontiersmen and New England sailors, and the imprisonment and public disgrace of two deserters. Washington seemed to him almost supernatural.

After the evacuation, Trask returned home. In early 1777, now a veteran of twelve, he entered the privateering service, and before the war was over he had made ten voyages on privateers and naval vessels. He participated in the disastrous Penobscot expedition, was captured three times, impressed into the British service once, and exchanged twice. In 1782 he and some companions managed to escape from a prison ship at Halifax, Nova Scotia.

He remained in Gloucester, Massachusetts, throughout his life. He applied successfully for his pension in 1845.

In the year of our Lord 1775, having completed the tenth year of my age the fifth day of February of that year, I volunteered in the service of the United States as a soldier in a company commanded by Capt. John Low, Lieutenant, I believe his name was, Eveleth, Lieutenant Trask, Ensign Cooper, and Sergeant Major Widger in the regiment commanded by Colonel Mansfield, Lieutenant Colonel Hutchinson, and Major Putnam. In my application to the secretary's office for a certificate of service, I stated that the enlistment took place at Beverly, and the certificate itself purports the same, but the fact is, as I believe, took place in Gloucester, as Lieutenant Trask, my father, procured a number of recruits there as well as other places, and Beverly was assigned for their meeting, and from thence marched to headquarters.

The precise time of the enlistment or that of joining the encampment of the army, my memory does not save me, and I can only state that Captain Low and the officers under him as well as the soldiers were bivouacked and under light tents during the summer months and part of the autumn. When cold weather set in we were put under barracks and quartered on Winter Hill during this period. I had various duties assigned me such as the care of the baggage and the property of the mess. When the officers were called on duty, which was daily the case, either to mount guard, or fatigue duties in fortifying the camp, the entrenchment of which had a line of continuity from Winter Hill to Watertown when finished, my duty alternately was to take the edibles prepared at the mess to the officers on duty, which in some instance [were] miles distant. The above particulars and those hereafter given are solely on the belief that they are in accordance with the requirements of the Pension Commission when documentary evidence should be found insufficient to establish the claims of the applicant.

My knowledge of the general officers of the army during this first term of service was quite limited. General Greene I knew well, mounted on a white horse, made frequent visits of inspection to our regiment, from which I infer I was attached to the brigade he commanded. Major General Lee I also knew, from the circumstance of his angry threats to cane an officer of considerable grade in the army for unsoldierly conduct and the high excitement the fact created among the officers of the army.

From the foregoing statement and accompanying certificate, I confidently expect will elicit full credence to its truth, for I do not know that a single individual now [is] in existence who served with me in the company or the regiment to which I was attached. This term of service expired the thirty-first December, 1775. If a certificate of discharge was given, Lieutenant Trask, my father, must have received it, as he did my rations as well as wages, whatever may have been paid. Personally I never received either.

The day immediately following the expiration of my first term of service, I recommenced my duty in the service of the United States for another term the first day of January, 1776, having previously engaged so to do some day in the month of December 1775, great exertions having been made by all the patriotic officers who had determined to continue in the service of the country to induce the soldiers to reenlist for another term during the whole of said month, this period being looked for with intense anxiety and frightful apprehensions, lest the enemy should take advantage that the time of disbanding one army and forming another gave them and make a sortie from Boston and Bunker Hill and attack the then half-finished works defended by a force so greatly diminished, and seemed to be the only theme of discussion among the officers. The company I enlisted to serve in was under the command of Capt. John Baker, Lieutenant Pearce, Lieutenant Trask, Ensign Cooper, in the regiment, I believe in numerical order twenty-seventh, under the command of Colonel Hutchinson, Lieutenant Colonel Holding, and Major Putnam and Surgeon Welch.

How long this regiment remained quartered on Winter Hill, I am unable to say. Sometime before the winter months of 1776 ended, the regiment was ordered to remove to Cambridge, the officers of which were quartered in the second story of the college buildings. It was at this encampment I saw for the first time the commander-in-chief, General Washington. A description of the peculiar circumstances under which it took place may not be thought foreign to the object of the present narrative but tend to illustrate not only the intrepidity and physical as well as mental power of the commandant-in-chief, but measurably show the low state of discipline then in the army, and the great difficulty of raising it to a proper standard.

A day or two preceding the incident I am about to relate, a rifle corps had come into camp from Virginia, made up of recruits from the backwoods and mountains of that state, in a uniform dress totally different from that of the regiments raised on the seaboard and interior of New England. Their white linen frocks, ruffled and fringed, excited the curiosity of the whole army, particularly to the Marblehead regiment, who were always full of fun and mischief. [They] looked with scorn on such an rustic uniform when compared to their own round jackets and fishers' trousers, [and they] directly confronted from fifty to an hundred of the riflemen who were viewing the college buildings. Their first manifestations were ridicule and derision, which the riflemen bore with more patience than their wont, but resort being made to snow, which then covered the ground, these soft missives were interchanged but a few minutes before both parties closed, and a fierce struggle commenced with biting and gouging on the one part, and knockdown on the other part with as much apparent fury as the most deadly enmity could create. Reinforced by their friends, in less than five minutes more than a thousand combatants were on the field, struggling for the mastery.

At this juncture General Washington made his appearance, whether by accident or design I never knew. I only saw him and his colored servant, both mounted. With the spring of a deer, he leaped from his saddle, threw the reins of his bridle into the hands of his servant, and rushed into the thickest of the melee, with an iron grip seized two tall, brawny, athletic, savage-looking riflemen by the throat, keeping them at arm's length, alternately shaking and talking to them. In this position the eye of the belligerents caught sight of the general. Its effect on them was instantaneous flight at the top of their speed in all directions from the scene of the conflict. Less than fifteen minutes time had elapsed from the commencement of the row before the general and his two criminals were the only occupants of the field of action. Here bloodshed, imprisonment, trials by court-martial were happily prevented, and hostile feelings between the different corps of the army extinguished by the physical and mental energies timely exerted by one individual.

The regiment continued to be quartered in and about the college buildings without any occurrence worthy of remark, except the occasional interchange of shot and shells with the enemy from the advanced works, until part of the army was marched to take possession of Dorchester Heights, and some days after, in the month of March, the main body of the army was put in motion sometime in the night, marched into Boston about the dawning of day, when the last of the enemy were leaving it. Hutchinson's regiment remained but a short time in Boston before it was removed to Dorchester. While in Boston, the spirit of insubordination then in the army broke out in a mutiny. It was, however, without much difficulty promptly quelled and the ringleaders seized, tried, convicted, and condemned by a court-martial, two of them to be shot, both of whom belonged to the Marblehead regiment.

The criminals were heavily ironed and strongly guarded and were by the sentence to be so kept until the day of execution. The door of the prison, by order, was left open during the daytime, with free permission to receive the visit of all, whether drawn by friendship or curiosity. Of the latter, nearly the whole army availed themselves of the liberty given. When I visited them, I learned they were both natives of Marblehead and both married men, and their wives, respectable-looking women, had taken up their temporary abode in the same prison with their husbands, the ghastly countenances of the latter on which the deepest contrition portrayed, the tears of penitence coming down their rough cheeks, made impressions on a young mind not easily effaced. The stern purposes of Washington were inflexible to the prayers and supplications of the friends of the criminals. He continued to receive in silence all solicitations in their favor until those purposes were attained. He then freely granted the unexpected pardon.

The exact time the quarters of our regiment were taken up at Dorchester I am unable to say. It was, however, somewhere about the latter part of March or forepart of April. From these quarters the regiment was not removed until orders came for part of the regiment to take up their march for New York, which I believe was about the middle or latter part of summer, '76. Few occurrences worthy of notice took place at this station. The enemy held possession of Castle William for the first few days, during which time this section of the army was occupied in perfecting the forts on the heights, throwing up breastworks, and planting batteries on the point of nearest approach to the Castle, between which shot and shells were daily exchanged without much damage to either party until the enemy evacuated the Castle and took refuge in their shipping then laying in Nantasket Road. Here the regiment first passed musters, but few at the examination were dismissed the service, and these were for incorrigible crimes and imbecility of mind.

It was here I witnessed for the first time public punishment inflicted in the regiment. Five or six soldiers were condemned to be flogged for the crime, I believe, of being concerned in the mutiny at Boston. This incident was impressed on my memory with increased force from the interest made to exonerate Major

Putnam's son from his share of the duty of applying the cat to the naked backs of the criminals that fell to him as a drummer in the regiment. A year or two older than myself, he was, however, obliged to submit and take his share of the unpleasant duty with his colleagues.

One other occurrence of general notoriety while the regiment was located at Dorchester I have in distinct recollection, by which an alarm was given and the regiment turned out in the forepart of the night. The alarm was occasioned by the flashes of musketry with continuous succession in the harbor of Boston, which was afterwards known to be an action between the boats sent from the enemies' ships from Nantasket Roads and an American privateer commanded by Captain Mugford, who was killed in the action, not before, however, he had filled two of the boats with water by seizing the masts with his own hands and holding them broadside to the rapid current which runs over the flats on which the schooner lay fast aground with three or four sheets but with only nineteen all told to defend her. Attempting the same on a third boat, he lost his life, but secured the safety of the vessel and the crew.

It was from Dorchester in one of the summer months, for the first time since I entered the army, I visited by permission my maternal parent, who then resided but a short distance from the camp. Sometime in the course of the summer, part of the army took up its march for New York, in which some of the companies of Hutchinson's regiment were included. Captain Baker's company was one of the last which quit the works in and about Dorchester, when orders came for the residue of the regiment to march. I was directed by my father to return home and hold myself ready to start when I received orders so to do. What time this took place, I can only judge from the weather, which was exceedingly hot and debilitating, nor do I know the date of my discharge from the army, whether it was at the period I have just alluded, or at the time my father quit the army, prostrated by sickness brought on by hardships and privations incident to a retreating army scantily supplied, as my father never returned to the army, being confined to his room nearly two years by the same sickness he brought home with him. I conjecture that my discharge was the same date as his own, he having the supervision of all my concerns with the service. He received my pay and rations, if any pay was given and receipted therefor, as well as clothing.

In the early part of the year 1777, I entered the sea service, privateer schooner *Speedwell,* Philemon Haskell commander. Cruised in and about the banks of Newfoundland and captured four prizes; all arrived safe at Gloucester. The latter part of the same year, was fitted and commissioned as a letter of marque, the same vessel and same commander; went to Martinique and returned in safety. Early in the year 1778 I entered on board the ship *Black Prince* of Salem, Capt. Elias Smith, Lieutenants Bordman and Nathaniel West. A few days out, captured after a smart action a brig of sixteen guns commanded by a lieutenant of the British navy. Cruised off the coast of Ireland, and in the Irish Channel captured many prizes. Sent seven home; all arrived safe.

In the autumn of the same year, the same ship sailed on second cruise under the command of Nathaniel West (previously lieutenant). Not many days out, fell in with an English privateer, the *Ladies Adventure,* mounting twenty guns. Not suspecting our character, she was unprepared, and shot poured into her with such rapidity, prevented all preparation for action. She surrendered without firing a gun. We cruised in the Bay [of] Biscay, took one more prize, went into Bilboa [Bilbao] to refit, sailed again, crossed the bay, cruised off the Land's End, the south and west coast of Ireland, captured some thirteen prizes, some of which were recaptured, and returned with the ship in safety to Salem early in the spring of 1779.

The *Black Prince,* shortly after her arrival at Salem from the latter cruise, was taken into the service of the Bay State and Capt. Nathaniel West appointed commander, Carlton, first lieutenant, and B. Crowninshield, second lieutenant. On board this ship I entered a volunteer, I believe in April 1779, and sailed from Salem the forepart of summer of said year and arrived at an eastern port I believe then called Townsend, where we lay many days waiting the arrival of other armed vessels and transports destined for the expedition to Penobscot. I continued on board this ship until she was blown up at the head of navigation on Penobscot River, from whence, with many others, I escaped to the dense forests and traveled through the wilderness about three hundred miles with a pack on my shoulders containing a light blanket, a small piece of rusty pork, a few biscuits, a bottle wine, and one shirt, wending my way across streams and through underbrush until the second day's march my shoes gave way. The rest of the way I performed on my bare feet until I reached home, which I infer from the following incident was the month of September, '79. The day preceding my arrival home I had traveled the whole day, at least until late in the afternoon, without breaking my fast. Between Beverly and Ipswich, I met a company of farmers returning from their labors in the salt marshes, who learning my wants, spread before me the payments of their luck. It was at that period of time a universal custom to cut and cure salt fodder in the low tides of September. If this inference should be considered correct, I shall then have passed six months in this unfortunate service.

Late in October, 1779, I again volunteered in the ship *Rambler,* twenty guns, of Beverly, Capt. Benjamin Lovett commander, Nathaniel Swazy, first lieutenant. Cruised on the Atlantic, Bay [of] Biscay, and entered Bilboa in December, where the ship was visited by the Honorable John Adams and his son John Quincy on their way through Spain to Paris. Sailed from thence the latter part of January, 1780. In one of the heavy gales of that severe winter, we were partially dismasted, lost main yard and mizzenmast. Arrived at Beverly the following March.

1780. Early in April, I again sailed in the brig *Wilkes* of Gloucester, fourteen guns, commanded by Capt. Job Knight. Took two prizes and sent home. Afterwards captured by the *Ferry,* sloop of war. Carried into St. John's, Newfoundland, where I was forced from the prison ship at the point of the bayonet on board the *Vestal* frigate and compelled to do duty until the arrival of Admiral Edwards, whose humanity, at the instances of a pathetic petition, ordered that I should with fourteen others be returned to the prison ship. Soon after, an exchange of prisoners took place. I returned home under the cartel.

In the winter of 1781 I sailed in the brig *Garland* of Newburyport, letter marque, Captain Knap, for Martinique. On the return voyage, captured and carried into Bermuda. After some months' detention, I returned home under the cartel flag of exchange. In the summer of 1781 I served in making two voyages in safety to Martinique and back, first in the brig *Ranger,* Captain Knight, letter of marque, second in small brig from Gloucester, Captain Hough.

In the spring of 1782 I entered on board the ship *Betsy,* eighteen guns, of Gloucester, petty officer Capt. Joseph Porter commander. Second day out, captured by the *Perseverance* and *Ceres* frigates, the former rated forty-four, the first of that class ever launched from the navy yards of Great Britain. Here we experienced the full force of the insolent pride and lofty arrogance so prevalent in the navy and army of Great Britain at that period. On board the *Perseverance* the prisoners were driven down under the haulup deck, their only beds large ironbound water casks, with a stifled, impure air to respire. Only four in the daytime and one at night were allowed to leave this dungeon to catch the pure air or answer the calls of nature. In about a fortnight we were relieved from these impurities to be thrust into a filthy prison ship at Halifax, a large old condemned East Indiaman. On her three decks were housed, or entombed, some hundreds of our countrymen, many of whom had been her occupants for three long years. The gloomy aspect of the ship, the cadaverous appearance of the prisoners, made death preferable to a lengthy abode in this horrific Avernus.

With spirits still alert and energies unrelaxed, the eighth day of confinement, two of our intrepid companions and expert swimmers swam in ice-cold water two miles to a fortified island and brought off, in the obscurity of a foggy evening, two boats within breath hearing of a sentinel. The smaller of the boats, unperceived, reached the ship, into which I was the last to enter. At that moment the alarm was given to the guard, and a volley of about forty muskets was poured in us before we had pulled a stroke. Only one ball entered the boat. Before a recharge could be made, we were hid in the obscurity of the night and succeeded, by hauling our boat on uninhabited islands in the daytime and embracing the night for progression, in making good our escape. After a fortnight of great suffering, we got on board of an American cruiser and reached our home a little over a month from the time we left it.

1782. I afterwards sailed in the brig *Congress,* letter marque, Captain Clark. Latter part of the same year, I sailed in the ship *Ruby,* Captain Babson, both strongly armed, the latter eighteen guns; both voyages to West Indies, and both return safe with valuable cargoes. In the winter of 1782, again sailed in ship *Ruby,* Captain Babson, to Guadeloupe, where news of peace reached and where we lay until it took effect in those latitudes.

It will be perceived by the foregoing narrative I was in active service, public and private, from the commencement of the Revolutionary War to its end about eight years: in the army of the United States under enlistment one year and eight months, and in active service until the last of the [regiment was] moved from the encampment of Dorchester to New York; that I was in the sea service of the United States about six months.

AMERICA TRIUMPHANT and BRITANNIA in DISTRESS

EXPLANATION.

I America ſitting on that quarter of the globe with the Flag of the United States diſplayed over her head; holding in one hand the Olive branch, inviting the ſhips of all nations to partake of her commerce; and in the other hand ſup-porting the Cap of Liberty.

II Fame proclaiming the joyful news to all the world.

III Britannia weeping at the loſs of the trade of America, atten-ded with an evil genius.

IV The British flag ſtruck, on her ſtrong Fortreſses.

V French, Spaniſh, Dutch, &c. ſhipping in the harbours of America.

VI A view of New-York, wherein is exhibited the Trator Arnold, taken with remorſe for ſelling hi[illegible], and Judas like hanging himſelf.

INDEX